Activist Origins of Political Ambition

Why do people run for office with opposition parties in electoral authoritarian regimes, where the risks of running are high, and the chances of victory are bleak? In *Activist Origins of Political Ambition*, Keith Weghorst offers a theory that candidacy decisions are set in motion in early life events and that civic activism experiences and careers in civil society organizations funnel aspirants towards opposition candidacy in electoral authoritarian regimes. The book also adapts existing explanations of candidacy decisions derived from advanced democracies that can be applied to electoral authoritarian contexts. The mixed-methods research design features an in-depth study of Tanzania using original survey data, sequence methods, archival research, and qualitative data combined with an analysis of legislators across authoritarian and democratic regimes in Africa. A first-of-its kind study, the book's account of the origins of candidacy motivations offers contributions to its study in autocracies, as well as in leading democracies and the United States.

KEITH WEGHORST was Assistant Professor of Political Science at the V-Dem Institute in the Department of Political Science at University of Gothenburg. His research focused on political opposition, legislatures, and civil society in electoral autocracies, with a regional specialization in sub-Saharan Africa.

Activist Origins of Political Ambition

Opposition Candidacy in Africa's Electoral Authoritarian Regimes

KEITH WEGHORST

Göteborgs Universitet

CAMBRIDGE
UNIVERSITY PRESS

CAMBRIDGE
UNIVERSITY PRESS

Shaftesbury Road, Cambridge CB2 8EA, United Kingdom

One Liberty Plaza, 20th Floor, New York, NY 10006, USA

477 Williamstown Road, Port Melbourne, VIC 3207, Australia

314–321, 3rd Floor, Plot 3, Splendor Forum, Jasola District Centre, New Delhi – 110025, India

103 Penang Road, #05–06/07, Visioncrest Commercial, Singapore 238467

Cambridge University Press is part of Cambridge University Press & Assessment, a department of the University of Cambridge.

We share the University's mission to contribute to society through the pursuit of education, learning and research at the highest international levels of excellence.

www.cambridge.org
Information on this title: www.cambridge.org/9781009011518

DOI: 10.1017/9781009019705

First published 2022
First paperback edition 2024

A catalogue record for this publication is available from the British Library

ISBN   978-1-316-51992-9   Hardback
ISBN   978-1-009-01151-8   Paperback

Contents

Figures

Tables

Acknowledgments

A lesson about success is found in a number of Swahili *methali* that highlight the role of collaboration and cooperation: *Panapo Wengi, hapaharibiki neno* ("Where there are many, nothing goes wrong"), *Mti pekee haujengi* ("One tree alone cannot build anything"), *Kusaidiana ni mali* ("Helping one another is wealth"), among others. There is wisdom in this view and it absolutely applies to the experience of writing this book. This manuscript is the final output of a process of intellectual growth and development that started before I attended graduate school and evolved through graduate training, a postgraduate research position, and experiences as a junior faculty member. I have been motivated by the puzzle of why opposition candidates run for office in Africa's electoral authoritarian regimes for about ten years and this intellectual curiosity could not have resulted in a book without the sustained and countless contributions collaborators, colleagues, friends, and family have made to me and to my work. This book is a reflection of those efforts.

I want to start by recognizing the Tanzanians without whom this book project would not have been possible. The book centers around three prominent Tanzanian politicians whom I hold in the highest regard: Ismail Jussa Ladhu, January Makamba, and James Mbatia. Each is principled, driven by a commitment to improve the lives of Tanzanians, and has made tremendous sacrifices in pursuit of that goal. Over the years I have been working on this project, they willingly shared their time with me in order to tell their stories. While the book's narrative differentiates pathways to opposition versus ruling party candidacy, I hope it is clear that all three should inspire hope about the quality and types of leaders that can emerge in electoral authoritarian settings. I am particularly grateful for the friendship I have developed with Jussa over years of working in Zanzibar. Many other leaders and activists from CHADEMA, CUF (and later ACT-Wazalendo), NCCR-Mageuzi, and CCM shared with me their passion for politics and their personal stories of how they came to be involved in public life in Tanzania and hundreds participated in the survey the empirical analysis of the book centers on.

Many research assistants contributed to the book, especially in the survey effort. This includes an enumerator team at the Parliament of Tanzania (Fidel Hassan, Deman Yusuph, Richard Alphone, and Paul Lousulie) and the Zanzibar House of Representatives (Riziki Pembe Juma, Abdallah Ali Abeid). Yulli Jeremia has also helped my work tremendously – as an enumerator, field supervisor, and research coordinator. Additionally, non-legislator surveys were carried out with the support of party activists in CHADEMA and Civic United Front: Silas Bwire, Victor Kingu, Innocent J. Kisanyage, Edward M. Makabayo, Bonifasia Mapunda, and Aminata Saguti.

A number of Tanzanian academics also supported me in various ways throughout my years working in Tanzania, including Mohammed Bakari, Benson Bana, Max Mmuya, and Bashiru Ally at the Department of Political Science and Public Administration at the University of Dar es Salaam and Vice Chancellor Dr. Idris Ahmada Rai at the State University of Zanzibar. Early on in the project, Aikande Kwayu was especially helpful in connecting me with political figures in Northern Tanzania and sharing her academic and personal perspectives on Tanzanian politics.

Finally, though he is a Wisconsinite by birth, most Tanzanians who know "Makame" Sterling Roop would welcome him as one of their own. I am indebted for his support in Zanzibar as a colleague and coauthor. His connections and access to guarded political networks unlocked much of what was accomplished in my fieldwork and his expertise on the internal workings of party politics in Tanzania is exceptionally rare. His companionship on the "Wazee" basketball team in Zanzibar and on various marathons and half marathons in Tanzania and elsewhere have been of even greater meaning over the decade we have known each other – *Njia in rafiki.*

This project began as my dissertation at the University of Florida, under the supervision of Staffan Lindberg and Michael Bernhard. Thanks to Dr. L for his mentorship, from coursework and coauthorship to my apprenticeship on the grill at Friday "Firesites." Thanks to Michael Bernhard whose sharp wit taught me to think on my feet. Both shaped my project through my graduate training and in their feedback on countless ideas and iterations of this project. They learned how to get the best work out of me and have remained supportive and engaged with me in the early stages of my career. Göran Hydén had formally retired before I arrived in Gainesville, but he remains a towering intellectual figure in Tanzania. His willingness to read early drafts of my work and introduce me to colleagues at the University of Dar es Salaam early in my PhD (many of whom he had trained) were incredibly valuable.

Thanks also to Ben Smith, a dissertation committee member, one of my first instructors at the University of Florida and the reason I will always be able to explain my book to my grandmother. The Department of Political Science at Florida has a uniquely collaborative faculty who supported my work, including other dissertation committee members Bryon Moraski, Charles Peek, and Ken Wald, as well as faculty members Michael Martinez and Dan Smith. The Center for African Studies is one of the world's premier homes for the study of Africa. I greatly miss the vibrance of the African studies community there and the opportunities it provided to interact with scholars from sub-Saharan Africa and for interdisciplinary exchange. Tremendous gratitude is owed to Leo Villalon and Todd Leedy, who led the center during my time in Gainesville. Thanks also to Scott Feinstein, Will Hicks, and Dominic Listanti for the ways their friendship shaped my development as a scholar in these pages and outside of them. As an institution, the University of Florida provided significant financial and logistical support for this project.

The kernels of my interest in autocracy in Africa go back to my time as an undergraduate at Northwestern University, where Will Reno showed me how exciting researching politics in Africa could be. I owe my expertise in Tanzania to the experience studying African Studies at UCLA. Katrina Daly Thompson helped me learn Swahili and to see it for its cultural, social, and political power, a perspective that is found throughout these pages. Without her mentorship, I doubt I would have been able to navigate the Tanzanian political research environment. At critical times of doubt, both Will and Katrina gave me confidence to pursue a PhD in Political Science.

During the research and writing process, I was fortunate to spend time at the Kellogg Institute of the University of Notre Dame. Michael Coppedge was tremendously supportive during my time there, Guillermo Trejo's feedback shaped how I view the nexus of civil society activism and political parties, and the Measuring Democracy working group there generated feedback on early versions of this project. New York University's

Wilf Family Department of Politics welcomed me into their academic community while I prepared dissertation grant applications.

Much of this book was written in my time on the faculty of political science at Vanderbilt University. I have been lucky to work in a department that is as intellectually rigorous as it is welcoming and warm. Many colleagues from my time at Vanderbilt influenced this book in various ways; I am especially grateful to Amanda Clayton, Dave Lewis, Jon Hiskey, John Sides, Tariq Thachil, Alan Wiseman, and Liz Zechmeister for feedback at various stages of the project. Allison Anoll and Sharece Thrower were supportive "accountability buddies" as we pushed our book projects forward. I also benefited from the intellectual exchanges with Africanist faculty, especially Gregory Barz and Moses Ochonu. Vanderbilt provided material support for the book project at the department, college, and university levels. A special thanks to Noam Lupu for substantive feedback, mentorship in navigating the book revision and publication process, and friendship throughout.

I was fortunate to have the opportunity to be a visiting scholar at the Varieties of Democracy (V-Dem) Institute at the University of Gothenburg during my work on this book. V-Dem is a one-of-a-kind place for scholars interested in the shape of democracy in the twenty-first century and I am grateful for the insights shared by its faculty, as well as other visiting scholars in residence during my visits. As I was completing this book, I joined the faculty of V-Dem and the Department of Political Science at the University of Gothenburg and am incredibly excited to begin a new chapter of my career working with them.

The scholars who have supported me throughout this work are too many to count. Ken Greene, Allen Hicken, Nic van de Walle, and Rachel Beatty Riedl participated in a full-day book workshop and were instrumental in shaping the revisions reflected in this manuscript. The same is true for two anonymous reviewers at Cambridge University Press.

My collaboration with Karisa Cloward on studying the linkages between NGO careers and candidacy in Africa broadly has helped refine my thinking about what makes candidacy dynamics in authoritarian regimes similar and different from democracies in the subcontinent. I learned about sequence methods from Matthew Charles Wilson and he was incredibly helpful in my early stages of using them. I think Leo Arriola and Rachel Beatty Riedl are tied for the award of "Most Times Served as Discussant" for components of this book, making even more impressive the creative insight and fresh contributions they offered each time they read my work.

Others who provided valuable feedback include Jaimie Bleck, Matthias Bogaards, Jen Brass, Sarah Brierley, Ruth Carlitz, Danny Choi, Michaela Collard, Jeffery Conroy-Krutz, Kim Yi Dionne, Anna Gryzmala-Busse, Jessica Gottlieb, Shelby Grossman, Robin Harding, Adam Harris, José Antonio Hernández-Company, Kevin Fridy, Willa Friedman, Matthew Gichohi Catherine Kelly, Dominika Koter, Eric Kramon, Adrienne Lebas, Ellen Lust, Andrew Little, Melanie Manion, John McCauley, Michael Miller, Yonatan Morse, Sigrun Marie Moss, Mathias Poertner, Dan Paget, Lise Rakner, Amanda Robinson, Ora John Reuter, Merete Seeberg, Dan Slater, Elizabeth Sperber, Kharis Templemann, Aili Mari Tripp, Kjetil Tronvoll, Michael Wahman, Shana Warren, Yael Zeria, and Brigitte Zimmerman. Many of these connections were made at meetings where the work was presented; thanks to the organizers of MGAPE, CAPERS, and MWEPS, an ad-hoc "conference within a conference" at the annual meeting of the Southern Political Science Association, and panel organizers, participants, and attendees at many annual meetings of the African Studies Association, American Political Science Association, International Studies Association, and Midwest Political Science Association.

The production team at Cambridge University Press has made the publication process smooth and rewarding. Particular thanks to my editors Rachel Blaifeder and Sara Doskow for their support, enthusiasm, and patience.

Writing this book has been a personal journey for me and I am proud that what resulted is a reflection of my voice and who I am as a scholar. At some point in my career, I set my sights on externally oriented professional goals of what I thought it would mean to be successful and anchored my personal ambitions to that vision. In doing so, I lost track of why I pursued this career, what made me unique as a scholar, and, more fundamentally, what I had to contribute to the world. While comparison is the core enterprise of what we do as political scientists, applying that frame of thinking to professional development and achievements really can, as the saying goes, steal the joy that comes with doing this work. I'm grateful for the support of mentors and advisors for critical guidance on course corrections within my career. Close friendships have helped me achieve greater balance in my life and my family has been steadfastly supportive throughout.

I am also lucky to have discovered running as an outlet to reflect, manage stress, and prioritize physical and mental health. Running has taught me many lessons applicable to my career and my life, including the value of process-based goals, knowing when to push myself (and when not to), navigating doubt and discomfort, and the power of community. To those who I have shared miles with, including coworkers in my department, colleagues at annual conferences, friends in my local running community, and my teammates in Rogue Running's Renegades Worldwide training group: thank you. It has meant more than you probably know.

My family has been unwavering in their support and understanding throughout the process of writing this book. I attribute my initial interest in Africa to my mother, whose work as an artist and tapestry weaver exposed me and my siblings to the vibrant fiber arts of West Africa and how seemingly simple objects often carry complex historical, social, and political meaning. Her passion inspires the personal touch of this narrative and its creativity. I credit my father for giving me the desire to "know" and to approach challenges – within a research question and in my life – through goal-oriented problem-solving. My parents' dedication to social justice has instilled in me the desire to understand the adversity that others face in their lives and generate knowledge that helps in part to alleviate it. As teachers, my brother and sister have shown me the value and reward of pursuing a career in education.

Thanks to my partner in life, Kristin Michelitch. Kristin is an exceptional scholar and her feedback on countless versions of this project is imprinted throughout the pages of this volume. I remain amazed at all of the improbable, random events that aligned for us to first meet at a summer workshop in Ghana and the journey we've navigated together since. I cannot imagine my life without the inspiration that Kristin provides and the appetite for adventure she brings to team Michelhorst. You are my best friend. I am so lucky to share life's mountains and valleys with such a caring companion.

And finally, nothing but love to our daughters Josephine Moto and Margot Moyo. Josephine, I see in you the curiosity to ask why the world is how it is and the passion to bend it to your will (in a good way ... mostly). Margot, over your first months, your love for smiles and laughter have brightened every day.

Running against All Odds

Kukimbia si kufika
To run is not to reach your destination.

Swahili Proverb

January Makamba and Ismail Ladhu Jussa first formally met in 2010 in the *Bunge* building on Dar es Salaam Avenue in Dodoma. A small, dusty city at the geographic center of Tanzania, Dodoma is where the *Bunge* (Parliament) has met since the country's capital was relocated from Dar es Salaam in the 1970s at the height of Tanzania's political and economic development vision known as *Ujamaa*. About two kilometers east of the legislature lies the green and yellow painted headquarters of Chama Cha Mapinduzi (CCM), situated between *Madaraka* ("power/mandate") and *Mwangaza* ("light") Avenues. Most would say that, having governed for more than half a century, the halls of the CCM building are where the *madaraka* of Tanzania's government really lies.

That January Makamba and Ismail Jussa would come to meet in Dodoma seems inevitable. They were rising stars in their parties – the CCM and the opposition party Civic United Front (CUF), respectively – and, to many, central figures of Tanzania's political future. They were informally introduced in Dar es Salaam years earlier in a sit-down arranged by a wealthy businessman and CCM financier. Both were also in Dodoma at the behest of the same person: then Tanzanian President Jakaya Mrisho Kikwete. The reason that each was in Dodoma differed: Ismail Jussa to advance the core ideological issue that defined his politics and January Makamba to solve the political headache that was costing CCM internal party cohesion and votes on election day – Zanzibar's autonomy within Tanzania. Their pathways to Dodoma were also different.

January Makamba knew Dodoma well. After leading Kikwete's successful 2005 presidential campaign, he became the president's personal assistant at age thirty-one. As a child, he spent time in Dodoma as his father Yusuf Makamba – a leader in Tanzania's war with Uganda – climbed the political ranks. By January's fifth birthday, his father had secured a position in CCM's secretariat. Yusuf would eventually serve as the party's secretary-general (2007–2011). January first joined CCM as a "Young Pioneer" in primary school and described his ascendency to political prominence within the party as a matter of course.

Jussa – the name Ismail Ladhu Jussa prefers to use – was in Dodoma because he was plucked out of Zanzibar by President Kikwete to represent Zanzibari opposition's interests in negotiating efforts to enhance peace and stability in the archipelago. The issue of Zanzibar's autonomy within the Tanzanian union defines the politics of CUF and is one that activists have fought and died for since Tanzania was created in the 1960s. Jussa's brief stint in Dodoma was not an effort to co-opt a staunch regime challenger. The government gave up on silencing him long before, when he turned down its first attempt to buy him out in his twenties in spectacular fashion. Approached by an elder, respected CCM leader who offered roughly US$ 25,000 to join CCM or quit politics – about 150 times the country's per capita GDP at the time – he responded with a lament that the elder had decided "to be used as a pimp."

When Jussa was born – in August 1971 – there was no political opposition in Tanzania. By the time multipartyism had been reintroduced, he had already been arrested for his civic activism as a student in pursuit of the dream of a prosperous, empowered Zanzibar. When the 2020 elections concluded – a contest marred by significant election fraud and intimidation – he reaffirmed his lifelong commitment to the betterment of Zanzibar from a hospital bed, saying he was "ready to make any sacrifice needed to make sure Zanzibar regains its freedom and our people live in a free and a just system." Police had kidnapped him on election day and broke his leg and shoulder during a multiday interrogation.

Like Jussa, James Mbatia's path into the opposition stood at the intersection of student activism, personal costs of political participation, and political reform. A founding member of Tanzania's National Convention for Construction and Reform – Mageuzi (NCCR-Mageuzi; NCCR, for short), politics found their way to James Mbatia, rather than the other way around. As an engineering student nearing graduation from the University of Dar es Salaam, he was expelled as a student activist not for political activism but for pushing the university to provide better conditions for students. The expulsion changed him – his career path to engineering derailed and he was displaced from his civic and social networks on campus. More fundamentally, his willingness to fight the system reemerged in the only alternative venue available at the time: opposition parties.

This book asks the following question: *Why do people run for the legislature for opposition parties in electoral authoritarian regimes?* On one hand, there appears to be little to be gained from running on opposition tickets in those settings: ruling parties will do nearly anything to hold onto power, and it is opposition candidates who pay the costs of campaigns thwarted by the government and the political, economic, and even physical repression that comes with fighting an authoritarian regime. When opposition candidates do win seats in the Parliament, they face ruling party majorities and supermajorities that undermine them. On the other hand, any chance of forcing those regimes out of office or into accepting reforms that curb corruption, deepen human rights, promote development, and protect civil liberties requires that formidable challengers bear the risks that come with candidacy and skillfully navigate their environment to enact change.

What we know about candidacy to date mostly comes from democracies and concludes that candidates weigh cost-benefit expectations regarding what they get out of being a legislator. This framework in its current form cannot explain candidacy in electoral authoritarian regimes. This is significant because regimes like that in Tanzania – where ruling party politics reign supreme – are not exceptions: they are the norm. Electoral authoritarianism is the most prevalent form of governance found in the developing world. The majority of countries in sub-Saharan Africa are electoral authoritarian regimes, and it is in the subcontinent where the greatest number of the world's electoral authoritarian regimes are found. Every single year, candidates around the globe stand for opposition parties in authoritarian elections to fight for a better future that is more fair, just, and democratic, and yet, we as scholars cannot explain why. Approaches to political ambition that cannot account for the authoritarian character of contemporary elections ignore the most important normative questions about the fate of democracy in the twenty-first century.

My book offers an explanation of opposition candidacy in electoral authoritarian settings that emphasizes the role of early life experiences with civic activism and vocational careers in the civil society sector in shaping later decisions to run for the opposition years or decades down the road. It follows Jussa, January, and James through experiences long before they considered running for office. It shows that Ismail Jussa and James Mbatia followed a path of civic activism and that this engagement translated later into opposition candidacy. January Makamba's early life experiences in party politics positioned him to run for CCM, a phenomenon I call "career partisanship." Their accounts combine with surveys of hundreds of legislative aspirants, the biographies of more than 700 Tanzanian legislators, qualitative interviews, and archival data to provide a rich, in-depth narrative of the politics of Tanzania, where the second longest-standing ruling party in the world currently governs.[1]

The book illustrates how political paths not only shape the candidacy options available to prospective office seekers but also the goals they hope to achieve in doing so. I reveal that the prevailing framework that casts candidates as strategic decision makers can be adapted to electoral authoritarian settings, but what shapes the cost-benefit calculations in that approach all ties back to early life experiences with civic versus political party activism. Experiences in civic activism early in life underlie a desire to seek policy-oriented benefits that running for opposition parties can deliver, even in electoral defeat.

Who runs for office and why they run are the two most essential questions for elections, representation, and political accountability in democracies. They are even more important in electoral authoritarian regimes because the answers determine whether those regimes stand any chance of growing into democracies in the future.

1.1 THE PUZZLE OF OPPOSITION CANDIDACY

Even Democratic Elections Favor Incumbents and Ruling Parties

Theories of why political actors participate as voters and candidates commonly focus on some combination of calculated costs and benefits of action. It is generally assumed that the benefits motivating any given candidate hinge on their chance of winning. Theorizing that candidacy motivations rest on the chances of defeating incumbent officeholders and governing parties, however, is problematic. In the history of democracy, governing party defeat via the ballot box is uncommon. In electoral

---

[1] CCM's reign is second only to the People's Action Party, which has ruled Singapore since 1959.

authoritarian regimes, such outcomes are even rarer. In consideration of these dynamics alone, why political actors would fight important but, ultimately, losing battles at the ballot box is not at all obvious.

Elections in general have always strongly favored the incumbent party. From 1788 through 2011, there were 2,230 contested elections held in the world. Nearly 1,500 of them resulted in victory for the incumbent government. Opposition success rates in the first half of the twentieth century were less than 20 percent and in the nineteenth century rarely more than 10 percent.[2] Examples of long-standing incumbent parties abound in democracies, particularly in Europe. Sweden's Socialdemokratiska Arbetarpartiet was elected democratically to rule uninterrupted for forty-four years. Only two parties held government in Austria from 1945 to 2000: the Austrian People's Party for twenty-five years, followed by thirty-five years of the Sozialdemokratische Partei Österreichs. Liechtenstein has experienced two periods of party government lasting more than twenty years; the same holds true for Luxembourg. Christian Democrats governed Italy for more than three decades after the Second World War, and the list goes on.[3] It is true that opposition-induced turnover has been on the rise in the past half century. Nonetheless, nearly a third of the countries around the world have never experienced a turnover in the party in power through the ballot box (Przeworski 2015, 102).

At the level of the legislative candidate, the rates of incumbent success are similarly high. Reelection rates of standing congressional representatives in the United States rarely fall below 80 percent and House of Representatives reelection rates hover around 90 percent (Jackson 1994*a*, 40–41). Standing legislators have regularly won 80 to 85 percent of reelection campaigns in Germany (Boll 1994, 165) and Denmark (Pedersen 1994, 221). Perhaps the lowest odds facing challenger candidates are where individual incumbency and party hegemony align: during the forty years of the Liberal Democratic Party's rule in Japan, the reelection rates of LDP incumbents averaged nearly 80 percent (Reed 1994, 282). The same holds for the Labor/Mapai tenure of thirty years, when 65 percent or more of incumbent legislators were elected in each election for the Israeli Knesset (Arian 1994). In Taiwan, a prototypical dominant party

---

[2] Calculated by the author based on Version 1 (September 1, 2011) of Przeworski et al.'s (2011) "Political Institutions and Political Events" (PIPE) dataset.

[3] These statistics are reported in Templemann (2014*b*) and drawn from an original dataset created by that author.

system, "permanent representatives" who established the legislature in 1945 remained in office through the 1990s (Templemann 2014*a*), and the new seats introduced went to members who proved to be resilient in subsequent elections (Jackson 1994*b*, 270).

In sub-Saharan Africa, ruling parties have remained in control via the ballot box: across all multiparty elections held in Africa, less than twenty percent of them yielded turnover of the party in power. The legislature of Botswana – considered by many observers as one of Africa's exemplary democracies and rated a 2 or 2.5 ("free") by Freedom House from 1998 to 2020 – has been ruled for nearly fifty years by a single political party that will continue to govern at least until 2024. At the level of the individual legislator, rates of incumbent return to the legislature are comparably lower. Much is driven by internal party competition and reelection rates increase with the strength of legislative institutions (Opalo 2019).

Opposition Chances Are Worse under Electoral Authoritarianism...

Electoral authoritarian regimes are settings in which ruling parties are subjected to electoral contests at regular intervals, but such competitions are so heavily stacked in favor of incumbents that the opposition has little chance to win. According to Schedler (2006, 3),

Under electoral authoritarianism, elections are broadly inclusive (they are held under universal suffrage), as well as minimally pluralistic (opposition parties are allowed to run), minimally competitive (opposition parties, while denied victory, are allowed to win votes and seats), and minimally open (opposition parties are not subject to massive repression, although they may experience repressive treatment in selective and intermittent ways).

In the aggregate, these conditions mean that there is little or no potential for the opposition to defeat incumbents and ruling parties. From 1980 to 2014, only 13 percent of elections in authoritarian regimes have resulted in a change in the ruling party (Lucardi 2015). This is not surprising, as elections in such settings feature "hyper-incumbency advantages" (Greene 2007, 39) and are manipulated so much they cannot be classified as democratic (Schedler 2006). Prospects for the opposition are marginally better when challenger parties collaborate through preelectoral coalitions (Wahman 2013); however, when they do not, parties fare even worse: odds of victory drop below one in ten (Lucardi 2015). In notable cases, the opposition manages to wrest power out of the hands of the authoritarian guard. The most studied example is Mexico's Partido Revolucionario Institucional (PRI), which governed for seventy-one years uninterrupted. Against a rising tide of discontent and waning access to state resources, it was finally defeated in 2000 (Greene 2007). In Africa, the Parti Socialiste du Sénégal (PS) lost control of the presidency and the legislature in Senegal after 2000. Such outcomes are exceptions, rather than the norm. Even if opposition is strong and appears poised to defeat incumbents, it may not be permitted to do so.

First, incumbents who are facing possible defeat may intervene to ensure victory. Such was the case in the 2015 elections in Zanzibar, a semiautonomous region of Tanzania where Chama Cha Mapinduzi faced strong challenges from CUF. As official results from the Zanzibar Electoral Commission trickled in by constituency, parallel tallies showed opposition victory was imminent. After validating some 60 percent of constituencies, the commission suspended counting and annulled the polls. The opposition ultimately boycotted the new election held months later, marking the second time CUF had been robbed of victory at the vote-counting stage in Zanzibar's multiparty history (Burgess 2009). Gabon's 2016 presidential elections offer another contemporary example where incumbents may appear to lose elections and still manufacture a victory through the tools of authoritarian rule such as fraudulent counting and manipulating election management bodies (Obangome 2016).

Second, incumbents who are voted out of power may simply not concede defeat. Incumbents may lose and admit loss but simply refuse to step down. Of the 660 instances in the global history of elections from 1788 to 2011 where opposition parties defeated incumbent governments, 57 of them never saw the opposition winner take office (Przeworski 2015). The incumbent government instead remained in power. Stated differently, even when the opposition wins an election officially, there is almost a 10 percent chance it will never make it to the state house or government. Gambia's 2016 presidential elections nearly followed this narrative. After conceding defeat to the opposition, incumbent President Yahya Jammeh backtracked and instead insisted that the victory of his challenger Adama Barrow was fraudulent. He remained in power for nearly two additional months until international actors negotiated his exit (Bleck and van de Walle 2018, 3). Laurent Gbagbo remained in power for a year after his 2010 election defeat in Côte d'Ivoire until he was deposed by the military with the support of the United Nations and France.

Third, incumbents who anticipate defeat in an impending election may delay or indefinitely suspend elections or selectively ban opposition parties. Elections and competition are only guaranteed to the extent that they serve the goals of ruling regimes. Leaders may shutter electoral institutions altogether after learning that fraud and repression alone will not guarantee victory (Thompson and Kuntz 2006).

Alongside the prospects of electoral defeat, it is also notable that opposition challengers in electoral authoritarian regimes bear the risk of a different kind of loss. Opposition candidates and supporters risk repression and physical harm, especially around election times. Using violence against opposition candidates may be electorally advantageous in that it represses dissent and protest (Brass 2003, Charurvedi 2005), mobilizes supporters (Wilkinson 2004), and/or captures new voters (Collier and Vicente 2014, Wilkinson and Haid 2009).[4] Some candidates who are poised to defeat incumbents may never take office because they lose their homes, businesses, or lives.

In sum, the opposition's prospects are poor in electoral authoritarian regimes. Incumbency advantages predominate in many types of regimes, and the asymmetries of competition are especially severe in authoritarian settings. Even in the rare event that the opposition is strong enough to rival the ruling party, incumbents can ignore election results or cancel the polls. Little of the promise of competition that electoral authoritarian regimes offer the opposition is guaranteed.

…Yet, Opposition Candidacy Is Ubiquitous

Given the barriers to success in electoral authoritarian regimes, opposition candidacy seems like it should be an empirical irregularity. A review of authoritarian elections in the world shows the opposite: opposition candidates proliferate in legislative contests. Figure 1.1 illustrates this pattern, visualizing constituency-level election data from countries around the world. The figure is created with data from the Constituency-Level Election Archive (CLEA), a resource that records constituency-level election data from more than 1,800 elections in 162 countries. Focusing on majoritarian systems, I calculated the average number of candidates per constituency for each legislative election included in the CLEA dataset. Making the conservative assumption that ruling parties run candidates in every constituency, I estimated the average number of opposition

---

[4] Straus and Taylor (2012), for example, estimate 58 percent of elections in Africa from 1990 to 2007 featured repression and about 20 percent of them resulted in twenty or more deaths (Bekoe 2012).

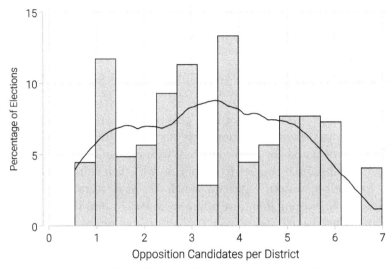

FIGURE I.I Opposition candidacy in authoritarian elections

candidates as the total number of candidates minus one. The figure shows the distribution of national averages of opposition candidates per constituency for single-member district systems across electoral authoritarian regimes.[5]

In contrast to foundational work in political science that predicts two-party competition in single-member district settings (Duverger 1954), Figure 1.1 shows that the average number of *opposition* candidates in single-member districts is much higher. In competitive democracies the fourth or fifth candidate in a race or, nationally, the fourth or fifth most powerful party, has little chance to win. In electoral authoritarian regimes the prospects of opposition victory are even lower. And yet, the average number of opposition candidates for the legislature in these regimes is between three and four.

We know that electoral authoritarian settings are ones in which parameters of benefits of office, prospects of victory, and costs of running for office differ in ways that should predict low rates of opposition candidacy. And yet, we see that these regimes actually feature more opposition

---

[5] This figure uses Wahman and Teorell's (2013) regime classification scheme because of its superior data coverage in contemporary elections. Elsewhere, I rely on Morse's (2019) approach, which focuses on sub-Saharan Africa, and Schedler (2013), which runs from 1972 to 2004. The figure does not include mixed-member systems with both majoritarian and proportional constituencies.

challengers than democracies do. These two seemingly incompatible facts shape the puzzle this book engages.

Election challengers often face little chance of victory but they endure. Even in settings where opposition supporters are not regularly targeted by the government and are allowed to exist without significant interference, they face substantial barriers to victory. So why then would anyone ever run for the opposition in general, much less in electoral authoritarian regimes? The existing literature offers some insight into the motivations of candidates that can be adapted to the puzzle of opposition candidacy in electoral authoritarian regimes.

The Rational Office Seeker

For decades, scholars have looked for the answer to the question of political candidacy in the same place: the rational, utility-maximizing assumptions underlying many theories of political behavior, including participation and candidacy. They rest on the idea that political actors consider the costs and benefits of a given set of choices and act upon whichever choice will deliver the greatest expected benefit. Strategic consideration of political ambition guides the decisions of prospective candidates (Aldrich 2011, Schlesinger 1966). Throughout the book, I generally refer to this approach as the strategic candidacy framework.

This theoretical approach has dominated studies of why people run for office in advanced democracies and this is for good reason: politicians generally act strategically and manifest behavior consistent with their political goals. Black (1972), Rohde (1979), and others offer that actors consider running with a political party and compare the expected utility of a number of alternatives; this provides a framework in which opposition versus ruling party candidacy decisions can be analyzed. The payoff of running is shaped by the benefits of winning and holding office, the costs of campaigning, and the chances of winning.

This approach has some intuitive appeal but it cannot tell us much about opposition candidacy. The disadvantages that opposition parties and their candidates face under electoral authoritarianism are constitutive of those regimes. An "uneven playing field" is the critical feature that distinguishes them from democracies (Levitsky and Way 2010*a*). Even opposition candidates who manage to overcome the significant hurdles erected before them and actually win offices still benefit less than ruling party members of parliament (MPs). Incumbent strangleholds over coffers deprive the opposition of the material benefits of office. Ruling party supermajorities thwart opposition lawmakers through legal and extralegal avenues. The costs of running are substantial. Candidates cannot rely on financial support from opposition parties, and challengers in electoral authoritarian regimes routinely face interference with financial affairs, extrajudicial arrests, and sometimes personal injury and death.

Strategic Defection

An explanation of opposition candidacy most closely related to strategic calculations of the benefits, costs, and prospects of candidacy offers that individuals hold expectations about the future that impact current candidacy decisions. This literature argues that opposition candidates emerge at critical times of ruling party weakness and are not political outsiders. They come from within the ruling elite as defectors. This intuition draws from research on democratic transitions that has long recognized that the breakdown of authoritarian regimes is "the consequence – direct or indirect – of important divisions within the authoritarian regime itself" (O'Donnell and Schmitter 1986, 19).[6]

Some work has supported this account of ruling party defection by demonstrating the relative frequency with which it occurs. For example, about 19 percent of executive elections in authoritarian regimes from 1946 to 2004 featured at least one opposition candidate who defected from the ruling party. When defections occur and the opposition fields candidates cooperatively, the odds of incumbent defeat are one in four, twice what they are absent those conditions (Lucardi 2015). When electoral institutions foment ruling elite factionalism, defection can contribute to the downfall of long-standing authoritarian parties (Langston 2006). Ruling party defections dilute the "image of invincibility" of the governing party and directly impact the probability of opposition victory (Magaloni 2006). The incentives to defect to challenger parties are particularly high during an economic crisis (Reuter and Gandhi 2011). If this constrains the public resources available for use by the ruling party, it may help balance the disadvantages of running for the opposition versus the ruling party (Greene 2007).

---

[6] Geddes (1999) and Przeworski (1991) raise similar points.

Strategic defection offers a convincing explanation of why opposition candidates may run for office. However, it does not account for what was revealed earlier: opposition candidates proliferate in elections across time, across regimes, and no matter the prospects of the party in power. Candidacy thus remains incompletely explained.

Co-optation

A significant literature on authoritarianism focuses on the role of elections in prolonging regime duration by creating opportunities to co-opt challengers (Gandhi and Przeworski 2007). It speaks to co-optation at three distinctive levels: the legislature, political parties, and individual candidates. Most accounts are focused on the creation of legislatures as a co-optation strategy whereby the targeted group is represented by broad opposition forces – formal and informal – rather than specific individuals, groups, or political parties. Legislatures institutionalize dissent by credibly guaranteeing a modicum of representation and influence to the opposition, while silencing the opposition's dissent to formal parliamentary proceedings (Gandhi 2008). Legislatures permit the ruling party to constrain and contain potentially critical political elites, while regulating the process of candidate entry through access to the spoils of office. Authoritarian elections, in this view, constitute a contest over access to state resources rather than a space for policy making (Lust-Okar 2009, Lust-Okar 2005). In this view, co-optation means that opposition forces concede some capacity to challenge the legitimacy of the regime outright in exchange for access to some of those resources. To borrow Schedler's (2006) concept of the "nested game," the opposition has sacrificed some stakes in the overarching competition with the government over the rules of the regime in exchange for guarantees for the less consequential but more immediate game of electoral competition. Growing reliance on this lower-level game as the primary arena of competition makes opposition complicit with, if not dependent on, the sustained rule of the authoritarian regime (Gandhi and Lust-Okar 2009). At the same time, evidence indicates that parliaments can become powerful checks on executives, presumably a role that was not envisioned when the executives created them in the first place and is driven instead by the accumulation of power outside the statehouse (Collard 2019, Opalo 2019).

Others point to co-optation at the level of the political party. Weak and poorly institutionalized opposition parties have proliferated in sub-Saharan Africa (Rakner and van de Walle 2009*b*); while parties in some countries are solidifying (Weghorst and Bernhard 2015), the weakness of opposition is baked into an authoritarian regime's strategy toward managing opponents (Riedl 2014). Many opposition parties operate as shells for the ambition of individual elites and are organizationally flimsy. An array of so-called briefcase parties only exist as institutions on papers held by the head of the "party" (Kelly 2019) with little on-the-ground presence (Randall and Svasand 2002). In this perspective, parties are filled with spurned ruling party elites and primarily exist as vehicles to return to the party (Morse 2015) or for amassing resources through avenues that do not exist in civil society, where the combination of ethnic salience and heterogeneity lends itself to highly localized parties (Wahman 2017). Organizations of these types are hardly capable of winning meaningful political power and, so the thinking goes, they attempt to extract material resources from the ruling party because that is the best option available to them.

At the individual level, opposition candidacy is explained by a logic similar to that of the party-level story: rent-seeking behavior demonstrated by individuals who desire clientelistic goods. By standing on an opposition ticket, a candidate can illustrate their power to the incumbent party and that they are sufficiently valuable to be bought off (Frantz and Kendall-Tayler 2014, Gandhi 2008, Gandhi and Przeworski 2007). Scholars claim that the opposition attracts rent seekers because policy goals are generally not attainable for the opposition and, if achieved, are attributed to the ruling party (Reuter and Robertson 2015). Thus, strong ideologists are argued to be unlikely to run for office for the opposition, as doing so is "both ideologically distasteful and a poor investment for ardent oppositions of the ruling government" (Lust-Okar 2009, 239).

It is absolutely the case that some opposition parties exist simply to amass resources from the ruling party, and the leaders of those parties are extracting whatever they can from the government. This, after all, is the dominant narrative of African politics that has been written and reiterated from Chabal and Daloz (1999) to the scholarship of the current day. It is also the case that many opposition parties are electorally weak, but electoral performance is a bad heuristic for opposition viability because election outcomes are endogenous to the strategy of authoritarian rule.

Some opposition parties are strong on formal organizational, conflict mediation, and linkages dimensions that lend credibility to opposition (LeBas 2011, 25). These parties – whose messaging resonates with voters and who have built experience and reputation over time and space – are viable challengers to the regime (LeBas 2011, Rakner and van de Walle 2009*b*, Wahman 2017). There is little empirical evidence that these parties are rent-seeking, that they are willing to accept the terms of competition dictated by the government, or that their candidates are responsive to co-optation overtures. The opposition has comparative advantages in criticizing the government for rampant corruption and being overrun with such rent-seeking behavior, and they appear to be capitalizing on it (Bleck and van de Walle 2018, 213–215).

Most insight on candidate-level co-optation comes from a handful of case studies outside sub-Saharan Africa. Ultimately, my book is about the individuals who choose to run for legislative office on the ballots of durable and strong opposition parties. In developing my theory of opposition candidacy in the next chapter, I will detail a number of reasons why co-optation is fundamentally incompatible with the aspirants who stand for those types of political parties, the ones that matter for the future of democracy and authoritarianism in Africa. Indeed, the most systematic evidence we have about co-optation in autocracies convincingly demonstrates these kinds of opposition parties are very unlikely to be co-opted (Kavasoglu 2021).

Ideology

The guiding appeal of candidacy in each of the previously discussed approaches is the promise of material gains from running for office. The final explanation in the literature takes the most distinctive view toward candidacy in proposing that some prospective candidates are driven by nonmaterial aspirations. They instead run as candidates to advance ideological goals. This account is advanced most persuasively by Greene (2007), who demonstrates that opposition candidacy may facilitate expressive benefits like demanding democratization, human rights, the rule of law, or in some cases extremist or niche policies. The account of opposition candidacy advanced in my book builds upon this foundation. I aim to explain not just that individuals are motivated by different goals or that opposition parties facilitate obtaining different candidacy goals, but from where differences in political goals and benefits of running for office originate. Why do staunch proponents of ideology take on those views in the first place? The theoretical approach of this book weds insights about the origins of political ambition to an understanding of how this shapes later candidacy calculations.

Legacies of Single-Party Rule

Finally, two related, yet distinctive, macro-level accounts of the origins of competitive party politics and party institutionalization in Africa offer insight germane to theorizing individual-level decision making under electoral authoritarianism. In both accounts, party-level dynamics at the onset of multiparty rule take on character from the antecedent era of single-party rule. Riedl (2014) argues that party systems in Africa are shaped by legacies of single-party rule. When authoritarian governments marginalized rival social and political actors by creating their own substitute institutions instead of incorporating those rivals, they played a less central role in setting up the multiparty system. The resulting framework was less regulated and this promotes less institutionalized political parties. The implication for candidacy is that variation in the difficulties of opposition candidacy is due to legacies of the party system.

Speaking directly to opposition mobilization, LeBas (2011) offers that strong opposition parties emerge when they draw upon mobilization structures in society that existed before multiparty transitions. This allows them to build broad, national constituencies with extensive linkages to voters and to stoke conflict with ruling parties. In the case of Zimbabwe, this takes the form of trade unions but may include other civic organizations. In many ways, the claims of my book are complementary to those of LeBas (2011), offering micro-level evidence related to opposition strength from the perspective of candidates.

1.3 THE ARGUMENT IN BRIEF

The theory guiding this book centers on three core ideas. First, most research on candidacy considers the decision to run in a snapshot moment ahead of an election. I instead argue that candidacy decisions are best understood as the result of years- sometimes decades-long paths in public and private life that impose strong path dependencies on candidacy decisions. Specifically, civic activism and careers in the civil society organization (CSO) and nongovernmental organization (NGO) sectors forge pathways to opposition candidacy, while cultivating experience through political party activism – what I call career partisanship – that leads to ruling party candidacy.

Second, the strategic model of candidacy can be innovated to account for opposition candidacy in electoral authoritarian contexts. My book does so by expanding on the parameters of that model – benefits of office, chances of election, and costs of candidacy – such that opposition candidacy can actually be attractive to some aspirants. Due to hyper-incumbency advantages and access to state resources, opposition parties simply cannot compete on the ground of providing material benefits to aspirants and legislators. The benefits they offer aspirants and the ease of winning party nominations compared with the ruling party make opposition candidacy more appealing under the strategic candidacy framework.

Third, the civic and party activist experiences that precede candidacy ambition directly shape strategic candidacy calculations. I show that civic activism versus career partisanship impacts the benefits candidates seek from office, their expectations regarding electoral victory, and their willingness to pay nonfinancial costs of running for office. Experiences with civic activism boost nomination and election prospects, increase the value of ideological and policy benefits, underlie the belief that there are benefits in losing elections, and increase the willingness to bear the risks of running for office. It is ultimately life experiences that shape long-term paths to candidacy and how they make sense of the strategic considerations facing individuals when aspirants do decide if they will run for office.

Civic Activism and Career Partisanship

Neither Ismail Jussa nor James Mbatia ever planned on entering politics. To this day, James Mbatia holds that the manner in which multipartyism returned to Tanzania in the 1990s was far too rushed, and the government needed to slow reforms to allow government challengers to develop. He nonetheless has been in the opposition since 1992. It was only after he was expelled from the University of Dar es Salaam that he found himself in the June 21 and June 22, 1991 meetings of the NCCR-Mageuzi's steering committee leading the push to multipartyism and broader government reforms. Although he remains the longest-standing member of the party that grew from the convention, it is deeply personal experiences with student and civic activism that brought him there. His drive in Tanzanian politics remains now as it has been since 1991: to fundamentally reform the constitution no matter win or lose for his own personal political stake.

Similarly, while Jussa was active civically in his youth in Zanzibar, he was far from weighing political ambition. It was later – through experiences in secondary school and afterward studying law in the United

Kingdom – that his social and political activism pushed him toward legislative office. These experiences laid bare to him fundamental political injustices in Tanzania: the policies that defined the role of Zanzibar in the Tanzanian state. Unable to return home in between semesters for fear the Tanzanian government would revoke his passport over pro-Zanzibari activism, he came to see the solutions to those problems came through policy change in the legislature.

By contrast, January Makamba was essentially a member of CCM from birth. He was first formally involved in primary school and officially joined the party's youth wing at age fifteen. He advanced rapidly within the party, due to both his father's lifelong commitment to the political party and his own steadfast loyalty to former President Jakaya Kikwete. He describes his eventual emergence in politics as an advisor to the president at age thirty-one as "inevitable." He first ran for office in 2010; in a period of five years, he became an MP, a cabinet minister, and was one of the final five nomination seekers for the 2015 CCM presidency at age of forty-one. By 2010, he had paid sufficient dues to the party and his political stakes were tied to CCM.

These three accounts suggest a path dependence into candidacy and that the real kernel of candidacy lies in initial decisions to become involved in politics in the first place. Thus, rather than narrowing our focus on expressive ambition (candidates presenting themselves for office), we need to trace candidacy to a more "nascent" form of ambition that inspires initial considerations of candidacy (Fox and Lawless 2005, 644). I argue that understanding individuals' lifetime trajectories is very important for explaining ruling party versus opposition candidacy in electoral authoritarian regimes. The most defining feature of life trajectory that differentiates opposition versus ruling party candidates in such environments is demonstrating civic activism versus career partisanship.

Civic activists and opposition parties are natural allies: from a policy-outcome perspective, they pursue broadly similar goals like protecting human rights, alleviating poverty, and promoting transparency. Opposition parties have distinct advantages over civic activists in shaping policies directly through political channels, but have limited resources to allocate to training and recruiting candidates, mobilizing supporters during elections, and basic infrastructure like offices, phone banks, and so on. Civil society organizations have advantages in financial and organizational resources, public visibility and name recognition, and network and mobilization infrastructure, but cannot directly change government policy. These complementarities mean that opposition parties and civic activists coalesce to form "social-electoral coalitions" (Trejo 2014) where opposition parties recruit civic activists to run for office. Civic activism experiences therefore establish pathways to later opposition candidacy.

The goal of my book is to explain opposition candidacy for legislatures; to comprehensively do so, I must also understand alternative routes to power through the ruling party. For this pathway, I propose career partisanship as a new concept akin to the trajectory of a career politician (Mattozzi and Merlo 2008, Sousa and Canon 1992), where individuals come to "live off" this career as a vocation (Weber 1921). Career partisanship is the process by which individuals come to rely on partisanship as their key source of political capital and as a means of primary or supplementary financial gain. Entry into the ruling party at an early age – in party-sponsored soccer teams, youth programs, and so on – and later party service are critical factors leading to candidacy that occur long before individuals act on running for office. Ruling party candidacy is preceded by partisanship, service in local party politics, and further participation in elite party circles years before more advanced opportunities like candidacy exist (Reuter and Turvosky 2014). These activities are important to ruling party elites because they signify commitment and loyalty, which head off internal factionalism that can break the party.

The empirical analysis presented in this book affirms the role civic activism plays in legislative candidacy for opposition parties, while career partisanship underlies running for the ruling party. These analyses span two chapters of the book and draw upon original survey data collected from legislators, sequence analysis of biographical, vocational, and political careers of an additional 700 Tanzanian lawmakers, and extensive qualitative interviews with the major players in Tanzanian politics. These are complemented by years of my own experience on the ground and a wealth of archival resources collected through the process. The traditions in the study of candidacy explain what factors a prospective candidate weighs at the moment of leaping into candidacy (or not), but we have almost no idea how they ended up at that crossroads. The tale we often tell of a political career and candidacy only begins at the conclusion of the story; my book sheds light on that journey.

Adapting the Strategic Candidacy Model

It is possible to explain opposition candidacy in electoral authoritarian regimes using the predominant rationalist account that conceives of candidacy as a choice driven by cost-benefit calculations at the moment an aspirant decides whether or not to run. Doing so, however, requires adding greater depth to each parameter in the framework.

The existing approach conceives of the probability of victory as driven by election prospects; instead, I take into account the combined prospects of nomination and election. While election victory is more difficult for opposition candidates in electoral authoritarian regimes compared with their ruling party rivals, securing nominations is much easier. The comparable ease of making it onto an electoral ballot offsets some of the electoral disadvantages opposition candidates face.

The benefits consideration in the conventional approach generally assumes candidates want material benefits and that those benefits are only delivered by holding office. I point to how opposition parties in electoral authoritarian regimes offer different benefits to prospective legislators, and politicians also vary in terms of what they want out of running for office. Drawing from survey data and in-depth interviews, the book will show that opposition candidates place greater value on nonmaterial benefits associated with office and, further, that opposition parties are better positioned to deliver those benefits. In settings where being in the opposition all but shuts off access to material benefits of legislative service, the compatibility between what opposition candidates want and what opposition parties offer is key to adapting the strategic framework.

Following Greene (2007), I also argue that prospective candidates may gain something out of losing elections and that these gains are uniquely suited for opposition candidates. Unsuccessful election contests may provide the campaign experience and know-how that is needed for later success. These are the very types of skills that opposition parties cannot provide through conventional channels of candidate recruitment and training. By contrast, losing as a ruling party candidate in spite of all of the advantages the party enjoys can end a political career. The act of expressing commitment to policy positions and standing up for a cause can provide value to candidates, even if they lose the election. As the book will show, these kinds of expressive gains from losing elections are more common among opposition candidates and also are more compatible with the nonmaterial, ideologically driven benefits opposition candidates seek. In the context of the strategic framework, this expanded understanding of benefits ultimately means the probability of opposition candidates obtaining benefits from candidacy is greater than just the odds of nomination and election victory.

The strategic candidacy framework conceives of costs as campaign expenditures and this requires adaptation for electoral authoritarian contexts. Costs may also relate to the heightened prominence that comes with candidacy, particularly for unsuccessful government challengers who are subsequently punished by the authoritarian regime. These nonmaterial costs can be high, but empirical analysis shows will show that opposition candidates demonstrate much greater willingness to pay those costs.

Linking Activism to the Strategic Model

The third tenet of my theory ties the two previous components together and emphasizes the path dependent nature of civic activism's role in shaping candidacy decisions. I contend that each parameter of the adapted strategic candidacy model I offer – the prospects of nomination and election, the benefits of winning and losing elections, and nonmaterial costs of running for office – are directly shaped by experiences in civic activism. Drawing from the insight of legislators, candidates, nomination seekers, and prospective aspirants who chose not to run, the chapters of the book offer evidence that civic activism drives perceived and actual election success for opposition candidates, shapes which benefits candidates seek, and influences consent to accept the high risks associated with running for a challenger party. It is possible to innovate the strategy candidacy framework to account for opposition candidacy under electoral authoritarianism, but the reasons for this strategic choice are found in the paths to candidacy ahead of that choice.

1.4 CONTRIBUTIONS

This book joins a growing literature on electoral authoritarian regimes and contributes to this scholarship. While the importance of authoritarian rule in the twenty-first century is undeniable, these regimes are commonly secretive and closed to outside observers, meaning insight provided by scholars and policy makers is not commonly drawn directly from first-hand elite accounts. In this tradition of current work on electoral authoritarianism, "authoritarian institutions do exactly what their creators want them to do" (Pepinsky 2014, 632).[7] Theories about political

---

[7] Meng's (2020) book stands out from this practice, offering an account where the authoritarian leaders' early decisions about executive constraints have counter-intuitive

decision making, particularly opposition activism, are generated at the elite level but often rely on subnational elite or citizen-level perspectives to draw conclusions about regime-level dynamics, perhaps because of the closed nature of authoritarian research environments. My book follows national-level political elites – potential legislators, especially those who may run for the opposition – as they navigate through the environment of authoritarian institutions, a setting that is elaborately detailed through rich archival and qualitative interview data. It theorizes their experiences, strategies, and decision making and then evaluates that theory using systematic, quantitative data on their choices and experiences. In this way, it bridges a deep divide in scholarship between the focus on political institutions and the behavior of political actors.

This approach allows my book to make sense of something that has been largely overlooked in this literature: opposition candidacy for legislative office. Opposition parties and their candidates are generally treated as ancillary or unimportant in electoral authoritarian regimes. As Morse (2012) notes regarding Levitsky and Way (2010a, 186-187), "Using the metaphor of the 'three little pigs,' they argue that it is the strength of the 'house' (regime) that matters, not the fact that there are 'wolves' (oppositions)." Applying an analogy of playing cards, the opposition participates knowing the deck is stacked and can do little but play with the hand dealt, as this is the only game the house is willing to play. With few exceptions, discussion of the political opposition as theoretically distinctive actors is rare and secondary. This is even more pronounced in sub-Saharan Africa – a point raised by Rakner and van de Walle (2009b). When scholars do consider what opposition actors may want, many point to material rewards such as access to the state and the role of "competitive clientelism" (Lust-Okar 2009), while few suggest they are driven to shape both electoral outcomes and the overall framework of strategic competition over political power (Schedler 2006).

What I hope is clear at this point is that in spite of the institutional disadvantages that are defining characteristics of electoral authoritarian regimes, opposition actors must be taken seriously. Ruling parties may hold the power to resist pressure from challengers; however, when the opposition acts in unity to mobilize civil society, it can induce political

downstream consequences for those leaders. She demonstrates that autocrats who are initially strong can resist institutionalized constraints like powerful cabinets, term limits, and succession rules but that foregoing these constraints ultimately results in less durable autocracy.

change (Kaya and Bernhard 2013). The opposition in electoral authoritarian regimes can and sometimes does win. Several of sub-Saharan Africa's most competitive regimes first experienced episodes of electoral authoritarian rule, and the strategies of opposition actors then impact what those parties do in government now.[8] Even absent victory, tens of thousands of candidates run on the legislative tickets of opposition parties around the globe each year; the existing explanations why this is so are deeply unsatisfying.

My account links civic activism as a long-term pathway to opposition candidacy and also establishes a framework of candidacy decision making that emphasizes nonmaterial drivers of political candidacy ambition, a motivation that links back to civic activist experiences. By contrast, ruling party candidacy under electoral authoritarianism conforms to much of what the "new institutionalism" in electoral authoritarian scholarship anticipates: career partisanship channels political ambition into the ruling party and manages the process of candidate emergence, thus allowing electoral and party institutions to operate in service of the elites who implement them. Elites who do run for the ruling party are constrained by selection procedures; when they do get onto electoral ballots, they seek the material spoils of office that ruling parties are equipped to offer. These insights are important and inform four critical academic and policy literatures. I discuss each in the text that immediately follows.

Performance and Accountability

Elections regularize political competition and draw rival factions to stand in opposition to incumbent governments. Political theorists and scholars have long attributed this to the power of elections to induce alternation. As far back as Athenian democracy, the principles of "freedom consisted not in obeying only oneself but in obeying today someone in whose [position] one would be tomorrow" (Manin 1997, 17). Elections are more than a system of rule in which parties compete; the most meaningful quality of elections is whether and how often they induce parties to take turns losing (Przeworski 1991). What ruling parties would do if they lost an election – concede defeat or suspend elections altogether – can only be known once it occurs (Przeworski, Stokes, and Manin 2000, 22).

---

[8] Based on Morse's (2019) typology, Ghana and Kenya stand out in this regard.

Without the assumption of one (or many) opposition challenger(s), few existing theories of governance and elections yield novel conclusions. Voters choose from a theoretically infinite slate of candidates or party policies arrayed spatially on policy dimensions (Congleton 2002, Downs 1957). Moral hazard and adverse selection problems steeped in political accountability cannot be overcome without choice. When incumbents face no punishment for failing to deliver on public goods (Rogoff 1990) and little pressure to articulate policy preferences (Ferejohn 1986), they have little reason to pursue citizen interests (Barro 1973). Elected leaders who compete in contested versus uncontested constituencies perform better in office across a number of outcomes and settings.

Challengers are critical in electoral authoritarian settings in a number of ways. First, though competition in the aggregate may be weak, regional pockets or other forms of subnational opposition can be important features that shape the national level of contestation (Dahl 1971, 11–13). Second, incumbents regularly overestimate the popularity of their challengers and may consequently improve performance. In electoral authoritarian regimes, ruling party politicians are more responsive to constituent demands and performance evaluations when they face a challenger from another party (Grossman and Michelitch 2018). Ruling parties may also attempt to marginalize the opposition and dilute their support by offering platforms that incorporate opposition policy issues (Greene 2008), thereby improving citizen-level outcomes. Thus, even if readers find nothing of interest in this volume with regard to the long-term prospects of democracy in electoral authoritarian regimes, there is value in understanding opposition candidacy for the sake of authoritarian government accountability.

Civil Society, Party Building, and Democracy

A long tradition of scholarship on democracy has pointed to the role of civic actors in mobilizing against autocratic regimes. In the Colour Revolutions, for example, public protests over election fraud at the hands of autocrats ultimately forced those autocrats to leave office (Beissinger 2007). Successful transitions in post-Communist Europe and Eurasia relied on the opposition's ability to "build ties with organizations in civil society in order to pursue the common goal of free and fair elections" (Bunce and Wolchik 2011, 254–255). This notion underlies the "socioelectoral coalitions" Trejo (2014) argues form between opposition parties and civic actors surrounding authoritarian elections. Statistical evidence affirms the collaborative role of opposition and civil society in elections; as Schedler (2008, 198) finds, "parties strong and bold enough to take their followers to the streets have impressive chances of reducing official margins of victory."

Opposition parties can link to civil society organizations and civic activism networks for more than just mobilization: my book will show their complementarities extend to candidates and elections if parties are able to draw upon the mobilization capacity of civic networks. Indeed, foundational concepts like party system "freeze" (Lipset and Rokkan 1967) are based on the idea that political parties are founded around existing social cleavages in society like religious organizations and labor groups. Successful Western European parties used these preexisting organizations to rally supporters and coordinate political choice (Boix 2007, Kalyvas 1996).

While accounts of electoral reforms in sub-Saharan Africa in the 1990s identify the key role of citizen mobilization (e.g., Bratton and van de Walle 1997); Riedl (2014) convincingly demonstrates that civil society in contemporary Africa is hampered by the legacies of single-party rule: ruling cadres that incorporated existing rivals into the regime rather than subverting them through new structures were able to manage and oversee transitions to multipartyism. In doing so, they maintained a persistent influence over emergent political challengers, leading to more regime stability and more institutionalized political parties. Tanzania is an example where the single-party state developed parallel institutions to completely marginalize alternative sources of political power and, in doing so, completely flattened civil society. My book thus shows that even under worst-case scenario conditions for robust civil society and well-institutionalized opposition political parties, civil society organizations and civic activism can underlie opposition candidacy motivations.

This conclusion has important implications for policy makers. Every year, foreign governments and other international donors spend billions of dollars to support the development of democracy throughout the globe. These donors choose where they invest their resources and need to know what levers are most effective for promoting short- and long-term political change. My book suggests that resources dedicated to direct party support like financial aid, training and capacity-building workshops, and networking opportunities from partner/sibling members of global party alliances (e.g., the National Democratic Institute and the International Republican Institute in the United States; Fredrich-Ebert-Stiftung in Germany) may be better allocated elsewhere. The same is true for foreign governments whose financial support comes with conditionalities tied to opening the political party environment. Political parties in electoral authoritarian regimes are subject to widespread interference from the government, while in these settings civil society operates with comparably fewer restraints. Efforts to strengthen civic space and civil society actors may be easier to effectively implement in these regimes. This provides opposition parties with sources of mobilization capacity to draw upon in future elections. More fundamentally, if pathways to candidacy begin long before the manifestation of candidacy ambitions, then activities like candidacy training workshops put on by an international actor are missing the key entry point to engage prospective candidates. Engaging in capacity building at the stage of expressed interest in candidacy is analogous to focusing on planting a single, mature tree with the expectation of it yielding a future forest; promoting civil society activism reaches potential future opposition legislators earlier in candidacy pipelines and is more like planting hundreds or thousands of seedlings that may each grow into a robust tree.

Relatedly, the volume also offers a wrinkle to the "democratization by elections" thesis that consecutive elections have the causal power to improve democracy, even if the elections themselves are poor quality. That civic actors learn to better challenge the government in power and opposition parties improve their ability to mobilize voters and campaign are two distinctive mechanisms through which holding elections promotes democratic growth (Lindberg 2006*b*). If opposition parties draw from civic activists to field candidates and mobilize supporters, then these two mechanisms feed on each other. Going back to motivations of policy makers to support democracy, there appear to be multiple possible pathways through which investments in civil society strengthening programming can improve democratic outcomes.

African Politics

This book is the first to comprehensively document the decision-making process regarding candidacy for national legislatures in Africa. African regimes are overwhelmingly presidential, and this has important consequences for the comparable strength of Africa's legislatures (van de Walle 2003), which scholars mostly overlooked until recently. Legislatures are of critical importance in Africa and often the main point of interaction between citizens and the state. Legislators in Africa play a prominent role in lawmaking and oversight, but they are also seen as the primary agents of economic development in the eyes of voters. More than simply representative institutions, authoritarian legislatures can evolve into more empowered institutions over time (Collard 2019) and check executive power (Opalo 2019), particularly if their members are oriented toward political reform (Barkan 2009). Legislatures and legislative elections are – alongside media and the judiciary – the primary arenas of contestation in which opponents can challenge authoritarian regimes (Levitsky and Way 2010b, 58–60). Legislatures are where the opposition has the chance to win some legislative seats and to show their character as potential alternatives to the government. In Africa, opposition parties gain greater vote share in legislative elections than they do in presidential ones (Rakner and van de Walle 2009b, 209). Legislatures are institutions that serve as focal points of opposition activism and coordination (Levitsky and Way 2002) and can induce antecedent autocratic governments into further liberal reforms and ultimately democratic transition (Fish 2006). My book also provides unparalleled insight into the institutions that shape the candidacy process, including documenting what candidate selection looks like with actual results from primaries and detailed data on campaign expenditures, finance, and mobilization strategy.

The narrative of what drives political behavior in Africa emphasizes material motivations, rent seeking, and clientelism. Political parties are viewed as institutionally weak with little to differentiate them regarding policy views or ideology. Only recently have scholars noted that opposition parties and candidates may differ from their ruling party counterparts in their willingness to deploy policy messaging and discourse to mobilize voters (Bleck and van de Walle 2018, 213–215). My book shows that at the candidate level, opposition actors are more motivated by policy-related and ideological goals and that opposition parties are better equipped to provide those benefits. Chapter 10 – the final empirical chapter of the book – affirms that across Africa's electoral authoritarian regimes and dominant party democracies, opposition legislators differ greatly from ruling party MPs on legislative policy dimensions: across executive oversight, budgetary procedures, lawmaking, and local development. This suggests an important reframing of how we think about policy making and ideology under the conditions of electoral hegemony that predominate across sub-Saharan Africa. The emphasis opposition places on promoting democracy, criticizing incumbents, and expanding social pluralism is, in fact, the domain of policy making over which they can exercise control. The opposition may share much in common with the ruling party in terms of on-the-ground campaign rhetoric, but that is the game they are meant to lose. The higher-level contest in the nested game of electoral authoritarianism – the competition over the rules that structure the system and entrench the ruling party in power – is where the opposition's policy gains are most consequential and where their efforts are oriented.

The book offers an in-depth investigation of the puzzle of opposition candidacy through a rich and multifaceted research study anchored in Tanzania, which features the longest-standing ruling party in Africa and second-longest in the world today. While there is interest in Tanzania, it is often dismissed by scholars who see it as unique and not worth comparison: the dominant role of politicized ethnic and religious cleavages in Africa is more muted there; it features a ruling party that invested in party-state building in a way that few African regimes had; Tanzania's first President Julius K. Nyerere's single-party regime, while just as economically disastrous as those of other peers in the postcolonial era, left behind a level of nationalism uncommon to the subcontinent. The picture that is becoming clearer from the emergent research on Tanzania – Carlitz (2017), Carlitz and McLellan (2021), Collard (2019), Croke (2017), Kwayu (2015), Morse (2019), Paget (2020), Rosenzweig (2018), Tsubura (2018), among others – is not that these legacies make Tanzania unique.

My volume, like many of the other works coming out of Tanzania, shows the opposite: theoretical and empirical insights derived from Tanzania travel well to other comparative contexts in Africa and more broadly among electoral authoritarian regimes. It may be that Tanzania is viewed by some as too peculiar to warrant greater engagement because the research environment is more difficult than many more commonly studied countries. The challenges of collecting high-quality qualitative and quantitative research is especially pronounced for studying national-level political elites. Swahili is the *lingua franca* and a language with layers of complex meaning; fluency is critical to building trust and rapport that underlie informative and revealing qualitative interviews. Government authorities tightly regulate research permissions for academics, and they enforce compliance in ways that researchers in other settings may evade. Parties and candidates may be closed off for their own reasons, including suspicion of outsiders and fear of exposing their internal workings. My book presents survey data that is one-of-a-kind both in Tanzania and in the study of African politics. It is one of only two surveys conducted with Tanzanian MPs in Tanzania's quarter century of multiparty politics,[9] and the only survey conducted in the Zanzibar House of Representatives in the existence of the institution. It is the only survey ever conducted with candidate aspirants who are not legislators (losing candidates, losing nomination seekers, prospective "noncandidates") in Tanzania and, one of only a handful of studies with surveys of non-MP legislative aspirants in Africa.[10] Interviews with party elites and documents like political party primary returns were obtained from connections developed over the decade this project has spanned.

Collecting difficult to obtain data is not a particularly meaningful contribution to the study of African politics in its own right, but doing so points to how deep engagement in a case over time, especially one with high barriers to entry, can yield novel empirical strategies. In the book, I employ quantitative methods for studying behavioral implications of path dependence in the form of sequence analysis of civic activism and career partisanship. Path dependence is a phenomenon that pervades political decision making, and the careers of politicians and scholars have shown the role of underlying "nascent" political ambition in downstream candidacy choices, but the application of sequence methods to studying paths is rare.[11] My surveys utilize *methali*, cultural proverbs that offer novel ways of measuring attitudes toward risk and time that address underlying ethical and measurement concerns associated with conventional behavioral measures. Retrospective survey reports of candidacy ambition and the beginning of paths toward candidacy are subject to several sources of bias; the use of innovative techniques like the life history calendar and carefully designed survey instruments can address these issues. I hope I show that lower-tech solutions to measurement and identification problems unlocked by knowledge of existing social practices, norms, and institutions are powerful.[12] This is particularly important in sub-Saharan Africa, where there exist oral and aural traditions of sharing information about political and social values.

---

[9] The African Legislature Project is the other; it surveyed fifty legislators. Most other legislator surveys were conducted prior to or shortly after independence. See, for example, Hopkins (1970) and McGowan and Bolland (1971).

[10] Cloward and Weghorst's (2019) work on legislative aspirants in Kenya's 2017 elections is another.

[11] MacKenzie's (2015) study of American legislators uses sequence methods.

[12] Kramon and Weghorst (2019) raise a similar point with regard to survey questionnaire design.

Candidacy and Careers across Regime Contexts

The study of candidacy mostly focuses on the United States. To make sense of candidacy decisions in different regions and regimes, scholars may employ one of two strategies. One approach is to follow the model in the American politics subfield and develop a theory that is rooted in the specificities of a given case. Theoretical scope and externally valid empirical findings are fundamental concerns for scholars of comparative politics – particularly those working in countries in the Global South – so this tactic is not productive for broadening our knowledge of candidacy. The alternative strategy is to engage existing theories on their own terms and innovate and adapt them to be externally valid, for example, bridge building. My book seeks to do this in the study of candidacy. Rational models of candidacy ambition have typically embedded within them assumptions about the dynamics of electoral prospects, benefits of office, and costs of competition that do not track well outside established democracies with advanced economies. While my volume will leave the reader with the impression that pathways to candidacy through civic activism and career partisanship are more powerful drivers of candidacy decisions in electoral authoritarian regimes, it also speaks to this existing literature and contributes in three ways.

First, it introduces additional parameters into the strategic candidacy that account for imbalanced nomination and election competition,[13] choice specificity in benefits based on candidate preferences over benefit types and party capacity to deliver them, benefits derived from losing nominations and elections, and an expanded understanding of nonmaterial, non-campaign costs associated with campaigns. This expanded understanding of benefits can be particularly useful outside contexts of electoral authoritarian regimes, including advanced democracies. Second, my theory of pathways into political office and the way in which candidacy is shaped by prior life and career experiences speaks to a growing literature on the role of pre-candidacy experiences in shaping ambition. From Fox and Lawless's (2005) work on how "nascent ambition" accounts for why women choose to run (or not) for office in the United States to a resurgence of interest in how career background impacts representation (Carnes and Lupu 2015), shifting our focus from the moment of strategic decision making to the precipitating events that led to the decision is valuable for understanding candidacy across comparative

---

[13] I am not the first to do this in non-US contexts: see Greene (2007).

contexts. Relatedly, my book shows that doing so can help elucidate why strategic actors evaluate the utility of a given decision in the way that they do. That is, the work provides insight on what populates the parameters of strategic choice related to candidacy. Such an account not only tells us why someone runs for office on the basis of an array of factors that shape that decision, but also establishes why that individual cares about those particular factors at all in the first place.

1.5 ORGANIZATION OF THE BOOK

Why do individuals run for the legislature on opposition tickets in electoral authoritarian regimes? In the rest of this book, I answer this question in the context of Tanzania, where Africa's longest-ruling party has governed for more than fifty years. I do so by drawing upon survey data collected from members of Tanzania's two legislatures, as well as from losing candidates, unsuccessful nomination seekers, and prospective candidates. I augment these data with archival research, in-depth interviews with political elites, and a database of the CVs of more than 700 Tanzanian politicians. The book's narrative is carried by my own words, as well as the voices of current faces of Tanzanian politicians: January Makamba, Ismail Jussa, and James Mbatia.

Chapter 2 further explicates my theory of opposition candidacy in electoral authoritarian regimes. It reviews existing explanations of why individuals present themselves for office and offers insight on how such applications might apply to nondemocratic settings. It then unpacks my theory of the origins of candidacy in civic activism and career partisanship. The chapter exposes how many differences observed between ruling party and opposition candidates can be uncovered by turning the clock back on candidacy to the processes prior to elections.

Chapter 3 provides more detail on the analytical strategy for evaluating the theory. It discusses electoral authoritarianism broadly and contextualizes the case of Tanzania among two sets of peers: contemporary electoral authoritarian regimes in Africa and historically important electoral authoritarian regimes in other regions of the world. It then provides more detail on the history of Tanzania as it relates to its system of government and makes an argument for why Tanzania is an ideal case to study these dynamics. I discuss scope conditions of the theory and external validity of the case as well, particularly regarding the types of opposition parties I study and the strength of CCM as a political party. The chapter details the data resources I draw upon to test the theory guiding the book and provides a centralized discussion of the measurement and analysis strategies used in later chapters.

Chapters 4 through 10 form the empirically driven section of the book. Chapters 4–9 address implications of existing literature and original theory by empirical analysis of data from Tanzania. The final empirical chapter considers the applicability of my theory to other electoral regimes in Africa, testing scope conditions of the theory across regime type and competitiveness.

Chapter 4 focuses on the first stage of my theory of candidacy by looking to prospective candidates' journeys into politics. It studies how early experiences with civic activism and career partisanship shape why individuals run for office. The central statistical analyses in this chapter demonstrate that civic activism in the form of grassroots mobilization experience and membership and leadership in civic associations are associated with substantially higher chances of running as a part of the opposition. Career partisanship, by contrast, points to ruling party candidacy. In the chapter's narrative, we hear extensively from January, Jussa, and James on how experiences in their formative years led to where they are today and anchor their experiences with the stories of other candidates and information about the civil society sector in Tanzania and formative linkages between opposition parties and that sector.

Chapter 5 also evaluates the impact of civic activism and career partisanship on opposition versus ruling party candidacy with a different empirical resource and approach. Drawing on biographical records of more than 700 past and present Tanzanian legislators, I use sequence analysis to assess how vocational and political careers prior to candidacy shape party choice when aspiring to run for office. Sequence methods are relatively new to the social sciences but are powerful for studying path dependencies like life trajectories into legislative office. Using these techniques, I establish that vocational careers spent in the CSO/NGO sector are significantly more commonly found among opposition legislators, while lawmakers from CCM have much more career experience in paid political party positions and government jobs of a political character. The chapter also carries out a detailed sequence analysis of career partisanship in different forms, including low-level party service and progressive advancement within a political party. It rules out party service as a prominent path to the opposition, showing instead that the political careers of CCM MPs are much more similar to these operationalizations of career partisanship.

Chapters 6 through 9 are dedicated to the parameters of the modified strategic candidacy framework – probability of nomination, probability of election, benefits, and costs. Each chapter studies a parameter in its own right and evaluates its role in candidacy decisions in electoral authoritarian regimes with evidence from Tanzania. They also establish how civic activism impacts the parameter of focus in that chapter to reinforce how early life trajectories drive opposition candidacy decision making represented in those parameters.

Chapter 6 investigates what shapes nomination prospects in electoral authoritarian regimes. It briefly reviews the scope of candidate selection techniques available to parties and describes the procedures used by political parties in Tanzania. Drawing on survey data from nomination seekers and archives of actual primary results, the key intuition from the first portion of this chapter is that nominations are comparably much easier to obtain for Tanzania's opposition aspirants compared with those from CCM, and this is the case across a host of subjective and objective indicators. I also study the role of civic activism on nomination choices and outcomes for opposition actors. Survey data show that among prospective candidates in the opposition who consider legislative candidacy, those with greater civic activism experiences are more likely to follow through on their desire to run for office. And while nominations are easier to win in the opposition compared with CCM, among nomination seekers in the opposition, those with more civic activism experience had better chances of getting nominated.

Chapter 7 studies what shapes the prospects of being elected to office in electoral authoritarian regimes. In these regimes, incumbency stacks elections in favor of ruling party candidates; this is validated by data that show higher campaign expenditures for ruling party winners. However, I also highlight how opposition candidates can overcome these financial disadvantages through effective election campaign strategies and elucidate which tactics distinguish opposition winners from losers. I unpack the role civic activism plays in shaping campaign strategy, which correlates with better election prospects on both subjective and objective dimensions. The impact of election expenditures on opposition candidate success is conditional on civic activism; no amount of money opposition candidates lacking links to civic associations spend on their campaign boosts their prospects of victory, while spending has a substantively meaningful influence on success even at modest levels of activism. The chapter points to the role of civic activism in transferring mobilization capacity and infrastructure from civic to campaign spaces.

Chapter 8 addresses differences between prospective candidates in terms of the benefits they seek from office. Through several analyses of Tanzanian survey data, I show differences between ruling party and opposition candidates in terms of benefits sought, evaluations of party proficiency in delivering benefits, and perceived benefits of losing election contests. The analyses provide evidence that opposition legislators value ideological benefits of office and that these can be obtained, even when losing elections. This supports the adaptation of the strategic candidacy framework I offer. I also establish how civic activism versus career partisanship underlies the differences in which benefits matter to prospective candidates. While civic activists are more motivated by ideological and policy benefits, career partisans value those benefits less and instead place greater emphasis on material benefits.

Chapter 9 concentrates on the final parameter of the strategic candidacy framework: costs. It turns attention to the costs outside campaign expenditures that are particularly associated with candidacy in authoritarian regimes and studies the variable willingness of prospective candidates to bear the risks of candidacy and to wait for long-term objectives of political change. The chapter employs a novel approach toward measuring risk attitudes and time perspectives using cultural proverbs. The reader will be familiar with these *methali* by this chapter, as each of the previous chapters features them at its opening. Analysis of these *methali* links risk tolerance and longer time horizons and opposition candidates. Civic activism is also linked to risk tolerance, echoing scholarship arguing that risk begets risk. Opposition candidacy may emerge out of civic activism because early experiences in civil society amplify the willingness of activists to challenge incumbent governments no matter the costs.

Chapter 10 explores the external validity of my findings and assesses scope conditions of the theory and its broader applicability across other African countries. Using data from sixteen countries included in the African Legislatures Project (ALP), I analyze surveys from national legislators to address whether my findings regarding paths into opposition versus ruling party candidacy extend to other cases. This includes countries that are most similar to Tanzania in terms of electoral authoritarianism (e.g., Burkina Faso, Mozambique, Uganda, and Zimbabwe), ones featuring less violence and repression but still dominated by a longstanding ruling party (Botswana, Lesotho, Nigeria, Namibia, and South Africa), and other regimes that are both more democratic and competitive (Benin, Ghana, Kenya, Malawi, Senegal, and Zambia). The analysis in this chapter affirms that the civic activism pipeline to the opposition can be found in other electoral authoritarian contexts but not democratic regimes, pointing to the role that civil society plays in cultivating political ambition in settings where challenger parties are weak and subject to regular antagonism from the government. There is suggestive evidence of career partisanship as well, particularly in terms of the enforcement of party discipline by electoral authoritarian ruling parties. Opposition legislators in electoral authoritarian regimes and in dominant party democracies differ greatly from ruling party MPs on policy dimensions, holding distinctive views over development, legislative mandates, and more.

Chapter 11 concludes. It summarizes the main findings and highlights broader contributions to political science and the policy world for understanding electoral politics of authoritarian regimes and their paths to democracy. It ends by charting a future agenda of research for studying opposition growth and development in electoral authoritarian settings.

2

A Theory of Opposition Candidacy

Nimekula asali udogoni, utamu ungali gegoni.
I ate honey in my childhood, and its sweetness is still in my tooth.

Mtu huenda na uchao, hendi na uchwao
A person travels with dawn, not the sunset.

Why do individuals run on opposition tickets in electoral authoritarian regimes? This chapter introduces the theory that guides the book. It begins by conceptualizing electoral authoritarian rule and the structural conditions that shape political competition in such regimes. It then reviews the existing literature explaining candidacy – a strategic candidacy framework primarily anchored in competitive, advanced democracies – and highlights how it travel poorly to the structures of political competition in electoral authoritarian regimes. The remainder of the chapter is spent on two efforts to theorize opposition candidacy. First, I step back from the calculation of candidacy decisions and focus on longer-term paths that lead individuals to those decisions. I argue that split-second, in-the-moment choices to run for the opposition versus the ruling party are not really choices at all. They are influenced by long-term path dependencies arising from early civic versus party activism. Second, I return to the strategic candidacy model to add theoretical depth to this approach such that opposition candidacy under electoral authoritarianism can be explained. I conclude the chapter by linking these two theoretical components. The critical differences that underlie strategic calculations over candidacy for opposition versus ruling parties – nomination and election prospects, benefits sought from candidacy, gains attributed to losing elections, and risk tolerance – are directly attributable to these early life experiences with civic activism versus career partisanship.

2.1 ELECTORAL AUTHORITARIANISM

"Electoral authoritarianism" is the concept most commonly used to describe modern nondemocratic regimes that hold regular elections (Morse 2012). The feature distinguishing electoral authoritarian regimes from other more "closed" authoritarian regimes is executive and legislative elections; they are "constitutive of the political game" (Schedler 2006, 12).

As the key node of competition (Levitsky and Way 2002), elections form an "uneven playing field" of political competition (Levitsky and Way 2010a) where "hyper-incumbency advantages" prevail (Greene 2007). More concretely, these regimes and their elections

> violate the liberal-democratic principles of freedom and fairness so profoundly and systematically as to render elections instruments of authoritarian rule, rather than "instruments of democracy" (Powell 2000). … [E]lectoral contests are subject to state manipulation so severe, widespread and systematic that they do not qualify as democratic. (Schedler 2006, 3)

Schedler (2006, 3) explains that the types of manipulation employed in these regimes range from election fraud and corruption financing of campaigns to more benign tools like discriminatory electoral rules and restricted access to media.

Elections are thus the most important feature of political competition in electoral authoritarian regimes, but one in which the opposition has little chance of defeating incumbent governments at the ballot box. Further, elections in these settings are not free or fair such that the observed election outcome is reflective of the product of incumbent support and violations of election integrity.[1] However, employing the concept of a "nested game," Schedler (2006) notes that even if election outcomes are essentially predetermined, they create an entire institutional structure for challenging the very rules of political competition. This creates additional opportunities within elections and in institutions that are impacted by elections (legislatures, parties, etc.) to contest the political terrain.

---

[1] Schedler (2006) formalizes this as $v = p^*i$, where the integrity of elections $i \neq 1$ ensures that popular preferences p differ from observed voting outcomes v.

Table 2.1 summarizes insights from the existing literature on the dynamics of political competition in electoral authoritarian regimes.[2] This table will help ground the environment of political competition for readers less familiar with electoral authoritarian settings.

Several other concepts share theoretical terrain and many applicable cases with electoral authoritarianism. Most prominently, these are competitive authoritarian regimes and dominant party regimes. Theoretically, "competitive" are distinguished from "electoral" authoritarian regimes on the basis of how competitive the regime is. In practice these distinctions are murky and the set of cases identified as competitive authoritarian mostly overlap with those independently categorized as electoral authoritarian. Dominant party regimes are classified on the basis of electoral performance where the ruling party controls government across several elections, generally with some threshold of "dominance" based on winning legislative majorities or supermajorities . Typically, this category includes regimes that are otherwise democratic (e.g., Botswana) as well as electoral authoritarian regimes (Bogaards 2008). An additional dimension cross-cuts the authoritarian distinction – "hegemony" – which takes on conflicting meanings in the literature. The theoretical frame used in this book focuses on electoral authoritarian regimes, but the theory I develop applies to electoral authoritarian regimes broadly, which encompass both competitive authoritarian regimes as well as ones that are more hegemonic. I discuss scope conditions related to the theory and external validity of the empirical evaluation in the next chapter, which lays out the empirical strategy of the book.

2.2 EXISTING THEORIES OF CANDIDACY

Existing theories of candidacy offer some insight on the puzzle of individual-level motivations to run for office. As will become clear, these accounts alone are insufficient to explain opposition candidacy in nondemocratic settings. However, they do offer a useful framework and key insights into where such a theory should begin. In this section, I review the state of knowledge on candidacy broadly using a rational choice framework. I then develop an original theory in Sections 2.3, 2.4, and 2.5. Section 2.3 explores the roots of candidacy ambition and how background experiences in civic activism and career

---

[2] In some cases, the referenced studies describe different types of nondemocratic regimes, but the insight applies equally to electoral authoritarian settings.

TABLE 2.1 *Political competition in electoral authoritarian regimes*

- Election Competition:
    - Elections help ruling parties/leaders consolidate elite power (Geddes 2005) and strong autocrats institutionalize legislatures (Opalo 2019), restrain opponents (Gandhi and Lust-Okar 2009, Lust-Okar 2005), gather information about their strength (Cox 2009, Geddes 2005, Little 2014), signal to supporters (Boix and Svolik 2013) and challengers (Rozenas 2011), and derive legitimacy domestically (Pepinsky 2007, Schedler 2002) and internationally (Levitsky and Way 2010*a*). In combination with party development, they manage elites and factionalism (Morse 2019).
    - Opposition parties are expected to lose elections but may win seats and votes.
    - Ruling parties do occasionally lose but may remain in power by "stealing" elections (Thompson and Kuntz 2006).
    - Ruling parties have significant resources to invest strategically against challengers (in campaigns, clientelism).
    - Opposition parties lend legitimacy to regimes by participating in elections (Gandhi and Lust-Okar 2009, Schedler 2006).
    - Opposition can delegitimize regimes by boycotting elections or protesting results (Schedler 2006).
    - Ruling parties reinforce clientelistic dependencies with voters to discourage opposition voting (Gandhi and Lust-Okar 2009); they rely on vote buying, selective fraud, disenfranchisement, and malapportionment.
    - Opposition campaign strategies that address systemic disadvantages along the lines of resources; experience; and voter recruitment, cohesion, and coordination will aid success.
- Opposition Parties:
    - Party building on existing mobilization structures shapes success (LeBas 2011).
    - Opposition cohesion is rare and difficult; shaped by structural and institutional constraints (van de Walle 2006).
    - Election performance, transition prospects, and regime liberalization are poor absent coalitions and coordination (Howard and Roessler 2006, Lucardi 2015, Wahman 2013).
    - Opposition supporters face coordination dilemmas over which parties to support inside and outside elections (Magaloni 2006).
    - Ruling parties may sponsor or create "fake" opposition actors to undermine credible opposition candidates and ban or restrict certain opposition candidates or parties (Schedler 2006).
    - Ruling parties may attempt to defuse or co-opt challengers (Lust-Okar 2005).
    - Institutionally organized opposition parties and ones ideologically distinct from ruling party are least likely to be co-opted (Kavasoglu 2021).

(Continued.)

- Opposition parties enjoy some limited autonomy (Schedler 2006) but are weakly institutionalized (Bogaards 2008).

- Officeholding and Policy:
  - Regimes permit legislatures little influence on policy outcomes; legislatures serve as theaters of resource distribution for supporters (Gandhi and Lust-Okar 2009).
  - Ruling parties build maximal winning coalitions and legislative supermajorities to marginalize opposition influence (Magaloni 2006).
  - Ruling parties use policy positions to further divide opposition and promote opposition's ideological extremism (Greene 2008).
  - Legislatures vary in their autonomy and strength relative to the executive (Fish 2006).

- Repression:
  - Ruling parties threaten and selectively apply repression against opponents (Schedler 2006).
  - Civil liberties are violated; "in some regimes overt repression – including the arrest of opposition leaders, the killing of opposition activists, and violent repression of protest – is widespread, pushing regimes to the brink of full authoritarianism (Levitsky and Way 2010a, 8-9).
  - Ruling parties apply "punishment regimes" that withhold resources from opposition supporters (Magaloni 2006, Weinstein 2011).

- Nonpolitical Careers:
  - A government-run public sector and government-owned industry dominate the economy and reinforce ruling party supremacy (Greene 2007, Scheiner 2006).
  - Fear of financial reprisal limits opposition access to private resources (Arriola 2013).
  - Ruling party candidacy promotes rotation between private and public sector business and career opportunities (Treux 2014).

partisanship shape downstream candidacy decisions. Section 2.4 returns to the strategic candidacy framework and introduces modifications to it so that opposition candidacy can be explained in electoral authoritarian regimes with this dominant approach. Section 2.5 ties these two pieces of theory development together, highlighting how the ways individuals calculate strategic prospects of candidacy and what they value in doing can be linked directly to civic activism and career partisanship experiences.

Theory 1: Ambitious Politics and the Micrologic of Legislative Candidacy

The prevailing wisdom as to why individuals become legislative candidates in advanced democracies is that they are calculating and ambitious politicians (Aldrich 2011, Schlesinger 1966) and are motivated by career prospects, policy objectives, and the prestige of political office (Fenno 1973). They join parties because parties help candidates reach their goals by increasing election chances (Downs 1957).

This strategic candidacy framework that explains the decision to run for office is formalized by Black (1972) as the following:

$$U(0) = (PB) - C$$

where B represents the benefit a legislator obtains from office. P captures the probability that the candidate will be elected to that office, or what Kazee (1980, 80) describes as "how hopeful (or hopeless) the political situation" facing the candidate is. C is the cost of seeking election. For most researchers, this most readily means campaign costs but does not preclude other sorts of costs associated with becoming a candidate. The resulting intuition is that if the expected utility of being a candidate $U(0)$ is positive and greater than the benefits that would accrue from utilizing resources A_i in an alternative manner [e.g., $U(0) > U(A_i)$], the individual will seek candidacy. Consequent evidence from Black and others shows that in highly competitive districts (where P is low and C in campaign costs is high), only individuals who expect to gain a lot from office choose to compete.[3] Research on US elected representatives shows that individuals seeking legislative office do so with ambitions to hold these positions of power and that the ambition extends vertically to offices of higher prestige (Aldrich 2011, Maestas, Fulton, Maisel, and Stone 2006, Palmer and Simon 2003, Rohde 1979). These approaches generally assume benefits offered across parties are homogeneous and primarily derived from legislative office, which simplifies the decision of choosing between any two political parties to considering only the variable costs of competing and chances of winning with each party.

The framework simply cannot explain opposition candidacy in electoral authoritarian contexts in this stripped-down form. The opposition is supposed to lose elections by design, material benefits of office mostly

---

[3] Paraphrasing Matthews (1984, 561).

accrue to members of the ruling party, and the financial and nonmaterial, non-campaign costs of opposition candidacy can be extremely high. It can be adapted to account for opposition candidacy in these settings, and I will do so in developing my theory in this chapter.

Theory 2: Co-optation

Chapter 1 introduced the perspective that opposition candidates contest elections to gain material goods for themselves and their constituents. Thus, the reason they compete as candidates in opposition parties is to get co-opted by incumbents. In this view, competing in an election generates public knowledge about a candidate's level of support and can facilitate that candidate's co-optation at an informationally efficient market price. Entry into the opposition party is easy and partisan attachment to the opposition weak.

Accounts of elite decision making in electoral authoritarian regimes rely on functionalist logic, and opposition actors are treated as residual – performing their duties in the environment created for them by autocratic rulers. With few exceptions,[4] discussion of the political opposition as theoretically distinctive actors is rare and secondary. This pattern is even more pronounced in the discussion of Africa's political opposition.[5]

Yet, scholars rarely illustrate that co-optation "works" for incumbent parties by reducing dissent and bringing on board opposition candidates.[6] Kosterina (2017) finds that the presidential candidate of an opposition party is co-opted by the ruling party in about 25 percent of electoral authoritarian regimes, the majority of them in sub-Saharan Africa. Stated differently, the overwhelming majority of electoral authoritarian regimes do not co-opt any presidential candidates from the opposition; those that do may only reward one candidate through co-optation. The most comprehensive study on opposition co-optation in legislative elections reaches similar conclusions. In nearly every year in since 1970, the majority of opposition parties competing in electoral authoritarian regimes around the world are not co-opted (Kavasoglu 2021).

There are a number of shortcomings of the co-optation theory. First, if the explanation of why opposition actors seek co-optation is that

---

[4] Greene (2007), Magaloni (2006).
[5] A point raised in Rakner and van de Walle (2009a).
[6] Notably, Reuter and Robertson (2012) link legislative co-optation with lower levels of political dissent in Russia, providing some evidence of this.

authoritarian leaders create power-sharing institutions to co-opt challengers, motivations of opposition candidates cannot be disentangled from the strategies of autocrats. Pepinsky (2014) raises the more general challenge of teasing out the causal impact of authoritarian institutions independently of the motivations of the leaders who create them; theorizing with this concern in mind is essential.

Second, for an incumbent party to improve its electoral standing by co-opting candidates, a co-opted candidate is assumed to be followed by their supporters. This is a strong assumption and there are good reasons to suspect that co-optation of this form does not actually work. By choosing to support the opposition, citizens have already forgone many of the goods the ruling party can offer. Thus, if leaders of opposition parties seek cooperation with ruling parties, opposition party activists may simply replace the compromised leader with one who will more effectively resist co-optation (Buckles 2019). The logic of materially driven co-optation motives is further challenged by evidence that ruling authoritarian parties discourage opposition by employing a "punishment regime" that withholds developmental and private goods from constituencies with opposition support (Magaloni 2006, Weinstein 2011). Finally, given that many ethnic groups "nest" within African political parties (Horowitz 2015) – a setting where electoral authoritarian regimes abound – the general expectation is that voter – candidate ties to parties are rather stable.

Third, more than half of electoral authoritarian regimes regulate defection through laws that restrict party switching, which directly impacts their ability to co-opt elites.[7] This is a substantially greater rate than advanced democracies (8 percent do so), new democracies (14 percent), and more severely closed autocracies (11 percent) (Janda 2009). More than 60 percent of Africa's electoral authoritarian regimes have such laws (Goeke and Hartmann 2011). Lastly, ruling regimes need not co-opt everyone; there still remains the puzzle of candidacy for individuals the ruling party will never attempt to co-opt.

It is undeniably true that some opposition parties, including some found in electoral authoritarian regimes, are created to win favor with the ruling party and to extract resources from the state. This is especially the case in settings with weak private sectors, leading "ambitious young men and women to view politics as the most realistic channel for upward mobility" (Rakner and van de Walle 2009*a*, 217).

---

[7] Twenty-five of forty-nine electoral authoritarian regimes have such laws. Coded by author based on Benstead (2008), Janda (2009), Nikolenyi (2011), O'Brien and Shomer (2013).

However, it is also similarly irrefutable that there are oppositions with promise to meaningfully challenge ruling parties, even if their chances of doing so at the ballot box are poor in the short run. As I will show in the the next chapter, most electoral authoritarian regimes feature some number of opposition parties that are "real" parties in the sense that they form permanent linkages with societal actors possessing mobilization capacity, establish physical and institutional footprints, develop organizational strength, and take on distinctive policy positions. Kavasoglu's (2021) research on opposition co-optation in legislative elections reveals that these very types of opposition parties have been the least likely to be co-opted over the last half century of authoritarian elections.

Thus, theories that opposition candidacy arises from desires to be co-opted by the ruling party at first glance seem sensible. However, when taking into consideration why and how the co-optation process takes place and holding these theories to empirical evaluation, it becomes clear that this does not capture the overall landscape of opposition candidacy in electoral authoritarian regimes.

Theory 3: Strategic Defection

A third theory introduced in Chapter 1 claims that prospective candidates strategically defect to the opposition when incumbents appear weak (Magaloni 2006). Simply put, prospective candidates see the "writing on the wall" when ruling party defeat is imminent. While a promising framework to apply to candidacy decisions, categorizing which defections are strategic and which are foolish requires post hoc justification based on subsequent electoral outcomes. The theory's counterfactual is dubious, based on the high numbers of opposition candidates observed in electoral authoritarian regimes. Whether the ruling party is strong or weakening, opposition parties frequently run candidates in as many constituencies as financially and logistically possible. If opposition candidates defect strategically, we should instead see variation in candidates running for the opposition over time and at peak moments of regime weakness. This narrow interpretation of strategic behavior is thus valuable but can only account for opposition candidacy under some circumstances.

Theory 4: Ideological Differences

The final account portrays individuals who join the opposition as "ideologists."[8] Ideological attachments and medium and long-term policy

---

[8] Following Eisenstadt (2000), Greene (2007), and Shefter (1994).

platforms can lure candidates to the opposition, and individuals can gain expressive benefits of espousing and influencing policy views independent of candidacy outcomes (Greene 2007). As LeBas (2011, 47) notes, "Many individuals involve themselves in opposition not only because they expect success, but because it is *meaningful* to them ... informants underlined the moral necessity of resistances, even if such resistance was doomed." My theory disentangles two related components in this account – the benefits candidates want and the conditions under which they can obtain them – in developing a more robust version of the strategic candidacy model.

2.3   ORIGINAL THEORY: POLITICAL PATHS TO AMBITION

I now develop an original theory in three stages. The first will turn back in time to the histories that led to the decision-making moment of candidacy and candidacy ambitions in the first place. The second step will speak directly to existing literature on strategic candidacy decisions and adapt it to nondemocratic settings. While engaging the preceding literature on its own terms up front is important, I will present the theory in the temporal order that it follows for several reasons. The first stage is more critical for understanding candidacy. Deciding to run as an opposition candidate is rare, and shedding light on what makes aspirants contemplate candidacy in the first place is a critical part of understanding what makes opposition candidates unique. It tells us what long-term factors might influence the choice set available to prospective candidates. Introducing the first stage of the theory also informs how prospective candidates calculate their benefits and costs of running for office. More specifically, long-term civic activism experiences actually shape what matters to prospective opposition candidates when deciding whether or not to run. The third stage of theory development further microfounds the strategic framework in past life experiences. It establishes that the way prospective candidates value decision-making parameters like benefits of running for and holding office is driven by these experiences.

Candidacy Paths: Civic Activism and Career Partisanship

Strategic calculations based on costs, benefits, and chances of electoral success are made at the moment of seeking nomination and candidacy. Consequently, nearly all research on candidacy overlooks how events long beforehand shape decisions to run for office. Yet, the literature appears to concede this narrow focus is not tenable. For example, scholars have shown that certain preexisting characteristics are also associated with candidacy, including social identity categories (e.g., male, majority ethnic group)[9] and certain careers (e.g., lawyers (Moncrief, Squire, and Jewell 2000)). Further, political service precedes candidacy so frequently that the "career politician" is one of only two commonly observed trajectories into the legislatures of modern democracies (Mattozzi and Merlo 2008, Sousa and Canon 1992). Others have described "nascent ambition," or the onset stages in "the candidate emergence process ... not motivated by political opportunity structure, but by attitudinal dispositions and personal experiences that facilitate or stunt the likelihood of even thinking about running for office" (Lawless 2012, 50). Thus, we have observed in advanced democracies political experiences that take place prior to expressing motivation to become a legislator (so-called expressive ambition).

Understanding what sows the seeds of interest in candidacy in electoral authoritarian regimes can shed light on why and when prospective opposition candidates seek office and, further, differences in the types of experiences that prime an individual for ruling party versus opposition candidacy. In contrast to advanced democracies, however, formal political and party experiences may not be a useful tool for government challengers given the limited pluralism of electoral authoritarian regimes and their more authoritarian predecessors. I thus contend there exist two distinctive paths to candidacy and, in addition, that they lead to different outcomes.

Life experiences in civic activism propel individuals toward candidacy with the opposition, while party experiences as career partisanship lead to ruling party candidacy. Figure 2.1 visually depicts the nature of this path dependency, whereby these two channels into candidacy impact the choices aspirants make when deciding to run for office. I will now define the civic activism and career partisanship pathways to political office.

Opposition Paths: Civic Activism

The role of social capital in political participation is well established in political science: individuals who are members of social organizations are more likely to engage in political activities (Brehm and Rahn 1997, Klesner 2007, Putnam 1993, Quintelier 2008, Teorell 2003, and many others). It reasonably follows that greater social capital in the form of

---

[9] See Bobo and Gilliam (1990), Fox and Lawless (2004), Norris (1997).

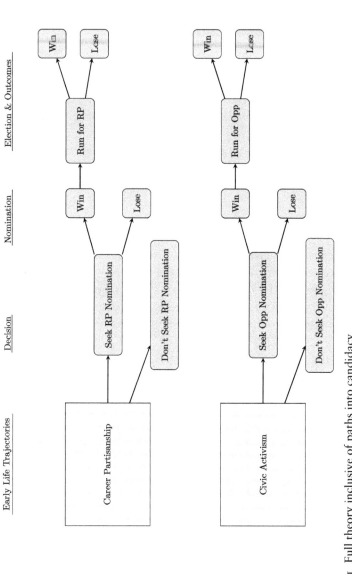

Figure 2.1 Full theory inclusive of paths into candidacy

Note: RP = Ruling Party, Opp = Opposition

membership in civic organizations would also enhance the likelihood of seeking political office, as greater social group linkages improve the opportunity structure for winning office. Scholars have demonstrated that both citizen-level political participation and for candidacy seeking, social group membership has an additive effect: the number of organizations one is a member of, not the strength of responsibility or type of organization, contributes to higher rates of political activity (Mishler 1978, Teorell 2003). Indeed, civil society is a "school for the training of democratic citizens" (Bermeo 2003, 9).

The relationship between civic activism and subsequent engagement in higher-risk political participation is well documented. Rather than the idea that activists moderate to centrist politics after achieving their goals – what Tarrow (1998, 167) calls a myth perpetuated by popular narratives – the opposite is the case. Communist activists at the forefront of 1960s mobilization later supported more radical action than counterparts from generations that followed (Lange, Irvin, and Tarrow 1989). Riders of the "Freedom Summer" during the civil rights movement were primarily young liberal students, not radical activists. The experiences of the Freedom Summers led them into subsequent lives of higher-risk activism (McAdam 1990).

Civic networks of activism have close ties with political parties in all types of regimes. Indeed, Diamond (1994, 9) envisions a critical role for civil society in consolidated democracies to recruit, train, and groom future leaders and potential candidates for office. The emergence of these leaders is often

a long-term byproduct of the successful functioning of civil society organizations as their leaders and activists gain skills and self-confidence that qualify them well for service in government and party politics. They learn how to organize and motivate people, debate issues, raise and account for funds, craft budgets, publicize programs, administer staffs, canvass for support, negotiate agreements and build coalitions. At the same time, their work on behalf of their constituency or of what they see to be the public interest, and their articulation of clear and compelling policy alternatives, may gain for them a wider political following. Interest groups, social movements, and community efforts of various kinds may therefore train, toughen and thrust into public notice a richer (and more representative) array of potential new political leaders than might otherwise be recruited by political parties.

This link is especially important in nondemocratic and transitioning regimes as well. In many nondemocratic settings, spaces of political and civic pluralism are closed and rendered defective (Linz and Stepan 1996).

Civil society can play a critical role in introducing a new set of potential leaders. When transitions stall and opposition is ineffective, civic activists can revitalize the leadership landscape. Thus, stagnant democratic growth in Africa may result from how a lack of "thickness" of civil society contributes to a thin crop of qualified leadership. Civil society is especially important when one or multiple groups are marginalized in the public sphere (Diamond 1994, 9).

Extensive research demonstrates that civic organizations play a significant role in challenging authoritarian institutions. Most fundamentally, civic organizations can form the bedrock of strong opposition parties (LeBas 2011). The organizational structure of certain civic associations like churches and labor unions often facilitates effective political mobilization in contentious politics (Lohmann 1994, Smith 1996), and this has been shown in Africa's electoral autocracies (Bratton and van de Walle 1997, Konings 2003, Larmer 2006, LeBas 2011, Love 2006). Individuals who are well networked socially are extremely valuable electorally because they offer candidate valence that poorly institutionalized parties cannot.

For leaders of emerging opposition parties, a lack of resources, capacity, and experience means the parties are unable to groom career partisans to become opposition candidates. Instead, they recruit experienced activists from nonpartisan organizations to run for office (Verba, Schlozman, and Brady 1995). Drawing upon the resources of civic organizations is strategically appealing for opposition elites. Civic activists have high public visibility and civil society organizations feature strong network and mobilization structures (McAdam, McCarthy, and Zald 1996, McAdam, Tarrow, and Tilly 2001, McClurg 2003, Siegel 2009) built upon preexisting cleavages in society (LeBas 2011). Such groups also enjoy more autonomy from the government than the formal opposition does, allowing them to more effectively organize against the party in power (Arriola 2013, Brownlee 2007, Riedl 2014, Smith 2004). What results are *social-electoral coalitions* where opposition parties seek out candidates who are able to "lead popular mobilization during election campaigns" (Trejo 2014, 331). In exchange, these individuals gain a prominent avenue to raise grievances against the government (Beissinger 2007, Bunce and Wolchik 2011). There may also be longer-term generational effects due to socialization against the ruling regimes (Greene 2007). Thus, participation in civic activism provides later incentives to run for office to advance goals aligning with opposition candidacy. In many ways, my argument about paths to candidacy nests well alongside that of LeBas (2011), who finds opposition party strength is driven by the ability of such parties to build from existing social mobilizations structures. Focusing primarily on trade unions as the source of opposition party strength in Zimbabwe, she argues such structures had "autonomy from the state, organizational resources, independent ties to mass constituencies, and a great deal of political visibility. These mobilizing structures could later be co-opted by opposition parties, given these parties a greater ability to mobilize voters" (LeBas 2011, 37).

The literature documents pipelines to opposition candidacy from three types of domestic civic groups relevant to the Tanzanian case: (1) religious organizations, (2) the student movement, and (3) advocacy organizations. In other settings, opposition candidates often emerge from trade unions. Because Tanzanian labor organizations remain informally tied to government, I do not explore the pathway from organized labor to opposition in this book. International actors may also play a role.[10]

Religious organizations facilitate transitions to democracy (Gyimah-Boadi 1996) and aid oppositional forces arising in the subsequent era (LeBas 2011, Smith 1996, Tarrow 1992). Religious institutions command tremendous capacity to organize supporters and deliver supporters *en masse*. They enjoy a powerful voice and a claim to legitimacy when pushing for democratic concessions (Levitsky and Way 2010a, 114). They also operate independently of the state and political elites, because their actions are not often explicitly anti-government. This makes it "considerably more difficult for ... the executive to identify who among these [religious] elites might ultimately prove to be a threat" (McGlinchey 2011, 117). Reflecting on the role of religious leaders in the US civil rights movement, Fredrickson (1996, 261) notes that "unlike professors and teachers, for example, they were not employed by white-dominated or funded institutions. Unlike doctors, lawyers, and businessmen they did not engage in activities subject to government control or regulation." Churches occupy a physical space in which opposition activists can be prepared for politics (Fredrickson 1996, 262).

When leaders of religious organizations venture into politics, they have placed authoritarian regimes in crisis. In Malawi, the decision of Catholic

---

[10] Most prominently, international actors can form relationships with activists on the ground through transnational society linkages. In doing so, they allow opposition movements to put pressure on or otherwise impact the incentive structures of costs of being in the opposition, which can lead to victory (Levitsky and Way 2005). Activists learn from one another across contexts through their interconnectedness and acquire techniques that lead to candidate success that can be replicated in other settings (Beissinger 2007).

bishops to issue a letter critical of the government led to protests, students revolts, and strikes (Levitsky and Way 2010*a*). In Kenya, the National Council of Churches of Kenya (NCCK) led the country's resistance to ruling party Kenya African Nation Union (KANU) under President Daniel Arap Moi, as well as reforms of ballot secrecy (Gyimah-Boadi 1996). Zimbabwe's primary opposition party – the Movement for Democratic Change (MDC) – grew out of a constitutional reform movement in which religious organizations played a critical part (Levitsky and Way 2010*a*). Religious organizations are particularly well suited for opposition activists and parties that are not viable, at least in the short run. Opposition candidates' goals align with the views of religious leaders because they share being reform oriented and holding longer-term time horizons: "not about governing in the near future but about building a movement, articulating an agenda, and using the limited openings that elections can offer" (Brown 2012, 25).

The second type of civic activism that facilitates candidacy emerges on university campuses. Student movements played a vital role in the wave democratization that swept across sub-Saharan Africa during 1990s (Bratton and van de Walle 1997). The origins of pressure to democratize can even be traced to universities and their student movements during the 1970s (Shivji 2004). Professors also serve as critics and mobilizers against the regime, intellectual supporters of democratization, and individuals with leadership, organizational, and research skills (Gyimah-Boadi 1996).

In addition to serving as advocates for democracy, student and faculty leaders often end up involved in pursuing these goals politically as leaders. Student activism may lead to participation in student government, which offers direct roles in university-level decision making (Luescher-Mamashela 2005), experience in running campaigns and representing diverse community interests (Bloom, Canning, and Chan 2005), and organizing public demonstrations (Hinton 2002). Students in these environments demonstrate higher levels of support for and knowledge of democracy, helping align them with the policy goals of opposition parties. In short, universities provide opportunities to engage in pro-democratic behavior and master skills needed to run effective campaigns for office. Thus, student activism often leads to later candidacy ambitions.

The final type I focus on is advocacy organizations. These include local, segmented grassroots organizations that give citizens local influence over government that later facilitates formalizing demands of government through political organizations (Cornwall and Coelho 2007, Goldfrank

2007, Heller 2001). Such organizations been significant in nineteenth- and twentieth-century democratization (Brockett 1991, Calhoun 1993, d'Anieri, Ernst, and Kier 1990, Ndegwa 1996, Schneider 1991). Grass-roots organizations can also play a role in fomenting political empowerment and activism in ways that translate into downstream political participation (Goldman and Little 2015). I also consider women's rights groups and public advocacy organizations, which include educational improvement NGOs and legal/human rights organizations. Research notes that these groups can link to international and transnational NGOs to pressure incumbent governments to reform (Keck and Sikkink 1998), especially on issues like women's representation (Bauer 2008, Bush 2011, Krook 2010).

How Civic Activism Differs from Ethnic Voting

Readers familiar with electoral politics in sub-Saharan Africa may note that the reasoning underlying civic activism's role in candidacy shares some terrain with the scholarship on ethnic politics. That opposition parties draw from existing social organizations with mobilization capacity, and candidates emerge from these types of organizations because their goals overlap with those of the political party echoes arguments regarding the affiliation of ethnolinguistic groups with political parties. The idea that ethnicity is the predominant dimension by which voters, candidates, and parties operate is pervasive in accounts of African politics. There is growing evidence of substantial variation in the political salience of ethnicity as a mobilization cleavage across sub-Saharan Africa. Bleck and van de Walle (2018, 229–230) point to many recent studies that challenge the centrality of ethnicity in politics. It is not my goal to dispute or validate whether the role of ethnicity in African politics deserves the attention it has received, but rather to distinguish civic activism pathways to candidacy from the mobilization of co-ethnic candidates in ethnic parties.

Political parties in sub-Saharan Africa that are built on ethnic cleavages wholly nest ethnic groups within their party; the thinking goes that from the perspective of a party that is organizationally or institutionally weak, it can harness the social ties within ethnic groups to mobilize members of those ethnic groups to support co-ethnic candidates of that party. My account differs from this approach in a couple of critical ways. First, ethnically based parties are viewed as policy vacant. Following other predominant narratives about African politics, the sole goal political parties organized around ethnicity have in winning power is to extract and redistribute material and financial resources for that group, the foundation of political clientelism. At the level of the individual candidate, this offers little opportunity for opposition legislators from such parties to seek non-material goods and ultimately places them in a role of mediating the exchange of financial goods from the state to the citizen. Civic activism pathways to opposition candidacy lead to candidates who pursue ideological and policy goals that are distinct from those of the ruling party, an outcome that does not fit with either candidate or party-level implications of ethnically organized parties. Electoral authoritarian regimes may encourage niche opposition parties, but niche or extreme policy dimensions are based on the nature of spatial policy competition in these regimes (Greene 2008), not in terms of niche appeal to a small subset of co-ethnics. The role of ethnicity as a pathway to office and its impact on political ambition points to material benefits and resembles ruling party candidacy, something I will expound upon shortly.

Second, civic activism is not just a pathway through that parties draw upon mobilization resources of civil society. Candidates themselves gain skill, training, and political know-how from their experiences in civil society. The narrative of ethnic politics suggests that mobilization capacity is intrinsic to ethnic groups, not honed and crafted by individuals within those groups. It is not clear how ethnic group membership transfers campaign skills to potential candidates for national legislative office or what type of variation within dimensions of ethnicity would translate into greater political ambition or ability.

Third, my theory of opposition candidacy focuses on parties that have the long-term national ambition to rival and eventually replace the incumbent government, even if these ambitions are unrealistic. Ethnic parties are more substantially tied to specific geographical areas, and building national-level support and intergroup coalitions is difficult under conditions of democracy. It would be even more challenging in electoral authoritarian regimes for opposition parties based on ethnicity to build bridges with other identity groups. Civic activist organizations can cultivate candidates with broad appeal across national-level issues, while recruitment and mobilization among co-ethnics are likely to reinforce limitations regarding national scope. As LeBas (2011, 25) notes, focusing on opposition parties with strong linkages to constituencies based on broad, common goals does not by definition prevent the inclusion of ethnically based political parties if they are otherwise organizationally strong. In practical terms, the kinds of opposition parties that can credibly challenge authoritarian governments are ones that can draw support across ethnic group lines.

Ruling Party Paths: Career Partisanship

Consistent with the notion of a career politician, political experience is a common way to gain access to legislative office and other higher-prestige positions (Sousa and Canon 1992, Mattozzi and Merlo 2008). Vertical advancement of this sort is common across many political systems in comparative settings (Field and Siavelis 2008, Norris 1997). An alternate path into politics is through political party offices. Both party service and political experience are important in determining who seeks nominations, but their relative weight depends on the party and on the political system. It is likely the case that party credentials are even more important when the party selectorate that chooses nominees is smaller, as personal connections and influence can be commodified for influence in a smoke-filled room.

Party service is also more valuable when less political experience is required to hold office and for groups that are historically disenfranchised in mainstream politics (Norris 1997). Party caucuses for women, for example, offer opportunities to learn skills necessary to be an effective legislator and help overcome biases against selecting female candidates (Studlar and McAllister 1991). Further, work within political parties places prospective candidates in close, repeated interaction with party gatekeepers who exercise control over who can become a legislative candidate (Gallagher 1988, Lovenduski and Norris 1993).

In electoral authoritarian regimes, political experience is of secondary importance to party activism. First, government positions that can offer political experience are dominated by the ruling party. Thus, prospective opposition nomination seekers have few opportunities to distinguish themselves from those who do not seek nominations. Moreover, ruling parties in these settings become extensions of the state so that the government apparatus operates largely in the service of the party. The government is therefore a highly partisan structure. Party service is important from the perspective of the ruling party because they signify commitment, loyalty, and attachment to a party. Ruling party commitments are critical because regime longevity hinges on maintaining intra-elite cohesion and preventing intraparty factionalism (Blaydes 2013, Brownlee 2007, Geddes 1999, Svolik 2009). Ruling party candidates are therefore regime loyalists "at the expense of cadres who are competent at making public policy and promoting economic development" (Reuter and Robertson 2012, 1023).

Entry into the ruling party at an early age – in party-sponsored soccer teams, youth programs, and so on – and later party service are critical factors leading to candidacy that occur long before individuals think about running for office. Paths to ruling party candidacy are preceded by partisanship, service in local party politics, and further participation in elite party circles years, sometimes decades, before candidacy decisions (Reuter and Turvosky 2014). Party service also allows party elites to encourage (or discourage) candidacy (Gallagher 1988, Lovenduski and Norris 1993). Thus, when individuals decide whether or not to run for office, career partisans have already traveled down a path leading to ruling party candidacy. Less active ruling party members and opposition and nonpartisans are not exposed to this avenue toward candidacy.

Career partisanship represents a commitment over time that exposes an individual to potential interests in candidacy. This leads to the expectation that ruling party nomination seekers in electoral authoritarian regimes will generally have more party experience than opposition candidates. This party experience will be reflected most in low-level positions – constituency offices, even perhaps *nyumba kumi* (ten household) branches, and regional service as well. Opposition candidates may demonstrate party service, but of two types: (1) where their skills contribute to otherwise low-capacity party offices (e.g., a professional accountant working in the party secretariat) or (2) where activity directly relates to election and mobilization goals (e.g., youth outreach). Such positions are more commonly found at the national level of the party. Temporally, any opposition party service is short lived, whereas career partisanship in the ruling party is reflective of long, grueling service in the bowels of a local party slowly cascading to more prominent regional or national positions. Aspiring ruling party candidates must "wait their turn" to run because the pool of qualified prospective candidates is larger than available positions. If fifteen or twenty years of party activism are required before being eligible in the eyes of a party, momentum for candidacy begins before candidacy is even considered.

In sum, decisions over candidacy are influenced by long-term life trajectories. While ruling party candidates demonstrate long-term partisan commitments, civic organizations help plant the seeds of civic activism that later grow into ambitions of opposition candidacy.

2.4 ORIGINAL THEORY: STRATEGIC CANDIDACY FRAMEWORK UNDER ELECTORAL AUTHORITARIANISM

As stated previously, it is essential to dialogue with existing literature on candidacy on its own terms. For this reason, the current section draws together prevailing wisdom on candidacy in democracies with insights on opposition activism and political competition under electoral authoritarianism. It employs the strategic candidacy framework and the same parameters of the parsimonious models of candidacy from democracies – probability of winning office *P*, benefits of office *B*, and costs of running *C*. Through this discussion, I offer a new version of the strategic candidacy model that can account for opposition candidacy in electoral authoritarian regimes.

P, *B*, and *C* of Elections in Electoral Authoritarian Regimes

The Probability *P* of Winning a Nomination

Most studies of candidacy focus on electoral competition. Yet, running for legislative office involves two separate contests: party nomination and general election. Indeed, winning over a party selectorate for nomination is a necessary first step that, "while obvious, is often ignored in analyses of candidates' prospects" (Stone and Maisel 2003, 952). Intraparty politics and competition are paramount to understanding candidacy because candidates must also take nomination prospects into account (Fox and Lawless 2004, Serra 2011, Stone and Maisel 2003) and also have a direct impact on election outcomes (Ichino and Nathan 2013, Indridason and Kristinsson 2015, Langston 2006, Serra 2011). Thus, a first innovation to the "ambitious politics" framework is to simply shift the decision-making point to the moment when individuals actually take action toward candidacy: nomination.

It has long been established that politicians strategically decide when to exit politics, hold their position, or seek higher-prestige posts (Moore and Hibbing 1998, Schansberg 1994). This also extends to decisions to run for office. As Fox and Lawless (2005, 645) note, if a "potential candidate does not deem himself/herself qualified to run for office, then considering a candidacy is probably unlikely."

Intraparty support also impacts motivations to seek office (Fox and Lawless 2004), especially in settings where party institutions wield significant power (Byrd 1963, Hibbing 1999). Parties dedicate more effort to selecting nominees and party leaders than they do to just about every other activity outside of raising finances and running elections (Gallagher 1988, 3). Such selections represent a contested terrain in which internal party conflict plays out (Gallagher 1988, 2). Just as electoral systems can shape interparty competition, candidate selection systems shape intraparty competition (Rahat and Hazan 2001). In terms of seeking candidacy, prospective politicians who think they have a good shot at winning a party nomination will seek office at higher rates.

The difficulty of obtaining nominations in electoral authoritarian regimes differs greatly by party based on election prospects. Mishler (1978, 586) posits that "the level of intraparty competition for nomination will increase with the party's prospects for victory." The inverse association between intra- and interparty competitiveness is commonly overlooked but is found as early as Key's (1964) work. Interplay of these two factors results in a parabolic relationship between a party's popularity and a prospective candidate's chances of becoming a legislator (Stone and Maisel 2003, 968). When one party dominates elections, nomination challenges severely limit the odds of holding office than those do not.

While we know little about candidate selection outside advanced democracies (Giollabhui 2013, Langston 2006, Wuhs 2006), insights can be gleaned from the nascent scholarship on candidate selection in electoral authoritarian regimes. First, an inverse relationship exists between election and nomination prospects, with ruling party contests featuring more nomination seekers. Case studies suggest that nomination selection is exclusive and centralized for ruling parties (Langston 2006, Wuhs 2006),[11] while more inclusive procedures are adopted in response to supporter demands for transparency. That Africa's ruling parties hold closed-member primaries to solicit member views but leave decision-making power to the party's secretariat (Ohman 2004) reflects this balance of central control versus supporter participation. Opposition parties tend to feature more decentralized procedures (Giollabhui 2013, Ohman 2004),[12] perhaps by default, since they do not face gatekeeping pressures like ruling parties do. Analysis of emergent data on candidate nomination procedures across all forty-nine countries in the subcontinent indicates that opposition parties nominate members through procedures that include larger selectorates.[13]

The Probability *P* of Winning an Election

In any given election, incumbents and ruling parties generally enjoy significant advantages. There are financial benefits of incumbency, and

---

[11] Mexico's PRI used *el dedazo* to select presidential candidates, where the outgoing president "tapped" or simply chose the next candidate (Greene 2007, Langston 2006, Wuhs 2006).

[12] Scholars argue this leads to nominating higher-valence candidates (Ichino and Nathan 2013, Serra 2011) and effective campaigners (Adams and Merrill III 2008).

[13] Based on analysis of Lührmann, Düpont, Higashijima, Kavasoglu, Marquardt, Bernhard, Doring, Hicken, Laebens, Lindberg, Neundorf, Reuter, Ruth-Lovell, Weghorst, Wiesehomeier, Wright, Alizada, Bederke, Gastaldi, Grahn, Hindle, Ilchenko, von Rümer, Pemstein and Seim's (2020) Party Identity and Organization dataset for ruling versus opposition parties in sub-Saharan Africa; analysis found in Appendix B.1.

campaign finance is among the most important keys to electoral victory (Arriola 2013, Jacobson 1986, Lust-Okar 2008, Stokes 2005, Treisman 1998). The incumbency advantage in Africa's electoral regimes is even more significant: access to government resources can legitimately be utilized to improve electoral prospects in the form of constituency-directed club goods and spending on "pork" (Basedau, Erdmann, and Mehler 2007, Joseph 1987, Kramon 2011, Lemarchand 1972, Lindberg 2003, 2012, van de Walle 2007, Vicente and Wantchekon 2009, Wantchekon 2003) and economies of "affection" attach citizens to politicians through networks of clientelistic exchange (Hyden 1980). In electoral authoritarian regimes, the prospects for opposition candidates to win an electoral contest are, all else equal, poorer than for ruling party candidates. Three overarching structural challenges impact opposition success in electoral authoritarian regimes: (1) resource asymmetries, (2) experiential deficiencies of campaign credibility and party capacity, and (3) citizen–voter coordination problems.

The ruling party enjoys advantages over challengers in mobilizing economic resources for campaigns. Competing in elections is costly and legislative candidates in Africa spend thousands of dollars of their own savings during election time just on personal contributions expected by their constituents.[14] In regimes with weak, poorly funded parties, candidates often bear large personal costs like voter handouts (Kramon 2011, Lindberg 2003, Wantchekon 2003), especially where electoral clientelism is widespread (Hicken 2011).

Ruling party advantages over challengers in mobilizing economic resources to finance campaigns are exacerbated in electoral authoritarian settings (Arriola 2013, Greene 2010, Greene 2007, Kasara 2006, van de Walle 2003). In electoral authoritarian regimes, the ruling party is often fused with the state. Ruling parties thus have "unlimited access to the government treasury."[15] Publicly owned companies, bloated civil service sectors, government allowances, budgetary control, and capacity for rent extraction are all tools available to ruling parties that further their resource advantages (Greene 2007). The impact of resource asymmetries in an environment where clientelism is an entrenched part of electoral politics is particularly acute: "incumbents can exploit their control of public

[14] Even in low-income countries, the "price to play" is quite high. In one instance, a Ghanaian member of parliament reported the cost of a party primary campaign at more than $300,000. For more on personal costs in African elections, see Lindberg (2003).

[15] Fombad (2004), quoted in Levitsky and Way (2010*a*, 259).

resources to offer the gifts expected during campaigns, their opposition counterparts must secure private resources to do the same" (Arriola 2013, 13). This is especially important if voters see the distribution of electoral gifts not as corruption but as signals of the credibility of a candidate (Kramon 2017).

Ruling parties use their legislative supermajorities to pass legislation that stacks the odds against opposition competitors financially, allocating government funds and media sources in ways that advantage the party in power. Strict campaign finance regulations may exist that only the ruling party can risk violating without fear of punishment.[16] The loss of access to public funds to direct to a party's electoral goals is cited as the cause of the downfall of long-ruling parties like Japan's LDP and Mexico's PRI (Greene 2007, Scheiner 2006). Leveling of resources between parties also enhances the ability of the opposition to cooperate. As Arriola (2013, 19) notes, "It is this asymmetry in the access to resources between incumbent and opposition – not the nature of ethnic cleavages or the specific arrangement of political institutions – that drives patterns of coalition formation across African countries."

The second structural barrier to opposition performance is experiential asymmetries – in terms of convincing voters of both their ability to govern and their capacity to manage themselves as a party organization. Autocrats who engineer transitions to multiparty electoral competition to stay in power, even when overseeing catastrophic economic and political performance, nonetheless hold one quality that all challengers lack: experience in government. Opposition parties may offer compelling platforms for what they would do if they took the reins of government. They may pronounce strong messages of uncompromising commitment to government reform and to changing the status quo. While such messages are credible in their sincerity, they lack evidence of the ability to implement them. In short, even when the market is ripe for a challenger party and that party offers precisely what voters want, these voters may still harbor doubts the opposition can implement its policies without experience in government.

At the party level, experiential disadvantages emerge as well. Opposition parties are frequently newly minted organizations with little capacity at their founding. Thus, the most basic challenge for these parties is to establish rules by which the organization is governed and functions. The

---

[16] Arriola (2013) raises this specific point with regard to election finance reform in Tanzania in his book's conclusion.

center of these parties is often filled with a mixture of elites expelled from the autocratic party and activists who accept the costs of participation in opposition. They often lack qualified administrative staff, a professionalized secretariat, and even individuals with sufficient legal and organizational skills to codify the rules and norms by which the party operates. They rarely have any party offices at their outset and must quickly establish their physical footprint. Maintaining cohesion in opposition parties in these regimes is difficult, as the challenges they face in recruiting party elites lead to severe generational conflicts over the party's direction, platforms, and goals and ultimately fracture parties (Greene 2007, 62). Activists may also perform poorly as managers of a political organization as compared to persons with decades of experience in government and professional organizations. These factors together make effective organization a difficult task for the opposition. Basic professionalization of a party secretariat, even "keeping the lights on" at the party's headquarters, can be challenging. Party conflict and keeping supporters believing in the viability of the opposition also loom as large challenges.

The third structural barrier for opposition candidate success is coordination among potential opposition voters. Opposition parties face significant obstacles to mobilizing voters because the threat of force at the hands of the ruling party discourages opposition supporters. The use of violence is a central indicator of electoral authoritarianism (Lindberg 2006b, 252). Thus, many voters who support the opposition are preference falsifiers, whereby they may support the opposition but fear to divulge such support or act on it (Jiang and Yang 2016, Kuran 1995), particularly when having experienced past violence (Young 2019). Any number of individuals might prefer to support the opposition party in an election, but they will only act on this given sufficient confidence that the opposition is viable or that they will not be singled out for casting a ballot for the opposition. This is what Magaloni (2006) calls a "mass coordination" dilemma, whereby latent support for the opposition does not materialize on election day. Research shows that willingness to vote for opposition candidates under such conditions is responsive to factors that boost beliefs in opposition viability, like support in social networks (Fafchamps and Gubert 2007, Wantchekon and Vermeersch 2005). Further, insight from advanced democracies suggests face-to-face contact with political mobilizers can boost participation (Green and Gerber 2004, Green, Gerber, and Nickerson 2003, Michelson, Bedolla, and McConnell 2009, Vicente 2008, Wantchekon 2003). This is true in sub-Saharan Africa as well (Brierley and Kramon 2020, Collier and Vicente 2014, Wantchekon 2003). Interaction with opposition elites may attenuate the fears an opposition sympathizer has to vote for that party. Thus, candidates who engage in or are willing to engage in or support door-to-door campaigning may fare better in elections.

What Legislative Aspirants Want: Benefits (B) of Running for Office

Seminal studies of candidacy conceive of benefits as material gains that all candidates value equally. Yet, Barber (1956) and Ziller et al. (1977) find self-esteem, social characteristics, and professional backgrounds like a law degree can differentiate the goals of legislative candidates. I join a minority of scholars arguing that there are multiple benefit types of office and candidates are heterogenous in how much they value them. I begin the discussion of benefits by highlighting what we have learned from advanced democracies, the context where the strategic candidacy model is most commonly applied. I then introduce knowledge from the sub-Saharan African context, which will make apparent the underlying differences between ruling party and opposition status. I bring to bear this geographical context to electoral authoritarian regimes to present a comprehensive picture of the structure of benefits for opposition candidates in electoral authoritarian regimes.

Benefits in Advanced Democracies

It is generally thought that benefits of office are obtained as compensation for performing formal legislative duties. Thus, the material goods associated with officeholding should not vary across a party's status in or out of government, the size of the party, constituency type, and so on. These benefits further should be homogeneous for all legislators. In addition to the material benefits of officeholding, the literatures notes that officeholding in advanced democracies may also provide benefits associated with performing the duties of legislating. In doing so, individuals engage in competitive, strategic interactions that may be personally rewarding or provide psychological benefits related to accomplishing goals associated with formal duties. This literature ties benefits of candidacy to officeholding, not to aspiring to hold office. As such, this literature anticipates no benefit from losing elections.

In addition to material benefits of officeholding, serving in the legislature can provide significant career advancement benefits. For private companies and enterprises, having access to government stakeholders who will listen to their interests and implement policies that are beneficial is critical. For this reason, holding a legislative seat may be of modest value formally – legislator salaries in advanced democracies are commonly lower than the income officeholders could earn in the private sector – but of significant value after leaving office. Evidence from the United Kingdom, for example, shows that Conservative MPs who ran for office ultimately doubled their wealth as a consequence of serving in the House of Commons not because of their legislative salaries but as a result of the positions they obtained during or after their terms – as political consultants, advisors on company boards, and so on. (Eggers and Hainmueller 2009). Similar evidence is found in less-developed democracies like India, particularly for high-prestige officeholders (e.g., ministers) and in federal states where corruption is more common (Fisman, Schulz, and Vig 2014). This benefit is generally viewed as accruing from officeholding, so this benefit should not be specific to a party affiliation under conditions of robust, interparty competition.

Benefits in Sub-Saharan Africa

Scholarship on political leaders in sub-Saharan Africa emphasizes that material goods are the primary resource that links voters to politicians. In this view, the forces of politics are shaped by neo-patrimonialism, by which "political authority in Africa is based on the giving and granting of favors, in an endless series of dyadic exchanges that go from the village level to the highest reaches of the central state" (van de Walle 2001, 51). In such regimes, "officeholders almost systematically appropriate public resources for their own uses" (van de Walle 2001, 52).

Importantly, the role of neo-patrimonialism – and how it drives materialist motivations for office seeking – is elemental. Rather than being an exception or a "rotten apple" phenomenon, patterns of material accumulation by political leaders "is a habitual part of everyday life, an expected element of every social transaction" (Chabal and Daloz 1999, 99). Inheriting weak, low-legitimacy, and low-capacity states upon colonial independence (Herbst 2000), political leaders placed solutions to political instability and power holding above economic concerns in resorting to this strategy (Ake 1996). Others argue that leaders have moral imperatives to seek and distribute resources to their own groups, particularly those who share ethnic identity, as a matter of "duty" (Ekeh 1975, 107); reciprocity norms between leaders and citizens are built on a social infrastructure and economic ties of "affection" (Hyden 1983). Even practices like clientelism and vote buying are commonly attributed to this sense of obligation. It also demonstrates politicians' quality and viability to voters (Kramon 2017, Lindberg 2003, Wantchekon 2003).

Politicians, for their part, benefit by creating citizens' dependencies so citizens view their fate as intrinsically linked to the continued rule of these leaders, a legacy that holds over into electoral politics (Gandhi and Lust-Okar 2009). This form of material consumption is frequently visible, by design. One well-known account offers a caricature of these dynamics:

> It is common on the continent to notice the greatest displays of luxury in an environment of poverty and squalor, most particularly in the urban areas. Magnificent mansions sit square in the middle of slum areas. Gleaming white limousines make their way down dank and filthy alleyways. ... So long as the newly rich are perceived to behave appropriately as patrons, they will be respected and admired, becoming in this way role models. As such, the accumulation of wealth is inherently linked to a notion of legitimacy which undermines the expected dynamics of class formation. (Chabal and Daloz 1999, 42–43)

In sum, it is well documented that political leaders in sub-Saharan Africa acquire material resources from officeholding. These resources are thought to be used for reinforcing political power through clientelistic distribution. There is an underlying assumption that elites also pilfer material goods for themselves, rather than simply serving as intermediaries between the state and citizens. However, these accounts do not focus specifically on whether legislative candidates to aim consume such resources.

A literature on the motivations of the African political elite more directly establishes the materially-driven goals of running for office. First, scholars note that "most of the material gains from clientelism are limited to the elite" (van de Walle 2003). Accounts supporting this often focus on the executive, particularly in autocracies. Zimbabwe's national reserve bank under Robert Mugabe's rule was "locally known as Big Bob's Take-away" (Thomson 2004, 205); Maryam Abacha was caught at the Lagos airport with thirty-eight suitcases filled with cash shortly after the death of her husband, Nigerian dictator Sani Abacha, and the offshore assets of numerous current and former leaders in Guinea, Zambia, Algeria, Democratic Republic of Congo, Ghana, Angola, Kenya, South Africa, Morocco, Nigeria, Congo, Rwanda, Sudan, Côte d'Ivoire, Egypt, and Botswana were exposed in the *Panama Papers* (Fabricus 2016). Research argues that even well-intentioned politicians become socialized into patterns of materialist consumption through path dependencies and the pervasive nature of clientelism (Lindberg 2003, 136).

Second, even the formal benefits of officeholding are significant. Legislators in South Africa and Nigeria earn nearly $200,000 per year, more than salaries in almost any other country in the world. Annual salaries between $75,000 and $150,000 are found in Kenya, Uganda, and Tanzania; in countries where salaries are formally taxed, legislators may be exempt or otherwise evade taxation (Fabricus 2016). Additional allowances that are not taxed can almost match the legislative salary, including car and fuel allowances approaching $50,000 per year, state-funded loan schemes, pensions, and medical coverages (Mwiti 2017). Uganda's parliament offers legislators a "living allowance" of $15,000 per annum, alone nearly twenty-five times the annual per capita GDP of the country. Parliamentarians commonly receive "sitting allowances" for attending legislative sessions, a per diem of sorts designed to support living expenses during proceedings.

Third, institutional design makes legislative positions critical to access executive power in jobs that can provide greater rents: cabinets in sub-Saharan Africa are frequently formed of legislators. In addition to weakening the oversight capacity of the legislature (Rotberg and Salahub 2013), cabinets provide direct channels for legislators to accrue additional financial resources. Cabinet membership and the related resources are thus viewed as part of a broader patronage strategy used by ruling parties; leaders who expand the size of their cabinet are less likely to be removed from office through a coup (Arriola 2009).

Fourth, political power comes with additional opportunities for personal enrichment and wealth accumulation within personal networks. A number of African legislatures feature what are commonly called "Local Development Funds" or "Constituency Development Funds" (CDFs), which are government earmarked funds for each legislator to ostensibly use for development projects in their constituency. These funds can be massive – a 2010 figure of Kenya's CDF estimated that each MP received nearly $800,000 per year; Sudan's was more than $300,000; and MPs in Malawi, Tanzania, and Uganda received on average between $5,000 and $25,000 (Baskin and Mezey 2014). CDFs also exist in Ghana, Namibia, Nigeria, Zambia, Liberia, and Zimbabwe (Baskin and Mezey 2014). They are discretionary, meaning that MPs can use them as their own private "slush funds" to reward both deserving and needed projects, as well as for constituency pork or clientelism (Barkan and Mattes 2014). In cases where funds disbursement is direct (as is true for in Tanzania, Uganda, and Zimbabwe), MPs are responsible for managing and distributing the funds directly, allowing ample opportunity for capture.

Of these four channels of material resources thought to motivate African legislators – (1) privately consuming public from the government, (2) formal benefits of officeholding, (3) access to plum positions in the executive, and (4) community slush funds for pork – at least the second and fourth are universally accessible and homogeneously delivered to officeholders, independent of whether or not an officeholder is in the ruling party versus the opposition, from a rural versus an urban constituency, a woman versus a man, and so on. By contrast, the first and third benefits are thought to accrue unequally. While there is some evidence that election strategy impacts the opposition's access to government resources (Arriola, Choi, and Lindberg 2018), it is generally thought the main beneficiaries of access to government coffers are those in government and, like in most regimes, positions in the executive branch are for those already in government. As Arriola (2013, 182) notes,

> Politicians who have served in government are the best placed to accumulate the wealth needed to attain and retain leadership status. Being in government typically enables those at the highest levels to appropriate land, acquire capital for business ventures or be placed on the boards of private firms... Candidates who have previously served in government should have a special advantage in this regard.

Importantly, Arriola (2013) more generally ties opposition's ability to compete to such experience and resources, something the opposition candidates sorely lack under electoral authoritarianism.

Aside from the material benefits of officeholding, the literature proposes little benefit of actually performing the duties of a legislator for most officeholders. While some "reformers" may seek to further empower legislative institutions, such individuals are generally rare (Barkan 2009). Consistent with literature from other settings, inherited wisdom on African legislators suggests their primary motivation is reelection. Similarly, since all four material benefits described in the preceding paragraphs require holding office, little benefit is anticipated from losing an election.

Benefits under Electoral Authoritarianism

Scholars theorize that legislative elections in electoral authoritarian regimes are contests of "competitive clientelism," whereby legislators vie for positions in government to extract rents for themselves and their supporters. The benefits of such positions are significant. As Lust-Okar (2009, 125–126) describes,

> In addition to the glamour and prestige of being in parliament and, for some, a hope that they can make a marginal contribution to the public welfare, members

TABLE 2.2 *Benefits of legislative office in Africa*

Benefit	Examples
Material Gains	MP salary/sitting allowance; tax/housing benefits for MPs; personal and familial enrichment; CDF/discretionary development; money for club good allocation to clients; preferential contract kickbacks
Prestige of Office	Local/regional popularity; personal/household autonomy (for women); NGO conferences in five star hotels; appearing on television
Ideology/Policy Aims	Shape/implement policy (democracy, rule of law, development); advance sociopolitical issues (women's rights, education, etc.); patriotic obligation
Career Opportunism	Access to other government jobs; experience/training for elected offices; develop political and business networks; "pay dues" to party for later ambitions; be co-opted into other party; join party "on the rise"

of parliament (MPs) also receive cars, drivers, offices, and a set of attractive benefits, and they gain direct access to government ministries that dole out public contracts. Candidates compete not only to obtain a position as a *wasta* [mediator] between citizens and the state, but also to obtain their own privileged access to state resources. Thus a factory owner-cum-MP may use his connections with the ministries to bypass import duties or to win large public contracts worth significant sums of money.

Semi-structured interviews for theory building highlight four types of benefits that legislative candidates in electoral authoritarian regimes seek. They can be cast as ideal types: material gains, prestige of office, ideology/policy aims, and career opportunism. The interviews suggest that candidates care about multiple benefits and value each differently in contrast to Payne and Woshinsky (1972), who argue that candidates carry one primary expected benefit of being in office. Table 2.2 sketches out candidate motivations across each ideal type, as drawn from these interviews.

Lust-Okar's (2009) quote also relays a view common to the literature on authoritarian regimes: elections are "winner take all" contests that the opposition has little chance of winning these resources. This literature allows little space for benefits to accrue from parliamentary activities like oversight or making laws (Lust-Okar 2009), as it would undermine these institutions as vehicles of co-optation. Greene's (2008) perspective is more consistent with my theory: opposition legislators may secure expressive benefits from fighting for their personal values and ideology. Opposition legislators may pursue policy goals of personal value more freely. Introducing heterogeneity in terms of what legislators want and how well parties deliver them helps move from a strategic candidacy approach that initially "leads us to a dead end" (Greene 2007, 121) when trying to explain candidacy under electoral authoritarianism to a more theoretically robust framework that can account for why some people run for the opposition.

Benefits (B) of Losing

In advanced democracies, the "divisive primary hypothesis" suggests that parties suffer electoral consequences for intraparty contests where one camp's supporters are alienated from the party when their preferred candidate is not selected (Makse and Sokhey 2010). One might expect that nomination losers may obtain conciliatory positions in the government administration in exchange for bringing their supporters back into the fold of the election.

The logic holds for electoral authoritarian regimes, where spurned elites are kept loyal through the distribution of conciliatory positions. Ruling party co-optation may take place in a way that delivers benefits, but at the level of losing nomination contests. A young challenger who gives a long-standing incumbent a "run for their money" is likely to garner more attention from the ruling party and perhaps obtain a privileged position in the local administration. This offers both the prestige of holding government office and a living stipend and other perks of working in the bureaucracy. They may also gain a party-based position that can afford different kinds of benefits to the candidate. There is further evidence that unsuccessful nomination seekers benefit by gaining voter valence, political experience, and conciliatory party positions (Makse and Sokhey 2010). Thus, one would suppose there to be some nonzero benefit for participating in this second stage along the path to candidacy. These so-called spoils of defeat do not, of course, outweigh the benefits of winning a nomination. They are also likely to be specific to ruling parties or otherwise highly competitive nomination contests.

As with losing nominations, individuals may benefit from running and losing an election contest. Research shows that candidates acquire benefits from losing elections due to "value-rationality" (Weber 1991), particularly if they aim to shape public debate about politics and development (Greene 2007, Magaloni 2006, Scheiner 2006). This aligns with intuitions on candidate and voter behavior in majority, run-off systems where a candidate eliminated in the first round can achieve policy-related goals if voters cast ballots strategically for a viable candidate who holds similar policy views or if viable candidates adopt policies of the person eliminated in the first round.[17] Opposition candidates in particular can benefit from showing that they can effectively mobilize voters and gain experience of running campaigns, which can boost their success in later attempts. Candidates generally may gain other perks like publicity/pundit gigs.

What resonates from these accounts is that benefits gained from losing a nomination or election are contingent on the difficulty of the contest. In electoral authoritarian regimes, these are ruling party primaries and opposition election campaigns. Individuals who see benefits in losing nominations are thus more likely to run for the ruling party; those who identify benefits of losing elections are more apt to become opposition candidates. Because this book is more focused on opposition candidacy, the main text will focus on benefits of losing elections, while consideration of benefits of losing nominations is found in the Appendix.

In sum, candidates may derive benefits from losing both election and nomination contests; differences in which benefits are obtained by opposition versus ruling party candidates mirror those discussed with regard to officeholding and performing legislative duties, whereby ruling party candidates primarily derive material and career opportunist benefits and opposition candidates prestige and ideological ones. A second difference is that the benefits of losing are pronounced for contests where winning is not expected; competitive candidates who are trounced in elections (ruling party) or nomination contests (opposition) they are expected to win stand to gain very little. Table 2.3 summarizes the preceding discussion regarding benefits of legislative candidacy, highlighting how the original theory guiding this book differs from existing scholarship.

Costs (C) of Running for Office: Money, Violence, Repression

The literature on elections generally holds that elections are strategic substitutes for violent conflict and repression – institutions that facilitate resolving contentious political conflict (Dunning 2011). In this view,

---

[17] See, for example, Bordignon, Nannicini and Tabellini (2016), Bouton (2013), and Bouton and Gratton (2015). In other contexts, candidates eliminated in the first round may extract something from the eventual winner if they back them in the runoff.

TABLE 2.3 *Benefits of candidacy: Literature and theory*

		Running (and Losing)	Officeholding	Legislative Service/Duties
Advanced Democracy (Literature)	Benefits	None	M, C	None
	Heterogeneity?	N/A	No	No
Africa Literature	Benefits	None	M	None
	Heterogeneity?	N/A	M: RP > Opp	N/A
Electoral Authoritarianism (My theory)	Benefits	**M, P, I, C**	**M,P,C**	**I,P**
	Heterogeneity?	Nom Loss Benefit: RP > Opp Elec Loss Benefit: RP < Opp	**M, C**: RP > Opp **P**: RP < Opp	**I**: RP < Opp **P**: RP < Opp

Material (M), Prestige (P), Ideology (I), Career (C), Ruling Party (RP), Opposition (Opp) political parties and their supporters form proto-armies and, when voting, citizens citizens cast "paper stones" to demonstrate support or opposition to the government (Przeworski and Sprague 1986). Election results thus approximate the likely outcome resulting from armed conflict between competing groups. In democracies, the costs of elections are economic ones not those of violence and repression. Costs in the form of campaign expenditure are discussed mostly under the parameter of election prospects, as it is well established that overall campaign spending is positively correlated with election success.

That said, there are personal and financial considerations surrounding campaigns that could factor into the cost parameter for candidates in electoral authoritarian regimes. On the opposition side, we know that opposition actors commonly lack independent sources of financial support and that it is hard for them to fundraise given that potential financiers fear government reprimand for supporting the opposition (Arriola 2013). Their personal outlay may then be higher as a proportion of their total campaign expense if opposition parties cannot deliver any resources to prospective candidates. Voters also have significant expectations of elected representatives to deliver financial resources, gifts, and development projects to their communities, and candidates are beholden to these expectations to deliver goods to them (Lindberg 2010). Research suggests this kind of "homestyle" constituency service is beneficial for both constituents and legislators (Barkan 2009, 1979, Fenno 1978). MPs who can marshal these kinds of resources are more likely to win reelection (Barkan and Mattes 2014).

My theory of candidacy in electoral authoritarian regimes mainly focuses on non-campaign costs, which disproportionately fall on opposition candidates. Under electoral authoritarianism, the selective use of violence and repression serves as an instrument of authoritarian control. Thus, violence and repression are complementary to elections. Violence may be electorally advantageous by repressing dissent and protest (Brass 2003, Charurvedi 2005), mobilizing supporters (Wilkinson 2004), and/or capturing new voters (Collier and Vicente 2014, Wilkinson and Haid 2009). Contests with fierce competition and small margins are likely to yield fighting (Chacón, Robinson and Torvik 2011).

Violence and repression are widespread in African elections, particularly under electoral authoritarianism. Studies estimate that 80 percent of African elections since 1980 have featured some combination of fraud, corruption, and violence (Bishop and Hoeffler 2014). Others suggest that somewhere around 60 percent of elections are repressive and between

20 percent and 25 percent of elections are "violent", as defined by some threshold of repression, violence, and deaths.[18] Across sub-Saharan Africa, nearly half of respondents in a recent Afrobarometer poll report fearing election violence (Mares and Young 2016).

Opposition forces that challenge authoritarian regimes face risks and nonfinancial costs outside elections (Kuran 1991, 1989, Levy 2010, Loveman 1998, Tarrow 1992). Electoral authoritarian regimes discourage opposition activity with "punishment regimes" that withhold developmental goods from opposition supporters (Magaloni 2006, Weinstein 2011). Opposition candidates in electoral authoritarian regimes also risk their financial status and personal security. Financing the opposition in electoral authoritarian regimes is said to "commit economic suicide" (Levitsky and Way 2010a, 249). Opposition leaders and elites are the primary targets of repression and violence in the months leading up to elections (Bhasin and Gandhi 2013) and in their immediate aftermath (Ash 2015). In electoral authoritarian regimes, "opposition figures have been arrested or disappeared, opposition candidates in parliamentary elections have been disqualified" (Kaya and Bernhard 2013, 745). Candidacy may actually cost a candidate's life (Bruhn 2012, Eisenstadt 2003). While the use of force needs to be restrained on a macro level so it does not completely dilute the legitimacy of *de jure* competitive elections and incite reciprocal violence from opposition forces (Carey and Lebo 2006, Tucker 2006) and embolden challengers (Kricheli, Livine, and Magaloni 2011), at the individual level, it remains a credible threat.

Attitudes toward risk impact candidacy decisions through how they shape costs. Violence and repression contribute to these costs, whereas risk attitudes and time perspectives have the power to discount or magnify them. Research has demonstrated that collective political action in authoritarian settings is driven by individuals who accept risk, particularly in earlier stages of challenges against the regime. It is the willingness of risk takers to engage in collective action and to do so publicly that explains why revolutions occur (Kuran 1991, 1989) and whether political protests (Levy 2010) and anti-government protests occur (Lohmann 1994, Loveman 1998), among other high-risk political activities (Tarrow 1992). Focal individuals in anti-incumbent movements hold longer-term time horizons, focusing on gains that may not be obtained immediately,

---

[18] Straus and Taylor (2012), for example, estimate 58 percent of elections from 1990 to 2007 feature repression and violence, while 19 percent feature events leading to at least twenty deaths. See also Bekoe (2012).

but over a series of repeated political interactions (Shefter 1994). How groups collectively view time horizons impacts their ability to engage in collective, cooperative political action and to reach political goals and outcomes (Bendor and Mookherjee 1987, Ostrom 1990).

Risk Tolerance and Time Perspectives among Opposition Candidates

Risk While not a direct cost function, political participation is constrained by perceptions and tolerance of risk (Kam 2012). This holds for political elites as well. Two prospective candidates who perceive identical odds of winning nominations across parties may not make the same decision to run for office. Candidates utilize different voter courtship strategies during campaigns depending on their level of risk aversion toward recruiting groups that offer more or less stable support (Cox and McCubbins 1986). Politicians behaving strategically may decide to forego running for office under conditions of high uncertainty over electoral competition if they do not wish to risk the downstream consequences of losing (Shepsle 1972).

Running for office in any setting incurs some risk – including financial risk – and the chances of losing. However, under electoral authoritarianism, the primary risk considerations are the nonfinancial costs of repression and violence associated with running for the opposition. By seeking opposition candidacy, one commits to take on the risks associated with standing against an authoritarian government. Risks range from modest ones, such as the consequences of losing an election contest, to severe ones, such as experiencing physical, social, or economic repression at the hand of the government, which may also be imposed upon a prospective candidate's family and friends and social and economic networks. What drives opposition candidate decision making is a combination of beliefs about the likelihood of such repression occurring and the willingness to risk the decisions that may induce such violence. Thus, risk attitudes can be conceptualized like a discount factor – a subjective weight individuals place on the repressive risks of running for office.

In comparing the willingness of citizens to take on such risks in the context of an electoral authoritarian regime, the literature demonstrates that opposition supporters – from voters to leaders – tend to be more willing to bear risk compared with ruling party candidates. This follows with the logic elucidated by Schedler (2013): when the political stakes are high, incumbent governments "dig in" and use their tools to manipulate the political system to sustain their rule.[19] Two arguments indicate why opposition candidates should demonstrate higher rates of tolerance for repressive risks.

First, it might be that opposition candidates as "outsiders" are wired differently and, *ex ante*, are more willing to accept repressive costs. Here, a broad literature across social scientific disciplines documents a robust relationship between socioeconomic inequality and risk profiles – from health decisions to engaging in violence, individuals who face political, social, or economic disadvantages are more likely to engage in higher-risk decisions and behaviors (Mishra and Novakowski 2016). In particular, the concept of "relative deprivation" – whereby an individual assesses their own state as inferior or disadvantageous compared with another individual or group of individuals and further views this inequality as unfair (Smith, Pettigrew, Pippin, and Bialosiewicz 2012) – offers a theory of how such inequalities translate into willingness to engage in high-risk political behavior (Gurr 1970, Muller and Seligson 1987). While empirical evidence regarding whether "relative deprivation" drives violent political behavior has been mixed, inequality between groups retains explanatory power, particularly regarding political decisions and outcomes in sub-Saharan Africa (Baldwin and Huber 2010).

This account would suggest opposition candidates manifest more risk tolerance if we offered evidence that opposition candidates systematically experienced greater rates of poverty, inequality, and so on. We know from the literature on electoral authoritarianism this is the case. Deprivation and the creation and reinforcement of inequality are critical strategies for regime maintenance, particularly in areas where nascent opposition support exists. Ruling parties use such strategies to forge citizen-government dependencies to discourage opposition sympathies (Gandhi and Lust-Okar 2009). It further documents that ruling parties economically punish areas where opposition support is concentrated (Magaloni 2006). In Tanzania, for example, the government systematically underfunds local governments and public service provision in areas with opposition support (Weinstein 2011).

Additional considerations support this view. Risk tolerance is associated with opposition participation generally: voters with greater risk

---

[19] Note that Schedler uses the terms "risk aversion" and "risk tolerance" but intends different meanings for them: he discusses willingness of autocratic leaders to tolerate the risk of insecurity of their power and whether they demonstrate aversion or tolerance of risk over challenges to this power in deciding to use more or less of the regime's manipulative capacity. See Schedler (2013, 281–284).

propensities are more likely to "gamble" on candidates and parties that offer less certain political policies or employ less conventional campaign strategies (Kam and Simas 2012). Under electoral authoritarianism, risk tolerance is correlated with greater propensity to vote for opposition candidates (Morgenstern and Zechmeister 2001); similar evidence emerges from dominant party systems that are democratic (Iida 2013). Further, politicians generally display greater tolerance of risk compared with citizens (Hess, von Scheve, Schupp, and Wagner 2013, Sheffer and Loewen 2019, Thomas, Hess, and Wagner 2017). Together, this suggests that opposition candidates should be less risk averse than their ruling party counterparts.

A second argument that opposition supporters are more risk tolerant looks to the motivations for running for office. My theory posits opposition candidates are significantly more motivated by ideological and policy goals related to broad societal advancement and change, as opposed to more individually focused material, prestige, or career benefits of office-seeking and officeholding. Political psychology shows that such goals – which broadly align with the concept of "altruism" – are associated with higher levels of demonstrated risk tolerance. As Fowler and Kam (2007, 816) note, "those who exhibit a sufficient degree of concern for the welfare of others will be willing to engage in costly political participation. Moreover, as people become more concerned for the welfare of others, they should experience greater benefit when political outcomes portend improvements for the welfare of others generally." Thus, it is possible that willingness to risk paying the costs of running for the opposition operates through altruism, whereby the benefits sought by such candidates are compatible with accepting the price of holding autocrats accountable.

Time The role of time horizons in authoritarian regimes has been considered to a more limited extent, focusing primarily on the decisions of autocratic elites and how much they value the future versus the present. This literature argues that leaders make political decisions in consideration of the expected duration of their rule (Wright 2008); when they expect longer periods of rule, they behave more like "stationary" than "roving" bandits (Olson 1993). Research shows that leaders who are more popular and face fewer challengers have longer time horizons regarding governance decisions (Beck et al. 2001). In sub-Saharan Africa, evidence of whether or not the time horizons of governments impact their actions is inconclusive (Dionne 2011).

Like Brownlee (2007), Dionne (2011), Beck et al. (2001), and Geddes (1999), I consider time horizons from the perspective of regime rule. In terms of candidacy, then, time horizons are shorter for ruling parties. As the regime is already in power, policies that it wishes to implement can be done with the ease provided by a legislative supermajority, and the spoils associated with office are already in place. Even short-term fluctuations in the availability of patronage and clientelistic goods to provide to supporters can spell out the trouble for the regime, as their absence strains intraparty cohesion and ruling party strength (Greene 2007, Scheiner 2006).

From the perspective of the opposition, access to power is limited in the short run. But what motivates the opposition – the belief that someday down the road opposition will take over office or, alternately, the ruling party will concede important reforms that open it to further citizen control – is only attainable in the longer term. Thus, the expectation is broadly that opposition party members have longer-term time horizons in the context of political activities. The road to opposition victory is long; consequently, opposition party supports are locked in for the long haul. This follows in the tradition of Shefter (1994) and Greene (2007), who focus on the lengthy commitments made by regime outsiders in the eventual displacement of the party in power.

In sum, opposition partisans, loyalists, noncandidates, candidates, and legislators are expected to be more willing to tolerate risk in political activities. They also are more likely to exercise patience over reaching political goals.

Summing Up: Strategic Candidacy in Electoral Authoritarian Regimes

Table 2.4 summarizes the main elements of my theory and how it differs from existing work. It reinforces the point that under electoral authoritarian settings, conventional models of candidacy cannot account for opposition. Adaptations to the theory in light of the conditions of political competition under electoral authoritarianism offer a solution.

2.5 LINKING THE THEORY'S PARTS TOGETHER

Thus far, I have argued that party versus civic activism imposes a path dependence on downstream candidacy decisions for prospective candidates, using an approach that suggests each of these two paths reinforces opportunity structures for prospective candidates that make candidacy with the ruling party versus the opposition more appealing. Civic activists

TABLE 2.4 *Strategic candidacy framework review*

Literature	Parameter	Key Points
Prevailing Wisdom	$P_{Election}$	No party choice/heterogeneity over P
	B_{Office}	Material; not specific to party/majority status; conferred by winning
	C_{Cost}	Primarily financial expense of running
	$P_{Nomination}$	n/a
	B_{Losing}	n/a
	$C_{RiskAttitudes}$	n/a
Original Theory	$P_{Election}$	Heterogeneity over P between party; across space
	$P_{Nomination}$	Generally, inversely related to $P_{Election}$
	B_{Office}	Multiple types; choice-specific
	B_{Losing}	May accrue in losing election and/or primary
	C_{Cost}	Includes personal expenses; other nonfinancial costs
	$C_{RiskAttitudes}$	Candidates vary in willingness to bear costs

travel down a path where opposition candidacy is a viable and desirable option, while career partisans find ruling party prospects welcoming. An additional impact of these paths on candidacy decisions remains: it has the potential to either shape or reflect what individuals value when considering candidacy.

LeBas's (2011) account of opposition party formation convincingly shows how civic activism impacts electoral prospects. Because civil society organizations have organizational capacity and mobilization experience, opposition candidates who can tap into those resources have better chances of being elected. Members and leaders of civic associations may see themselves as viable candidates if they conclude from frequent interactions with large numbers of other activists that they are popular among the electorate. Career partisanship can shape how prospective candidates rate their chances of electoral victory based on whether they think they will make it out of the nomination stage. Have they paid sufficient dues in the form of party service to win the support of the party?

Civic activism's impact on benefits of office can manifest in two ways: socialization and selection. Ismail Jussa's and James Mbatia's accounts offer evidence that both mechanisms can be at play at the same time. Jussa engaged in civic activism as a student and advocated for the political and economic empowerment of Zanzibar and explains why he was motivated to run for office and the benefits he sought in candidacy. His experiences in these activities led to the discovery that his goals had political dimensions and that legislative politics was the most effective way of pursuing them; in this sense, his experiences in civil society engagement transformed those goals though socialization. For James Mbatia, the role of activism of opposition candidacy appears guided more by selection: he advocated for constitutional reform as a student and, after being expelled, folded that into opposition candidacy advocacy because that was the remaining venue available to pursue that goal. Selection is more clearly at play in career partisanship, whereby individuals who may desire to run for office in the future realize there is strategic advantage in making early investments in a political party. The underlying benefits derived from ruling party candidacy – the material benefits of the spoils of office – are well known and so a desire for those benefits might tip someone toward career partisanship early on. At the same time, the legacies of institutions of single-party rule that expose people to party politics at a very early age suggest that socialization may also shape career partisanship's impact on benefits sought from candidacy. Exposure to ruling party legislators benefiting from material benefits can lead to developing a taste for private goods as a party functionary.

Experiences with civic activism can impact risk attitudes in a number of important ways. First, such civic engagement already constitutes high-risk political behavior in electoral authoritarian regimes, which can catalyze self-reinforcing cycles of activism. Across an array of settings and actors – from Freedom Riders in the southern United States to insurgents in Syria and victims of violence in Burundi – there is evidence that activism begets activism through risk tolerance: experience in lower-risk activist activities reduces barriers to later, riskier behavior (Hanaoka, Shigeoka, and Watanabe 2015, Larner and Keltner 2001, McAdam 1990, Voors, Nillesen, Vermip, Bulte, Lensink, and van Soest 2010, Whitt and Mironova n.d.).[20] Second, experiences of civic activism constitute a process by which potential opposition candidates gain skills, know-how, and confidence in their abilities as potential future leaders. This is how activists learn the "repertoire of contention," or *how* to engage in

---

[20] Notably, others find experience with violence heightens risk aversion (Brown, Montalva, Thomas and Velásquez 2019, Jakiela and Ozier 2018). However, it appears the behavioral consequences of such risk aversion are not permanent (Moya 2018). Importantly, Young (2019) demonstrates that past experience with repression may heighten expectations of future repression in Zimbabwe and thus reduce citizen willingness to dissent against authoritarian regimes. Perhaps greater risk tolerance of political leaders may mitigate this demonstrated effect of experience with repression.

protests against the regime (Tarrow 1993).[21] Furthermore, such experiences can boost beliefs in internal and external efficacy. Confidence in one's own efficacy in politics is associated with opposition participation in electoral authoritarian regimes in Africa (Young 2019). Third, life trajectories in civic activism may foster social identities tied to such activism. Social identification with groups that participate in politics is associated with greater political activism (Fowler and Kam 2007), including costlier actions (Huddy, Mason, and Aaroe 2015). Civic activism may also play an information role: prospective opposition candidates learn about their viability and potential to win, allowing them to overcome coordination dilemmas that otherwise constrain participation (Magaloni 2006). Finally, when initial steps on the path of anti-incumbent political action took place before challenger parties were permitted, challengers evolved from organizations leading protests under single-party rule. Activists may have already accepted risks associated with predecessor organizations (unions, etc.) prior to candidacy that hold over into the competitive era (LeBas 2011).

CONCLUSION

This book began with a puzzle for which the literature has almost no answer: why would anyone rational ever run on opposition tickets? I have offered a theory that directly engages with the strategic candidacy tradition that emphasizes cost-benefit calculations. In this view, prospective candidates weigh the chances of winning a nomination, chances of winning an election, the benefits of political participation (seeking and or winning office), and the costs of seeking office. While these innovations lead to strategic rationales under which opposition candidacy emerges in electoral authoritarian regimes, it misses the more critical driver. Thus, the second theoretical contribution to candidacy shifts focus to a time far before candidacy strategies are actually developed: early experiences and life moments. Participation of individuals in civic activism versus career partisanship prior to candidacy decisions imposes path dependencies on those choices and directly impacts how they evaluate the various elements of candidacy strategy. With this theory in place, the next chapter moves on to discuss the electoral authoritarianism in the world and the empirical strategy used to evaluate the book's theory in Tanzania.

---

[21] Here, Tarrow's (1993) discussion draws extensively on Tilly (1978) and Tilly (1986).

3

Electoral Authoritarianism in Tanzania

Jeraha uliganga sharti ulione.
To treat a wound you must see it.

Kusikia si kuona.
Hearing is not seeing.

This first half of this chapter grounds the concept of electoral authoritarianism in contemporary empirical realities and contextualizes the case of Tanzania along the dimensions of toleration/repression and electoral hegemony of the ruling party. Introducing Tanzania's Chama Cha Mapinduzi (CCM) to readers highlights its longevity and organizational strength, but the chapter shows that the modal ruling party in electoral authoritarian regimes looks more like CCM in terms of its permanent physical footprint than it differs. Similarly, the opposition parties I focus on in this volume look much like the opposition found in electoral autocracies around the world.

The second half of the chapter summarizes the book's novel empirical approach. I review the in-depth, qualitative interviews that formed the bedrock of my theory and laid the groundwork for a multifaceted survey data collection strategy. The survey included over 25 percent of Tanzania's legislators from the 2010–2015 term and several hundred interviews with losing candidates, unsuccessful nomination seekers, and prospective noncandidates from the 2010 elections. The breadth of the data collection strategy is the first of its kind and is uniquely positioned to evaluate the question of why some people make high-risk decisions like running for office with the opposition, while others choose not to. The chapter also discusses specific survey measures employed to address the challenges of tapping the core element of my theory, including pathways to candidacy, benefits sought from candidacy, and risk attitudes. The final section of the chapter addresses remaining concerns regarding biases arising from survey data. I reach the conclusion that most of these concerns have been effectively mitigated through sophisticated survey design complemented by contextual expertise.

3.1 ELECTORAL AUTHORITARIANISM IN AFRICA

Multiparty elections in sub-Saharan Africa are characterized, just as the history of elections throughout the world, by high rates of incumbent success and bleak opposition prospects. While the government turnover rates are on the rise,[1] the spoils of victory staying with governing parties is the norm. The reelection rate of governing parties in Africa's multiparty elections is about 80 percent and dozens of sub-Saharan African governments have held power for either three elected terms in a row or fifteen years straight. While an exceptional few of these dominant party regimes are democratic – notably those in Botswana and South Africa – the majority of countries in sub-Saharan Africa are electoral authoritarian regimes (Miller 2015, Schedler 2002). Furthermore, somewhere between 35 and 55 percent of the world's contemporary electoral authoritarian regimes are found in sub-Saharan Africa, depending on coding criteria.[2]

Morse (2019) offers the most detailed account of electoral authoritarianism in Africa to date. In his approach, electoral authoritarian regimes must meet two criteria. They must be "electoral" – having held two consecutive elections for the legislature and executive – and they must be "authoritarian," in that they fail to meet a minimal threshold of democracy based on political rights. Electoral authoritarianism is further subdivided into regimes that are more or less competitive electorally (non-hegemonic or hegemonic) and ones that are more or less repressive (repressive or tolerant). Morse (2019) defines hegemony as winning consecutive elections with a legislative supermajority or 70 percent of the presidential vote.[3] Electoral authoritarian regimes can have variable levels

---

[1] Lindberg (2006a), Lindberg (2009), Weghorst and Lindberg (2011).

[2] Schedler (2002, 47) shows that sub-Saharan Africa accounted for 45 percent of such regimes found around the world; thirteen of Levitsky and Way's (2010a) thirty-five cases of competitive authoritarianism are African.

[3] Hegemonic party "distinctions are neither consistently used nor clear" (Morse 2012, 171–172) and include criteria that a dominant party "usually" wins (Ware 1996); is

of repression, violence, and the like but provided they hold elections, this does not push them out of electoral authoritarianism. Under these criteria, twenty-eight countries in sub-Saharan Africa have experienced electoral authoritarianism since 1990 and seventeen have sustained its rule up to the present day. Most episodes of electoral authoritarian rule fall under the category of repressive hegemony, while tolerant hegemonies are found in periods of rule in Burkina Faso, Mozambique, Senegal, Seychelles, and Tanzania.

Regimes vary in terms of their tolerance and hegemony, but a number of other features make exploring legislative elections and legislators in sub-Saharan Africa's electoral authoritarian regimes attractive. Broadly, democratic and autocratic regimes alike across Africa share a number of important characteristics. First, the modal regime in the continent experienced brief, if any, multiparty politics after colonial transition and quickly shifted to mono- or no-party dictatorships. When the surge of protests brought the third wave of democratization to the continent in the late 1980s and 1990s (Bratton and van de Walle 1997), legacies of weak state development under and after colonialism and underdeveloped civil societies were shared by most countries (Levitsky and Way 2010*a*). Multiparty elections were among the first instances of widespread political participation in these regimes – in contrast to Latin American regimes, where elections predated periods of dictatorship (Weghorst and Bernhard 2015). Political parties consequently were ill equipped to organize outside of channels of personalism and clientelism (van de Walle 2003).

Similarities in institutional design across sub-Saharan Africa also allow more externally valid theory development. The overwhelming majority of regimes in sub-Saharan Africa are presidential or semi-presidential, with only five parliamentary systems of forty-nine regimes. Adopted electoral systems were mainly inherited from colonial predecessors, meaning that many former French colonies have systems of proportional representation, while former British colonies are most commonly majoritarian (Manning 2005). The theory evaluated in this book best fits the electoral logic of single-member district systems. Most multiparty transitions that were engineered by authoritarian parties feature that party still competing in subsequent elections. Political parties – both challengers and incumbents – are widely considered organizationally

stronger than rivals (Sartori 1976); wins some electoral threshold in a given election (Diamond 2002, Donno 2013, Howard and Roessler 2006); or is in power for some number of years, terms, or both (Blondel 1968, Bogaards 2004, Greene 2007, Sartori 1976).

weak and offer voters little in terms of political alternatives, instead campaigning largely on valence issues (Bleck and van de Walle 2013). Scholarship is evolving to recognize the sophistication of voters in Africa,[4] but the decisions of voters remain constrained by limited access to political information.

In spite of these similarities, a number of important differences between regimes in Africa make their study particularly interesting. First, there has been important variation in outcomes of interparty competition throughout sub-Saharan Africa, particularly of late. While electoral authoritarianism still characterizes the norm in the regimes, regularized competition between established political parties is growing over time in many regimes (Weghorst and Bernhard 2015). Much of the variation in party systems can be traced to whether single-party governments incorporated existing political forces or built parallel institutions to rival them (Riedl 2014). Even in regimes where one party has ruled for an extended period of time, patterns of opposition contestation, coordination, and in some cases collapse differ widely (Bogaards 2008).

The theory I test in this book applies to electoral authoritarian regimes broadly – regimes that are not democratic but hold elections. Variation among electoral authoritarian regimes in terms of hegemony in the form of electoral dominance and repression can be directly accommodated within that theory. Provided they meet the condition of holding elections, the extent to which a government uses fraud, violence, and repression is embedded within the decisions over candidacy as does country- and individual-level variation in election prospects. As such, the universe of cases to which this theory most directly applies is the twenty-eight cases of electoral authoritarian rule in sub-Saharan Africa, as well as the electoral authoritarian regimes found in other regions of the world. Much of it should also should apply to dominant party authoritarian regimes. I will discuss scope conditions of my theory and the external validity of the Tanzanian case after introducing the regime context in greater detail.

3.2 ELECTORAL AUTHORITARIANISM IN TANZANIA

Tanzania's deviance from electoral democracy has been noted by many scholars. It has been designated as "competitive authoritarian" (Levitsky and Way 2010*a*) and "electoral authoritarian" (Lindberg 2006*b*,

---

[4] See Bratton, Bhavnani, and Chen (2011), Ellis (2014), Lindberg (2012), Weghorst and Lindberg (2013), for example.

Morse 2012, 2019), where the party in power has "not been subjected to serious electoral competition" (Rakner and van de Walle 2009*b*, 208). Others have described Tanzania as "ambiguous" (Diamond 2002), "hegemonic" (Magaloni 2006), and a "fluid dominant" party system (van Eerd 2010).

After Tanganyika received its independence from Britain in 1961, then-leader Julius Nyerere established the Tanganyikan African National Union (TANU). As a movement-based party with its origins in the struggle against colonial rule (Smith 2005), upon independence it embarked on one of the more extensive party-building projects in the history of sub-Saharan Africa (Bienen 1967, Levitsky and Way 2010*a*). This accelerated with the integration of the Zanzibar archipelago to form Tanzania following the overthrow of the Zanzibari sultan in 1964, one year after Zanzibar became independent from Britain. Thus was born Tanzania, the political force later rebranded as Chama Cha Mapinduzi (CCM), and the era of single-party dominance that defines the relationship between the two.[5] Through this and the subsequent period, CCM came to control nearly all political, social, and economic life throughout the country (Barkan 1994, Hyden 1999, Msekwa 2006, Mmuya and Chaligha 1994).

Tanzania implemented a series of elite-driven and donor-supported democratic reforms in the early 1990s. Described as "top-down democratization" (Hyden 1999, 143), these changes were initiated by Julius Nyerere. He stepped down from the presidency in 1985, but continued to lead CCM as its chairman until 1990 and remained a revered political figure until his death in 1999 (Maliyamkoko 2002). In spite of reintroducing multiparty competition and diluting the formal power of the presidency, CCM has remained electorally dominant in legislative elections. The 1995 polls featured some electoral irregularities, failures by the National Electoral Commission to provide ample voting materials, and government assistance for campaigns directed almost entirely to CCM (Kaya 2004, TEMCO 1997). Observers deemed this to hinder the opposition but alone it did not guarantee its defeat (TEMCO 1997), with the potential exception of Zanzibar (Burgess 2009). In a sense, this election was

---

[5] Chama Cha Mapinduzi means "Revolutionary Party," in reference to the Zanzibari Revolution in 1964. The revolution led to the formation of the United Republic of Tanzania from mainland Tanganyika and the Zanzibari archipelago and the single-party rule of TANU in mainland Tanzania and the Afro Shirazi Party (ASP) in Zanzibar. They largely operated as sibling parties until TANU and ASP were formally integrated in 1977 when they were reestablished as Chama Cha Mapinduzi.

the "abetura"[6] for opposition parties in Tanzania, an ephemeral moment to rival the governing party that quickly passed. The subsequent elections in Tanzania have varied in their repressiveness, but none of the six polls held from 1995 through 2020 have broken CCM's supermajority in the *Bunge* or their majority in Zanzibar's House of Representatives. After the widely criticized polls of 2020 were certified by the country's electoral management board, CCM held over 90 percent of seats in the parliament.

Studying these dynamics in Tanzania is critical. While many study Tanzania – particularly its dynamics of development[7] – far fewer scholars study dynamics of elections and authoritarian rule in this setting.[8] Yet, Tanzania's electoral authoritarian regime resembles patterns of competition in nascent political systems in Africa and around the world. CCM is Africa's longest-ruling party and has been in power since Tanganyika's and Zanzibar's independence (1961; 1964, respectively).[9] It won six multiparty elections from 1995 to 2020, and has been minimally impacted by interparty challenges (Hyden 1999). A key difference at the macro level is that opposition in Zanzibar has succeeded in breaking into government through a power-sharing agreement in 2010. Opposition party Civic United Front (CUF) would have won the 2015 elections there outright had the polls not been extra-constitutionally annulled by an election official after votes from roughly 60 percent of constituencies were certified. Until the 2020 polls, the opposition had made modest but steady gains across each parliamentary election. This allows for exploring longitudinal and cross-sectional patterns of interparty competition.

In the remainder of this section, I describe electoral authoritarianism in Tanzania along the two dimensions of variation within those regimes identified by Morse (2019): toleration/repression and hegemony. In the context of candidacy and the modifications to the strategic candidacy framework I propose, repression most directly impacts costs, while hegemony shapes election prospects and the benefits of running for office.

---

[6] Joseph (1998) coined this term to refer to the brief opening for democratic governance in sub-Saharan Africa during the early 1990s, after which authoritarian rule was re-entrenched.

[7] Iconic works include Barkan (1994), Bienen (1967), Chaligha, Mattes, Bratton and Davids (2002), Hyden (1980), Miguel (2004), Weinstein (2011).

[8] Notable contemporary research includes Carlitz and McLellan (2021), Collard (2019), Hyden (1999), Maliyamkoko (2002), Mmuya and Chaligha (1994), Morse (2019), Paget (2017), Rosenzweig (2018), Smith (2005), Tripp (2000), Weinstein (2011).

[9] Including its two predecessors, mainland Tanzania's TANU and Zanzibar's ASP.

Toleration and Repression in Tanzania

The narrative of Tanzania among scholars and policy makers for most of the last 30 years portrays the country as peaceful, and the ruling party has enjoyed its tenure in power under multipartyism primarily through delivering moderate but consistent economic growth, maintaining a positive public image, and fending off a weak and poorly organized opposition. Zanzibar is viewed as the potential exception to what others see as a fairly benign authoritarianism. Yet, it features both a capacity to engage in coercion (Levitsky and Way 2010a, 254) and a willingness to use it for political ends. The presence of government security forces pervades opposition activities. Election rallies from 1995 forward have featured strong oversight from police (Kaya 2004) and police also intervene and cancel rallies under claims they were improperly announced or permitted (Ewald 2013). More recently, the government has opted to outright prohibit political rallies, allowing only small-level constituency meetings (Staff 2016). Elections themselves generally feature limited but dispersed use of violence against voters and candidates (TEMCO 1997, TEMCO 2000, TEMCO 2006). This force at the government's disposal has become increasingly apparent since 2010 (Paget 2017), and the contemporary public view toward Tanzania has shifted since the election of President John Pombe Magufuli. In his first term, Magufuli significantly increased the government's repressive capacity through legislation that clamped down on political dissent, reduced transparency, restricting civic engagement, and muzzled print, digital, and social media.

The 2020 elections marked the most visible example of repression since multiparty elections were reintroduced in the 1990s. In the lead-up to the elections, opposition leaders were harassed, detained, and attacked by government actors and other unknown assailants. The country's electoral management charged the opposition's leading presidential candidate Tundu Lissu with sedition and banned him from campaigning in the final stretch ahead of the elections. Prominent international election observation missions were either not welcomed to oversee the polls or were denied accreditation (Odula 2020). On the days surrounding the elections, the government harnessed its enhanced cybersecurity capacity to throttle or outright block access to social media platforms like WhatsApp and Twitter and campaign tools like bulk SMS messaging (Karombo 2020).[10] In

---

[10] During President Magufuli's first term, Tanzania signed cybersecurity agreements with South Korea and Israel, as well as with private firms (Goldberg 2018, Lugongo 2017).

the immediate aftermath of the elections, at least twenty people died at the hands of the government. Opposition leaders went into hiding and others were arrested; as many as 300 activists were detained (Burke 2020). Ismail Jussa was abducted by police and in the subsequent days rumored to be dead. He emerged several days later after the police had brutalized him during interrogation, resulting in four leg fractures and five fractures in his shoulder (Muchena 2020).

John Pombe Magufuli died on March 17, 2021, reportedly as a result of a chronic heart condition for which he wore a pacemaker. Many suspect he contracted the novel coronavirus COVID-19, a pandemic which his administration had largely ignored.[11] In the weeks leading up to his death, several members of his cabinet were hospitalized with conditions consistent with COVID-19 infections and his Chief Secretary died in early February. Vice-President Samia Suluhu has succeeded Magufuli as President of Tanzania.

At the time of writing, it remains to be seen whether Suluhu's administration will further efforts to crack down on political and civil space in Tanzania or if they will plateau under her leadership. Magufuli disappeared from public eye nearly three weeks before his death was announced. During this period, the government managed to keep information regarding his health status from leaking to the public. Even days before his death, Prime Minister Kassim Majaliwa issued a public statement that the president was "strong and working hard as usual." The ability of the government to close ranks and prohibit the spread of information about Magufuli's condition indicates the depth of the government's control over civic space and the information environment in Tanzania. This suggests the current repressive capacity is one Tanzania has long possessed and will maintain in the future, rather than something specific to the presidency of John Pombe Magufuli.

Tanzania's Repression in Comparative Perspective

Tanzania is similar to other present-day electoral authoritarian regimes as well as iconic examples from the literature. I demonstrate this by reference to the extent to which the regime imposes nonfinancial costs on citizens and politicians. Following Morse (2019), I draw upon an index

---

[11] Magufuli denied the severity of the pandemic's impact on Tanzania, did not report infection statistics to the WHO through most of 2020 and into 2021, rejected deliveries of COVID-19 vaccine, expressed general distrust toward international health actors, and at one point, claimed prayer had eradicated the virus.

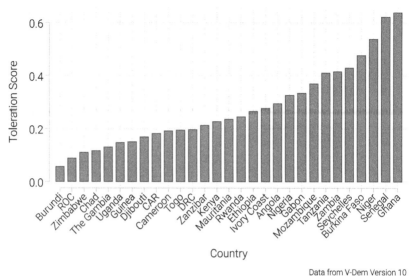

Country

Data from V-Dem Version 10

FIGURE 3.1 Toleration index for Africa's electoral authoritarian regimes

of toleration that captures the extent to which an electoral authoritarian regime tolerates competition and dissent from political and civic actors. I use V-Dem data, which combine indicators of government use of physical violence outside the context of elections, freeness and fairness of elections, freedom of association, and freedom of expression. The index is created as described in Morse (2019). It forms a continuum that ranges from 0 to 1, where higher values indicate greater tolerance and less repression.[12]

First, I situate Tanzania's ruling party among other electoral authoritarian regimes in sub-Saharan Africa during the twenty-first century. Figure 3.1 focuses primarily on African examples and shows the average value of the Toleration Index across the duration of each regime.

Figure 3.1 shows that the most direct generalizations from this study will speak to regimes where repression is a credible weapon in the ruling party's toolbox, but one used modestly and with discretion. This

---

[12] The tolerance index is reproduced following Morse's (2019) aggregation formula, which is Electoral Toleration = 0.5 x (Physical Violence x Clean Elections x Freedom of Association x Freedom of Expression) + 0.5 x (0.4 x Physical Violence + 0.3 x Clean Elections x+ 0.15 x Freedom of Association + 0.15 x Freedom of Expression). Minor differences in values here compared to Morse (2019) can be attributed to the source data: annual coding updates performed by V-Dem include previously coded years, meaning the country-year value of a particular indicator is retroactively subject to a modicum of change each subsequent coding year.

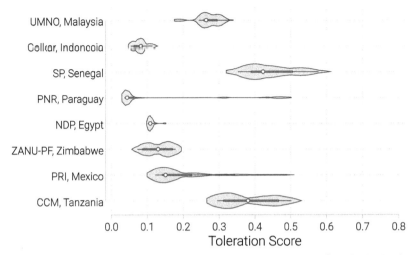

FIGURE 3.2 Toleration index for notable electoral authoritarian regimes

places Tanzania among fairly tolerant peers like Burkina Faso, Mozambique, Nigeria, and Seychelles. The Toleration Index value for Zanzibar specifically is comparably lower and situates it closer to less tolerant, contemporary electoral authoritarian regimes like those in Rwanda, Ethiopia, and Cameroon. Still, even in the archipelago, CCM uses repression and coercion sparingly compared to more brutal regimes like that in Zimbabwe, where past elections featured widespread violence and the government "abducted and tortured hundreds of MDC supporters [and] the government was able to use coercive force to systematically preempt or thwart protest" (Levitsky and Way 2010a, 243–246).

A second effort looks to Tanzania alongside some of history's best-known electoral authoritarian regimes. Once again, comparisons are based on the index of toleration introduced by Morse (2019). The goal here is to gain a broader understanding of how much a regime's tenure is defined by the use of violence to reinforce its power over decades of rule. Using violin plots, Figure 3.2 shows the central tendencies of the Toleration Index for a number of electoral authoritarian regimes. Each violin plot indicates the median score during the time that party was in power, as well as the distribution of scores throughout the regime's tenure.[13]

---

[13] Duration of rule is coded as follows: UMNO 1960–2018; Golkar 1965–1998; SP 1978–2000; ANR-PC 1954–1999; NDP 1981–2011; PRI 1929–2000; ZANU-PF 1987–present; CCM 1961–present. Regime codings are based on Schedler (2013), with context-specific adjustments to duration of rule.

In the figure, one observes that the level of toleration by CCM is somewhat higher but comparable to other electoral authoritarian regimes. The primary difference lies in the spread of the data, highlighted by the shaded Kernel density distributions. While the median level of toleration sits between 0.1 and 0.2 for several of these regimes, the willingness of ZANU-PF and the Socialist Party of Senegal to engage in violence against citizens and crackdowns on campaigns are much greater at certain times, similar to Tanzania. This is represented by the wider distribution of the variable for those regimes.

Tanzania's regime is one where violence is only one possible strategy of regime rule and thus CCM better resembles other cases. The Socialist Party of Senegal, for example, is noted as having inherited a strong military force and early on utilized violence against opposition. Over time, however, it relied more heavily on its resource and institutional advantages to engineer political support without resorting to repression (Galvan 2001, Villalon 1994). Like CCM in Tanzania, UMNO in Malaysia possesses a strong, penetrating party apparatus with extensive membership and presence down to the ten-household unit (Levitsky and Way 2010a, 320). The strong party structure combined with internal party cohesion permitted the select use of violent repression – notably during the onset of the *Reformasi* protest movement against the government in the late 1990s – combined with increased patronage distribution and more benign authoritarian techniques of harassment to fracture the opposition into electoral defeat (Brownlee 2007, 152). These included calling early elections for an unprepared opposition (Brownlee 2007, 129) and banning popular, nongovernmental publications (Slater 2003). Situating the case of Tanzania in the broader literature will find more promise with comparisons to such regimes.

In sum, Tanzania's electoral authoritarian regime and lessons derived about candidacy there can speak to a number of other electoral regimes found around the world. While the costs of competition and, more broadly, willingness of the ruling party to use violence as a political tool are more limited in Tanzania than in contemporary and historical cases of authoritarian rule, it compares well to a number of regimes in Africa and elsewhere. Thus, contemporary Tanzanian politics can inform scholars of electoral authoritarian regimes about general tendencies of ruling parties in these settings but only to the extent that ruling elites are not relying on violence as a central tool to gain or re-entrench regime support. Having established this, the chapter moves to discuss hegemony in Tanzania's legislatures.

Electoral Hegemony in Tanzania's Legislatures

Tanzania features two legislatures. The first is a national parliament known as the *Bunge*. The 2010–2015 Parliament of Tanzania was composed of 239 directly elected seats from single-member districts, 50 constituencies were located in Zanzibar and the remaining 189 in mainland Tanzania. It featured an additional 112 seats and of these, the majority were women's special seats that were allocated to each political party proportional to its percentage of constituency seats.[14] While designed to increase women's representation, these seats advantage the governing party because they enhance disproportionality. Additional seats come from presidential appointment, appointments from Zanzibar, and the attorney general, who serves as an ex-officio member. The legislature added 25 single-member district seats in 2015; and on the eve of the 2020 elections, the chamber had 393 total members. Institutionally, the Tanzanian parliament has grown progressively stronger and more independent over time, particularly in the early twenty-first century (Collard 2019).

Opposition parties have performed poorly in each of the six multiparty elections in Tanzania, but had posted incremental progress prior to the 2020 polls. In 2015, the opposition candidates won about 45 percent of total votes cast for the legislature and secured about 25 percent of the constituencies, compared with 22 percent in 2010, less than 15 percent in 2005, and about 7 percent in 2000 (Msekwa 2006, TEMCO 2015, TEMCO 2006, TEMCO 2000). The prospects of specific opposition parties have changed over time as well: CUF won the most constituency seats from 1995 through 2010, while CHADEMA took the lead in 2015. The 2015 outcomes, in part, reflect the preelectoral UKAWA alliance made by several opposition parties to jointly field a single legislative candidate per constituency. The 2020 elections marked a dramatic shift away from the opposition's consolidated gains. Official results indicted a blowout – with CCM securing 256 of the 263 constituency seats and an additional 94 of 113 quota seats reserved for female members, or nearly 93 percent of the 377 seats selected in 2020. These results were widely viewed as fraudulent and criticized by the United States and other Western actors. The results included entirely implausible changes in vote shares – in some races,

---

[14] The number of parliamentary seats had been as high as 357 between the 2010 and 2015 elections, but it then dropped due to deaths and further because the president may appoint a number appointees with a constitutionally specified maximum but may fill them at their discretion and has seldom utilized all of the positions.

official returns CCM secured were over 50 percentage points higher than their 2015 performance – multiple constituencies even shared identical vote totals and distributions.[15]

In addition to the Parliament of Tanzania, a second legislature in Tanzania is located in Zanzibar. In 2010, the Zanzibar House of Representatives (*Baraza la Wawakilishi*) contained fifty constituency seats and an additional thirty-two allocated by appointment and for reserved women's seats allocated in the same manner as for the parliament. The fifty constituencies were identical to the fifty parliamentary constituencies, but the House of Representatives has a limited mandate in Zanzibar's semiautonomous government. That mandate is for what are considered "non-Union" issues (e.g., education and health, but not immigration, currency, or military) within the boundaries of Zanzibar. Four House of Representatives seats were added for the 2015 elections. Zanzibari politics have historically been more competitive; this is owed in part to the legacies of immediate post-independence rule and the institutional memory of the Afro Shirazi party's political foes. Indeed, the Zanzibar revolution that ushered ASP-soon-to-be-CCM into power deposed a popularly elected coalition of the Zanzibar Nationalist Party (ZNP) and Zanzibar and Pemba People's Party (ZPPP), the latter of which is associated with the opposition's contemporary stronghold in Pemba.

The 2010 election resulted in CUF controlling about 40 percent of the total seats in the Zanzibari legislature, having won twenty-two of the fifty constituencies and an additional nine reserved seats for female members. The term was unique in that it formed a power-sharing Government of National Unity and members from both parties were nominated for cabinet posts. The 2015 elections were held under conditions that were widely viewed as the most peaceful and transparent under multipartyism, but the results were canceled by Zanzibar's electoral management body, the Zanzibar Electoral Commission (ZEC).[16] ZEC had tabulated the

---

[15] Newala Urban and Tarime Urban, for example, both announced returns in the presidential elections of 19,975 votes for Magufuli and 11,955 votes for CHADEMA's candidate Tundu Lissu.

[16] ZEC is responsible for elections for Zanzibari positions (president of Zanzibar and House of Representatives) and voter registration of Zanzibaris, while Tanzania's National Electoral Commission (NEC) is in charge of election management for the Tanzanian presidency, the parliament, and *diwani* (local councilors). In practice, the two commissions work together on election management in Zanzibar and results are cast in the same location on the same day, while the votes for each position are tabulated and aggregated by the respective commission.

results and publicly announced thirty-one of the fifty-four constituencies' returns. In these districts, they performed better than the previous elections in 2010. The remaining 23 constituencies were all located in Pemba, where CUF's popularity is greatest. These factors together ensured the final count would deliver CUF the Zanzibari presidency and a legislative majority. Parallel tallies of election returns from all 54 constituencies confirmed this. CUF strategically announced its tabulations in a press conference at which presidential candidate Seif Shariff Hamad, usually known as Maalim Seif, "called on ZEC to declare the winner because we knew if ZEC delayed, they would manipulate the results and declare [CCM] the winner."[17] ZEC responded with allegations of massive voter fraud and annulled the polls, rescheduling a new election for early 2016. The opposition boycotted the election; thus, CCM held 97 percent of the eighty-eight total seats in the legislature through 2020, with three seats filled from tiny opposition parties TADEA, AFP, and ADC through government appointment.

The 2020 elections marked the opposition's return to electoral competition in Zanzibar. The principal actors competing were the same, but running under the banner of ACT-Wazalendo. As described in greater detail shortly, divisions between the mainland and Zanzibari factions of CUF resulted in CUF-Zanzibar recamping *en masse* with ACT-Wazalendo. As with the overall Tanzanian polls, the 2020 elections were disputed and criticized as fraudulent. In the presidential contest, Maalim Seif's official vote share of 19.8 percent is less than half of what he secured in each of the previous five elections he contested. Zanzibar Electoral Commission official results claimed CCM won 46 of the 50 House of Representatives constituencies. With an additional 22 of the 25 seats reserved for women's representatives and presidential appointees going to CCM, the ruling party secured over 90 percent of seats in the legislature. After the elections, Seif turned his attention to reforming the government to guard against manipulation in future elections by reprising his role from 2010 through 2015 as first vice-president of the power-sharing Government of National Unity. The potential impact of his efforts to institute safeguards for the integrity of future legislative elections will never be known; Maalim Seif was hospitalized in Zanzibar in late January 2021 after contracting the novel coronavirus COVID-19 and died a few weeks later.

---

[17] Interview, Maalim Seif. Washington, DC, June 14, 2016.

Tanzania's Main Political Parties

Chama Cha Mapinduzi

Tanzania has never experienced a turnover in party in power and has been governed by various forms of the same political party since its independence: Chama Cha Mapinduzi. CCM originated as the Tanganyika African National Union (TANU), which was among the most institutionalized state structures in Tanganyika after independence. Its development as a political party organization rapidly increased following the Arusha Declaration (1967), in which President Julius Nyerere laid the groundwork for a national political, economic, and social vision known as *ujamaa*. In a decade, the party had created thousands of party offices, formed party-sponsored worker cooperatives and women and youth organizations, and established a highly localized footprint of the party known as *nyumba kumi*, whereby the party had some form of leadership for every ten-household "cell" in the nation. Party staff from the national to the cell leaders were paid for their duties (Morse 2019).

The name Chama Cha Mapinduzi came about when TANU formally merged with the Afro-Shirazi Party (ASP) in Zanzibar. ASP was founded in the late 1950s to promote the interests of lower and working classes in a Zanzibari Sultanate where most land and wealth were concentrated among people of Omani descent. Its name reflected this political and economic alliance – the "Afro" refers to descent from the continent Africa and *Shirazi* indicates mixed African and Iranian lineage, although the distinction was socioeconomic in that it implied non-elite (non-Omani) economic status. ASP was most popular in Unguja, a legacy that maps onto CCM support in the larger of Zanzibar's two main islands today. Its main rival was the Zanzibar Nationalist Party (ZNP), which aimed to protect the interests of the Sultanate and large-scale spice farmers who drove Zanzibar's export market. The Zanzibari revolution brought about several changes: it deposed the government of ZNP and the Zanzibar and Pemba People's Party (ZPPP; notably the party of later CUF co-founder Seif Shariff Hamad), put ASP in power, and led to the creation of Tanzania as a union of Zanzibar and mainland Tanzania. The politics of the revolution and its consequences define contemporary Tanzanian politics: the name "Tanzania" is a portmanteau of Tanganyika and Zanzibar and the moniker of Tanzania's ruling party "Party of the revolution" refers to the Zanzibar revolution and ASP's role in it.

Most recognize CCM and TANU/ASP as sibling parties in the same family because of the nature of single-party rule: the 1965 constitution that formalized single-party rule established TANU's domain as the mainland and ASP's in Zanzibar. Their respective leaders – Amani Abeid Karume and Julius Nyerere – ruled in collaboration. ASP's localized party penetration was similar to that of TANU, and it held internal elections. Julius Nyerere proposed joining the parties in 1975, and the formal merger took place on the twentieth anniversary of ASP's foundation in February 1977 (Burgess 2009).

There were meaningful differences between ASP and TANU: ASP's decision-making body was the party's Revolutionary Council, which governed in a way that was less open and deliberative (Othman and Peter 2006) than TANU's national congress (Morse 2019). Karume's political programs were distinct from Nyerere's, and he remained skeptical of mainland interference in Zanzibar (Burgess 2009). But Karume was assassinated in 1972 – some suspect Nyerere played a role in the orchestration – and his successor gradually steered the party toward coalescence with TANU. Because the legacies of TANU and ASP are so intensely intertwined, the leadership of both worked cooperatively within the structure of the Tanzanian union, and the organizations were similar structurally; the period of ASP/TANU rule through its form as CCM is viewed as continuous.

After the merger, CCM further established itself as a credible ruling party by investing significantly in building party institutions and infrastructure such that the party influenced the daily life of citizens nationwide (Morse 2019, 103). Political competition for the legislature persisted, through contests between members of the ruling party under majoritarian. Within this framework, elections were competitive and legitimate; incumbents were ousted with rates similar to those in established, two-party democracies (Hyden and Leys 1972, Maliyamkoko 2002). Under multiparty rule, CCM has remained institutionally strong and mechanisms for resolving fierce internal rivalry have evolved over time to keep the party from falling into turmoil (Morse 2019).

CHADEMA

Chama cha Demokrasia na Maendeleo (Party for Development and Democracy) was founded by Edwin Mtei, who served as Nyerere's minister of finance from 1977 to 1979. He submitted his resignation – in his telling, while Nyerere was simultaneously preparing to fire him – over disagreement regarding International Monetary Fund (IMF) loan conditionalities. Mtei saw the economic reforms the IMF required as necessary to pull Tanzania out of economic crisis, while Nyerere viewed them as a return to an economic form of Western colonialism. Later as an executive at the IMF in the 1980s, Mtei navigated Tanzania through structural adjustment before establishing CHADEMA in 1992. The party's roots matched these ideological origins – a center-right party focused on free market economic policies that actively courted the support of the business community. Mtei was an estate coffee farmer and sought backing from commercial farmers, and the party was regionally anchored in the northern areas of Kilimanjaro and Moshi. It attempted to establish a nationwide physical footprint at its inception but lacked resources to build party infrastructure locally or to expand outward from these regions for roughly a decade; it ran on donations, membership dues, and Mtei's personal resources. Staff from juniors to the executive committee were volunteers (Mtei 2009, 207).

The party succeeded in strengthening its electoral performance and institutional footprint over time, particularly under the leadership of Freeman Mbowe as chairman and Dr. Wilbrod Slaa as secretary-general in the early 2000s. Institutionally, *CHADEMA ni Tawi* ("CHADEMA is the Branch") marked the party's attempt to develop a nationwide branch structure similar to what CCM had inherited from the single-party state. By 2010, its evolution into *CHADEMA ni Msingi* ("CHADEMA is the Root/Foundation") strived to set up 17,000 branches nationwide (Paget 2019a). It has also diversified its appeal to voters, drawing considerable support from youth and urbanites. The contemporary policies of the party harken back to its original orientation toward market economics and reforms to improve development.

The party has suffered growing pains, particularly in the context of the 2015 elections. Zitto Kabwe – one of Tanzania's youngest yet most popular parliamentarians regardless of party – rose quickly within CHADEMA after his election to parliament and was the party's deputy secretary-general until 2013. After unsuccessfully challenging Freeman Mbowe for the party's chairmanship in 2009 (Ewald 2013), he was accused of a similar plot ahead of the 2015 elections and stripped of his positions, including deputy leadership of the formal opposition in the *Bunge*. Zitto would go on to found ACT-Wazalendo, described shortly, but not before his challenge of the expulsion ran through Tanzania's court system.

More critically, the decision of CHADEMA to accept former CCM Prime Minister Edward Lowassa as the party's presidential candidate – and the sole candidate fielded by a preelectoral alliance UKAWA that included CHADEMA, CUF, and NCCR – fractured the party's leadership. Lowassa's was the most prominent CCM defection under multipartyism, and he was tremendously popular among the electorate. However, he is stained by corruption scandals that led to his downfall as prime minister in 2008: this, along with massive expenditure to support his attempt to win CCM's presidential nomination in 2015, led CCM's Ethics Committee to cut him from consideration for its presidential ticket (Morse 2019, 151–152). The party's Secretary-General Wilbrod Slaa briefly disappeared from public view after the nomination and subsequently resigned from CHADEMA and left the country. Recounting his decision, he states, "it was impossible for me to remain in a party that has abandoned its own policies and beliefs … He was a part of the list of shame I announced during my days as an opposition politician so it was difficult to be part of the team that would clear his image" (Kamagai 2018).

In the 2020 elections, Tundu Lissu – a prominent legal activist whose pathway to becoming an MP will be discussed in later chapters – stood for the presidency as CHADEMA's candidate in 2020. He returned to Tanzania in July 2020 after three years abroad, recovering from an assassination attempt in which he was shot sixteen times. Other opposition parties planned to field Lissu as a coalition candidate in 2020, but were prohibited from doing over administrative requirements surrounding coalitions. In practice, ACT-Wazalendo endorsed Lissu and told its members to vote for him over their own candidate (Ng'Wanakilala 2020).

Civic United Front (CUF)

Civic United Front (CUF) was registered as a political party in 1993. The party came about through the amalgamation – of both political forces and their namesakes – of the Zanzibar United Front and related *Kamahuru* (Kamati ya Mweleko ya Vyama Huru/Committee to Promote Multipartyism) led by Shabaan Khamis Mloo, Ali Haji Pandu, Seif Shariff Hamad, and the Civic Movement of James Mapalala in mainland Tanzania. In ideological matters, the party has emphasized *utajirisho* ("enrichment") policies consistent with center-left economic programs that combine economic reform with pro-poor, redistributive actions. Within CUF, however, there was substantial difference between the roots of support and the goals of the two factions that formed the party. The current state of affairs of the party are baked into this foundation.

James Mapalala had been a vocal opponent of Nyerere since the 1960s; as a journalist reporting on government abuses, he was expelled from TANU in 1968. He spent most of the subsequent quarter century advocating against single-party rule in spite of being harassed and jailed for doing so (Msuya 2012, Nyanto 2020). For the Zanzibar side, the politics were more directly oriented toward the structure of Tanzania itself. Maalim Seif was the chief minister of Zanzibar until the late 1980s, when he was stripped of the position and had his CCM party membership revoked. As chief minister, Seif sought bilateral agreements with the Omani government and other Muslim-majority countries and this, in his view, led his rivals to create a narrative that he sought to resubmit Zanzibar to Arab rulers who had been deposed: the Sultanate of Zanzibar in the 1964 Zanzibar revolution (Burgess 2009, 253–254). CUF-Zanzibar has, since its formation, asserted that the structure of the Union disadvantages Zanzibar and needs to reformed to boost its autonomy. Seif and many other CUF leaders maintain that the Union itself is not legal because it was never actually ratified by the ASP's Revolutionary Council that governed Zanzibar (Burgess 2009, 191–192).

This makes for a political balancing act that the party has struggled to navigate and is the source of significant intraparty strife. The unifying focus of promoting greater Zanzibari autonomy is electorally powerful for CUF-Zanzibar but is also a liability for the national party. It allows CCM to invoke ASP's role as liberator in the Zanzibar revolution and claim that CUF is a religious (roughly 97 percent of Zanzibaris practice Islam) and "Arab" party, casting CUF as a continuation of the two founding political parties (ZNP/ZNPP) that rivaled the Afro-Shirazi Party (Bakari 2001), and a force that seeks to return to a time when non-secular, foreign interests dominated part of Tanzania. Tension between the mainland and Zanzibar led to the expulsion of James Mapalala from CUF leadership shortly after the party's founding (Msuya 2012): fast-forwarding to the 2010 elections, the tensions represented by CUF's leader Ibrahim Lipumba and Maalim Seif in Zanzibar became untenable. In Lipumba's eyes, a reformed Union was valuable and could help Zanzibar better resolve conflict and crises and build consensus over economic and political issues between government and opposition. Increasingly, to Seif, the Union was the source of the problem.

The chasm between the two factions of the party – and, perhaps even more so, the factions' leaders Lipumba and Seif – broke the party in the aftermath of the 2015 elections. Like Slaa of CHADEMA, Lipumba resigned from his party leadership position when Lowassa was selected as the presidential candidate for the 2015 opposition alliance UKAWA, claiming it was "deviating from [CUF's] original principles and embracing people who a few months ago were fiercely opposed to the alliance" (Mwakyusa 2015). While Lipumba would later seek to return to CUF leadership in 2016 after Lowassa had been defeated, Seif and CUF Zanzibar viewed Lipumba's actions – which reportedly included breaking into the party's headquarters and stealing financial resources from Zanzibar's side of the party – as unforgivable, calling him a "traitor" on live television (Mesomapya 2017). The government played a role in stoking the conflict when the registrar of political parties sided with Lipumba. After a multiyear court battle, Civic United Front-Zanzibar essentially dissolved and the political force that was the party moved *en masse* to join the new opposition party ACT-Wazalendo after a period of quiet negotiations between Zitto Kabwe and Maalim Seif (Kabendera 2019*b*). The change in many ways is cosmetic for Zanzibar's party, especially because CUF as a party institution did not own many of the CUF assets in Zanzibar. Put succinctly by Ismail Jussa, the offices that were once painted light blue for CUF got a new coat of paint for the purple tone of ACT: "they've turned purple because all of the offices are now flying purple flags." What this means for CUF in mainland Tanzania remains to be seen; it has historically performed well in several regions of central and coastal mainland Tanzania.

NCCR-Mageuzi

NCCR-Mageuzi stands for the National Convention for Construction and Reform – Mageuzi. At the of transition to multiparty politics, it was the most promising new opposition party, having "demonstrat[ed] a high degree of organizational competence, internal cohesion and commitment to their party's course" (Mmuya and Chaligha 1994, 59). The party purports to represent the poorest among Tanzanians and promotes socialist economic policy (Ewald 2013, 362); however, it originally drew substantial support from the young and educated, especially on university campuses in the early 1990s (Mmuya and Chaligha 1994, 61). The party has been a victim of factionalism since the days of its foundation – its first chairman Mabere Marando sought to shutter NCCR and form a new party even before the first elections; its 1995 presidential candidate Augustine Mrema left to form the Tanzania Labour Party in 1999 (Ewald 2013).

NCCR held four parliamentary seats in 2010; the face of the party is James Mbatia, who is seen by both ruling party and opposition legislators as a sort of messenger between the two camps. Mbatia operates the Tanzania Centre for Democracy, which is an NGO designed to facilitate cooperation between member political parties (CCM, CHADEMA, CUF, NCCR, and ACT) in a lower-stakes environment outside parliament.

ACT-Wazalendo

ACT-Wazalendo – the Alliance for Change and Transparency-"Patriots" – is the newcomer of Tanzanian political parties. It was founded in 2014 by Member of Parliament Zitto Kabwe after he was expelled from CHADEMA leadership. The party emphasizes anti-corruption and transparency, which are consistent with the legacies of Zitto Kabwe as the legislature's fierce government watchdog.

The party had little footprint in the 2015 elections aside from Zitto Kabwe but grew rapidly between 2015 and 2020. Absorbing the opposition in Zanzibar guarantees it significant presence in both mainland Tanzania and Zanzibar. In the lead-up to the 2020 elections, the party won over a high-profile defector Bernard Membe – who was among the final five candidates for CCM's 2015 presidential candidate. ACT-Wazalendo attempted to formalize a coalition with opposition party CHADEMA to field Tundu Lissu as their joint candidate for presidency; when they were prevented from doing, the party publicly endorsed Lissu and told ACT voters to cast their ballots for him. In 2020, it fielded candidates in the majority of parliamentary constituencies and all of Zanzibar's House of Representatives contests.

My book studies candidacy decisions that took place during or prior to the 2010 elections in Tanzania, before ACT-Wazalendo existed. Thus, I do not engage with ACT much in the main text, except in reference to its contemporary leaders to clarify the former versus party of opposition leaders, including Ismail Jussa, Zitto Kabwe, and Maalim Seif.

External Validity of the Tanzanian Case

The preceding discussion has established that Tanzania is similar to other electoral authoritarian regimes within Africa and in other regions on the dimensions of toleration/repression. It also fits among many hegemonic regimes in that the executive and parliament are controlled by a single party for several elections. In consideration of these characteristics, an evaluation of my theory of opposition candidacy using the case of Tanzania is not subject to substantially limiting external validity concerns. With regard to candidacy paths to the opposition, civic activism as a channel through which political ambition for the opposition is cultivated operates with few resources available to opposition parties and the constrained political environment in which such parties exist. Those environmental factors are defined by the level of repression the government imposes on rivals and are constitutive of the authoritarian component of electoral authoritarianism. For this reason, what I find in evaluating my theory with the Tanzanian case regarding civic activism and opposition candidacy should apply broadly to electoral authoritarian regimes.

My version of the strategic candidacy framework can also capture variation of the repressiveness within the category of electoral authoritarian regimes. Since costs of candidacy are conceived as including nonmaterial, non-campaign costs, the risks of being a government critic in these settings are directly incorporated into the decision making of aspiring candidates. The same is true for differences in the stranglehold a ruling party has over seats in the legislature. I evaluate my theory in a setting that includes subnational variation whereby the Zanzibari House of Representatives is comparably more competitive than the Parliament of Tanzania. If my theory only applied to legislatures in which a ruling party controls a supermajority of the legislature, for example, it would not be supported by evidence from Zanzibar. More fundamentally, like repression, competitiveness is directly factored into the candidate decision-making framework and thus variation in this factor is accommodated within the framework of the theory.

The two sources of potential limitations arise from the nature of the political parties themselves: opposition parties that are viable, serious, and possess national ambition and ruling parties that are credible and institutionalized.

Opposition Parties

I study a specific kind of opposition in this book, and it impacts the decisions opposition candidates make. CHADEMA and CUF are opposition parties with regional footholds but national presence and national ambition. Both field candidates in the majority of mainland constituencies.[18] CUF fields candidates in every constituency in Zanzibar. These parties articulate national policy platforms and conduct electoral campaigns

---

[18] In 2015, this was not the case due to intra-opposition coordination to field a single UKAWA candidate per constituency, a condition to which both CHADEMA and CUF agreed.

across the country. These are not "briefcase parties" or the highly "fluid" oppositions scholars have noted (Lindberg 2007, van Eerd 2010). NCCR is much weaker nationally but was Tanzania's primary opposition party in early multipartyism and held national ambition in its origins.

What distinguishes these parties as serious or credible is fluid and likely to depend on context. Following LeBas (2011, 25–26), the types of opposition parties that my theory engages have formal structures with organizational capacity, intraparty decision-making mechanisms, and established linkages with supporters. One systematic way to assess the comparability of the types of opposition parties my theory speaks to and related limitations of evaluating the theory with aspirants from CHADEMA, CUF, and NCCR is to analyze party-level data on opposition parties' physical and social institutionalization in electoral authoritarian regimes.

Varities of Democracy (V-Dem) collects data about political parties within countries and documents their performance, political orientation, and organizational features over time. Three indicators related to political party structure can help identify the comparability of CHADEMA, CUF, and NCCR to opposition in other electoral authoritarian regimes. The first regards physical infrastructure and captures whether a party maintains a permanent office presence – that is, party offices that operate outside periods of elections – at the local level. Country experts rate political parties from zero to four, where higher values indicate a greater proportion of municipalities with permanent local party offices. A second indicator is related to organizational strength. This measure captures whether the party has a presence of personnel and activists in local communities outside electoral periods. Here, higher levels of strength are associated with a larger, more comprehensive presence. A third taps into mobilization capacity of the party in the form of linkages to social organizations, including religious associations, cooperatives, professional and business associations, and other social groups. It ranges from conditions where parties have no connections to prominent social organizations to exercising dominant control over them. These are precisely the kinds of organizations that I theorize cultivate opposition candidacy. If we were to see CHADEMA, CUF, and NCCR as parties that are at the extreme values of any of these indicators, it would point to limited external validity of the findings of my book at the party level.

Figure 3.3 shows the distribution of opposition parties across these three measures for all legislative elections in authoritarian regimes

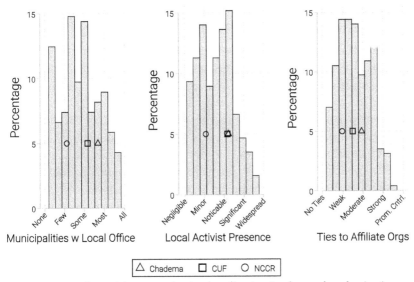

FIGURE 3.3 Opposition party institutionalization in electoral authoritarian regimes

worldwide from 1980 to 2002, as identified by Schedler (2009).[19] Covering 123 legislative elections in 51 regimes, each histogram summarizes the physical infrastructure, organizational strength, and mobilization capacity of roughly 250 party-observations.[20] In each panel, I plot the average values of CHADEMA, CUF, and NCCR for the given indicator. What the figure shows is that CUF and CHADEMA are broadly representative of opposition parties in electoral authoritarian regimes. CHADEMA comes out as the highest of the three Tanzanian parties on each measure and is slightly above the central tendency of electoral authoritarian opposition for these variables, which fits with the view that its contemporary party-building efforts have significantly improved membership, branch coverage, and local linkages of the party (Paget 2019*a*). CUF falls closer to the average party across the world of electoral authoritarian regimes, while NCCR is below average. NCCR was promising at the advent of multipartyism, but its prospects were never met with institutional growth, as these data reflect.

[19] Patterns are similar if including both legislative and presidential elections during this period.
[20] Parties appear multiple times but observations are distinct; they are coded by party-election year and are not constant over time.

Ruling Parties

Tanzania's CCM also stands apart from parties in many other electoral authoritarian regimes in that it is well institutionalized, featuring a well-organized central party apparatus matched with extensive local party development and leadership down to the level of every tenth household. This has two implications regarding external validity, one related to career partisanship and the other to strategic candidacy decisions.

Career partisanship is conceived as a process of cultivating political capital and accruing resources in a party that is later mobilized into candidacy ambition; this pathway points toward ruling party candidacy. For this pathway to operate, it requires a meaningful party. In cases where a party is more of a name and brand than an institution or its physical existence is confined to the capital city, then the party does not have positions for supporters to fill, and there are no party institutions through which leadership ambition is cultivated. It is possible that some form of career partisanship could exist lacking such parties if alternative institutions of power are nested within a ruling party – perhaps ethnolinguistic identity groups – but it is most likely to be found where strong parties exist.

The list of electoral authoritarian regimes with these types of strong ruling parties is not long – Morse's (2019) detailed typology identifies Tanzania's peers as Mozambique, Seychelles, and Senegal. Others point to Rwanda, Uganda, Ethiopia, Zimbabwe, Cape Verde, and Namibia as regimes with institutionally robust ruling parties (Bauer 2001, LeBas 2011, Levitsky and Way 2010*a*, Loxton 2015, Lyons 2016), though both Rwanda and Uganda have yet to survive a change in party leader. Outside Africa, a higher number electoral authoritarian cases feature strong ruling parties with well-developed, local institutions. Malaysia's UMNO, for example, had more than 16,000 branches and a ten-cell structure similar to that of CCM (Levitsky and Way 2010*a*, 64), Mexico's PRI featured a nationwide footprint (Eisenstadt 2000, Greene 2007, Langston 2006, Magaloni 2006), and the Socialist Party of Serbia had a robust party branch structure and, like CCM, created party institutions that linked to the workplace (Levitsky and Way 2010*a*, 105). Other comparable cases on the dimension of an effective, institutionalized ruling party include Indonesia's Golkar (Smith 2005), El Salvador's ARENA, Nicaragua, Paraguay, and Bulgaria (Levitsky and Way 2010*a*, Loxton 2015, Miller 2020, Smith 2005).

We can gain some traction on the uniqueness of Tanzania's case by returning to the party-level V-Dem data regarding the permanent presence of local party offices. Figure 3.4 visualizes patterns of party

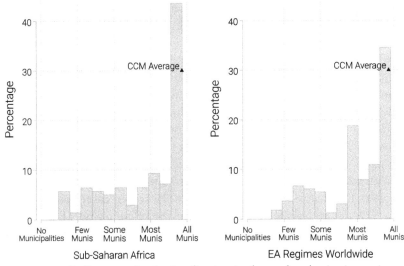

FIGURE 3.4 Ruling party institutionalization in electoral authoritarian regimes: Permanent local party offices

institutionalization on this dimension among ruling parties in Africa's twenty-eight electoral authoritarian regimes identified by Morse (2019), as well as the broader global set presented in Schedler (2009). Both panels of the figure are histograms showing the distribution of ratings of governing parties across authoritarian elections during this period and plots where on this party institutionalization measure Tanzania's ruling party falls.

The figure illustrates two main points. First, it is absolutely the case that Chama Cha Mapinduzi is highly institutionalized, as the preceding discussion has noted. Second, and more important for the purposes of establishing external validity, a high level of downward penetration of authoritarian ruling parties – at least in the form of permanent physical infrastructure – is the norm. In sub-Saharan Africa, more than forty percent of ruling parties in authoritarian regimes have/had permanent local offices nationwide, while globally about a third of them do. It is with these types of cases that my theory's component of career partisanship is most likely to be applicable. It is also likely that career partisanship is found in regimes where ruling parties are hegemonic, but the regime itself is more democratic – in Botswana and South Africa and outside of Africa in settings like Taiwan. The extent to which a party exercises control over candidate nominations or the formality of those procedures may also play out differently across regimes, but nomination prospects are incorporated into my strategic candidacy framework.

In sum, Tanzania is an ideal case for testing a theory about opposition candidacy in which both long-term trajectories from civic activism into political ambition and short-term calculations over benefits of running; nomination and election prospects; and the nonmaterial, non-campaign costs of running against the authoritarian regime drive candidacy decisions. My theory also aims to account for the alternative choices facing potential candidates: not running for office or running with the ruling party. With regard to ruling party ambition, the strategic candidacy framework I offer is broadly applicable to authoritarian regimes, including ones that feature weak ruling parties. However, career partisanship as a pathway to legislative candidacy for the ruling party is likely to be limited to settings with strong ruling parties that are institutionalized and have a physical footprint across the country.

3.3 EMPIRICAL APPROACH AND DATA RESOURCES

I evaluate my theory of opposition candidacy with a multifaceted approach, made possible by extensive experience in Tanzania and robust networks with party and political elites there. Fluency in Swahili combined with more than three years of on-the-ground field experience yield a mixed-method empirical strategy that combines qualitative theory-building interviews; survey data focused on candidacy decisions and life histories; and documents on political careers, party organization, and party competition, all supplemented with the perspectives of political actors engaging in candidacy decisions themselves. This section summarizes the overarching data collection strategy.

Qualitative Interviews

Initial stages of fieldwork began in 2010 with extensive qualitative interviews with political and party elites. This phase of data collection primarily spanned 2010–2013, with first efforts aimed at vetting the book's theory of candidacy decision making with leaders and elites of the political parties in Tanzania. These interviews also helped refine the design of the survey described shortly.

Relationships in Zanzibar were initially cultivated in 2010; I was a long-term election observer based in Wete, Pemba (an opposition stronghold in the smaller of Zanzibar's two main islands) during the voter registration process, a subsequent referendum, and later for the October 2010 national elections. During this period, I regularly met with party officials and political leaders. I also was a collaborator on a government-supported good governance initiative in 2011, through which I regularly interacted with cabinet members, civil servants, nearly every member of the legislature, and the institution's speaker and clerk.

In mainland Tanzania, I developed relationships through a combination of snowball sampling techniques and direct contact. I first met many CUF leaders from mainland Tanzania while in Zanzibar, who were later available to meet in Dar es Salaam at the party's headquarters. CHADEMA interviewees were recruited through personal connections to party leaders from the party's strongholds (Moshi and the Kilimanjaro region), as well as direct visits to the party's headquarters in Dar es Salaam. Most interviews with CCM leaders were conducted on the premises of the *Bunge*; the party's headquarters in Dodoma; or regional offices in Zanzibar, Dar es Salaam, and Arusha. Interviews with mainland Tanzanian government officials were conducted through direct, in-person recruitment and parliamentary interviews and permissions were planned at the Dar es Salaam legislative office ahead of parliamentary sessions in Dodoma.

I interviewed the leadership of all the parties featured in this volume, as well as the heads of relevant government institutions (e.g., electoral commission, Clerk of Parliament) and leading Tanzanian intellectuals. In total, I conducted approximately 120 qualitative interviews during this period.

Table 3.1 lists interviews that were conducted from 2010 to 2013, prior to carrying out the survey. Interviewees are identified by name, position, or both. Position and party are indicated for the time when they were interviewed. Additional supplementary qualitative interviews have been carried out since this period. These are used in the text to ground interpretation of statistical analyses and to further expound upon the core intuitions of the book.

Longer-form interviews with Ismail Jussa, January Makamba, and James Mbatia that shape the book's narrative were carried out over several years: face-to-face in Dodoma, Dar es Salaam, Zanzibar, and even the United States, as well as by phone. For the stylistic purposes of narrative flow, I generally do not cite quotes from these interviews with specific times, locations, or dates in the text.

TABLE 3.1 *Qualitative interviewees*

CCM	CHADEMA	CUF	NCCR	Nonparty
		Key Figures		
SG Abdoulrahim Kinana	SG Wilbrod Slaa	SG Lipumba	SG Mbatia	
DSG Vuai Ali Vuai	PS Zitto Kabwe	DSG Julius Mtatiro		
DSG Feroz	PS John J. Mnyika	DSG Ismail Jussa		
PS Pandu Ameir Kificho	PS John Heche	PS Salim Bimani		
M Mporogonyi	PS Deogratis Munishi	M (ZNZ) (8)		
M (ZNZ) (6)				
		Elites		
Deputy Press Secretary	Head of Security	Dir. Elections (ZNZ)		Dir. Elections (TZ)
Press Secretary (ZNZ)	MPs (4)	Dir. Region (ZNZ) (5)	MPs(1)	Dir. IT, Elections (TZ)
MPs (12)		MPs(4)		Dir. Elections (ZNZ)
HOR (26)		HOR(24)		Prof. Benson Bana, UDSM
Dir. Region (ZNZ) (5)				Prof. Max Mmuya, UDSM
				Prof. Chris Maina, UDSM
				Prof. Mohammed Bakari, UDSM

Abbreviations: (D)SG-(Deputy) Secretary-General/Chair; PS-Party Secretariat; M(S)-Minister (Shadow); MP(ZNZ)-Member of Parliament TZ/(ZNZ); HOR-House of Representatives; Dir.-Director; Prof.-Professor; UDSM-University of Dar es Salaam

Survey Data

I carried out a survey that included legislators, losing legislative candidates, unsuccessful nomination seekers, and prospective candidates who chose not to run. Much of the detail regarding sample strategy and representativeness is found in Appendix A. Substantively, survey questions were grouped into conceptual modules and the position of the modules in the survey generally followed the candidacy process: (1) personal background characteristics and upbringing, (2) party and civic organization memberships, (3) personal and political influences, (4) a life history calendar recording individual political and civic activism histories, (5) reasons regarding the decision to run for office (or not), (6) attitudes toward risk and time horizons, (7) party nomination experiences and perceptions, and (8) election experiences and perceptions. Noncandidates were also asked about youth and women's wings activities. The survey concluded with a battery of questions related to political party funding, challenges, and strategies. These were the questions included mostly for internal party use that were asked to incentivize political party buy-in.

A study of candidacy involves the question of whether someone runs for office; thus, the population of interest in addressing this question includes both individuals who chose to aspire to run for office and potential aspirants for office who chose not to seek to run. The least ambiguous members of this population are individuals who aspire to run for office, are nominated by a political party to run in the general election, and subsequently win their election contest. Those individuals are easily identifiable because they are current or former officeholders.

Equally unambiguous members of this population are election losers and nomination seekers. These groups include individuals who did not successfully become legislators but undertook the key action of expressing ambition to run for office by pursuing nomination from a political party. While unambiguously members of the relevant population, they are not as easily identifiable. Generally speaking, election losers should be identified by official election returns, but electoral data from electoral authoritarian regimes may be incomplete or inaccurate. The identifiability of nomination seekers has greater potential to be problematic, as party nomination procedures and outcomes are often opaque and candidate screening mechanisms may rely on informal exclusions that risk understating the population size of office seekers.

The greatest challenge for a study of the decision to run for office lies with determining who belongs to the population of individuals with

TABLE 3.2 *Nomination seeking and candidate emergence*

Election Status	Target Population?	Survey Data
Election Winner	✓	Legislator
Election Loser	✓	Candidate/noncandidate
Nomination Loser	✓	Candidate/noncandidate
Non-Aspirant, Considered Aspiring	✓	Candidate/noncandidate
Non-Aspirant, Did Not Consider	☒	n/a

genuine aspirations to run but choose not to; membership in this population subset is ambiguous: what constitutes "genuine aspirations" to run, absent actually doing so?. It is also difficult to identify individuals who wish to run for office but may never communicate with anyone else about this motivation. Without a creative sampling frame to overcome this challenge, such individuals are difficult to differentiate from the majority of citizens who never took action to run for office because they never had any desire to do so. While this problem is common to studies of contentious political behavior (e.g., why do some people protest?), its consequences are particularly acute for studies of phenomena like candidacy ambition that are rare among the general population.[21]

The nature of this population of interest thus requires a multipronged survey sampling frame to adequately test the theory. For this book, I carried out two surveys that are described in the pages that follow. Table 3.2 provides an overview of the different population subgroups of interest for evaluating a theory of candidacy and identifies which survey data collection effort targeted that population subgroup.

Legislator Survey

The most easily identifiable members of the population of interest are election winners – members of Tanzania's two legislatures. The survey was fielded at the Parliament of Tanzania and the Zanzibar House of Representatives, with interviews conducted on the grounds of the legislature or, in some cases, in the surrounding areas (hotels, cafes, restaurants,

---

[21] Bernhard, Shames, and Teele's (2021) study of women's candidacy in the United States focuses on participants in a candidacy training program offered by Emerge America. The program is both selective and rigorous, meaning that all participants possess candidacy ambition they may credibly act on and roughly half of Emerge graduates do run for office.

informal or formal party meeting areas). Survey interviews were carried out during the annual budget sessions in 2013, April–June for the parliament and June-August for the Zanzibar House of Representatives. Enumerators conducted interviews face-to-face and collected data with tablets using iSurvey.

Members of the 2010–2015 Parliament and House of Representations most recently were elected in 2010, in which 289 directly elected seats from single-member district constituencies were up for grabs – 239 for the Tanzanian parliament and 50 for the Zanzibari legislature. This means that roughly 800 candidates competed in single-member district constituencies for parties that won one or more seat in the legislatures. Aspirants are not permitted to contest elections as independents and require a party nomination to compete for and sit in the legislature, which may benefit the opposition (Rakner and van de Walle 2009a). Of the 289 single-member district seats, the opposition won 75 of them (27.6 percent), 35 in the Zanzibari legislature and 92 in the *Bunge*.

An additional 102 seats were indirectly elected for Tanzania's parliament through a women's reserved-seats quota whereby seats are allocated to parties proportional to election performance in the single-member districts; how parties filled these quota seats varied somewhat by party, but the processes were competitive and carried out internally prior to election day. Zanzibar's 2010 election featured twenty such reserved women's seats. Legislators who were either directly elected or indirectly elected through these gender quotas were included in the study, whereas non-elected, appointee members were not.[22]

Candidate/Noncandidate Survey

In addition to the legislator survey, I carried out a survey among other subgroups of the relevant population with the two main opposition parties that contested Tanzania's 2010 elections. I summarize the data collection effort here; extensive detail on the sampling procedure is found in Appendix A.[23] The survey focused geographically on the regions where the respective parties regularly field candidates in most or all

---

[22] Twenty-five additional seats may be filled by appointees. (Thirteen are in Parliament: up seven discretionary appointments the president may or may not fill; five members appointed from Zanzibar; and the attorney-general (ex-officio). There are twelve in Zanzibar: up to ten presidential nominees, the attorney general (ex-officio), and, the speaker if he/she they are not already a member of the legislature.)

[23] I attempted to conduct a similar research effort with the ruling party. It presented significant barriers to carrying out the project through its infrastructure and alternative approaches were infeasible.

constituencies and win some legislative seats. Paper questionnaires were distributed to respondents at district and regional political party offices and completed on-site. I trained two junior party research staff members for each of the two parties. They served as research assistants, floating around the offices to address clarifying questions while respondents completed the instruments and managing communication and instrument collection protocols described shortly.

Three groups of individuals were invited to participate in this survey: candidates for the legislature who lost in the 2010 elections (row 2 in Table 3.2), nomination seekers who were not selected by their party as candidates (row 3), and individuals who considered but did not seek candidacy in the 2010 elections (row 4). Membership in the latter group was determined by meeting two criteria. First, an individual must have demonstrated ambition to run for office without taking the steps to formally seek to run. Specifically, an individual must have collected a party nomination form in advance of the 2010 elections – a procedure by which they signaled intention to run for office by collecting signatures of supporters – but *ultimately did not submit the form or withdrew from consideration prior to party nominations.* This indicates a credible desire to aspire to run for office, but also that the individual formally chose *not to* aspire to run in the election, addressing the underlying ambiguity issue related to surveying this population subgroup. Second, an individual must be a member of their respective party's women's or youth wing. This second criterion was driven by practical considerations in terms of identifying members of this population subgroup and being able to assemble participants for this portion of the survey.

The processes of recruitment for and implementation of this survey differed slightly by party but shared the following steps in common. First, collaboration between the researcher and a member of the party's secretariat provided a draft copy of the survey instrument for their consideration. They were given the opportunity to strike objectionable questions and to add questions as they saw fit. To encourage party buy-in, each party also had a section dedicated to questions specifically designed for internal consumption by the party's secretariat. Parties suggested only minor modifications, meaning the risk of collusion at the party level to bias responses is low.

Second, after formally approving the questionnaire, a timeline was developed for when each party office would be visited. Regional and, in some cases, district offices were informed days prior to that office's data collection session.

Third, the research assistants traveled to each district or regional political office where the survey was to be conducted. The heads of these offices then utilized their party infrastructure to ensure party members belonging to these three groups (election loser, nomination loser, non-aspirants who considered running) reported to the office on the scheduled survey day. On that day, research assistants distributed the questionnaires, fielded respondents' clarifying questions, and collected the surveys when they were completed. They also carried out additional screening on the day surveys were administered to ensure that respondents were actually members of their particular subgroup. Party offices outside the national headquarters did not receive the questionnaires until the enumerators reached the office, minimizing the likelihood that local party officials would impact survey responses or otherwise interfere with the survey in any way. Upon completion of the surveys, the enumerators stored the questionnaires in a secure manner and proceeded to the next site to prepare for the next day. Party visits were planned in a manner that minimized transit time between offices and were geographically sequential.

Additional Data Resources

Legislator Biographical Profiles and CVs

I collected the CV and biographical data of 725 members of Tanzania's Parliament and Zanzibar's House of Representatives. Much of the information was collected from an e-government platform for the Tanzanian Parliament that includes extensive personal background information. Most importantly, the bios use a standardized format with fields for employment history as well as political experience; this ensures that the type of information and where various political and vocational experiences are reported in their histories are consistent across the biographical data. This resource covers legislators who entered the *Bunge* in 2000, 2005, and 2010. Zanzibar's House of Representatives was preparing but had not yet launched an e-government platform with this information at the time I was gathering data. I was able to compile the underlying CVs submitted by members of the 2010 House of Representatives that went into the development of Zanzibar's platform; these CVs followed the same format as those for the Tanzanian Parliament. For CVs with missing data fields, I augmented legislator biographical data with primary source documents from party and public records when possible.

Tanzania Election Data

Election results from the 2005 and 2010 elections for Zanzibar's House of Representatives and the 2000, 2005, and 20010 elections for Tanzania's Parliament were obtained directly from the IT department of the Zanzibar Electoral Commission and Tanzania's National Electoral Commission. These data are used throughout various sections of the book. They also provided data on whether or not incumbent candidates ran again and if they were reelected.

Party Primary Data

I obtained the results of 2010 primary contests in Zanzibar from both CCM and CUF that indicate the winning percentage of the candidate who won the primary, the number of candidates who stood in the contest, and the identification of the winner. These data cover twenty-nine CCM constituencies and forty-one of Zanzibar's fifty constituencies for CUF. The CCM data are more detailed, including the distribution of votes across all candidates. CUF members indicated that these data exist somewhere in an archive for the remaining nine constituencies in Zanzibar, while others informed me that the results had accidentally been destroyed or the electronic files recording the results had been corrupted for the parliamentary contests. Data on primary turnovers in mainland Tanzania were collected from media articles, popular social media like online forums, and research by civic organizations that monitor government performance like *Twaweza*.

3.4 ANALYTICAL STRATEGY

In this section, I provide an overview of how the data resources I draw upon are used to evaluate the theory across the following six chapters. Analytical details like model specification and estimation technique are addressed in each chapter. The discussion here is designed to familiarize the reader with the central measures that will appear throughout the book and to describe the process through which the measures were collected and created.

Survey Measures of Civic Activism and Career Partisanship

The Life History Calendar

A key barrier to understanding the impact of civic activism versus career partisanship on candidacy decisions is an analytical one: researchers only observe prospective candidates after they manifest candidacy ambitions. The journey to politics, however, may have begun years or decades prior. The life history calendar approach can improve data collected about these types of retrospective life events. Life history calendars (also called event history calendars) are grid-form questionnaires, where one axis shows a time interval (years, decades, etc.) and the other a list of activities, memberships, and life events (Axinn, Pearce, and Ghimire 1999). Often, life history calendars are organized in a manner that allows a researcher to simultaneously collect important background information about monumental life events and also strengthen respondents' ability to recall other information of interest surrounding these strong memories. To my knowledge, this is the second work in political science to ever use this technique.[24]

My life history calendar collected information regarding the first time an individual engaged in civic activism and career partisanship, as well as when several other important political and personal life events occurred. This conceptualizes trajectories as investments – how much time an individual puts into party service and civic activism – with the assumption that investing longer in an activity indicates its greater significance in one's background. Thus, this variable is measured as the duration (in years) from when they first did each of the activities to when they sought to run for office. If opposition nomination seekers demonstrate more civic activism, they will differ in where they invested their time and energy. To capture civic activism, respondents were asked to indicate the first time they organized a local grassroots community meeting. This variable will be referred to as "Grassroots Organizing." By contrast, CCM nomination seekers are expected to demonstrate more career partisanship. For career partisanship, respondents were asked to indicate the first time they (1) took a membership card of their current party; (2) wore campaign "fulana," such as t-shirts, hats, and so on of their current party; and (3) understood the ideology of their party. I rely on the first variable and describe it in analyses as "Party Membership."[25]

---

[24] See Zeria's (2019) research on youth organization membership and later participation in the Palestinian National Movement.

[25] Respondents were also asked anchoring questions (the first time they became interested in public affairs, chose a career, and held a leadership position outside politics), questions regarding activities they participated in multiple times (participated in protest, took a leadership seminar), and questions aiming to validate the life history calendar by collecting information available from other sources (years served in the party's secretariat).

Other Measures of Civic Activism and Career Partisanship

In addition to time invested in civic activism and party service, the type of position and/or organizational membership also matter and thus are measured distinctively. Civic activism is captured through an index that records the total number of organization types an individual was a part of prior to candidacy ambition. Respondents were asked to indicate from a list of social group membership organization types whether or not they were a leader, official member, unofficial member, or not a member of an organization in that domain at the time of or prior to considering candidacy. A respondent's value for this variable increases by one for each type of organization they were a member of (unofficial, official) and two for leadership from the following: (1) religious organization, (2) women's organization, (3) labor union, (4) professional association, (5) neighborhood/community/grassroots organization, and (6) student/university council. This variable is named "Civic Activism Index" in analyses. Conceptually, this measure balances sensitivity to the depth of civic activism (by distinguishing membership from leadership) and the breadth of such activism across multiple domains, which could be specific to contextual factors like timing, age, locality, and organizational specialization. This measure does not necessarily capture the number of organizations – if an individual who was a leader in one women's organization is counted the same as one who may have led six women's organizations – but rather the range of civic activism across type and interest area.[26]

Career partisanship is captured with a series of dichotomous variables that identify whether an individual had held positions in their political party prior to aspiring to candidacy. In the event that the individual had candidacy ambitions in more than one party (e.g., ran for office with one party and subsequently switched to another), data were collected on party positions in all parties in which candidacy ambition manifested. The information presented in this chapter, however, regards the party in which those individuals first aspired to office.[27] Party variables are

---

[26] Several alternative approaches are possible and detailed throughout Appendix B.2, following chapter-by-chapter analyses. Generally speaking, the findings are robust alternative measures. Disaggregated patterns for religious, women's, student, and grassroots groups also map onto the more detailed, contextual discussion of Tanzania across chapters.

[27] Instances where respondents considered candidacy in one party but did not aspire to run and subsequently switched to an alternative party and ran for office in the same election cycle were extremely rare.

identified in the results discussion as "Party Leader" followed by the relevant office/level. Following the conventions of candidacy studies from advanced democracies that argue candidates are progressively ambitious from local to national office, I also include an indicator of nonpartisan, local government political experience: "Local Govt experience."

Sequence Measures of Civic Activism and Career Partisanship

Chapter 5 uses the legislator biographical profiles to construct sequences of vocational career background and political party experience to assess the prevalence of civic activism and career partisanship among the broader set of more than 700 Tanzanian legislators. These sequence data are structured in a way that resembles cross-sectional, time-series data in long format. Each sequence is uniquely identified with one variable (here, a legislator), a second variable orders a sequence with a discrete time unit (years), and a third variable contains the sequence attribute – the substantive information of interest (Blanchard 2013). Each sequence contains two types of information. First, an *element* represents the value or state of a sequence in a single time unit. Second, sequences contain *episodes*, which describe each group of consecutive, identical elements. The totality of episodes together forms a sequence. Unlike conventional time-series, cross-sectional analyses where an observation-year (e.g., a person in a given year) is treated as the unit of analysis, the concept of a sequence considers the entirety of a respondent's or case's related events/states together as a single observation (a sequence).

Sequence analysis is ideal for studying phenomena where a given piece of information is best understood in relation to others in its sequence and when comparing the trajectories of one observation to another is theoretically appropriate. Applications of sequence methods in the social sciences include the study of pathways through schooling (Brzinsky-Fay 2007, Dietrich, Andersson, and Salmela-Aro 2014, McVicar and Anyadike-Danes 2002), life course and family development (Martin, Schoon, and Ross 2008, Oris and Ritschard 2014), and vocational careers (Abbott and Hrycak 1990, Blair-Loy 1999, Pollock, Antcliff, and Ralphs 2002). While not commonly used in political science, sequence analysis has promise for studying political phenomena featuring path and temporal dependence (Gryzmala-Busse 2011). Sequence methods have been used to study legislatures (Borghetto 2014) and legislative output (Abbott and DeViney 1992), as well as activism (Fillieule and Blanchard 2011) and democratic transitions (Wilson 2014).

For the vocational career background analysis, each legislator's sequence begins the year they first held a job and tracks their employment year by year until they enter the legislature for the first time. In Chapter 5, I use vocational career sequences to create three key variables. I capture civic activism as the proportion of total career years spent in positions in the nongovernmental and civil society organization sector. Career partisanship is measured similarly, but for career years it is paid jobs in political parties. I also calculate a measure of political positions – jobs in government that are political in nature (e.g., government spokesperson, electoral commission director) and not professional or civil service-related public employment (e.g., public school teacher, doctor at a government-run hospital).

I conduct a more granular analysis of career partisanship in Chapter 5 using a measure that includes all party service reported as political experience for each legislator. This sequence begins at political adulthood (eighteen years of age) for all legislators and runs until they enter Parliament or the House of Representatives. There are six possible levels – ward (sub-constituency), constituency, district, region, secretariat, and central committee – within each of the six office levels, positions are further divided based on whether they are low- or high-prestige positions. Appendix B.3 provides much more technical detail regarding this variable; analyses in the main text simplify the sequences into four possible elements: no party service, local service, subnational (regional/district) service, or national service.

I analyze descriptively with regard to the number of distinct positions within party service and their duration. The core statistical analysis of career partisanship sequences uses a method called "optimal matching," a procedure that compares sequences and estimates the (dis)similarity between two sequences (Levenshtein 1966). The method works by determining the distance between two sequences, measured as the number of arithmetical operations carried out on one sequence – in the form of inserting, substituting, and deleting elements – to make it identical to another (Gautheir, Buhlmann, and Blanchard 2014). Higher optimal matching scores indicate greater distance and thus greater dissimilarity between two sequences. In Chapter 5, I calculate the dissimilarity of the career partisanship sequences of Tanzanian legislators compared with three ideal types that correspond with my theory with regard to career partisanship: a lengthy period of local party service; a lengthy period of national-level party service; and one featuring local, then subnational, then national party service.

Measuring Benefits

To assess whether or not individuals in the opposition versus ruling party and candidates versus noncandidates have different views toward the expected benefits of office, the Legislator Survey and Candidate/Noncandidate Survey presented individuals with a series of questions regarding reasons why an individual might seek office across the four ideal types: material gains, prestige of office, ideology/policy aims, and career opportunism. Specifically, respondents considered four lists of five reasons why an individual might run for office. For each reason, respondents identified from their own perspective how important each reason was at the moment when they first considered seeking candidacy with the response options that ranged from to being very important to not being important at all. Respondents were also asked from each list of five items to identify which among them were the first and second most important reasons for seeking office when they first considered doing so. Table 3.3 shows English-language translations of the five statements corresponding with each of the four motivation types.

A key feature of this second version of the question design was that respondents (1) had a finite number of reasons they could identify as important and (2) each group of items contained at least one item corresponding with each of the ideal types. Each time a respondent identified a reason as the first most important, it was analogous to a respondent conferring two tokens to the ideal type corresponding with the reason (material gains, prestige of office, ideology/policy aims, career opportunism). The second most important reason was analogous to allocating one token. In total, each ideal type could have been allocated a possible nine tokens, had an individual chosen that ideal type as important every opportunity. The lists contained one reason that captured each of the four ideal-type reasons to seek candidacy. The fifth item was also an ideal type item so that each respondent had one opportunity to indicate each ideal type twice. The lists were organized as shown in Table 3.4. I created lists of a similar fashion regarding reasons to choose to not run for office; the analysis of those responses matches what is presented in the main text and is discussed and analyzed entirely in Appendix B.6.

Measuring Risk and Time Perspectives with *Methali*

Most studies that utilize the concepts of risk tolerance/aversion and time horizons arise from the broad political economy literature. Underlying

TABLE 3.3 *Reasons for seeking candidacy, survey items*

Benefit type	Statement
Material Gains	Getting salary Making sure development funds go to your area Building prominence through distributing community gifts Making sure your family and friends benefit from development projects Traveling internationally for political business
Prestige of Office	Being a prominent party representative Giving public statements on the news Being invited to workshops about politics Interacting with NGOs and international donors Becoming famous
Ideology/Policy Aims	Investigating why Tanzanians (Zanzibaris) lack government services Implementing policies that reflect your views about the economy Strengthening role of government oversight Enhancing minority rights and representation Reducing government size and largesse
Career Opportunism	Preparing for a different government job Building a personal business network Getting leadership training and experience Being in the party with government influence Building reputation as successful leader

TABLE 3.4 *Reasons for seeking candidacy*

	List One	List Two	List Three	List Four
Item 1	Material	Material	Career	Ideology
Item 2	Material	Ideology	Material	Prestige
Item 3	Prestige	Career	Ideology	Career
Item 4	Ideology	Prestige	Career	Material
Item 5	Career	Prestige	Prestige	Ideology

this research is the idea that individual preferences over a set of outcomes are shaped not just by the end goals themselves but also by attitudes toward how long it takes to achieve those outcomes and the certainty with which they can be reached (Netzer 2009, Rogers 1994). Individuals may discount the utility of various outcomes and penalize those that are far in the future or unlikely to be realized. Empirically, research on risk tolerance and time horizons has been confined mostly to behavioral games carried out in laboratory settings. Many of these studies explore risk, not because the goal is understanding risk for substantive purposes but instead to compare and control for differences in the motivations of individuals when participating in behavioral games (both experimental and non-experimental) that use financial incentives (Morton and Williams 2010).[28]

Prevailing Approaches toward Measuring Risk and Time Attitudes

Research on risk typically uses a lottery approach, whereby respondents are presented with a series of choices over which payouts they prefer. Risk is captured by manipulating two factors: the amount of the payout and the certainty a participant receives that payout. Such studies often present respondents with an array of options associated with a low-risk and a high-risk profile, where individuals compare smaller payouts with high rates of attainment versus payouts of higher value where the chance of obtaining that payout is lower (Holt and Laury 2002, 2005). Others ask respondents to identify a point at which they world prefer a lower risk versus a higher risk to pinpoint the precise risk trade-off for each respondent (Tanaka, Camerer, and Nguyen 2010).

The political economy convention toward time and time horizons also seeks to assess how individuals discount outcomes that occur in the future, versus those that can be realized more immediately. Behavioral games for assessing time horizons take a similar approach to that of lotteries: a respondent considers whether they would prefer some sum of money today or a larger sum of money at some point in the future. Within this practice, scholars use experimental and non-experimental designs to assess the point at which a respondent is indifferent between the value of an outcome today and one of greater value obtained at a time in the future. The difference in the magnitude of the utilities is used to calculate a "discount rate," which captures the extent to which a respondent devalues future gains.

While the majority of this research has been carried out with university students in the United States and Western Europe, behavioral lottery games have also been implemented in sub-Saharan Africa, including in

---

[28] See also Cox and Harrison (2008) for a discussion of this.

Rwanda and Burundi (Jacobson and Petrie 2007, Voors et al. 2010). Nonetheless, for the purposes of understanding candidacy decisions, these approaches to risk and time horizons are problematic for many reasons. Implementing games with financial incentives with national legislators presents ethical and practical challenges.

Being a legislator is very lucrative in most African countries and presenting political elites with meaningful financial incentives to make inferences about risk and time perspectives of prospective politicians is cost prohibitive; games with smaller sums are less likely to tap into the underlying risk attitude because they are not ecologically valid (Morton and Williams 2010). Using financial incentives in behavioral games with elites in electoral authoritarian regimes in this study could appear as distributing financial resources to political parties, which poses real risk to research teams in electoral authoritarian environments. Finally, assessing risk and time perspectives through the lens of material or financial stakes is too narrow for electoral authoritarian regimes. Decisions to seek candidacy in an authoritarian regime are associated with financial, social, political, and material risks. Ideally a measure of risk aversion and time perspectives would be broader than the narrow economic sense.

Alternative Approach: Culture Expressions and Proverbs

As an alternative to behavioral measures of risk aversion and time horizons, I rely on an individual's attitudes toward common cultural expressions. Specifically, I assess how they perceive frequently used proverbs whose meaning communicates lessons about time horizons, risk attitudes, and other aspects of strategic behavior. Cultural tradition and ritual play an important role in understanding strategic actor behavior and cultural institutions ranging from common language (Laitin 1994) to minutiae like seating configurations of political assemblies (Chwe 2001) and facilitate collective action and political decision making. This is reflected in a culture's literature and its folklore (Chwe 2009).

Use of cultural expressions focuses on East African proverbs known as *methali*. The role of figurative and metaphorical speech as an important element of cultural communication and meaning is well documented in the context of Tanzania and sub-Saharan Africa broadly (Hymes 1968, Mutembei 2011, Timanywa 2017, Thompson 2013). Embedded in such forms of speech are important social and historical lessons that speak to the shared experience of cultural groups and nations. Swahili-language *methali* are widely used in East Africa with particular prominence in Tanzania, where the language of government is Swahili. These proverbs are ubiquitous in common speech and found extensively in literature and poetry (Kalugila and Lodhi 1980). They are also printed on *kaanga*, which is the first and still most ubiquitous printed cloth in East Africa. Each *kaanga* bears a proverb associated with the pattern of the cloth or the reason for which one might, for example, gift the cloth to another person. As such, *methali* are used as a means of communication, even in a nonverbal manner (Beck 2005).

Cultural media like *methali* have played an important role in politics throughout Tanzania's history. Even prior to decolonization, ceremonies of song and dance contributed to political mobilization on the eve of transition to independence (Ranger 1975). Upon independence, Tanzania turned to culture – language, poetry, dance, and proverbs – to solve many of the national unification problems of a highly heterogeneous society. This first began with the creation of a Ministry of Culture and a nation-alization project broadly known as *Ujamaa*. Swahili was established as the language of government, school instruction, and the arts, and this Swahilization blended the realms of public and political life with language where *methali* played an important role. As Askew (2002, 65) notes, "local discourse throughout the country on the streets, in the newspapers, and on the radio is peppered with Swahili proverbs."

The Swahili proverb *kidole kimoja hakivunji chawa* ("One finger can-not kill a louse") was of common use during the era of collectivism and Tanzania's brand of African socialism under single-party rule (Ruotos-alainen 2009) and still holds meaning of cooperative political effort now (Kelsall, Lange, Mesaki, and Mmuya 2005). The ruling party in Tanzania has utilized such cultural tools, in addition to hiring writers, poets, and more recently hip-hop performers to produce art in praise of the regime. On the eve of multiparty politics in Tanzania, *methali* also featured in movements against the government. One notable example, musicians in the historically underdeveloped region of Tanga were commissioned to perform for a presidential visit. They only managed to play a few stanzas of a critical song named after the *methali Ubaya Kauna Kwao* ("Evil Has No Home") before government officials discontinued the performance (Askew 2002, 229–233). Other examples point to the role of *methali* in evaluating political choice: that Augustine Mrema – well-suited to fight endemic corruption in government – emerged as a presidential frontrun-ner in 1995 was celebrated in song with the proverb *Pumu zimepata mkohozi* ("Asthma has found one who coughs") (Askew 2002, 348).

In sum, exploring risk and time perspectives in the contexts of decisions of legislative candidacy is difficult using common approaches toward measuring these phenomena. Lottery-type behavioral games face a number of logistical and theoretical challenges in such settings. Swahili cultural proverbs offer a novel way to explore risk and time perspectives in the context of decisions of legislative candidacy.

Potential Biases and Their Implications

Much of what motivated my data collection strategy was addressing underlying measurement problems at the stage of design, especially for capturing benefits preferences and risk/time attitudes. Still, relying on self-reported survey measures regarding candidacy decisions is subject to unavoidable potential biases driven by both unintentional and intentional misreporting by respondents. Broadly speaking, these fall into three bias types: unintentional biases driven by retrospective recall, biases driven by retrospective updating that may be intentional or unintentional, and intentional bias whereby respondents are reluctant to divulge unpopular or socially inappropriate attitudes or behaviors. I will address each of these three sources of bias, discuss their implications for the empirical analysis in the chapters that follow, and steps I have taken to alleviate them.

Challenges of Recalling Past Attitudes and Events

The latency of measurement is problematic for survey data, especially when collecting data about past decisions and influences that preceded those decisions. Both issues are potentially present in my study. The strategic decision to run for office was made in the past for all study participants and for some many years prior. The civic activism and career partisanship paths to candidacy ambition stretch back even further. Surveys about political life histories can only collect data in the present, once the path to political office has been completed and long after it began. This can lead to recall problems, whereby aspirants cannot remember pieces of information that are important but temporally distant. Even when respondents aim to honestly report answers to retrospective survey questions, the additional effort required to optimally answer is greater (Tourangeau 1984), which might lead participants to satisfice and offer responses that are low quality but that will seem satisfactory to the researcher (Krosnick 1991).

This issue is a source of measurement error in that it can lead to lower-quality data but should not bias any of the findings presented in the chapters that follow. How recall challenges impact responses should not be based on which party someone ran for or their experiences that led up to it. Nonetheless, the survey had design features that aimed at reducing the demands of retrospective recall. First, the survey structure followed the flow of the theory and, in a sense, it walked participants through their candidacy experience from pathways to ambition through nominations and then campaigns. Second, questions about the very first stages of candidacy paths regarding civic activism and career partisanship used the life history calendar. Such calendars are shown to yield more reliable and complete data on social and economic histories than do conventional survey formats (Belli, Shay, and Stafford 2001). Researchers also note high rates of response consistency when carrying out panel surveys and comparing responses to direct questions from previous panels to data elicited through life history calendars at later stages (Freedman, Thornton, Camburn, Alwin, and Young-DeMarco 1988). I can directly compare some information collected with my life history calendar to the same information from the biographical records of twenty-seven Tanzanian legislators and the correlation between the two is nearly perfect.[29] Beginning the substantively meaningful parts of the survey interview with the life history calendar also helped ground subsequent questions about political candidacy. The life history calendar requires thinking about specific life events and their timing in a way that sparks introspection. This eases the burden of further recall about subsequent events emanating from what is represented in the life history calendar.

Past Candidacy Experiences and Potential Survey Bias

A more prominent concern for the sake of bias is that study participants might retrospectively update attitudes on the basis of events that have transpired over time. This potential for bias is present in current day assessments of prospects of winning election and nomination contests that have already happened; views toward how well political parties provide various benefits after having already decided on a party; and how much one values a given benefit of office after, for example, realizing the benefit they originally wanted in office is not one they have managed to secure.

A solution common to all of these concerns is careful survey design and deliberate and repeated anchoring throughout the survey. The life history calendar encourages respondents to think about the first time they ran for office. Throughout the survey, questions cued respondents to specifically

---

[29] Correlation in the duration of career partisanship between the two sources has a Pearson's R of 0.9959.

consider and answer on the basis of their first attempt to run. It was clear in the field that the first attempt is the most impactful for aspirants; even if they lose, that first experience of defeat and lessons from it remain as strong memories.

Using *methali* to measure risk attitudes guards against this form of retrospective updating. The meaning of culturally embedded expressions does not vary at the individual level over time in the same way that financial status does. Political discourse is steeped with metaphorical concepts and *methali* are a core part of that medium of expression across contexts and time. With regard to benefit preferences changing in response to initially wanting benefits that are later revealed to be unattainable, retrospective updating is possible. To lead to bias, it would have to impact the opposition differently than it does the ruling party. It is more likely that this updating is idiosyncratic and specific to a given individual's own, personal experience, which creates statistical noise but not bias. There may also be a homogenizing effect of serving as a legislator, whereby opposition and ruling party figures become more similar to one another as a consequence of formal political service, compared with how they operated and what motivated them on their path into legislative service. This should work against finding differences between opposition and ruling party aspirants but could make opposition winners look more different from opposition aspirants who lost elections, nominations, or did not run.

Retrospective updating may be particularly common when respondents learn something from their experiences: a candidate may dramatically overestimate their election odds but after being defeated handily is likely to reassess what their odds were in that election. That same is true for nomination contests. While this phenomenon is unavoidable with subjective views, it is drawing on objective data regarding nomination and election outcomes.

Social Desirability Bias

Social desirability bias is a phenomenon whereby survey respondents underreport behaviors and attitudes that are illegal, unpopular, or otherwise unflattering to divulge to others. This impacts a wide array of topics related to elections, including discriminatory attitudes toward candidates (Kane, Craig, and Wald 2004, Kuklinski, Cobb, and Gilens 1997, Streb, Burrell, Fredrick, and Genovese 2008, Tourangeau and Yan 2007), not turning out to vote (Holbrook and Krosnick 2010), and engaging in vote buying exchanges (Corstange 2010, Gonzalez-Ocantos, de Jonge, Meléndez, Osorio, and Nickerson 2011, Kramon and Weghorst 2019). Social desirability biases are not likely to be present in empirical evaluations of my theory of how civic activism and career partisanship shape candidacy ambition, but they are possible in the modified strategic candidacy framework I evaluate.

The first area of concern is benefits sought from office. It is likely that all candidates know seeking material goods from office is an undesirable thing to admit. Opposition candidates who represent parties that are driven by commitments to anti-corruption and rule of law stand against the kinds of government largesse these policies produce, while ruling party candidates know their party is stained by the financial corruption scandals that the opposition criticizes them for. From an inferential perspective, this would lead to bias if only one of the two groups felt compelled to underrepresent the value they place on material goods. If everyone sees divulging the idea that material benefits drive candidacy decisions as undesirable, this would bias all responses downward; however, this bias could not account for differences we see between opposition and ruling party legislators.[30]

The second relates to campaign tactics. Divulging that one spent massive resources on a political campaign can be embarrassing if defeated. More concerning is reporting spending if the amounts were above rates permitted by campaign finance rules or if they point to the influence of behind-the-scenes financiers who may be cultivating political favor. To collect as accurate information as possible about campaign expenditure, I asked about total, party-funded, and self-funded campaign expenditures to address concerns about funds sourcing. Legislators who completed the survey on tablets were also given the option of entering the information themselves rather than verbally reporting the amount to an enumerator. For each expenditure question, participants were given the option to provide an actual campaign amount *or* to answer an ordinal question with expenditure bands. Most respondents answered the ordinal version of the question, consistent with other research on campaigns expenditure in Africa (Lindberg 2003, 2010). At higher levels of the ordinal variable, expenditure bands were larger and invariably only ruling party candidates reported such high expenditures, which compresses gaps between ruling party and opposition. Among higher levels of the ordinal scale were values that were above the legal expenditure limit and the final values were higher than plausible expenditure levels, while the lowest level was

---

[30] Bias could be present if one group overreported and the other underreported, but with regard to preferences over material benefits, this scenario is implausible.

essentially no expenditure. Respondents may feel more comfortable giving true responses if they are not near the ends of an ordinal scale, which is addressed by including these extreme values at the ends of the measure. Even if social desirability bias impacts campaign expenditure reports, the implications of the bias work against the findings I present in later chapters because, if anything, they are likely to understate the differences between opposition and ruling party candidates in the study.

To sum up, potential concerns regarding bias are present in any study with analyses based on self-reported survey data. The design of the survey I analyze in this book helps greatly in circumventing many of the most damaging issues from an inferential perspective. Other measurement errors inherent to the topics the survey addresses like campaign expenditure or benefits of office present unavoidable biases that impact responses on the whole, but they should not systematically impact ruling party and opposition legislators in a way that overstates what I will find in the chapters that follow.

CONCLUSION

This chapter has situated Tanzania among other electoral authoritarian regimes in Africa and the rest of the world. It also has provided more context on what is at stake in elections there, focusing on the country's two legislatures. Lastly, I detailed the empirical strategy of the book and the data sources which that be used to evaluate the theory I developed in Chapter 2. The next six chapters of the book test this theory. The chapter that immediately follows begins where the paths of many aspiring candidates in authoritarian regimes start: in their personal and professional backgrounds in the years and decades before deciding to run for office.

4

Roots of Ambition: Civic Activism and Career Partisanship

Hata mbuyu huanza mchicha
Even the baobab begins as a sprout.

Mtu hujua atokako haisi aendako
People know where they came from; they are ignorant about where they are going.

Tundu Lissu is an outspoken government critic and opposition leader who was elected to Parliament from Singida West in 2010 and reelected in 2015. He narrowly survived being shot sixteen times outside his home during the midday break of a legislative session in 2017.[1] Long before Parliament and the assassination attempt, Tundu Lissu was first and foremost engaged in legal activism as a researcher and attorney for Tanzanian advocacy NGO Lawyer's Environmental Action Team (LEAT). Hailing from Singida, a region with increasing foreign interest in mining precious metals and gemstones, Lissu led LEAT's public charge against the government over the extrajudicial killings of peasant gold-miners in the Bulyanhulu mine located in the neighboring region of Shinyanga. LEAT claimed the government, which was struggling to evict local, small-scale miners before transferring mining rights to a Canadian company, intentionally sealed active mine shafts with bulldozers and in doing so buried fifty-two Tanzanians alive. Tundu Lissu was charged with sedition and incitement over

---

[1] He was stripped of his parliamentary seat in 2019 by the chamber's speaker due to his "unknown whereabouts" while he recovered from his injuries abroad, meaning at the time of writing he was no longer a parliamentarian (Kabendera 2019*a*).

the claims, the first of many times he would face charges and arrest for his commitment to human rights and environmental advocacy. His pre-parliamentary career also included researching and coauthoring the *Orodha ya Mafisadi* or "List of Shame," a 2007 document that detailed corruption allegations against eleven prominent CCM politicians. The list rocked the government. It included the standing president, the prime minister, the leader of the central bank, and several other government leaders and led to several resignations (Mohammed 2015).

Captain John Damiano Komba's path to the *Bunge* could not have been more different. From 2005 until his death in February 2015, he represented Mbinga Mashariki, located in Southern Tanzania along the Mozambican border. Komba joined Tanzania's army *Jeshi la Wananchi Tanzania* (Tanzania People's Defense Forces, JWTZ) in 1977. He served in the Kagera War that deposed Ugandan dictator Idi Amin in 1978 and afterward he was picked for an atypical but critical role in the army: he was the leader of the musical/cultural troupe within the military branch. He led the troupe around the country performing *kwaya*, nationalist adaptions of colonial-era choir music meant to generate enthusiasm and loyalty for the single-party state and ruling party (Barz 2003, Edmonson 2007). He later directed Tanzania One Theatre (TOT), a government-backed performance group created to promote CCM and entrench its position under multiparty rule (Askew 2002). In these capacities, he composed a number of CCM praise anthems and election campaign songs, including "CCM ni Nambari Wani" ("CCM is Number #1"). By the time he secured his first nomination for Parliament in 2005, he had been CCM's chief of culture for more than a decade, an eighteen-year member of the party's National Executive Committee, and a close confidant of the outgoing and incoming Tanzanian Presidents Benjamin Mkapa and Jakaya Kikwete.

The next several chapters of this book empirically test a theory of opposition candidacy in electoral authoritarian regimes. Chapters 6 through 9 will evaluate whether modifications to the strategic candidacy framework that attribute political ambition to cost-benefit calculations can account for opposition candidacy. Before the split-second moment in which candidacy decisions are calculated, however, years or potentially decades of political and vocational career trajectories shape the desire to run. In this chapter, I focus on two distinctive life trajectories – civic activism versus career partisanship – with path dependencies that chart courses to the opposition versus ruling party. In subsequent chapters, I will also show how these backgrounds impact opposition versus ruling party ambition to run for office through a second channel, whereby cost-benefit calculations of candidacy decisions are impacted by these past life trajectories.

The accounts of Tundu Lissu and the late John Komba illustrate the key message to take away from this chapter: both voluntarily chose to run for office and, in doing so, weighed the trade-offs of running or not running for office. However, the choice to run with the opposition or the CCM is less a product of this strategic consideration and far more a consequence of the life experiences leading them to the decision in the first place. Tundu Lissu's journey to Parliament is shaped by a clarity of purpose. As he notes,

I [had] been in the trenches for 20 years and have the battle scars to prove it. So when I went to parliament I had already become quite notorious for always championing causes against the high and mighty and against the government's abuses (Ashly 2020).

How could someone run for a governing party whose contemporary leaders topped his "list of shame" for corruption and malfeasance? Captain Komba had written and sung the soundtrack of more than thirty years of CCM's dominance on the campaign trail and in government. "CCM ni Nambari Wani" may have informed the strategic weight Komba placed on the chances of winning an election contest as a CCM candidate, but having written this anthem tells us more about the path dependence of that choice.

The evidence in the chapter that follows will reinforce the message that the decision to run for the opposition can be explained in terms of rational, strategic calculations, but this explanation ultimately misses the point. Paths to office are shaped by the sequences of events in life, work, and politics that lead to the choice to run for office.

This chapter is divided into four sections. First, I review the concepts of civic activism and career partisanship introduced in Chapter 2 and recapitulate how these life trajectories shape opposition versus ruling party candidacy. I then review the life history calendar, a survey data collection technique used to gather information about pre-parliamentary life events of Tanzanian legislators. Section 4.2 presents the main empirical analysis of the chapter, drawn from a survey with 132 Tanzanian legislators. Section 4.3 uses additional survey data to further unpack evidence of civic activism versus career partisanship. Section 4.4 contextualizes these results with in-depth discussion of Tanzania and by returning to the narratives of James Mbatia, Ismail Jussa, and January Makamba.

4.1 OPPOSITION VERSUS RULING PARTY PATHS TO CANDIDACY

Chapter 2 proposed that decisions to aspire to legislative office for the ruling party and opposition are shaped by cost-benefit calculations but also that those calculations are secondary to longer-term personal and professional background experiences that form the lens through which individuals view and engage with politics. I offered two distinctive paths that shape how individuals come to the decision to run for office (or not) and argued that each of these has distinct consequences in terms of the party for which candidacy ambitions grow.

On one hand, the experiences that plant the seeds of opposition candidacy are found in careers and histories of civic activism through the formation of "socio-electoral coalitions" of civic and opposition organizations (Trejo 2014). The importance of civil society for democracy is broadly recognized, as political civil society and civic activism serve to train citizens to exercise their rights, vocalize demands to political leaders, and hold government accountable (Dahl 1971). In electoral authoritarian regimes, opposition parties fight for the legal enshrinement of these principles during elections and outside of them (Schedler 2006). Civic groups do the same, but with more autonomy and less interference from the government compared with the formal opposition (Arriola 2013, Brownlee 2007, Riedl 2014, Smith 2004). This overlap creates supply- and demand-side explanations of why opposition candidates emerge from civil society and NGO vocations.

From the perspective of opposition parties, candidates with these backgrounds are desirable because individually and as representatives of civic organizations, they have assets the parties lack. Resource-constrained opposition parties cannot offer prospective candidates leadership training, campaign management skills, or financial support for campaigns. Civic leadership already provides these skills and civic organizations can offer opposition candidates basic but vital administrative goods – phones, copiers, and office space. Civic activists also have high public visibility and experience, and civil society organizations feature strong network and mobilization structures (McAdam, Tarrow, and Tilly 2001, McAdam, McCarthy, and Zald 1996, McClurg 2003, Siegel 2009) built upon preexisting cleavages in society (LeBas 2011), giving them experience applicable to campaign mobilization.

For prospective candidates with NGO vocational backgrounds, opposition parties offer opportunities to further pursue goals desired by civil society and a prominent avenue to raise grievances against the government (Beissinger 2007, Bunce and Wolchik 2011). Elections are critical moments in which electoral authoritarian regimes permit challengers additional leeway to criticize, meaning opposition candidacy can serve as a vehicle for civic activists to bring a level of visibility to their causes only possible through elections. This complementarity forges a candidacy path from the civil society sector into the opposition.

By contrast, ruling party candidacy aspirations in electoral authoritarian regimes follow years or decades of career partisanship. A form of political capital and experience, this account resembles the narrative of political careers in advanced democracies. In democracies, such careers are initially launched by "nascent ambition" (Lawless 2012) and then developed through progressive ambition, holding local, low-prestige political offices followed by more important, national political office. Such politicians are "professionals" and "insiders" in that their vocation is politics. Career partisanship differs, however, in terms of the substance of political capital that shapes ruling party candidacy ambitions. In electoral authoritarian regimes, "nascent ambition" is cultivated within the ruling party, and the progressive growth of a political career that facilitates candidacy ambitions and prospects takes place within the party. For such ruling parties, political experience in government for aspirants is secondary to the value of demonstrated loyalty to the party, in part because managing intraparty factionalism is paramount to regime longevity (Greene 2007). For candidates, career partisanship plants the seeds of candidacy aspirations through indoctrination, interaction with political leaders, and earning political party capital. Party service also provides prospective candidates with financial resources through formal means (e.g., salary for performing party office duties) and informal ones, like access to government favor and public resources for patronage. Through this process, career partisanship foments candidacy ambition and sets a path to ruling party candidacy. This path is particularly pronounced in high-prestige, low-level positions in hyper-local and constituency offices, marking a long, labor intensive path to candidacy. Opposition candidates may feature some party service in their backgrounds as well, but only insofar as they serve immediate electoral goals of parties – mobilizing voters or serving basic party functions at the national level (like bookkeeping, assisting presidential campaigns, etc.).

The primary goal of this chapter is to examine evidence of civic activism versus career partisanship to see if they point to differences in candidacy decisions. What does knowing about the nature of these two forms of pre-candidacy backgrounds in electoral authoritarian regimes tell us about the decisions of prospective candidates when choosing to run for office (or not)? The chapter now moves to the empirical strategy for answering this question with survey data and begins by discussing challenges and solutions for measuring these candidacy backgrounds.

Empirical Approach and Results

My theory anticipates that candidates who travel to office through the path of civic activism are likely to run for the opposition. By contrast, CCM candidates will have cultivated their political careers in a political party. The dependent variable is dichotomous and indicates whether a respondent is an opposition partisan. It is coded such that positively signed coefficients indicate a greater likelihood of being an opposition candidate. Analyses explore how early partisan and civic activism shape candidacy decisions and use standard logistic regression due to the intuitive interpretation of results and post-estimation analyses.[2]

Chapter 3 introduced the life history calendar as a solution to several related measurement challenges for documenting life trajectories retrospectively. I developed a life history calendar to collect information regarding the first time an individual engaged in civic activism versus career partisanship, as well as when several other important political and personal life events occurred. For civic activism, respondents were asked to indicate the first time they organized a local grassroots community meeting and for career partisanship when they first became an official member of a political party. I additionally capture civic activism through an additive index of associational membership and leadership positions and career partisanship with several indicator variables of leadership in party positions.

In the text that follows, I visually present the substantive effects of civic activism and career partisanship captured with survey measures of civic and party organization memberships (Figure 4.1) and the life history calendar (Figure 4.2), revealed through post-estimation analysis. Full results of the regression analyses are found in Appendix B.2.

---

[2] The findings are robust to the penalized-likelihood approach proposed by Firth (1993). This technique reduces potential bias in maximum-likelihood estimates where there is quasi- or complete separation in data (e.g., some variables or variable configurations may perfectly predict an outcome or binary event) by "using a penalized version of the likelihood function" (Rainey 2016, 339).

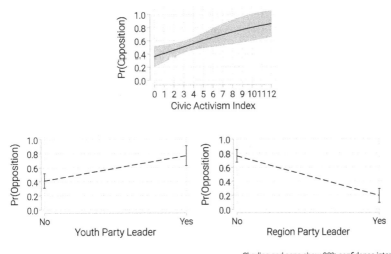

Shading and caps show 90% confidence interval

FIGURE 4.1 Civic activism versus career partisanship, membership variables

4.2 RESULTS

The results from multivariate regression show that opposition candidates come to candidacy through social activism. Looking to the role of civic engagement, each additional type of civic group to which an individual belongs or leads – religious, professional, union, community, student and women's organizations – is associated with about 30 percent greater odds of being an opposition candidate. This is visualized in the top panel of Figure 4.1. The civic activism measure from the life history calendar also supports this intuition in Figure 4.2. Each additional year since first organizing a grassroots community meeting is associated with about 13 percent greater odds of being an opposition legislator, as seen in Figure 4.2.

Ruling party legislators, by contrast, come to office through a path of party activism that allows them to develop ambition and be groomed for candidacy through a distinctly partisan lens. Other individuals – those who become opposition candidates or are not candidates at all – experience shorter partisan careers. The first observable manifestation of career partisanship is the amount of party service undertaken by prospective candidates before running for office. The direction of all but one party service coefficient is negative, which corresponds with the expectation that career partisans more frequently run with the ruling party. The predicted probability of regional party officers being opposition candidates is about 0.4 lower than for individuals who did not hold such posts; this captures the

underlying intuition of my theory: opposition candidates may occasionally serve in political parties, but in performing mission critical duties
at the top of the party, in the secretariat.[3] Ruling party aspirants, by
contrast, pass through the party machinery step-by-step; thus, it is ruling
party aspirants who perform service at this subnational level.

Perhaps surprisingly, results in Figure 4.1 also show that youth leaders are more likely to run for the opposition. This could indicate career
partisanship has heterogeneous effects that depend on the party position
and low versus high prestige of the position, a consideration I explore
later in the chapter in Section 4.3. These results support seminal qualitative research showing that Tanzania's ruling party has valued party
service in determining loyalty and fitness for office since single-party rule
(e.g., Hyden and Leys 1972). The importance of CCM party credentials
in candidacy lives on in the multiparty era.

The second observable aspect of career partisanship is a measure of the
number of years since an individual officially joined their current party.
Using the life history calendar, we observe that for each additional year
since taking a party card, the likelihood of being a ruling party legislator
increases by about 25 percent. This variable alone accounts for about 20
percent of variation in respondents' party affiliation. Figure 4.2 strikingly
shows that the probability of an individual joining the ruling party and
running for office immediately is nearly zero. Of fourteen respondents
who joined a party and ran for office in the same year, eleven (79 percent) were opposition candidates. The figure similarly illustrates that the
probability of running with the opposition approaches zero as the number of years since joining a party reaches its maximum value. Alternative
measures of career partisanship derived from the life history calendar –
the first time wearing party regalia (called *fulana* in Tanzania) and the
first time mastering party ideology – offer similar results.[4] Together, there
is robust support for the role of career partisanship for ruling parties
in electoral authoritarian regimes. This analysis offers strong support

---

[3] Party service variables for campaign leadership and local party offices are insignificant
but point in the same direction as regional leadership (away from opposition legislators).
Consistent with my theory of career partisanship, these measures are correlated, which
may account for these non-results. I test my theory of career partisanship positions at
different levels more comprehensively in Chapter 5, where I analyze entire sequences
of career partisanship. The coefficient for secretariat service is positively signed but not
significant.

[4] The life history calendar variables are highly correlated and, consequently, not included
in a single analysis together.

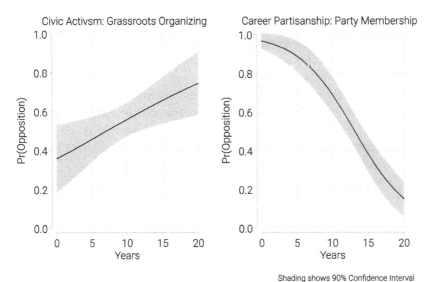

Shading shows 90% Confidence Interval

FIGURE 4.2 Civic activism versus career partisanship, life history calendar

for my theory that different paths to candidacy – civic activism versus career partisanship – have downstream consequences on candidates' party choice.

4.3 FURTHER SURVEY EVIDENCE

The immediately preceding survey results show two pathways, one to the opposition and one to the ruling party. However, they also suggest a potential channel from party to opposition tickets through the route of youth organizations. In this section, I unpack that further. I also elaborate on the idea that an absence of career partisanship precludes ruling party candidacy by comparing CCM legislators with former CCM members who did not run for the ruling party (and instead ran with the opposition).

Youth Partisanship in Opposition

First, I return to a finding from the previous analysis that showed a positive relationship between youth wing leadership and opposition candidacy. On one hand, youth wing leadership fits with the civic activism narrative in highlighting the particular skills of student leaders in winning over new recruits as well as grassroots support. One could instead claim that youth leadership is evidence of career partisanship, contrary to the theory I advanced. I now provide evidence that the pattern supports the former interpretation: youth wing leadership for the opposition under-lies youth recruitment strategies, a pillar of opposition voter and activist courtship. Opposition parties in Tanzania saturate university campuses, looking for new members and identifying potential leaders. Youth lead-ers recruit new members and, in doing so, gain greater valence among the electorate. This is symptomatic of the civic activism and youth connec-tion that will be discussed shortly with Ismail Jussa's and James Mbatia's narratives.

To support this intuition empirically, I use the candidate/noncandidate survey data, in which individuals credibly displayed interest in running for office in 2010 but ultimately chose not to act on that ambition. The survey included about 150 youth wing members from CHADEMA and Civic United Front. These surveys offer an insider perspective on how youth leadership fits alongside candidacy narratives. I focus on a question in the survey that asked respondents to identify the primary activity of the youth wing. Their answers are displayed in Figure 4.3. Respondents did note that learning party policy positions was important, consistent with evidence regarding the importance of ideology to opposition parties that is provided in the next chapter. More than 50 percent of respondents noted that most of what youth leaders do is recruiting new members and winning over defectors from the ruling party. An additional 7.6 percent pointed to participating in party rallies, a campaign mobilization tool that also resembles public protests that have characterized the civic activism of youth under multiparty politics. This evidence supports the intuition that youth party leadership for opposition candidates is consistent with the civic activism narrative and the role student leadership plays in opposition strategy.

Career Partisanship among CCM Members

This book is motivated by interest in opposition candidacy but under-standing that requires illuminating both civic activist pathways to the opposition and career partisanship routes to the ruling party. An ideal test of career partisanship would compare ruling party candidates with ruling party candidate hopefuls who did not run for office. While I lack non-legislator data from ruling party candidates, I can harness insight from nineteen opposition legislators I interviewed who were CCM defectors. They ran for the opposition but did not run for the ruling party before defecting to the opposition; thus, these former ruling party hopefuls can

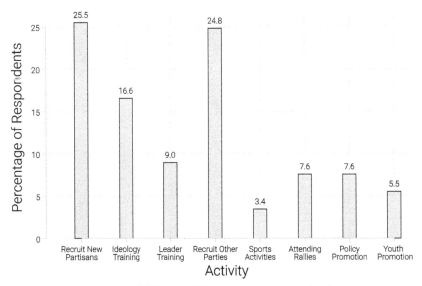

FIGURE 4.3 Main activities of opposition youth wings

be compared with successful ruling party candidates in terms of their service in the ruling party. What level of ruling party career partisanship did these individuals demonstrate before defecting to the opposition to run as candidates? Figure 4.4 differentiates the party service of sixty-four CCM legislator respondents from nineteen CCM defectors who ran as opposition candidates. Each bar shows the percentage of individuals from that group who had some service across different party offices and duties. The figure illustrates how starkly career partisanship differs between individuals who sought CCM nominations and those who did not. CCM candidates served in a substantially higher number of positions than these CCM noncandidates, from elite-level regional and central party offices down to local positions. Nearly all CCM legislators had positions on the campaign trail prior to running for office. This points to how interaction with party elites around elections can serve as a gateway to candidacy. Later chapters will show that campaign experience also features in opposition candidacy, but in service of different goals. These data generally reinforce the message that ruling party candidacy is unlocked by paths in career partisanship.

4.4 CONTEXTUALIZING RESULTS IN TANZANIA

Using survey data, I have shown that opposition candidates emerge from civil society backgrounds in Tanzania's electoral authoritarian regime.

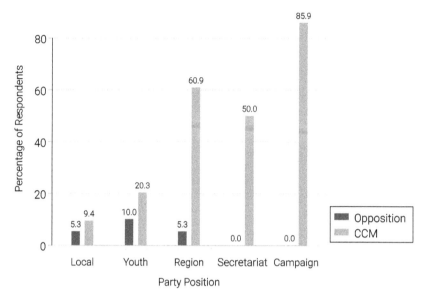

FIGURE 4.4 CCM positions held by CCM legislators and opposition legislators formerly in CCM

Under single-party rule, civil society was severely constrained and existed in service of CCM. Trade unions, women's organizations, and religious associations were regulated and commonly sponsored or controlled by the ruling party. Even musical groups and theater troupes performed at the behest of the ruling party and reinforced its political and social messaging (Askew 2002). This started changing with the liberalization of Tanzania's politics beginning in the early 1990s. Across Tanzania, civil society organizations catalyzed political reform during the onset of multipartyism and have served as consistent sources of political pressure for the government since (Shariff 1999). Civil society today broadly still reflects the flattening it experienced during CCM's single-party rule (Paget 2019a). This is especially true for unions and collectives that still have state-linked appendages (Ewald 2013) and lack the autonomy to form a base for opposition party mass mobilization at the citizen level (LeBas 2011). However, they do provide important avenues for candidacy emergence and are increasingly important in Tanzanian politics.

From 1990 to 1995, the number of registered NGOs exploded from 25 to 800; by 1997 there were more than 8,000 formal and informal NGOs (Tripp 2000). Because cooperatives, community-based organizations, and faith-based organizations are classified separately from NGOs, this estimate is conservative (Ewald 2013, 196). NGOs – as organizations that could empower voters and provide political representation – were treated by the government with skepticism and for good reason (Mercer 1999). More than 75 percent of the NGOs are located in three regions of Tanzania – Dar es Salaam, Arusha, and Kilimanjaro (AMAP 1997). These are the most populous regions of Tanzania but also the areas that saw contentious politics from youth strikes, anti-government demonstrations, and collective organization by labor unions, women's groups, and religious institutions in the late twentieth century. In Tanzania's 1995 elections, these also proved to be the areas in which opposition parties performed the best, in no small part because of establishing links with civic organizations whose grievances with government had reached a boiling point. This pattern endures today. While the focus of civic organizations and NGOs that feed opposition advocacy vary, three types have been particularly important: religious organizations; advocacy organizations dedicated to grassroots causes and national empowerment issues, and student government and youth movements.

Religious and faith-based organizations (FBOs) in Tanzania have historically played roles in contentious politics that foment opposition activism (Ewald 2013, Msekwa 2006), particularly in the three aforementioned regions. The Lutheran Church – which predominates in Northern Tanzania – was fractured over power struggles and corruption under the leadership of Jackson Kaaya in the 1990s. Kaaya was a CCM Regional Party Chairman of Arusha for two decades and a close ally of Julius Nyerere. Fallout from corruption scandals under his watch damaged CCM's reputation in the region and impacted pipelines to opposition leadership (Baroin 1996, 538). The crisis within the church was mediated by then-Minister of Home Affairs Augustino Mrema in favor of the church's predominant faction; in 1995, he was NCCR-Mageuzi's presidential candidate in large part because of the enthusiastic endorsement and support he received from the beneficiaries of this mediation. NCCR candidate Samwel Kisanga Akyoo's successful parliamentary race in 1995 was also bolstered by the Lutheran Church, as his brother had recently been made the bishop of the Meru Diocese within the Arusha region.

The importance of activism within the Lutheran Church continues to play a role in opposition candidacy, and endorsement by religious leaders in the region is critical to opposition success (Kelsall 2004, 46). CHADEMA leadership pipelines are linked to both the Lutheran Church (specifically the *Kanisa la Kinjili la Kilutheri Tanzania*, KKKT) and the Catholic Church. The party's leader until 2015 – previously a CHADEMA MP and its 2010 presidential candidate – is a former

Catholic priest. The Catholic Church publicly endorsed opposition candidates in past elections based on assessments of their "worthiness for office," in part due to their relationship with the church, a move criticized by the ruling party (Downie 2015). Muslim–Christian tensions also map onto opposition versus ruling party political cleavages (Bakari 2012). Tanzanian Muslims lament government discrimination beginning under Nyerere and continuing into the present; opposition party Civic United Front has succeeded in translating this anti-government grievance into political mobilization for supporters and candidates (Heilman and Kaiser 2002). After independence, Muslim organizations that provided education and health services were banned by the government and replaced with parastatal and party organizations at the hands of Nyerere (e.g., disbanding the East African Muslim Welfare Society in favor of *Baraza Kuu la Waislamu Tanzania* (National Muslim Council of Tanzana, BAKWATA)); CUF has attempted to reinvigorate connections with transnational religious organizations as a mobilization and fundraising strategy (Burgess 2009, 274–278).

The comparative literature documents that opposition candidates emerge from advocacy organizations, both local, segmented grassroots organizations and national groups with a particular focus on women's rights. They give citizens local influence over government that later facilitates formalizing demands through political organizations (Cornwall and Coelho 2007, Goldfrank 2007, Heller 2001) and have been significant in nineteenth- and twentieth-century democratization.[5] Tanzania's most prominent women's organization with opposition ties is BAWATA (*Baraza la Wanawake wa Tanzania*), an organization initially formed by the CCM party's women's wing. Ostensibly focused on mobilizing women at the grassroots level, the organization has been repeatedly threatened by the government with suspension (Kelsall 2004) for its support of opposition campaigns and candidates, particularly during the 1995 elections (Brown 2001). The Tanzania Media Women's Association (TAMWA) is another organization that plays a critical role in advocacy for issues that underlie opposition appeals, promoting a robust, independent media. It has co-organized workshops with international NGOs to train prospective political leaders in leadership skills and communicating information about women's issues (EISA 2005, Tripp 2000). Other rights-based organizations operate outside the context of gender and focus on issues related

---

[5] Brockett (1991), Calhoun (1993), d'Anieri, Ernst, and Kier (1990), Ndegwa (1996), and Schneider (1991).

to government accountability. For example, education NGO *HakiElimu* has produced critical evaluations of school performance, leading the government to dictate it "should not set its foot in Tanzanian schools again until it apologized for what was described as 'ridiculing government efforts in development of the education sector in the country'" (Ewald 2013, 198).

Lastly, universities have served as focal points in Tanzanian politics, both for opposition development and for ruling party attempts to influence campus affairs. During Tanzania's push for multiparty politics in the 1990s, students played a critical role, in particular student leaders at the University of Dar es Salaam (DARUSO, the Dar es Salaam University Student Organization). While campus activism during the 1970s and 1980s generally focused on university economics – student fees and allowances – students began to organize against the government through on-campus activities in the 1990s. They were supported in part by training and strategy-building activities carried out by international nongovernmental organizations and foreign governments (Luhanga 2009, 21). Through university activism led by DARUSO, students participated in boycotts, protests, and civil disobedience on campus, amid growing consequences for their contentious actions. DARUSO also led efforts to bring newly minted opposition parties to campus to meet with students as early as February 1992; for doing so, members were considered anti-government agitators and punished by the university (Luhanga 2009, 31). James Mbatia came to opposition politics through civic activism on the University of Dar es Salaam campus. His experience is identified – though not by name – by then-UDSM vice-chancellor Matthew Luhanga in Luhanga's memoir. He notes (disparagingly) of James Mbatia:

[O]ne engineering student who was within three months of completing his under-graduate studies would have been the first person ever from his clan to have completed university education. Yet by knowingly or unknowingly allowing themselves to be used by politicians, they messed up their lives. ... Some have become unsuccessful politicians (Luhanga 2009, 36)

James Mbatia remembers this experience very differently. His goals as a student activist were not to agitate politics on campus but rather to help develop the kind of political and civic engagement that multiparty democracy would require of its citizens. According to Mbatia, the multiparty transition was premature and "when multipartyism came in 1992, people weren't ready for it." Only when he was expelled did his activism turn political, a "post-mortem decision to fight the system" after he was unfairly removed from school. It was also through his student activism that he learned mobilization tactics, the very skills that were immediately put to use once he joined NCCR-Mageuzi. In addition to being selected to run the party's youth activities and mobilization, he became Tanzania's youngest parliamentarian at age thirty-one when he won his 1995 election campaign.

Ismail Jussa describes the origins of his political ambition in a similar light, with roots in rejection of party indoctrination early in school and later developing in stages of his secondary education in Forms 4 and 5. He noted this in a 2017 interview with me:

In 1986, I was in Form 2. The whole year in the subject of politics was to study the CCM constitution. We would be taught from chapter one to the last chapter of the CCM constitution. In a way, you have to memorize because there will be an exam at the end of the term and you're supposed to answer questions about the CCM constitution. That's how we were indoctrinated. By that time, that's when we started forming that resistance. We would now use the classrooms to challenge the teachers of *siasa* [politics].

Later, as Jussa reached adulthood and neared the end of secondary school, he became a student activist. He described in the same interview how this activism ultimately propelled his involvement in politics:

At that time, I was known to be stubborn at school because I would talk with teachers at Haile Selassie [secondary school] who were politically conscious. That developed into a movement and those of us who are in higher learning in Zanzibar, called Higher Learning institutions, started to form our own conscience. Formed and developed our own network of students who are bold enough to identify with what at the time was called "rebels" – those against the ruling party and the one party system. With myself and others from that time, for example, *Taasisi ya Kiswahili na Lugha Za Kigeni* (Swahili Institute and Foreign Languages) … Lumumba, Taasisi, Nkurumah Teachers Training College, Fidel Castro, secondary school in Pemba, Karume Technical college. We had some *washawishi* (influencers) like myself, the young people's champions in that rank. Those kind of things and trying to influence other students to join that movement. That's how I got involved.

When the idea of actually running for office came to him in 2010, he had already been a major player in advocacy for changing Zanzibar's role in the Tanzanian union. This issue of expanding or retracting Zanzibar's autonomy has driven the archipelago's politics since Tanzania was formed in 1964, and has undergirded a fierce, deep ideological divide between the opposition and CCM up to the present day. As much as Jussa was working for Civic United Front's leader Maalim Seif, he ultimately was engaging in activism surrounding Zanzibari nationalism and the so-called Union Issue. Jussa expounded upon this in an interview I conducted with him in 2019:

> When I contested the position in 2010, my name was very well known in Zanzibari politics for many, many years ... during the campaign that led to the multiparty system, during the early stage of multiparty system formation ... and all the processes like *Muafaka*.[6] For 2010, there was an extra thing because as you know and everybody knows one of the key issues if not the major factor of Zanzibar politics is the Union issue. ... I was in the forefront, one of the major spokespersons about those issues. I was very active and being the initiator of the process that made my name mentioned widely. My reason for contesting was being pushed by the people of Stone Town [Jussa's constituency]. They said "It is high time now. You've always played many roles behind the scenes but now we feel it is an honor for us the constituency to be represented by someone like you."

Student activism remains a critical pathway into politics and opposition candidacy. The DARUSO at the University of Dar es Salaam regularly leads protests on campus against both the government and the administration of the government-run institution. Although its activities and objections are commonly related to economic and student "pocketbook" issues, protests commonly invoke government corruption, poor incumbent leadership, and the ruling party as culpable. The government, in response, frequently laments the way in which opposition parties feed upon student advocacy (Mwollo-Ntallima 2011). Outside the DARUSO leadership, surveys of UDSM students indicate that nearly 75 percent of them engage in some form of activism like protesting, contacting government officials, writing letters to university administration, or participating in student political meetings (Mwollo-Ntallima 2011, 120). Student leaders disproportionately hold pro-democracy views that emphasize values aligned with opposition policy (Mwollo-Ntallima 2011, 130–134).

---

[6] *Muafaka 1(1999)*, *Muafaka II (2005)*, and ultimately the 2010 *Maridhiano* were three efforts to create stability, peace, and reconciliation between CCM and CUF in Zanzibar following the violence and turmoil surrounding national elections there. The *maridhiano* resulted in a power-sharing form of government affirmed by popular referendum and operating from 2010 to 2015. Ismail Jussa played an instrumental part in these proceedings, particularly in behind-the-scenes efforts to build consensus among the opposition, CCM-Zanzibar, and CCM-Tanzania over an acceptable form of power sharing.

In contemporary Tanzanian politics, universities are key recruitment areas for the opposition. CUF leader Ismail Jussa described this to me in 2017:

CHADEMA in alternative way, they have come up with what they call CHASO, CHADEMA Students Organization. ... They've opened CHADEMA branches in almost all of the higher learning institutions, their branches. Now they are organizing through those branches, which you cannot take over because this is a CHADEMA branch. There's Dar es Salaam, CHADEMA branch at Mzumbe Morogoro, CHADEMA branch at St. Augustine University. CHADEMA are using that to try to mobilize people.

He went on to note similar patterns for CUF in Zanzibar through its development even though the majorities of Tanzanian universities are located on the mainland:

It became typical of Zanzibari life that even the student politics somehow, though not formally said so, were seen as competition during student government elections between people who were seen as maybe pro CCM and pro CUF. ... It was becoming like a movement that was almost everywhere from Zanzibar University, from State University of Zanzibar SUZA, to the Chukwani College of Education. Other institutions that have branches in Zanzibar: From Zanzibar Institution of Financial Administration in Chwaka, ZIFA, to places like Mwalimu Nyerere Academy's Branch in Zanzibar and the Institute of Public Administration (IPA) which is run by the government ... it was going further down to high schools and even secondary education where there was a student government. Suddenly you find that almost all of them were won and therefore run by people who identify with CUF politics. That was really pissing off CCM. They saw that it was partly with all the strength and success that CUF had registered in the 2015 [national] elections. Afterward, student elections results were cancelled in universities and higher learning institutions simply because those people who won were not CCM. And they had a re-run, just like the national elections, to impose their own people because [CCM] is afraid ... CCM is struggling because they have realized [student governments] are really powerful in putting in place who can become a future leader.

Talking with Jussa, he rattles off example after example of the student activist turned opposition politician emerging now in the youth of CUF and later ACT in Zanzibar. Before Yusuf Makame was elected as an opposition MP in 2015, he was a leader of student associations at the State University of Zanzibar (SUZA) and Zanzibar University; his vocational career included leading TAHLISO, a civil society organization that assists and liaises with student governments across Tanzania's higher-learning institutions. Juma Kombo Hamad won a Parliament seat in Wingwi after being a student leader at SUZA. Others who did not win but ran for opposition passed through this same student engagement gateway in Zanzibar, including Khaleed Gwiji (Kiembe Samaki constituency), Nasra Nasef (Wawi constituency), Khaleed Said Sulieman, and many others.

In contrast to these opposition accounts, January Makamba's storied career in public office and his desire to run for office point back directly to his experience of party service. To a certain extent, much of the pathway was laid out ahead of him long before he contemplated running for office, even as a small child. His father Yusuf Makamba was a military leader turned political heavyweight who would ultimately lead CCM as its secretary-general. While the upbringing was not overtly political, it was "a bit of a tunnel in a way." He recalls seeing his father's activities in service of the party and the country as "important work. He had an official car, the official CCM flag. You knew he had people working for him so you know he is important."

January joined CCM's Young Pioneers organization in primary school, a group for young children to play together with their friends overlaid with lighter-touch party activities that were not deeply political – formal parades (*halaiki*) and ceremonies that included dancing, singing, and presenting a party scarf similar to those used in boy scouts, combined with some political education and indoctrination. January notes he was not very active in the program, even if he did serve in its national leadership. However, it was impactful for many future CCM leaders and in a conversation we had in 2019 he described how the party designed it to shape future leaders:

Initially, actually, it was set up to groom leaders by the party. You do Young Pioneers, you go to the youth league, then automatically you're there. The party is assured that its cadres had been trained since they were kids. ... You are recruited, you're taken, you become part of it. You select your leaders. It mimics the structure of the party. ... Because it has the structure, they had the chairman, the board. ... They point out: "This one will be a leader." Then, many CCM of my generation – the younger people who have come to be CCM leaders – they have come from that process.

He sees the pathway to office through party service as plainly as the data in this chapter show. As an admired leader in the new generation of CCM leaders, many young members of CCM seek him out for mentorship. Relaying his experiences with mentoring young politicians, January told me in an interview they come to him and say "I want to run in ten years. That's why I want to be part of politics now." But he also experienced the comparable difficulties of careers in party politics and political positions in government versus elected office. Sure, one had to fight for support of voters at election time, but for positions like the district and regional chairpersons of the party – the "reliance on this work for a livelihood" is filled with uncertainty over political futures and an "itinerant, unsettled" lifestyle for aspirant leaders and their families. He witnessed the bloat and rot in CCM and its consequences – "People without professionalism, ethics, no imagination, no creativity yet being key players in politics." Thus, while his "father was a politician almost all of his life, [he could] have a politician for a parent and still have the freedom to decide for yourself what you want to do" (Karugendo 2015, 16–17). For this reason and for his cynicism toward the life of a politician, January Makamba found an alternative route into politics.

January's political story had a groundwork laid early in the youth appendages of CCM, but it began in earnest when he started working for the Tanzanian government in pursuit of a graduate education. Needing financial support to pursue a master's degree at George Mason University, then President Benjamin Mkapa encouraged January to work for the government so that he would be eligible for a government employee scholarship to fund his studies in the United States. The timing of when January completed his degree was fortuitous: Tanzania began its term on the United Nations (UN) Security Council as he finished his Master's and he was able to successfully extend his time in the United States to work with Tanzania's UN delegation. In this capacity, he prepared policy briefs for government officials on the politics of the African Great Lakes region. His reporting on Burundi drew the attention of then-foreign minister Jakaya Kikwete, who had led peace negotiations in both Burundi and the Democratic Republic of Congo (DRC) during his ministerial term. When Kikwete decided to run for president, he plucked January from his position in the foreign ministry and brought him into the realm of party politics as the soon-to-be president's speech writer and campaign advisor. January later became Kikwete's aid, confidant, planner, and personal assistant – his "everything" man.

As the everything man for Jakaya Kikwete, Makamba tells me this is when he began to feel the pull to enter politics from his rewarding experiences on the presidential campaign trail.

What I saw on the trail, people waiting for three hours and that they came to it expecting him. The frenzy of the rallies, and the tour, with people on the roadside. All the cynicism I had really went out the window. I saw that this is very important stuff because of the reaction of the people toward the candidates and the political process.

Having seen both the good in politics – Kikwete as a good man who sought and succeeded in doing good things – and the bad that had taken over parts of CCM, Makamba summarized how this thinking transitioned into ambition to run for office "You know what, I want to demonstrate that this can be done differently. ... I am going to go out there and show it by running a proper campaign, mobilizing, inspiring people."

CONCLUSION

This chapter has evaluated the first component of my theory of opposition candidacy, showing that backgrounds in civic activism versus career partisanship impose path dependencies on later candidacy decisions. Activism in student government, religious groups, local grassroots associations, and advocacy organizations shape political ambition in a way that points to opposition parties. Opposition parties, for their part, draw upon civic activists who are committed to similar policy and ideological issues and have organizing experience, access to institutional resources, and mobilization capacity. By contrast, lifelong experiences rooted in political party activism are instrumental in promoting political ambition, but in a way that the accrued political capital can only be mobilized for ruling party candidacy. Survey data from legislators in Tanzania's Parliament and Zanzibar's House of Representatives supported these conclusions through analysis of memberships and leaderships in party positions and civic associations, as well as the years of experience in grassroots organization and formal partisanship, measured with the life history calendar. The opening accounts of Tundu Lissu and Captain John Komba, however, suggest that this analytical strategy may miss other dimensions of civic activism and career partisanship. Tundu Lissu spent several years of his vocational career working in environmental law and advocacy; Komba was employed by CCM. The next chapter expands the study of civic activism and career partisanship to a larger dataset of Tanzanian legislators and studies how career backgrounds impact candidacy decisions. It also carries out a more granular study of career partisanship that considers three forms of what career partisanship might look like in action.

5

From Roots to Branches: Career Pathways to Candidacy Choices

Kaukumbatie mnazi ukaupande, kazi uanze
Embrace the coconut tree and climb it; start work.

5.1 SEQUENCE ANALYSIS: POLITICAL AND VOCATIONAL CAREERS

Thus far, testing the book's theory has compared ruling party and opposition legislators in terms of cross-sectional differences regarding investments and experiences in civic activism versus career partisanship. The analysis in this chapter takes a new empirical approach by incorporating the timing and ordering of political and vocational career experience to more comprehensively compare paths into opposition versus ruling party candidacy. I do so by employing sequence analysis to study the employment background of legislators, as well as their histories of party service prior to entering the legislature. The analysis tracks these political careers to study career partisanship, capturing the influence of party positions as individuals hop from one position to another, in and out of leadership, and even potentially from one party to another to another or in and out of politics altogether. In this sense, partisanship as conceived in this book is a bundle of states an individual can exist in at any given time – holding a position in a regional party office or not, serving as the chair of a constituency office or not, and so on. I also study civic activism versus career partisanship in the context of employment, measuring how long an individual works in a given career sector and how this primes them for opposition versus ruling party candidacy. For disentangling how political events speed up, slow down, start, stop, and change over time, understanding timing and sequence is critical (Brzinsky-Fay and Kohler 2010, Gryzmala-Busse 2011, Mahoney 2000, Pierson 2000, Slater and Simmons 2010).

Sequence analysis is a method of processing and studying longitudinal data. The concept of a sequence considers the entirety of a respondent's or case's related events/states together as a single observation (a sequence). My theory argues that civic activism and career partisanship have path dependent consequences of candidacy decisions, meaning an individual's political and vocational career into office is a holistic trajectory that is best understood in comparison with the trajectories of others. Sequence methods account for one's entire path to the legislature and thus are ideally suited for evaluating the theory.

This chapter will analyze two sequences for each of roughly 725 Tanzanian legislators from Tanzania's second (2000–2005), third (2005–2010), and fourth (2010–2015) Parliaments and members of Zanzibar's House of Representatives from 2010–2015. The chapter will show that vocational career sequences in the CSO/NGO background are found at significantly higher rates among the opposition, while party employment and political government work are more common among CCM legislators. I also show that several possible conceptualizations of career partisanship all point to ruling party candidacy.

5.2 SEQUENCE ANALYSIS: PARTY, CSO/NGO, AND GOVERNMENT VOCATIONAL CAREERS

The first set of sequences is derived from employment history data. A vocational career sequence begins when an individual has their first job and terminates when that individual becomes a legislator. Careers are coded into sectors corresponding with (1) civic activism (NGOs, INGOs, advocacy organizations, etc.); (2) party employment – if an individual reported a party job explicitly in their "employment history" and distinctive from party service categorized in career partisanship sequences;[1] (3) political positions in government;[2] or (4) other, a residual category

---

[1] Party positions indicated under "political experience" on CV fields is not considered for coding vocational career sequences; party positions are only coded for career sequences if they are reported under "employment history," consistent with the party as vocation dimension of career partisanship.

[2] Positions in publicly run institutions are not considered political unless they primarily engage in a political or governmental-oriented capacity. Within the health sector, for

of positions in sectors like business, education, the legal sector, and
health. For the analyses presented in this section, career sequences are
transformed into variables that correspond with the percentage of total
years of a career spent working in a given sector (the CSO/NGO sector,
political party employment, and in government). Table 5.1 highlights several career sequences of Tanzanian legislators, more intuitively describing
the measures I use.

The top two sequences in Table 5.1 belong to CHADEMA MPs,
starting with Tundu Lissu. As noted before, Tundu Lissu worked with
the Lawyers' Environmental Action Team (LEAT) as a researcher and
attorney with an intervening period in Washington, DC with the environmental advocacy NGO World Resources Institute (WRI). These jobs
spanned 1998 through 2008. He began his career as a teacher (1990–
1991); prior to joining LEAT, he worked for D'Souza Chambers, a general
domestic and international legal services firm located in Arusha. His
career features two brief periods with no reported employment, shortly
before becoming an MP and while he was earning his law degree. Tundu
Lissu thus had seventeen years of employment; about 65 percent were in
an NGO/CSO and the remaining 35 percent in other sectors (education,
law).

Reverend Israel Natse has represented Karatu for CHADEMA, a constituency in the region of Arusha – "CHADEMA country," if there were
such a thing – an area where robust economic trade and tourism bol-
ster the party's organizational capacity. As his title indicates, Natse is
a priest in the northern diocese of the Lutheran Church. The church –
the *Kanisa la Kiinjili la Kilutheri Tanzania*/KKKT (Evangelical Lutheran
Church in Tanzania) – and its footprint are geographically concentrated
in Arusha, Kilimanjaro, and other adjacent northern regions, making an
ideal counterpart to a political party that shares many of its core values
of freedom and human dignity. His career had a brief hiatus while he
earned a divinity degree. After completing his degree, he worked within

example, a doctor at a public hospital is considered to be in the health sector, but the
public relations officer who represents that hospital on behalf of the government is considered to be in a government position. A private attorney defending a client works in
the legal sector (a category that falls under "Other" career sectors), while an attorney
who prosecutes the case, the police officers who may provide evidence during trial, and
the commissioner of the district in which the case takes place are government employees. As such, this category captures positions that are not held by technocratic or skilled
employees in publicly run institutions but generally are political positions within the
government. More detail is found in Appendix B.3.

TABLE 5.1 *Vocational career sequence examples*

	Career Years																											
	1	2	3	4	5	6	7	8	9	10	11	12	13	14	15	16	17	18	19	20	21	22	23	24	25	26	27	28
Tundu Lissu	O	O	N	N	O	O	O	O	O	C	C	C	C	C	C	C	C	C	N	N	-	-	-	-	-	-	-	-
Rev. Israel Natse	O	O	N	N	N	N	N	N	C	C	C	C	C	C	C	C	C	C	C	C	C	C	C	-	-	-	-	-
Capt Komba	O	G	G	G	G	G	G	G	G	G	G	G	G	G	G	P	P	P	P	P	P	P	P	P	P	P	P	-
Capt Chiligati	P	P	G	G	G	G	G	G	G	G	G	G	G	G	P	P	P	P	P	P	P	P	G	G	G	-	-	-

Notes: C=Civil Society Organization, P=Party, G=Government, O=Other, N=Non Sequences terminate when an individual enters the legislature the KKKT as a pastor and in various outreach and management capacities from 1994 until entering Parliament in 2010. Notably, the previous MP from Karatu was Wilbrod Peter Slaa. Slaa was CHADEMA's 2010 presidential candidate and a religious leader who honed his leadership craft in the Catholic Church as a youth leader and later a priest. The first years of Israel Natse's vocational career were spent in public education, while the remaining nearly seventeen years in the KKKT correspond with about 90 percent of his career in the NGO/CSO sector.

Captain John Damiano Komba's storied path to the legislature has already been introduced in some detail: the core of his early work was performed in the JWTZ, tasked with the responsibility of enhancing support of and allegiance to the state and the CCM through the music of *kwaya*, adapted from colonial church music but "adequately cleansed of foreign connotations via the twin process of politicization and secularization" (Askew 2002, 251). When Tanzania reintroduced multiparty politics, Komba took on a new position as the leader of Tanzania One Theatre (TOT), which in his view "was a response to the introduction of multipartyism for the purpose of promoting CCM" (Askew 2002, 252). TOT's songs and dances carefully echoed campaign slogans and messaging from CCM, often in staged competitions between TOT and other prominent performance groups that were more critical of the government. TOT was known to disrupt opposition rallies and use its superior audio equipment to overpower the rallies with CCM campaign materials, "a forceful reminder of the effectiveness of TOT as a weapon for CCM" (Edmonson 2007, 127). Of his twenty-nine-year career before becoming an MP, nearly half was in government employment, the same proportion in party work through TOT, and the remaining one year in public education.

Captain John Chiligati moved between party and government jobs prior to being elected to *Bunge* from Manyoni Mashariki in 2000. He served in the legislature for three terms including stints in cabinet positions and, in retirement, was appointed to the board of trustees of CCM. His first twenty-five years were spent in school – earning both officer's credentials in military training and a BA in public administration from the University of Dar es Salaam – after which he became a regional staff member of TANU/CCM in 1975. He temporarily left party service during the Kagera War and its aftermath, during which he was a platoon commander and subsequently an instructor at the military facility where he trained. He returned to working for CCM for ten years as a personal assistant in the office of the chairman of CCM under Julius Nyerere and in other administrative capacities in the party headquarters. In the final eight years of his pre-legislative career, he was appointed a commissioner of various districts of Tanzania. His twenty-six-year-long pre-parliamentary career was in party employment for fourteen of them (54 percent) and government for the remaining twelve (46 percent).

In addition to illustrating political party employment for ruling party candidates, it is notable that Captains Komba and Chiligati both worked for the government. While formal party employment is comparably less common as a vocation prior to parliament, a substantial number of MPs worked in political positions within the Tanzanian government before entering office. Both of these accounts reinforce what is known of both autocracies and democracies around the world – government employment is a characteristic of political insiders and political insiders have advantages in running for and winning elected office.

5.3 STATISTICAL ANALYSIS OF VOCATIONAL CAREERS

So what is the impact of vocational careers on candidacy choices in electoral authoritarian regime? A multivariate statistical analysis of the Tanzanian legislator biographical data can help answer this question. As with previous analyses, the outcome of interest is becoming an opposition MP versus an MP for the ruling party CCM, and I want explain this outcome probabilistically. Does spending some or all of one's career working for nongovernmental organizations and as civic activists increase the chances that an individual is an opposition MP? Are those who made their careers working for a political party or in political positions in the government less likely to be in the opposition? Figure 5.1 visualizes what the analyses of these three career variables show, while controlling for a number of other factors that might influence party choice. As before, the y-axes in the figures indicate the probability of being an opposition legislator. Rug plots run along the x-axis of each figure that show the distribution of values in the dataset to give a sense of the spread of the data across the three vocational backgrounds.[3]

The top of panel of Figure 5.1 shows just how much civic activist experiences shape motivations to run for the opposition. The average time of a career spent in this sector is a little less than 10 percent and at that level, the likelihood of being an opposition MP is similar at about 10 percent. As an individual's career becomes more heavily dominated by

---

[3] Full results are found in Appendix B.3.

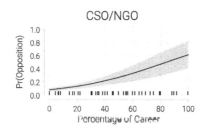

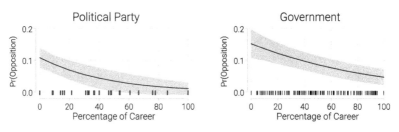

Shading shows 90% confidence interval. Rug plots show variable distributions.

FIGURE 5.1 Vocational career and opposition candidacy

CSO/NGO work, the odds that the individual represents the opposition in the legislature shoot up dramatically: increasing the percentage of a career in CSO work by one standard deviation corresponds with twice the chance of being in the opposition. The likelihood that individuals who spend all of their career in CSO/NGO work are opposition MPs is about 60 percent.

The nature of civic activist turned opposition MPs pathways varies widely, including local and international employers and a range of skills and sectors. Opposition MP Zitto Kabwe's career, for example, combined advocacy and activism experience with the National Youth Forum (NYF) and the Tanzania Gender Network Programme (TGNP) with more formal and politically useful training in the Fredrich Ebert Foundation associated with the Democratic Party in Germany. Other opposition legislators performed skilled, administrative, or research duties in organizations engaged in community development and health – from large organizations such as the Axios Foundation and Abbott Fund (Civic United Front's Kuruthum Jumanne Mchuchuli, a 2010 special seats MP) to local health advocates like KIWOHEDE (Kiota Women Health Development), where CHADEMA's Mhonga Said Muhwanya worked after a stint with global humanitarian relief organization International Rescue Committee (IRC). Religious organizations also feature in a number of opposition MPs' vocational backgrounds, particularly Catholic and mainline Protestant faiths.

Ruling party MPs are not completely lacking NGO or civic activist experiences, but the experience of CCM legislator Professor Anna Tibaijuka highlights how they differ. In the years immediately prior to becoming a legislator, she was the second-highest-ranking woman in the United Nations, including serving as the executive director of UN-HABITAT and a special envoy to the UN Secretary-General to report on a Zimbabwean government program to clear slums in urban areas.[4] She also was a tenured economics professor at the University of Dar es Salaam. Much of her initial international advocacy and policy experience came through government-sponsored/nominated delegations to various United Nations programs; her husband was a Tanzanian diplomat, serving as an ambassador for most of the 1990s. Professor Tibaijuka's pre-parliamentary career in international development and politics is remarkable and prestigious, but not one that would be expected to lead to anti-government activism or opposition candidacy.

Party work has the completely opposite effect of civic activism on opposition prospects, which is seen in the bottom left panel of Figure 5.1. For someone whose employment resembled that of Captains Komba and Chiligati – where roughly half of their careers was spent working in party service – the likelihood of that parliamentarian being from the opposition is about 4 percent. For those who worked their entire careers in a political party, there is basically no chance they represent the opposition. Within this sample of legislators, seventeen from CCM spent their entire careers working for CCM. For example, Mary Pius Chatanda, a women's seat appointee who entered Parliament in 2010 at the age of fifty-one spent all twenty-two years she was employed in various positions with CCM. When she was sixteen, Chatanda worked as a secretary in the party's youth organization *Umoja wa Vijana wa CCM* (UVCCM) and at the district and regional levels and later in the national party office. Her vocational career pathway mirrored career partisanship in CCM as well and this is especially common among women who were appointed to Parliament in women's quota reserved seats. We will return to Mary Chatanda's story in a later discussion.

Lastly, the bottom right panel of Figure 5.1 shows there is a significant, negative relationship between employment in political positions in government and becoming a legislator for the opposition. Recall that

---

[4] Interestingly, the UN report of Mugabe's "Operation Murambatsvina" was critical of the Zimbabwean government, suggesting ZANU-PF was disproportionately targeting urban areas with high rates of opposition support, a criticism Tanzania's opposition has echoed about policies of its own government.

government positions refer to a specific type of public employment that is political or related to the production of state power; they do not include positions held by technocratic or skilled employees in publicly run institutions (e.g., teachers and doctors at public schools and hospitals).

Work in government is comparably more common than the other two types of career experience, with nearly half of ruling party MPs working in government positions prior to entering the legislature and about 20 percent of opposition MPs. Nonetheless, incremental rises in the percentage of a career spent in government work corresponds with a marked decrease in the chances a legislator represents the opposition. Moving from spending one's entire career in a political position in government to spending no career years at all in such positions maps onto three times the likelihood of being an opposition MP.

This section has reinforced the overarching message that guides this chapter: opposition versus ruling party candidacy choices are not single-shot calculations, but journeys through which personal life experiences forge pathways to office that lead to the opposition or away from it. Vocational career data drawn from past and current Tanzanian legislators make clear the implications of working in civil society and nongovernmental organization: it provides a framework for political and social action that underlies the goals of the political opposition. By the time one considers running for office, as the stories of Ismail Jussa and James Mbatia, and others like Tundu Lissu and Zitto Kabwe show, the set of options for party choice has narrowed to challengers. Like all of these examples, bridges toward the ruling party have long-since been burned and even if they were not, the ruling party has little to offer to them. By contrast, both political party work and government employment establish avenues to ruling party candidacy for the legislature. In authoritarian regimes, the lines between political government jobs and those in the ruling party are often blurred, and CCM legislators often worked in both types of positions before entering Parliament and Zanzibar's House of Representatives. It is clear that when one has invested in institutions of the state and the regime, increasing benefits come from furthering the investment in the form of elected office in the ruling party.

5.4 STATISTICAL ANALYSIS OF POLITICAL PARTY CAREERS

The second set of sequences captures career partisanship and indicates for each individual whether or not they held a political party leadership position in a given year within their sequence. The purpose of this section is to augment our understanding of candidacy choices to run with the opposition and how they are shaped by activist pathways by further examining the alternative path to elected office: career partisanship. Unlike vocational careers, where spending a year in a given sector is zero-sum in that each year in activism means one fewer year available to work in a political position in government, political party careers are a little murkier: one may hold multiple positions in a party at a given time in a way that does not necessarily preclude other investments in, say, civic activism. The narratives of Ismail Jussa and James Mbatia certainly illustrate this is the case; they both were members of their respective party's secretariat before they became legislators. I have claimed that generally party service is less common among opposition legislators; when it occurs, as in the cases of Ismail Jussa and James Mbatia, it is qualitatively different from the concepts underlying career partisanship. This section further unpacks party service toward show how career partisanship is a path away from the opposition and to the ruling party.

I start by describing in more detail what constitutes a political party service sequence. This is derived from self-reports on legislator biographies. The bios have standardized fields and non-vocational party service is recorded under a "political experience" (as opposed to "employment history") field. The information reported in this field typically indicates the level of office within the party hierarchy, the years the position is/was held, and some additional information about the position, like title or department. I further simplify this information into one of four states: not having a party position or holding a position at either the local, subnational (district, regional), or national office of a political party.[5] Unlike a vocational career sequence, which begins at the time of formal employment, there is no natural "starting point" of a career partisanship sequence. I choose to begin each sequence when an individuals turns eighteen, the age at which most citizenship rights of adulthood are extended to Tanzanians. Starting the sequences at age eighteen will ignore some party service taking place before that age, for example, those who are involved in CCM's Pioneers program that begins in school. This may understate the prevalence of party service in particular for CCM MPs, who have more extensive party programming aimed at youth who are not yet eligible to vote, meaning estimates of the impact of party service on party choice for MPs is conservative. From age eighteen, each subsequent

---

[5] A more complex coding of party positions that includes six office levels and differentiates position types by their prestige underlies the more simplified version presented here; details of the full coding scheme are found in Appendix B.3.

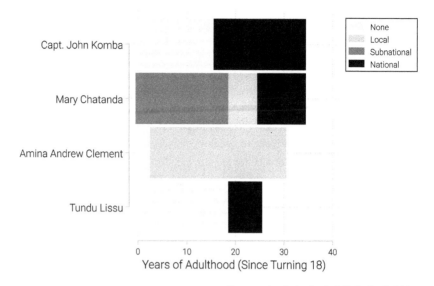

Sequences terminate when individual enters legislature

FIGURE 5.2 Career partisanship sequence examples

year within that sequence is characterized by whether or not that individual held a party position and, if so, the level within the party hierarchy where that position is located. A sequence ends when that individual enters the legislature, and variable sequence lengths correspond with MPs being different ages when entering office. Figure 5.2 depicts the career partisanship sequences of several CCM legislators and CHADEMA's Tundu Lissu.

The top of the figure shows the sequence of Captain John Komba, who was introduced earlier. Born in 1954, his sequence begins in 1972 when he turned eighteen. His military career – first in combat during the Kagera War and then as the musical director – was in service of the state and the ruling party, including writing and performing songs to celebrate and commemorate anniversaries of CCM's time in power. However, it was not until 1987 that he took on a formal position within the political party as a member of its National Executive Committee, the central decision-making board in the party's secretariat. His sequence is thus coded as featuring no party service from 1972 (year 0) till 1986 (year 15) and his national party position from 1987 until 2005, when he entered the Parliament of Tanzania.

Directly below his sequence that of is Mary Pius Chatanda. She began with the district- and regional-level positions in UVCCM at sixteen, as discussed earlier. She also performed a short stint in a high-prestige position in her *diwani* (ward); before entering *Bunge* in 2010, she was in the national leadership of *Umoja wa Wanawake-Tanzania* (UWT), the party's women's wing. In total, Mary Chatanda performed party service for thirty-six years before becoming an MP, thirty-four of which are represented in her sequence in Figure 5.2. This is emblematic of the extensive, dedicated service ruling party candidates demonstrate in electoral authoritarian regimes. Women's quota seat members in Tanzania are nominated by a party selectorate of women's wing members rather than directly elected by voters, elevating the premium of career partisanship in the eyes of UWT members responsible for choosing special seat nominees.

Amina Andrew Clement was also selected as a special seats member in 2010. Born in 1963, she became a party activist at the lowest level of CCM party organization at age twenty in 1983 – a *nyumba kumi* or "ten cells" leader. The ten cell is a political unit composed of ten households initially formulated in the 1960s under TANU rule and it remains a critical force in mobilization. As former CCM ideology and publicity secretary Nape Nnauye noted, "Our leaders at Ten-cell level ... move from house to house to offset opposition's indoctrination" (James 2015). After twenty years, she became the treasurer of the party for its *diwani* office. For the three years prior to being nominated to the *Bunge*, Clement was a campaigner and promoter in her constituency of Koani.

The final sequence is that of Tundu Lissu, the human rights and environmental activist turned opposition leader who has been a thorn in the side of the government during his career as a legislator. As described earlier, most of his experiences leading to politics occurred outside the context of party politics. He had a long career as an attorney and NGO activist in the Tanzania-based Lawyers' Environmental Action Team (LEAT), in addition to a three-year stint in the World Resources Institute, an international environmental advocacy NGO based in Washington, DC. His sequence does include a brief period of service in a political party – he became the director of law of CHADEMA in 2004 and served in that position in the six years prior to becoming Singida West's elected MP.

Many opposition MPs perform some party duties prior to becoming legislators; both Ismail Jussa and James Mbatia had mission-critical roles in Civic United Front and NCCR-Mageuzi, respectively, in advance of their legislative careers. What distinguishes those positions from the concept of career partisanship that underlies ruling party candidacy is that they are national, high-prestige, and highly skilled. Ismail Jussa was the personal assistant of CUF presidential candidate Maalim Seif for years because of their close, personal relationship and because of Jussa's deft and indispensable skills in navigating the political needs of the party and its leadership to deliver reform and change. Mary Chatanda's and Amina Clement's experiences were characterized by performing low-level "grunt work" for the party, while Captain Komba's service was explicitly tied to the image of the party and its popularity. By contrast, Tundu Lissu, Ismail Jussa, and James Mbatia harnessed skills derived from the professional experiences that enable the opposition to enhance its impact on goals bigger than any specific party, and those are delivered at the level of the party secretariat. January Makamba is not particularly representative of this career partisanship form, perhaps owing in part to his familial linkage to the power centers of CCM.

Analyzing Career Partisanship Sequences

I analyze these career partisanship sequences by focusing on three related questions: (1) Do career partisanship sequences reflect more extensive – in episodes of positions held – careers for opposition versus ruling party legislators? (2) Are career partisanship sequences longer for ruling party versus opposition legislators? (3) Are opposition and ruling party sequences more similar within versus across party? I proceed with these three questions sequentially.

Career Partisanship Extensiveness and Duration

First, I address whether sequence length differs for ruling party versus opposition legislators. I argued that demonstrating loyalty and developing political capital through party service were critical in shaping later ambitions to run for office with the ruling party. Survey data showed that a greater duration of formal partisanship was positively correlated with ruling party candidacy, as was service in regional party offices. Using legislative career sequences, I am able to more comprehensively study the impact of party service on candidacy.

The average CCM legislator had 1.8 episodes of party service; more than five percent of CCM legislators had five or more episodes. By contrast, opposition legislators averaged 1.5 episodes. This difference is statistically significant at conventional levels.[6] The most frequent form of

---

[6] A difference of means test comparing the CCM mean (1.802) with opposition mean (1.493) is significant, with a p-value of 0.015.

career partisanship for opposition legislators was *not having one* at all – that is, running for office without having served in any party position. Combined with legislators who held only one position prior to candidacy, this constitutes nearly two-thirds of opposition MPs. By contrast, CCM legislators most commonly held one position prior to candidacy, followed by the second most common pattern holding one position and switching to another.

A second indicator of party service focuses on the amount of time an individual invests within a political party. I measure the total number of years across all party positions an individual held prior to candidacy.[7] Here, too, we observe that stints of party service for opposition legislators are on average about two years shorter.[8] About 25 percent of ruling party legislators served more than fifteen years; 12 percent surpassed 20 years, compared with 15 percent and 2 percent of opposition legislators, respectively.

Studying the total years in which an individual held a party position and the number of episodes of party service focuses on features within the sequences of legislators. I conclude the discussion of career partisanship with analyses of partisanship sequences in their totality to evaluate the overall comparability of opposition versus ruling party candidates.

Career Partisanship Sequence Similarity

I have theorized that career partisanship is a legislative path away from the opposition and toward the ruling party. In elaborating this theory, and through the narratives of Tanzanian politicians, I highlighted two related versions of this journey. One fits the experience of Amina Andrew Clement, who entered low-level party service shortly after turning eighteen and remained there for three decades before successfully being nominated to *Bunge* by CCM in a women's quota seat. The other was Mary Chatanda's, one of incrementally climbing the ranks within the party for the chance to fight for a spot in Tanzania's Parliament. A third possible type of party service concentrates solely at the national level and/or in the party secretariat, something observed for both MPs like Captain John Komba and among opposition legislators like Ismail Jussa, James Mbatia, and Tundu Lissu.

I now carry out sequence analyses that draw upon these three pathways and use them as ideal types. The first is the low-status, long slog of

---

[7] This measurement excludes from analysis all individuals who held no positions at all.
[8] A difference of means test comparing the CCM mean (10.304) with the opposition mean (8.777) is significant, with a p-value of 0.040.

party service, holding a ward-level party position for the duration of the sequence. This account best captures the view of career partisanship as a long courtship between a distrustful ruling party fearful of disloyalty and dissent and a potential future candidate who is cultivating loyalty, access, and influence with a party during this commitment. A second ideal type is of the same length and captures a similar pattern of long-term cultivation of loyalty and trust, but through a ladder-climbing process spent in comparable time periods at each level. The third ideal type captures an unvaried pattern of party service, but at the highest levels of the party: the secretariat. The average legislator in the sample became an MP at age forty-nine, so these ideal-type sequences are twenty-nine years in length.

I analyze measures of similarity to these ideal-type sequences created through optimal matching. As introduced in Chapter 3, these measures capture how many arithmetic operations must be performed to make a legislator's career partisanship sequence identical to an ideal-type sequence. Each operation has a specified cost and, thus, the more different a sequence is from an ideal type, the higher the value.[9] Following previous analyses, the dependent variable of interest indicates if a legislator whether or not an opposition MP. If my theory is correct, higher optimal matching scores (indicating greater dissimilarity from the three ideal types) will be positively correlated with status as an opposition MP.

Figure 5.3 visualizes the results from analyses of the optimal matching data. Each panel within the figure strikingly illustrates the strong influence of career partisanship on legislative candidacy choices. The top panel of the figure corresponds with the ideal type of an unvaried period of low-level party service. The most similar observation in the dataset to this ideal type has about a 9 percent chance of being the opposition. As one becomes maximally dissimilar from the low-status ideal type, these odds jump to nearly 50 percent. The bottom-left panel corresponds with climbing the ladder of party service and the results are similar: those who are most different from ladder climbers like the ideal type are more likely to be opposition MPs (52 percent). Those most similar to career partisanship in the form of incrementally more prominent party service only have about one in nine odds of being an MP for a challenger party. Career partisanship at the elite, national-level party office separates opposition

---

[9] For analyses presented here, I use a substitution matrix that follows my theory in that larger movements (local to secretariat) are costlier than smaller ones (local to regional) but is symmetric (local to regional is the same as regional to local). I describe this approach and the robustness of alternatives in Appendix B.3.

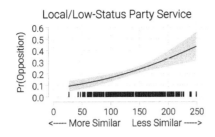

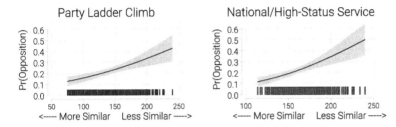

Shading shows 90% confidence interval. Rug plots show variable distributions.

FIGURE 5.3 Career partisanship and optimal matching distance

and CCM legislators even more than the other two ideal types. Going from the legislator who is most like the national-level party service ideal type to the one who is least like to corresponds with a seven fold greater probability of being an opposition MP (7 percent to 51 percent). This last result is important. While several of the opposition leaders whose experiences have guided this chapter and the text generally took on important, high-prestige positions in the secretariat of their parties before running for office, the legislators with extensive party service at the national level are on average the least likely to run for the opposition.

The sequence analysis presented here – considered alongside consideration of length and variable party service – coheres with what was borne out with legislator survey data. While the path to opposition is a channel through civic activism and careers in civil society and nongovernmental organizations, an alternate route to office from career partisanship in political and vocational backgrounds feeds into the ruling party. This is viewed across several forms of party service, including tenure in low-level offices, climbing across levels, and even at the elite national level. As the sequence analysis and narratives of Ismail Jussa and James Mbatia show, opposition candidacy sometimes reflects no party service; other times their sequences feature elite party service. Even that party service, though, is due to the skills and reputation developed by these individuals in civil society, through student activism and participation in other social organizations outside formal politics.

CONCLUSION

This chapter and the one that preceded it have illuminated the importance of early onset civic and political party activism in trajectories into political office. Most approaches to candidacy that emphasize "ambition" and strategic decision making focus on individuals after they have obtained office. Studying the role that civic activism versus career partisanship plays in candidacy decisions highlights how what appears to be strategic choices are actually owed to path dependencies forged in early life events. But these paths cannot alone explain why people act on underlying ambitions to become a legislator. After all, most civic activists and career partisans will never feel motivated to run for office and the subset of individuals who act on that ambition are even fewer. The next chapter is the first of four that will study the strategic choice to run for office and begins by looking at the first competition a prospective candidate must win to run for office: party nominations.

6

Winning Party Nomination Contests

Ngozi ya paa haikai watu wawili
The hide of a gazelle does not seat two people.

James Mbatia was integrally involved in the transition to multiparty politics in Tanzania during the 1990s and a founding member of NCCR-Maguezi. Thus, he won NCCR's nomination for his home constituency of Vunjo with ease in Tanzania's 1995 multiparty elections. By the time January Makamba and Ismail Jussa sought office, Mbatia's party had largely fallen out of political relevance and he had been out of Parliament for ten years. He nonetheless remains a titan among the first generation of opposition leaders in the country and has been nominated to the NCCR ticket in each of Tanzania's five multiparty elections to date.

Ismail Jussa's contest to win Civic United Front's nomination for the Zanzibar House of Representatives election in *Mji Mkongwe* (Stone Town) was more competitive than any of Mbatia's. Jussa told me in a 2019 interview that he decided he would run after he had been sought out by young constituents who "pushed" him to take the lead and he accepted their call. Even Stone Town's incumbent opposition house member Fatma Fereji encouraged him to vie for the seat; she could vacate the seat and remain in the legislature through a reserved quota seat for female legislators. Fereji ultimately remained in the contest – Jussa thinks she was persuaded by elders fearful of political change – but he still won nearly two-thirds of the primary vote. Two additional competitors secured a few percents of ballots, with the remaining 30 percent or so belonging to Fatma Fereji. Jussa told me that to win the party's nomination he "didn't really have to work that hard because it was a foregone conclusion that I was the choice of the people in Stone Town."

A number of factors made January Makamba's 2010 nomination easier than the norm for CCM. The son of CCM heavyweight Yusuf Makamba and the personal confidant and aide of Jakaya Kikwete, the incumbent president who was standing for reelection, January benefited from name recognition among CCM members who would vote in the primary for Bumbili. He was facing an incumbent who was vulnerable. William Shelukindo dominated three parliamentary elections (winning 91 percent, 87 percent, and 83 percent of the vote); was the fifth most active MP in *Bunge* from 2005 to 2010; and had support in the party, having served as a permanent secretary in the prime minister's office before entering Parliament. However, he relied heavily on these existing sources of support, in spite of his age (seventy-seven in 2010) and growing frustration among tea farmers over how he managed his purchasing cooperative. While Shelukindo was "taking people for granted," January was differentiating himself by recruiting new party members; mobilizing youth and women supporters; weaponizing tea politics; and emphasizing his youth, education, and party credentials. He ran an actual campaign to win the party nomination and the *kura za msingi* (primary) nomination contest was "like the actual [election] vote": the party produced professional ballots and aspirants canvassed, gave speeches, and sought support for nearly a month. In the end, he won with nearly 80 percent of the vote, beating out the incumbent and seven other hopefuls.

While his experience was easier than that of many, he mentors young CCM leaders regarding party service:

They wait, they invest, they work in a party because they know that that somehow will count when party nominations are decided. Yes, everybody knows that it's important to have that in your CV that they're being involved. ... For UVCCM, the rationale of its servicemen was that people pay at CCM and the country leaders, so some go through there. One of the criticisms of the decision making of getting into politics is that it is hard [to get into]. So, people use UVCCM and CCM as stepping stones as positions of leadership for member of parliament and so on. It has become common now.

The previous two chapters offered insights on how individuals' early-life experiences shape downstream decisions regarding candidacy. I now turn to understanding what shapes the calculations prospective candidates engage in when considering whether or not to run for office. As discussed in developing the book's theory, this effort will focus on the benefits of candidacy, the costs of candidacy aspirations, and the prospects of winning nomination and election contests. These parameters will shape this chapter and the three that follow it. The current chapter looks to the first institutional barrier to becoming a legislator after deciding to pursue that ambition: party nomination.

The experiences of Ismail Jussa, January Makamba, and James Mbatia will reverberate throughout analysis in the pages that follows. Opposition legislators face an easier route to ballots for the general elections. In many cases, aspirants face no opponents in the nomination process for a challenger party. There is variation within parties across space and time; Ismail Jussa's 2010 contest was comparably more competitive for an opposition contest in part because the incumbent was a standout in her own right – very few women in Zanzibar are directly elected to the legislature through constituency seats – and because the party performs strongly in Zanzibar's urban capital. Consistent with the intuition that nomination and election competition are inversely related, this was a competition that *should* have been more fierce than most opposition ones are. Critically, Jussa attributes his success in the contest and the relative ease by which he achieved it to his history of civic activism. From early student activism to his later involvement in the Zanzibari autonomy movement, he was the choice of Zanzibari's youth and this résumé is what led them to convince him to take party nomination forms. The same base of supporters delivered his nomination victory.

Makamba won a nomination by defeating William Shellukindo. This account illustrates several important lessons that the pages that follow will emphasize. Securing ruling party nominations in electoral authoritarian regimes is difficult and renomination even harder. In Tanzania, ruling party incumbent MP renomination rates are lower than 40 percent on average and in some years are lower than 30 percent. Shelukindo's vulnerability stemmed not from his performance as a legislator, which was stellar, but from his alienating local CCM supporters over constituency service issues and a concern that this was costing CCM support on election day. Moreover, while January Makamba's nomination experience may have been comparably easier than that of many CCM candidates, it still was quite difficult. He secured the nomination by running a professional campaign and capitalizing on the weaknesses of the incumbent's performance in the community. Yet, his educational, professional, and party credentials were unrivaled across the entire country, much more so within his own constituency. He had just left employment with the most powerful political figure and the leader of CCM, the first-term President Kikwete who was all but guaranteed a second. January's father helmed the party through many years of the single-party era. And yet, Makamba faced an incumbent MP and seven other competitors in the 2010 nomination contest. For someone of his party pedigree and political skill matched with an extensive, professional nomination campaign, he was about the best CCM members could ask from a leader. Based on these qualities, winning 80 percent of the vote frankly seems too low and is testament to a real ceiling of support any ruling party nomination seeker can secure.

The chapter begins by discussing insights on procedures parties use for candidate selection. It briefly summarizes candidate selection in Tanzania, an important step in unpacking the context in which candidate aspirants compete. I then analyze what shapes the probability of winning a nomination in the final three sections of the chapter. Next, I focus on aspirant perspectives toward candidate nomination prospects across parties and unpack the realities of nomination experiences of Tanzanian aspirants, drawing on insights from their own nomination contests. Finally, I link civic activism to nominations, showing that prospective candidates are more likely to seek nominations with opposition parties and also more likely to win them if they have greater experience and engagement with civic activism.

6.1 CANDIDATE SELECTION IN ELECTORAL AUTHORITARIAN REGIMES

How parties choose their candidates can help or hurt the party. In settings where clientelism is widespread, holding primaries is thought to benefit the opposition mainly because ruling parties stand to lose much more by following suit by nominating candidates via a primary. As the argument goes, primaries can lead to intraparty conflict over the outcome and losing primary candidates can defect to other parties or run as independents (Ichino and Nathan 2013). Moreover, opposition nomination seekers are not expected to distribute clientelism but ruling party counterparts are and thus may empty out campaign war chests prematurely before the general election. Therefore, in a scenario where all parties use similar selection procedures, primaries might help the opposition by hurting it less than they do the ruling party. Introducing party primaries can also provide an electoral bump for the candidates they yield.

Primaries emphasize broad popularity among the electorate (Carey and Polga-Hecimovich 2006) and require campaign skills (Serra 2011) more than selection via party leaders, and these assets translate into general election performance. But in electoral authoritarian regimes, this primary bonus for opposition parties may not hold. Opposition parties face such resource asymmetries that *any* money spent on primary campaigns has consequences for what can be marshaled to finance election campaigns. Due to inexperience, parties may bungle managing primaries and thus create the same costly fallout ruling parties face. Opposition candidate supply pipelines can lack trained, well-seasoned politicians and primaries can yield nominees who are popular but will not succeed as a legislator. This points to competing incentives for opposition parties to hold primary contests and a pathway to candidacy for qualified aspirants without significant barriers.

For ruling parties, various candidate selection methods also have different appeals. While primaries can be costly both economically and in the internal fallout their outcomes generate, they also have distinct advantages. Primaries allow the party to "bypass party activists to appeal to the rank-and-file voters" (Field and Siavelis 2008, 631). In majoritarian systems, the localized nature of primary contests helps parties respond to pressures to allow local participation and influence in politics and may minimize the collateral damage caused by spurned nomination seekers, who cannot claim being overlooked by party leaders and instead must attribute their lack of success to being unpopular in the eyes of everyday citizens.

The goal of using regular party members rather than activists to select leaders may be especially desirable if party discipline in the legislature is strong. Potential damage from legislators deviating from party policy goals is less likely simply because of their stranglehold over the legislature. With legislative majorities, and often supermajorities, the ability of a single legislator to influence policy away from the ruling party's goals is minimal. Party caucuses and whips can enforce intraparty discipline and punish deviators by stripping members of their posts.[1] This enforces party discipline within the legislature, alleviating potential consequences of allowing regular members to select candidates in primaries.

Another possible reason ruling parties use primaries to select their candidates is that primaries are a party's way of paying lip service to constituency demands while keeping final decisions about the fitness of

---

[1] This occurred to a former minister and CCM representative in Zanzibar in 2013. Mansoor Himid was removed from the party for promoting positions on constitutional reform that conflicted with the party's stated policy.

candidates at the party's center. This has historically been the case in Tanzania and is documented for the Botswana Democratic Party and the People's Democratic Party (of Nigeria), two dominant parties in sub-Saharan Africa (Ohman 2004). These parties hold primaries but the final candidate list is ratified by the party secretariat. As Rahat and Hazan (2001, 313) note,

> if the parties maintain, or reassert, control over certain phases in the candidate selection process, the phenomenon of democratization need not lead to a loss of control for the party organization, nor to a decline in its functional capacities ... the party can still remain the master of its internal fate.

Long-time ruling parties also introduce primaries when facing growing competition from opposition parties. They also devolve central party power through primaries, which may help hold opposition challengers at bay. Research points to this response by two long-term incumbent parties – in the case of the Partido Revolucionario Institucional in Mexico and the Norwegian Labour Party – which used the strategy when facing increasing pressure from opposition parties (Rahat and Hazan 2001). It also allows partisans to punish ruling party incumbents without costing the party voter support on election day.

6.2   CANDIDATE SELECTION IN TANZANIA

The first formalized legislative candidate selection procedures for Chama Cha Mapinduzi were introduced while the party was still operating in mainland Tanzania ("Tanganyika") as the Tanganyikan African National Union (TANU). Alongside Tanzania's shift to single-party rule in 1965, CCM/TANU constituted a system whereby its secretariat vetted and issued lists of approved candidates to compete against one another in constituency-level contests for legislative seats (Southall 2006, 234). Specifically, the 1965 constitution permitted "people some freedom of choice in electing their MPs. In each constituency the electorate [could] choose between two candidates officially selected by a district party conference consisting of approximately seventy-five local political leaders. The central party leadership retain[ed] the right to finally approve the candidates recommended by the local conferences" (Hyden and Leys 1972, 408).[2] Campaigns under these regulations were fairly restricted – with campaign

---

[2] Language is changed to past tense, reflecting that these rules applied at the time of publication of Hyden and Leys's (1972) article but do not any longer.

speeches limited to specific topics and exhibiting a significant amount of what Hyden and Leys (1972) call "political hygiene" (409) – they nonetheless led to the frequent defeat of prominent ministers at the hands of voters. Only 60 of 107 incumbent MPs stood for election in 1970 and of them, more than one-third of them lost their seats (Hyden and Leys 1972). Such legislative competitiveness continued even into the 1980s, when through a combination of party-candidate approval and the legislative elections themselves, nearly half of incumbent legislators did not return to office (Southall 2006, 234). In the 1986 party elections, a quarter of legislators lost their positions (Southall 2006, 242). Throughout this period, the presidency and chairmanship of CCM were voted upon by the National Executive Committee of the party (NEC-CCM (TZ))[3] during a party congress. Importantly, this process was credible to voters because it was systematically adhered to by the party (Morse 2019, 104).

From 1995 through the 2005 elections, Chama Cha Mapinduzi selected candidates through a multistage procedure, whereby the party's district committee produced a list of recommended candidates at its District Conference. These recommendations were sent for the Regional Committee's consideration at its Regional Conference and then finally passed along to the party secretariat, where CCM-NEC (TZ) produced the final list of candidates for active party members to consider before voting. CCM introduced a more direct primary system in 2007 that was implemented ahead of the 2010 elections (Ewald 2013). All CCM cardholders (it cost approximately $0.20) who could show their monthly membership fee was current ($0.06 per month) were allowed to participate in primary contests that were held at the branch level. CCM gave candidates specific guidelines regarding the nature of campaigning permitted and the time it could be carried out prior to the day of the primary. At each branch, candidates were allotted a few minutes to introduce themselves and to field questions from attendees. On August 1, 2010, all branches held primary elections that followed many practices of administering national elections – an "eligible voter" register, voting booths, and ballot boxes (Fjeldstad, Moss, Roop, and Weghorst 2010a, 5–7). Ballots were counted at the branch level and then sent to the district, where aggregation occurred under the supervision of party agents and leaders.

---

[3] To prevent confusion, "CCM-NEC (TZ)" designates the party's central organ for all of Tanzania, "CCM-NEC (ZNZ)" designates the party's central organ for Zanzibar, and "TZ-NEC" refers to the National Electoral Commission of Tanzania, which is tasked with voter registration and elections.

When counting was completed, results of the top three candidates were announced for some constituencies, while others were kept secret until the National Congress held by CCM-NEC (TZ) two weeks later. As a result of the primaries, 77 of 264 (almost 30 percent) incumbent legislators for CCM lost primary contests, including six members of the cabinet (Ewald 2013, 349). Then Deputy Secretary-General of CCM (Zanzibar) Ferouz reported that the primaries in Zanzibar had similar turnover rates, yielding "60 percent old faces and 40 percent new faces" (quoted in Fjeldstad et al. (2010a, 9)). The 2015 nominations had high turnover but lower rates than those seen in 2010: about 50 CCM MPs were ousted in primaries (Morse 2019, 153). They also featured a new local ethics vetting stage, modestly increasing constituency control over the preferential primary process (Morse 2019, 150). CCM retained preferential primaries in 2020 with similar results – 36 sitting MPs were voted out in polls at the constituency level, including cabinet members. The party exercised its power to determine who ultimately was on the election ballot in October 2020 and the decision of CCM's NEC to nullify some primary results and nominate alternate candidates was defended by CCM Ideology Secretary Humphrey Polepole as aiming to "protect the wider interests of the people, the party and the nation as a whole" (Namkwahe 2020). Notably, the size of the party's central government body NEC was been reduced by nearly half, in part due to an effort of President Magufuli to consolidate influence over the party and to further manage conflict and competition from the party's center outward (Andreoni 2017).

CUF uses primaries to select its parliamentary and local council (*diwani*) candidates (Ewald 2013), a system that was institutionalized in 2010. In Zanzibar, primary voters also may select their preferred Zanzibari presidential and House of Representatives candidates. Like CCM, participation in primaries is limited to members who have paid their party dues. Primaries are preferential insofar as CUF's National Executive Council (*Baraza Kuu*) has the final say in who represents the party in electoral contests. Unlike CCM, CUF's decision to overrule the preference of primary voters is generally due to candidate qualifications, particularly in Zanzibar where overall levels of educational attainment and candidate qualification are lower. As put by CUF's election director in Zanzibar, "sometimes we must remove the popular candidate simply because he/she lacks basic skills required to be a representatives member, sometimes as basic as reading and writing well."[4] The primaries themselves are organized in a fashion similar to those held by CCM.

[4] Then CUF Zanzibar election director Muhene Said Rashid, October 29, 2012.

CHADEMA uses branch- and constituency-based balloting processes to aggregate preferences of party members for their presidential, legislative, and councilor candidates. These rules were put into place in advance of the 2005 elections alongside a nationwide party mobilization and membership drive. The openness of the procedures in 2005 was comparably more democratic, as the primary decisions at the local level translated directly into the actual candidate selection process. In 2005, the party hosted conventions across national "zones," six areas of the country that each contained multiple regions of Tanzania.[5] In each of these zones, the party held large-scale rallies and a subsequent convention in which dues-paying members could vote for their preferred presidential and legislative candidates. These exercises were nonbinding. After the zonal conventions were completed, the party convened a special national conference in August 2005 to officially verify and endorse the preferences of primary voters for the coming elections (Mtei 2009, 211), just ahead of the official date set for the submission of candidate names to Tanzania's National Electoral Commission and the commencement of electoral campaigns. The procedure used in 2010 involved an upward cascading system by which names were submitted by constituency-level offices and taken into consideration first at the district level and subsequently at regional and national levels (Ewald 2013). The party secretariat ultimately decides which individuals will represent the party on the day of the elections.

New opposition party ACT-Wazalendo, founded by Zitto Kabwe in 2014 in advance of the 2015 elections, has grown in prominence since the beginning of this book project; this was accelerated by the nearly universal movement of CUF-Zanzibar leaders, members, and infrastructure into ACT. While the comparably small scale of the party did not require organized candidate selection methods across Tanzania, the party's constitution provides for constituency-level competition over nominations which are vetted in an upward-cascading fashion similar to CHADEMA (Sulley 2020).

This section has illustrated that the main parties in Tanzania utilize candidate selection procedures that combine elements of inclusiveness and decentralization with control still exercised from the party's center. CCM's decision to adopt member-based primaries in 2007 represents

---

[5] The amalgamation of regions into "zones" or "provinces" and the elimination of regional administration have been central to CHADEMA's election platform to reduce government expenditures and further devolve government to local structures.

TABLE 6.1 *Direction of candidate market, all MPs*

	Party Controls Market	Candidates Control Market	Mixture
CCM	58.0%	35.3%	6.7%
CUF	45.3%	30.7%	24.0%
CUF TZ	30.9%	52.8%	16.4%
CUF ZNZ	78.5%	10.7%	10.7%
CHADEMA	42.4%	32.9%	24.7%

Note: Difference of means tests for CCM versus CUF and CCM versus CHADEMA are significant at conventional levels ($p < .01$).

an instance of formally diluting power for the goals of reducing the consequences of selecting candidates unpopular with rank-and-file party members. The CCM system is far more well institutionalized, compared especially with those used by CHADEMA. To illustrate this summarily, I draw upon assessments from candidates themselves regarding nomination procedures used in Tanzania. Participants in the Legislator Survey reported if they believe the nature of candidate selection is "party-driven" or if qualified candidates can influence their fate by effectively marketing themselves to their party. The question captures an idea akin to a labor market where firms (parties) need employees (candidates) and employees in turn seek out positions in one or more firms.

Table 6.1 shows the distribution of responses to this question, where all respondents were asked to evaluate each party (their own and others) as to whether the party controls this market, candidates control it, or some mixture of both. As Table 6.1 shows, MPs from all parties saw the selection for CCM candidates as strongly controlled by the party. In opposition parties, where qualified candidates are fewer, it can be easier for one to stand out and perhaps utilize their value to the party to induce concessions like nominations. Table 6.1 distinguishes between CUF in mainland Tanzania where it is weaker and Zanzibar, where it won 49 percent of the presidential vote in 2010. Seeing CUF-Zanzibar's candidate selection procedures as regulated more by the party is also consistent with the argument that higher levels of electoral competition can induce parties to impose more regulation on the candidate market. By comparison to mainland Tanzania, legislators in Zanzibar also have lower levels of educational attainment and political qualifications, perhaps also explaining the central nature of CUF's Zanzibari candidate market.

6.3 CANDIDATE PERCEPTIONS OF NOMINATION PROCEDURES

Prospective candidates in electoral authoritarian regimes ultimately must decide whether or not to run for office and, when they do, to run on opposition or ruling party tickets. For the strategic candidacy framework to account for opposition candidacy under electoral authoritarianism, it must consider the joint probability of election and nomination victories: even if, all else equal, a ruling party seat is significantly easier to win, this election victory is conditional on nomination. This section explores perceptions of nomination procedures and the challenges of securing a nomination.

Chapter 2 cited scholarship showing nomination competitiveness is negatively correlated with election competitiveness: as a seat becomes easier to win in the general election for a given party, the contest for that party's nomination in that constituency becomes more difficult. It was further affirmed that for electoral authoritarian regimes and dominant party democracies where a ruling party monopolizes politics, the nomination and election trade-off exists nationally: ruling party nominations are generally more challenging (Giollabhui 2013, Langston 2006).

Participants in the Legislator Survey and Candidate/Noncandidate Survey were asked to assess the difficulties of primary contests in their party and other parties. Respondents also considered whether getting a nomination would have been harder or easier in other political parties. Opposition aspirants from the survey indicated nominations for CCM would have been harder at striking rates; about five in every six respondents said this.[6] By contrast, CCM members saw securing opposition nominations as less difficult than it was making it onto CCM ballots, with about two-thirds stating CUF nominations were easier and about 55 percent of respondents with respect to CHADEMA.[7] The lesson drawn from is that prospective candidates view opposition parties as easier to win a nomination than they do the ruling party. Asking respondents to evaluate all parties on this dimension allows us to consider why one party is more or less appealing than another. With the framework of strategic, utility-maximizing political leaders, this helps illustrate why prospective

---

[6] 84.1 percent of opposition legislators said getting a CCM nomination would have been more difficult; they viewed nominations in other opposition parties as about as hard as their nomination contest.

[7] 36.9 percent of CCM legislators said CUF nominations were harder; 46.7 percent of CCM legislators identified CHADEMA nominations as harder.

TABLE 6.2 *What barriers do nomination seekers face?*

	Number of Competitors	Competitor Quality	Nomination Procedures
CHADEMA Nom-Seekers	8%	23%	70%
CUF Nom-Seekers	7%	24%	70%
CCM Nom-Seeker	35%	16%	50%

Note: Differences of proportions for each category are significant at conventional levels.

candidates may prefer opposition parties in terms of the relative ease of nomination contests.

This affirms what we know of nominations in other electoral authoritarian regimes: difficulty of winning varies by party. We also have reason to believe they should vary by party. Some point to nomination difficulties being due to the number of competitors or others to the quality of aspirants (Key 1964, Mishler 1978, Stone and Maisel 2003). Procedures impact subjective perceptions of difficulty – a party insider, for example, might view less centralized and more inclusive procedures as a greater barrier to nominations because they dilute the role of party elites in selection, while a locally popular, upstart aspirant may prefer such procedures because of the role they give everyday citizens. So if all legislators recognize that CCM nominations are more difficult to obtain, why is that the case? Is the difficulty nomination seekers face for the opposition driven by different reasons? Traction on this comes from returning to the same group of people – all nomination seekers included in the study – and asking them to identify why nominations are hard to obtain for aspirants of a given party. They were asked to review each political party and to identify the source of difficulty of obtaining nomination for the groups identified. Answers are grouped so that we can have opposition perspectives on what barriers ruling party nomination seekers face in getting to an election ballot and ruling party legislators weigh in on what they think constrains opposition aspirants from getting onto the ballot for a challenger party. Table 6.2 summarizes the perspectives of Tanzanian politicians on this.

The first thing that is evident in Table 6.2 is that all candidates see the nomination policies and procedures as the primary constraint on nominees, regardless of the party. This should not be completely surprising – consistent with views of party control over the candidate market found in Table 6.1, the nomination process is not a complete free-for-all where upstart candidates can simply demand representation on party tickets and parties are supposed to play some role as gatekeepers over nominations. What is of note, however, is the marginal difference between opposition and CCM nominations. While it accounts for less than half of responses of what drives difficulty for CCM nomination seekers, it is nearly three-quarters of those seeking nominations in both CHADEMA and CUF. Opposition parties do not need to gatekeep to ensure party loyalty or keep rivals at bay (as is the case for ruling parties in electoral authoritarian regimes) but to intervene in primary outcomes over issues of basic competency. According to opposition leadership in Zanzibar, for example, relying on aspirants with local popularity means the party must sometimes intervene in primary outcomes of issues of basic competency and substitute an alternative candidate.[8] This insight highlights the second impression gleaned from Table 6.2. Candidate competency is a more significant concern for opposition party nominations than it is for the ruling party. Few view lacking qualifications as a barrier to getting onto ruling party tickets, whereas this is a potential issue for opposition aspirants.

Most strikingly in the table, however, is that nearly five times as many respondents identify the number of competitors as an impediment to nominations for the ruling party than do those seeking opposition nominations. The results in the table echo the experiences of James Mbatia, January Makamba, and Ismail Jussa that opened the chapter: a star candidate for CCM, one who would be appointed to the cabinet only two years into his legislative career, faced eight other competitors including a three-term incumbent who was among the legislature's most active members. He had to run an extensive and professional campaign to beat out those competitors. Ismail Jussa faced an incumbent, but one who had endorsed his decision to run and was bested without extensive campaigning. James Mbatia secured his party's endorsement easily; as a party leader, he entirely controlled the process by which his name moved from aspirant to nominee. Having laid out the structural environment that parties create to shape nominations, the next section further elaborates on the perspectives of candidates and their nomination experiences.

6.4 CANDIDATE EXPERIENCES WITH NOMINATIONS

My theory proposes that primaries are more competitive for the ruling party versus the opposition in electoral authoritarian regimes. I assess this with two measures: the vote share required to win a nomination and simply the number of competitors standing against a prospective candidate.

---

[8] CUF Zanzibar election director Muhene Said Rashid, October 29, 2012.

The first strategy for testing this uses primary data collected from Zanzibar on contests for the House of Representatives and for the Parliament of Tanzania. One approach toward measuring primary difficulty is to look at whether or not primaries produce "consensus" candidates or individuals who are chosen with the majority or more of selectorate members. If primary winners on average net larger proportions of the selectorate – nearly supermajorities – this would indicate that the competitiveness faced by a qualified prospective candidate is low. Analyses of these data indicate that the percentage of primary votes taken home by the individual selected to be that party's candidate is significantly higher for CUF than CCM. The percentage of ballots won in primaries for the opposition versus CCM in Zanzibar is a little less than 20 percentage points higher for Parliament (64 percent vs. 47 percent), and the margin is similar for the House of Representatives (66 percent vs. 51 percent).[9]

The second approach toward assessing the difficulty of obtaining a nomination is the sheer number of individuals who are competing. Given that parties often put in place basic requirements to participate – signature thresholds, small fees, and so on – this also serves as an indication of the number of at least modestly qualified candidates in a given constituency. In these surveys, respondents from Tanzania and Zanzibar were asked to report the number of individuals who were competing for the same party nomination within their constituency.[10]

This pattern also holds true for objective primary data collected from contests in Zanzibar, which recorded the number of candidates in 140 primary contests held in the lead-up to the 2010 elections there. The mean number of competitors for MP and House of Representatives primaries in CUF is about two fewer than the number faced by their counterparts from CCM. Perhaps even more strikingly, nearly one-third of the primary contests for CUF were run without an opponent at all. These differences are summarized in Table 6.3.

Thus, ruling party primaries are more competitive in terms of the average number of candidates, as well as the consensus winning candidates obtain at the nomination stage. This fits with the assessments of

---

[9] The differences in means between CCM and CUF nomination seekers are significant for both legislative bodies at p<.01.

[10] This question was restricted to constituency seat members, as women's special seats are allocated akin to a countrywide multimember district and divided among parties based on the seat distribution of Parliament. Women's seats are also often chosen at a higher administrative level, like the region or district.

TABLE 6.3 *Number of competitors faced in nomination contests*

	Mean Competitors (Survey)	Mean Competitors (Zanzibar MP Primaries)	Mean Competitors (Zanzibar HoR Primaries)
CCM	7.0	5.6	4.7
CUF	3.2	3.6	2.7
CHADEMA	2.5	–	–
NCCR	0.5	–	–

Note: Differences comparing opposition and ruling party nomination contests are significant at conventional levels.

candidates of the nomination process in analyses we saw earlier – in comparison with what makes it difficult for opposition nomination seekers to get a slot on the electoral ticket; the sheer number of opponents one faces is a key impediment for ruling party aspirants. Note also that the objective primary data come from Zanzibar – among the most competitive regions in all of Tanzania – and thus, opposition candidates for the general election have a genuine chance of being elected in many constituencies. While such fine-grained primary data are not available for opposition nominations in mainland Tanzania, one would expect them to look much more like the information presented here: the majority of contests are won with no competitor.

Finally, it is notable that the competitiveness of nominations also impacts reelection bids. Opposition legislators can expect to face strong electoral challenges to second and subsequent terms, as even modest gains in opposition prospects can signal weakness in the ruling party and erosion of its stranglehold over power. On the other hand, many ruling party constituencies are locked in for that party with little threat of opposition challenge. I collected biographical profiles of 725 legislators in Tanzania from 1995 to 2010 and of them, 204 failed reelection bids due to either electoral defeat or defeat in a primary contest.[11] Table 6.4 summarizes the ways Tanzanian legislators exited the legislature. It highlights how

---

[11] Primary turnover is coded based on interviews with party elites and several news sources. Defeat via elections is an instance where an incumbent stood in a subsequent elections and lost. "Did not contest" records instances where candidates retired, took on other political positions like an ambassadorship, or did not compete for other reasons like death.

TABLE 6.4 *Legislative turnover in Tanzania*

	Nomination Defeat	Election Defeat	Did Not Contest
CCM	57.2%	11.4%	31.4%
CUF	5.9%	11.8%	82.4
CHADEMA	0.00%	81.2%	18.8%
NCCR	0.0%	100.0%	0.0%

Note: Differences comparing opposition and ruling party nomination contests are significant at conventional levels.

competitive nominations are for governing parties in electoral authoritarian regimes like Tanzania in comparison with opposition parities. Even when including legislative turnovers due to retirement, more than half of turnovers for CCM legislators come from losing nomination bids. By contrast, CUF, CHADEMA, and NCCR were defeated mostly defeated via election or did not contest reelection at all.

Finding such high rates of internal party expulsion from candidacy by CCM at first may seem shocking. Viewed in the history of Tanzania's long ruling party, however, it should not be. Incumbents being punished for absence from the constituency at the selectorate stage has long been the tradition in Tanzania, with prominent ministers being pushed out of CCM office by party members even under singlepartyism (Hyden and Leys 1972, 413). Thus, the 1970 ouster of TANU (CCM) Finance Minister Amir Jamal under single-party rule bears much continuity with the 2010 defeat of incumbent finance minister and businessman Phillip Sarungi via party primary. Such purges reentrench trust in the ruling party (Hyden and Leys 1972, 413). Research in other African contexts finds similar patterns: incumbent defeat in the party selectorate is common (Opalo 2019); this is particularly true in authoritarian regimes with well-defined succession procedures (Morse 2019).

So far, this chapter has highlighted two related points. First, prospective candidates perceive nomination prospects as more challenging for the ruling party across the board, no matter the party they are a member of and no matter the constituency they are from. Second, these perceptions are affirmed by the realities of their nomination experiences: CCM aspirants face significantly more competitors and, even after having won a seat, face fierce renomination contests. Together, these inform why prospective candidates might choose to seek nominations in the opposition. However, it does not link how histories leading up to this decision-making moment in civic activism versus career partisanship influence nomination choices and, ultimately, whether or not the choice over party nomination seeking is a "true" choice. The final empirical section addresses this.

6.5 HOW CIVIC ACTIVISM IMPACTS NOMINATIONS

Potential legislative aspirants with histories of civic activism face three choices when deciding whether or not to run for office: seeking an opposition party nomination, trying to run with the ruling party, or deciding not to seek a nomination and instead pursue a goal other than candidacy. However, the nature of civic activism experiences constrains these choices.

The previous two chapters showed that experience with grassroots mobilization and higher levels of associational membership were significantly more common among opposition candidates, whereas ruling party legislators demonstrated greater levels of career partisanship. We have seen example after example of Tanzanian legislators whose civic activism and careers in civil society organizations have rendered paths to politics that only point to the opposition: for both push and pull reasons, the real choice was between running with the opposition or not running at all. These experiences also shape how potential nomination seekers weigh their decision to run for office and how they assess their prospects in a multitude of ways. Subsequent chapters show that experiences in such activism account for the benefits prospective legislators expect from running for office and what they are willing to pay in campaign and non-campaign costs to get them. The remainder of the current chapter analyzes the impact of civic activism on opposition nomination ambition and prospects and contrasts this with career partisanship.

Does civic activism influence perceptions or performance in nomination contests for potential opposition candidates? In this section, I detail the role of civic activism in shaping the strategic action and nomination perceptions and performance of prospective candidates in the opposition. I do so by exploiting two types of comparison of opposition respondents possible with the Legislator Survey and Candidate/Noncandidate Survey: (1) nomination seekers versus prospective candidates who did not seek nominations and (2) candidates (nomination winners) versus nomination losers.

How does civic activism impact nomination perceptions and experiences in nomination contests? To investigate this, I return to the measures

TABLE 6.5 *Civic activism and opposition nominations*

	Nomination Seekers	Non-Seekers	Significant?
Civic Activism Index	1.99	1.60	✓
Grassroots Organizing	6.90	4.33	✓
	Nomination Winners	Nomination Losers	
Civic Activism Index	2.70	1.47	✓
Grassroots Organizing	7.33	6.26	p=.15

of civic activism introduced in Chapter 4. The first is an index that aggregates the number of civic organization types a prospective candidate was a past or current member of at the time of considering running for office. Recall that higher values of this variable indicate membership and/or leadership in organizations across a greater number of domain types, including student government, religious organizations, labor unions, professional associations, and local grassroots organizations. For comparing nomination winners versus losers, this measure also includes women's organizations.[12] The second measure captures the number of years that elapsed between first organizing a grassroots community meeting and considering seeking a nomination to run for office and is derived from the life history calendar. Two comparisons of potential aspirants are useful to address the role of civic activism on candidacy decisions. Comparing those who sought nominations versus those who did not can tell us something about the candidate-side impact and how it shapes ambition to run; comparing nomination winners with losers can inform how civic activism shapes nomination prospects.

Table 6.5 summarizes the overarching findings from these two comparison types. The first regards the impact of civic activism on the ambition to run. Of all the individuals who took nomination forms, does civic activism have an impact on who submits the forms to seek nomination versus those who ultimately decide to not do so? The answer is yes. People who followed through on the motivation to run for office by submitting completed nomination forms had about 50 percent more – a statistically significant difference of a little more than two and a half years – experience with grassroots organizing than those who credibly

[12] This measure for the comparison of nomination seekers and non-seekers excludes women's organizations because more than half of the sample of those who did not seek nominations were recruited from women's wings of opposition parties. This group reported much higher rates of membership in women's organizations.

considered running but did not return those forms. Associational membership points in the same direction in that nomination seekers were represented in more organization types than those who did not follow through on seeking nomination. The magnitude of the difference is also significant. Looking further into the components of this measure suggests what really differentiates nomination seekers along civic associations is not membership, but leadership responsibility in those organizations.[13] Those who have held any leadership position across the civic organization types are more likely to act upon motivation to run for office and individuals who hold leadership positions in a greater number of civic sectors seek out nominations at greater rates. Consistent with contextual information on Tanzania, student leaders are particularly more likely to submit forms for nomination.

Civic activism also appears to help aspirants who submit forms actually win nominations, with some qualification. Both measures of civic activism point in the direction of this intuition, but one of them does not achieve statistical significance. In terms of associational membership, nomination seekers who successfully made it onto opposition party ballots were members and leaders of organizations across a higher number of organization types compared with those who did not successfully secure nomination. The difference is substantively meaningful – it is greater than the difference of joining one additional organization type or being an official member versus a leader in an organization. Separating out the index into components, activists across organization types are consistently more successful – those who held any leadership position, those who hold a higher number of leadership positions, and more active members and/or leaders of nearly all organization types.[14]

The evidence is also suggestive that aspirants who won opposition nominations may have more experience in grassroots organizations. The magnitude of difference (almost one year of experience) is not large enough to achieve statistical significance. However, it is close. Furthermore, associational membership data show that members and leaders of grassroots/neighborhood associations are significantly more likely to win nominations compared with those who are not members, offering support for the overall idea that participation in grassroots organizations promotes opposition nomination chances. Nomination seekers with unimpressive civic activism credentials may be less appealing in the eyes

[13] These analyses are found in Appendix B.4.
[14] Supporting analyses are found in Appendix B.4.

of an opposition party or its supporters, limiting their ability to translate ambition to a candidacy opportunity. Those individuals who do not have sufficient capital in civic organizations but also do not self-select out of nomination contests (e.g., non-seekers) succeed less than often their more civically active counterparts.

CONCLUSION

Winning nominations to run for office is the first stage of political competition prospective candidates face once they have decided to try to run for office. It is potentially the most important – if one does not win a nomination, anticipated election prospects simply do not matter. Rational choice models of candidate strategy must take into consideration this critical step along the candidacy path. Because ruling party nominations are difficult to obtain in electoral authoritarian regimes, the inverse relationship between nomination and election prospects helps flatten the competitive asymmetries between ruling party and opposition candidates. When legislators decide to vie for a party nomination, however, their past trajectories may predetermine their fate. Civic activism backgrounds drive opposition nomination ambition and success. The next chapter focuses on the second parameter of the strategic candidacy framework and what happens when individuals are nominated to run: the general elections.

7

Winning General Elections

Aliyetangulia katangulia; afuataye akazane
The one who is ahead is ahead; the one who follows must make an effort.

Simbiko haisimbuki ila kwa msukosuko
A thing that is firmly fixed cannot be dislodged except with much trouble.

Ismail Jussa has run in three elections for the House of Representatives in Zanzibar. His 2010 campaign was comparably easy for an opposition candidate. In the months preceding the October general election, he was the right-hand man of CUF presidential candidate Maalim Seif as they led the historic peace-building process in Zanzibar. The result was a power-sharing proposal for the winner and loser of the approaching elections, and it went to a popular referendum three months ahead of the general election. When Zanzibaris voted in support of forming a Government of National Unity two-to-one (and 88 percent voted "Yes" in Jussa's constituency), it seemed clear he was poised for success. CUF was strong in urban Stone Town and his CCM opponent was Simai Mohammed Said, a candidate who lost to CUF's Fatma Fereji in 2005. Simai's campaign underplayed CCM party messaging – given the relative unpopularity of the party in the constituency – and instead promoted his experience in several tourism-related businesses as evidence that he could deliver better development and quality of life in Stone Town to youth leaders to whom Jussa appealed. He sought support from key business leaders, bolstered by his success helming a consortium of tourism investors.

Jussa's 2010 campaign, by contrast, combined national (and national-ist) messaging with extensive canvassing. Keeping the campaign content national, he emphasized the missteps of CCM in government and offered a vision of a more autonomous Zanzibar. In his words, the core message was that "You need someone who is vocal and whose party represents the aspirations of the Zanzibari people. In Zanzibar, CCM can never speak for Zanzibaris because it received its orders from the mainland. ... [Change] can only be done if there will be change at the national level for the islands." He split his time during the 2010 elections between his own effort to win Stone Town's seat in the Zanzibari legislature and leading the presidential campaign of Maalim Seif.

Either speaking at their *barazas* or receiving questions from them, going house to house, like door to door campaign. These were the main efforts done by me and by teams of women and young people who would also assist. ... We would do this in stronger areas like Stone Town and others as well ... because when you support your own voters who are loyal to you, they also like seeing they are being appreciated and recognized.

Jussa won the election with about 74 percent of the vote.

Fast-forward to October 2015 and Jussa's star had continued to rise in Zanzibari politics and in his constituency in spite of a changing polit-ical environment. The Government of National Unity had failed to fully deliver on the massive expectations of political, economic, and social change Zanzibaris expected. The momentum for Zanzibari autonomy had been disrupted by CCM, most notably in derailing a nationwide effort to modernize Tanzania's constitution that proposed devolving greater authority to the archipelago. Against this backdrop, he still secured more than 70 percent of the vote but would never take his seat. As returns for the Zanzibari presidency trickled in and appeared to point to opposition victory, the polls were unilaterally annulled by the Zanzibar Electoral Commission over dubious claims of fraud (Roop and Weghorst 2016). CUF boycotted a subsequent replacement election in March 2016, meaning CCM won Jussa's seat, along with every other constituency in Zanzibar. In spite of the public boycott, the opposition was still antago-nized and harassed by the ruling party, government, and military (Roop and Weghorst 2016).

In the interim between 2015 and the 2020 elections, Jussa hesitated about whether or not he seek office again. In the end, he decided to run because there was important work for him to do in the legislature: ACT-Wazalendo's mainland leadership committed to pursuing Zanzibari autonomy and the House of Representatives is where those reforms could be advanced. He lost in an October 2020 national election that observers noted featured higher rates of fraud, intimidation, and violence than ever before seen in Tanzania's multiparty history. Jussa paid mightily for his candidacy – he was kidnapped by police and disappeared on election day, rumored to be dead. He emerged several days later with bones broken in nine different places, a reminder of the costs opposition candidates face that I will further explore in Chapter 9.

January Makamba's first election campaign was one in which victory was guaranteed: while the incumbent William Shellukindo had won more than 80 percent of the vote in all three of his contests, January faced no opposition candidate and ran unopposed. He still ran a significant and professional campaign, something he describes with modesty as his "just going to say 'hello'" and that "we're ready to do this." His campaign emphasized a combination of reaching out to "influential voices" in his constituency, something he had already done in his effort to defeat the incumbent in the CCM primary as well as holding rallies, a sort of "show of force" for his campaign and the ruling party.

Elections in electoral authoritarian regimes exist, in large part, as vehicles for the ruling party to continue to rule. Much of the literature on electoral competition under authoritarianism identifies structural conditions imposed upon opposition candidates and how those structures limit their success. Yet, unlike closed autocracies, the probability of election victory is not universally zero for opposition candidates. Opposition candidates can and do win some seats in legislative contests under authoritarianism, even if the more common outcome is losing. Opposition candidates may exercise some agency over their campaign trajectories – effectively campaigning or shrewdly using limited campaign resources, representing a constituency type that is popular among voters, or delivering effectively on campaign promises while in office, in spite of the significant barriers to doing so. However, the tale of Ismail Jussa's three elections shows that there are no guarantees that winning an election means securing a seat in authoritarian regimes. As authoritarian leader Anastazio Somoza reportedly once told a defeated electoral rival, "You poor s.o.b., perhaps you won the voting, but I won the counting."[1]

This chapter explores what shapes election prospects for opposition candidates. It primarily does so from a candidate-centered perspective,

---

[1] Quoted in Alvarez, Cheibub, Limongi, and Przeworski (1996, 25).

considering specifically what opposition versus ruling party candidates do to win election contests. It begins by illustrating the underlying disadvantage opposition candidates face: they have much less money to spend on campaigns. I then turn attention to tactics that opposition candidates can use to exploit comparative advantages on the campaign trail, showing how opposition candidates differ from CCM candidates and what tactics differentiate opposition winners from losers. The final section links civic activism to candidate strategy, showing how experiences in various civil society organizations influence campaign expenditures and ultimately campaign success. This chapter empirically narrows its focus, drawing analytical insight from a subset of participants in the Legislator Survey and the Candidate/Noncandidate Survey: those individuals who have experience running for office. In other words, our gaze will now fall on individuals who sought nominations and succeeded in obtaining them, going on to compete in an election.

7.1 HYPER-INCUMBENCY AND CAMPAIGN RESOURCES

How uneven is the playing field in which opposition candidates compete against governing party candidates? While many factors contribute to the disadvantages the opposition faces on the campaign trail – from not getting access or coverage to state-run media to government forces limiting or prohibiting campaign rallies or arresting and jailing candidates – the most direct indicator of ruling party "hyper-incumbency" is a simple financial one: campaign expenditure. After all, campaign spending is generally viewed as predictive of candidate success. Drawing from the Legislator Survey and the Candidate/Noncandidate Survey data, I compare personal and total expenditure of ruling party winners, opposition winners, and losing opposition candidates.

Candidates reported the expenditures of their first electoral campaign in one of two possible response avenues: an estimate of the actual expenditure or an ordinal variable featuring spending ranges. Figure 7.1 shows the average total amount of money spent on a candidate's election campaign the first time they ran for office. As anticipated, ruling party candidates have the most costly campaigns, with expenditures about 35 percent higher than those of opposition candidates. There is also support for the more general claim that better financed candidates are more likely to win elections: opposition winners spend more than opposition losers. These differences are significant at conventional levels.

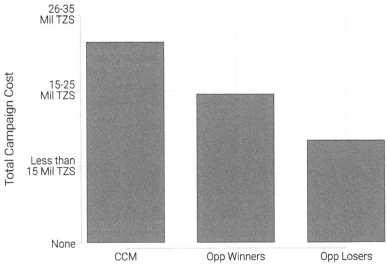

FIGURE 7.1 Total campaign expense

Some opposition candidates reported receiving modest sums from their party, while others emphatically reported they were not permitted to receive party funds in their district or constituency.[2] For opposition parties to attract enough financial support to finance candidates, they need nongovernmental channels of funds (Arriola 2013); Tanzania's opposition lacks these. Former Civic United Front Chairman Professor Ibrahim Haruna Lipumba notes,

Even when we get highly skilled – those with education, those who are elites – to compete in elections for us, they will feel like funding should be made available for them to stand in the elections. But the resources are extremely limited. So we need a candidate with financial support, but if you encourage his candidacy, which we must do in order to get the high-quality, capable candidates, he may expect the party to provide him with funds. (Interview at Lipumba's private residence, May 7, 2013)

Candidates from CCM, by contrast, received more significant financial support from their party. As one parliamentarian noted,

[2] The latter was reported in interviews with NCCR-Mageuzi member Moses Joseph Machali (May 7, 2013) and CHADEMA leader Zitto Zuberi Kabwe (May 7, 2013). Since the interviews, Zitto went on to found new opposition party ACT-Wazalendo, which Machali decamped to in 2015.

In the campaign, you are responsible for about 80% of the expenses or more. In my case, the campaign cost 65 million [Roughly $40,000]. Of that, the party contributed about five million shillings. The party does pay for some expenses, like print materials. But these are shirts for the president. If you want your own information on them, you will have to pay for them yourself. I used money on the salaries for campaigners, t-shirts for my own campaign. I also made my own posters, pamphlets, paid for a speaker system for rallies and radio advertising. These were all private expenses.[3]

7.2 OVERCOMING STRUCTURAL CONSTRAINTS THROUGH CAMPAIGN STRATEGY

Opposition in electoral authoritarian regimes faces significant disadvantages in terms of finance, experiential and organizational capacity, ability to mobilize supporters among the electorate, and potential for cooperation between parties in the opposition. Given these constraints, do opposition candidates campaign similarly to their adversaries in the ruling party or do they instead employ different approaches to turn supporters out to vote and win new supporters? I now explore in greater detail specific campaign tactics used by candidates.

Opposition candidates have fewer resources at their disposal to spend on campaigns, meaning that simply matching ruling party candidate strategy move for move is not likely to succeed. Instead, opposition parties must effectively allocate their efforts toward activities where they have comparative advantages and can work against the structural barriers that constrain their success. Tanzanian candidates who participated in the survey for this book were asked to identify what campaign tactics worked best for candidates from their party. Responses included the types of campaign activities (rallies, door-to-door canvassing, and courting local elites) and three types of campaign messaging (development promotion, critiquing underperformance, and distributing cash).

Rallies form the bedrock of political campaigns in many African countries, a fact that has been true since the first post-independence elections (Mackenzie and Robinson 1960) up to the present. Events of great pomp and circumstance, rallies bring together local constituents with national and local candidates for hours, sometimes even daylong programs of speeches in support of candidates and delivered by candidates combined with an assortment of performances by musicians, dancers, and actors in

---

[3] Interview with CCM first-term parliamentarian in Dodoma, February 6, 2013.

support of a candidate or party. Speeches focus on candidate characteristics like personal wealth and highlight "promises to deliver specific goods in that particular village" (Bleck and van de Walle 2018, 146), rather than divisive policy issues. The reasons for the content may include that the rallies are more prominently held in a party's stronghold constituencies where drumming up the enthusiasm of supporters to show up to the polls; canvassing is relied on more where they are trying to win over voters (Brierley and Kramon 2020). Rallies are very common in sub-Saharan Africa and especially in Tanzania, where Paget (2019*b*) estimates close to 70 percent of Tanzanians attend election rallies during the two months of formal campaigning ahead of elections, particularly localized ones. With regard to messaging, candidates across sub-Saharan Africa notably lack discussion of divisive policy issues; instead, incumbents highlight achievements, while challengers offer an alternative platform that emphasizes what the incumbents have done poorly (Bleck and van de Walle 2018).

Figure 7.2 displays responses regarding campaign tactics. Answers are transformed into indicators showing whether ruling party or opposition candidates use a tactic more. This figure plots the difference between the proportion of opposition respondents and ruling party responses with a hypothetical solid line indicating no difference. Points above this line

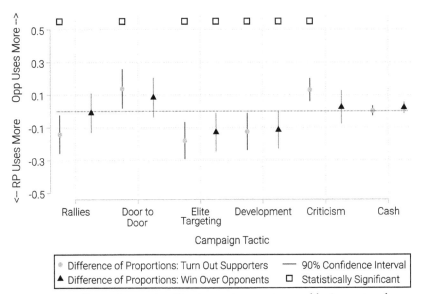

FIGURE 7.2 Campaign tactics: Turning out supporters and luring voters from other parties

mean opposition respondents reported the view more frequently and below the line, the ruling party did so. Differences that are significant at conventional levels are signified by the hollow box above a given response. The figure reveals a few critical differences between opposition and ruling party candidate strategies. Between the two distinctive groups of voters in the question posed to respondents – supporters in one's own party versus supporters of a different party – the opposition stands out from the ruling party more in terms of what gets their supporters out to the polls.

Looking at candidate perspectives in Tanzania, opposition challengers emphasize door-to-door canvassing as their central campaign technique, particularly for turning out supporters. This finding coheres with a recent public opinion survey showing that in the lead-up to the 2015 elections in Tanzania, CHADEMA canvassing had actually reached 500,000 more voters than that by CCM.[4] Door-to-door campaigning may reduce the fear or resistance an opposition sympathizer has to voting for the party and thus is an effective strategy for opposition candidates.[5] Opposition sympathizers can be found widely in these regimes, but the risks of supporting the opposition are nontrivial. Thus, even if an individual's true preference is to vote for an opposition candidate, they may choose to stay home out of fear of reprisal. Tanzanians still doubt the secrecy of the ballot – in the 2012 round of the Afrobarometer survey, more than 25 percent of respondents indicated there was some likelihood "that powerful people can find out how you voted, even though there is supposed to be a secret ballot in [their] country." This view is more prevalent among individuals who indicate they are opposition partisans, at around 30 percent. Canvassing can help overcome coordination dilemmas facing voters who are concerned about being "outed" as an opposition supporter, especially in settings where "neighbors or co-ethnics can be relied upon to monitor each other's behavior" (Birch 2007, 97). Canvassing is resource intensive, but only in terms of human resources in that it takes significant effort from candidates. Thus, what opposition can contribute to their campaigns in sweat and labor helps address resource asymmetries.

---

[4] As noted by Paget (2019a), the September 2015 Synovate poll showed 11.8 percent of voters were reached by CHADEMA's efforts, compared with 9.9 percent of respondents being contacted by CCM "face-to-face."

[5] Analysis of citizen survey data in Tanzania that I collected supports this as well; density of opposition support in social networks is correlated with opposition support.

The prevalence of canvassing also aligns with different campaign messaging strategies: opposition candidates more heavily rely on policy messaging that emphasizes criticism and alternative visions of government. By contrast, ruling party candidates rely on development promotion messaging to win over new voters and turn out their supporters. By contrast, opposition candidates rely on hammering incumbent governments for their poor track records to get their supporters out to the polls. These tactics help opposition candidates address experiential disadvantages, offering alternatives to voters. It is also the case that the campaign tactic of door-to-door canvassing is best suited for more detailed policy-driven appeals, meaning the messaging content fits well with the campaign approach.

Opposition candidates use rallies and elite targeting much less compared with CCM candidates and tout development records less. Rallies could be potentially fruitful for opposition candidates if they can shape public perceptions of their popularity – a well-attended opposition rally could convince voters a challenger candidate is viable. Indeed, this is the role they play for all candidates from the perspective of CCM MP January Makamba: "Rallies are normally a show of force. ... The rally is to show people how likely to win you are. You are psychologically telling people: *'Just come this way, because all these people are going to vote for me.'* We use rallies for that." Jussa described the rallies he carried out during his campaign as less critical than canvassing: while rallies were "a symbolic gesture of showing people that we've gone to their localities, what matters more is ... going house to house, 'door to door' campaigns, as we say."

However, they also are displays of public support for the opposition and thus may be high-risk activities. The police have arrested opposition candidates for holding rallies that were deemed "illegal," and opposition supporters may be harassed by the police and armed forces when attending or leaving rallies and other political events. CCM's extensive party branch structure is used for monitoring local political activities; while canvassing may be low-profile enough to evade local ruling party suspicion, rallies are certainly not (Croke 2017). A ban on most political assembly put into place during Magufuli's first term remains in place, rendering traditional rallies a political tool largely available only to the ruling party (Paget 2017).

Furthermore, rallies can be tremendously expensive. *Takrima* – "hospitality" given to voters when attending political events that is seen as distinct from vote buying – is common, even though it was banned after the 2005 elections. This entrenches CCM's hold on power because of the campaign resource disadvantage of the opposition (Croke 2017). Ruling party candidates invest a tremendous amount of resources in rallies, and this effort is found in citizen-level perspectives as well: Paget (2019b) finds that Tanzania citizens attended about twice as many rallies for CCM as they did for opposition party CHADEMA.

It is also unsurprising to see ruling party candidates rely more on wooing local elites; given many opposition voters may disguise their preferences to local elites, the ability of elites to mobilize opposition supporters is more constrained. The narrative of CCM legislator January Makamba drives this message home. In documenting his experience campaigning with Jakaya Kikwete, he highlights the tactics and the sheer scale of a ruling party campaign (albeit a presidential one):

> We traveled the road to every corner of our country except I think two or three districts. And in each district Mr. Kikwete spoke to the people at many external meetings and internal meetings of leaders...I learned from Mr. Kikwete that you can apply for a vote, explain your vision, your ideas and party policies without using critical or abusive language and still succeed. ... I also learned techniques and strategies to campaign for this great opportunity for the leadership of our country. I learned a lot about our party and its capacity even at the lowest party-levels. In the whole campaign, we focused on the policies of CCM without discussing opponents and still won lots of votes. I was acquainted with building brotherhood and friendship with many of our Party leaders across each corner of Tanzania, which it has been productive even when I decided to enter politics.[6]

These campaign tactics also help explain differences in campaign messaging between opposition and ruling party candidates. CCM aspirants rely on development promotion messaging to win over new voters and turn out their supporters and, as January Makamba's account relays, eschewed critical discourse. This is consistent with the notion that electorally dominant parties are ideologically flexible (Greene 2008) and, like many African parties, run on "apple pie" valence issues that do not differentiate them from platforms of other parties (Bleck and van de Walle 2010).

7.3 MAXIMIZING ELECTORAL RETURNS FROM CAMPAIGN EXPENDITURE

If opposition candidates are campaigning strategically, they must use their scarce resources in ways that maximize their value, address organizational and experiential deficits, and embolden opposition sympathizers to

---

[6] See Karugendo (2015, 64).

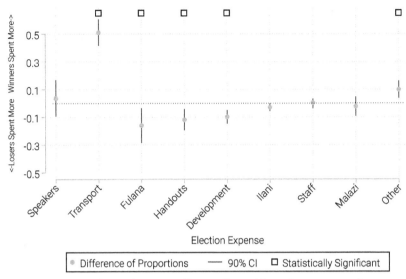

FIGURE 7.3 Campaign expenditures: Opposition winners versus losers

cast their ballots for their preferred candidate without fear of reprisal. So what kinds of campaign expenditures can deliver opposition candidates electoral success? To answer this question, I focus specifically on opposition candidates to shed light on whether the ways they spend campaign funds can distinguish opposition winners from losers. I asked opposition candidates to rank their campaign costs across expense types, ranging from material handouts and local development projects to transportation expenses and salaries of campaign staff. As with the preceding questions, respondents identified the most significant expenses they had during their first campaign for office. Here, I report their greatest and second-greatest expenses. The results from this analysis comparing opposition winners and losers are found in Figure 7.3. The figure is crafted as before, except in this figure, values above the solid line indicate opposition winners used more resources on a given expense item; values below the line indicate the expenditure was a higher priority among opposition candidates who lost.

Opposition winners outspent their opposition counterparts who lost on one key dimension: transportation. Why is this the case? The first reason is simply viability: campaigns with little or no chance to win are likely not large-scale enough to have or need resources to move candidates and their support workers across a constituency during campaigns. Indeed, ruling party legislators spent more than both opposition winners and losers on transport, meaning it is an expense that generally maps onto electoral success regardless of party. Second, transportation is especially valuable for parties that have weaker on-the-ground presence like Tanzania's opposition and instead must move resources around physically. CHADEMA's national campaign strategy has increasingly made use of the most capital-intensive transportation expense: in 2000 it used one helicopter; in 2005 and 2010 it employed two; and in 2015 the campaign operated a total of four helicopters, three exclusively for the use of parliamentary candidates. While CCM employed even more choppers in recent elections, it was emulating a technique perceived as giving the opposition an electoral advantage. CHADEMA's Philemon Ndesamburo was the first legislative candidate in Tanzania to solve Tanzania's infrastructural challenges of campaigning with aircraft in 2000 (Paget 2020). At the same time, the opposition has kept its eye on addressing the larger-scale problem of lack of localized party infrastructure that undergirds the need for transport. CHADEMA in particular has engaged in an extensive branch-building initiative following the 2010 elections. *CHADEMA ni Msingi* was an effort to open more than 17,000 party branches; during 2012–2014, the party trained more than 36,000 agents to be local representatives and advocates of the party (Paget 2019a). As one opposition candidate noted, it was as if "we had all built the houses together under Nyerere and, when it came to multiple parties, they kicked us out of the house and made us compete with them to get back inside of the house they had now claimed as their own."[7] While the opposition continues to build its own "house," successful candidates will need to use their campaign funds on transport to win.

Spending campaign resources promoting local development appears to be ineffective for opposition candidates. This finding ties back to what we saw earlier with regard to messaging of opposition versus ruling party candidates: experiential disadvantages and a lack of performance record mean development promotion messages are not credible in the eyes of voters. Tellingly, opposition candidates who employ harsh messaging critical of the government to win over new supporters are more likely to succeed in election contests.[8]

Most strikingly, we see that clientelism is not an effective strategy for opposition. Opposition candidates who spend their resources on cash

---

[7] Interview, Japhary Michael, Mayor of Moshi, CHADEMA partisan and former candidate.

[8] Analysis found in Appendix B.5.

handouts are simply less likely to win. This is sensible. After all, the legitimacy of the opposition as an alternative to CCM's corruption and mismanagement rides on its ability to look and act differently. CCM candidates give out *takrima* to supporters to turn out and may give money to opposition supporters to stay home – Tanzanian election monitors report that ruling party candidates exchanged cash for opposition supporters' voter identification cards, thus binding them to abstention (TEMCO 2015). Handouts are designed to create voter dependencies, but this does not stand to benefit the opposition since the dependencies point to the ruling party (Gandhi and Lust-Okar 2009) and challenger parties cannot enforce clientelistic reciprocation anyway.[9] The production and distribution of campaign materials like hats, t-shirts, posters, and the like – in Swahili *fulana* – are also negatively associated with opposition success. In one way, they are a handout in that they are distributed to political supporters. They are more benign than direct handouts and could address voter coordination challenges, whereby wearing party materials convinces others about the viability of a particular candidate or party; nonetheless, are associated with opposition loss. We will return to this later in the chapter.

Opposition candidates have less to spend on campaigns but use their limited funds to carry out door-to-door canvassing. While it appears that opposition candidates spend on technology that enhances voter coordination, this section showed that electoral handouts are clearly an ineffective strategy for challenger candidates. Opposition candidates who lost their election contest relied on *fulana* and handouts more than opposition winners or ruling party candidates. The final section of this chapter looks to candidate trajectories through civic activism and career partisanship and how they impact elections.

7.4 HOW CIVIC ACTIVISM IMPACTS ELECTION STRATEGY

The previous chapter showed that civic activism impacts the decision prospective candidates make when choosing to seek a nomination to run for office or to instead stay home. Civic activism was tied to opposition nomination prospects, whereby associational memberships in civic organizations and experience in grassroots mobilization were tied to deciding to seek opposition nomination and winning those nomination contests.

---

[9] See Kitschelt (2013).

Now, we turn to see how civic activism shapes opposition candidates election strategies.

How might civic activism influence how opposition candidates carry out election campaigns? Recall that the theory introduced in Chapter 2 proposed both candidate-supply and party-demand reasons for the link between activists and opposition parties. While much of the book has focused on how civic activism shapes the motivations of candidates, it is also the case that working in the NGO sector or leading various types of civic organizations benefits candidates in that it gives them skills and experiences that opposition parties need but cannot or do not provide to aspirants. Civil society provides a training ground for grooming potential future leaders and also helps them generate social capital. Civic organizations also have mobilization structures that can be used by opposition parties and also have resources that candidates and parties can draw upon to win campaigns (LeBas 2011). This leads to the expectation that civic activism can shape campaign success by increasing available resources, impacting campaign tactics, or changing expenditure priorities compared with other candidates. The section will address each of these matters in sequence.

First, though, we must establish whether civic activism actually helps candidates get elected generally. I focus on two outcome variables capturing election performance, one that is subjective and applies to all candidates (ruling party and opposition) and an objective one specific to opposition candidates. The first variable is a candidate's self-assessment of their election prospects. A second variable is simply whether or not the respondent won their election contest. To measure civic activism, I use the activism index derived from associational membership and leadership in civil society organizations, which better taps into the social capital and mobilization resources derived from civic activism.

Figure 7.4 drives home that civic activism translates into election success for opposition candidates. The left panel of the figure shows that subjective assessments of preelectoral chances rise with civic activism, tapping into a candidate's perceived chances of winning the contest as a consequence of their own résumé of community and social engagement. This feeds back to the underlying question of whether opposition candidacy can be explained as a strategic choice made by rational actors. The answer is yes: when calculating whether or not to run for office, the subjective value of one's probability of being elected P is shaped by having engaged in activism across religious, women's, professional, trade, student, and grassroots associations. The right panel shows that these

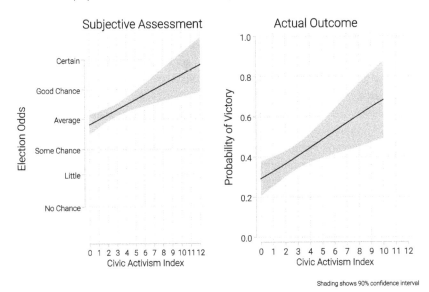

FIGURE 7.4 Civic activism and opposition victory

subjective assessments are validated on election day: greater civic activism is associated with better chances of actually being elected. The impact is substantively large: each additional value on the index translates into roughly a 4 percent better chance of being elected.

A number of potential mechanisms underlie the observed relationship between civic activism and opposition success. Civic activism could confer candidates popularity; prominent leaders in the civic sector by virtue of their activism work may simply be more recognizable and liked, making it easier to win over voters on election day or to draw upon networks of voters who are supportive of the causes advanced by the candidate as a civic leader. Civic activism work could also serve as a substitute for the experience opposition candidates lack; while an opposition candidate who works in service delivery NGOs cannot claim their party has effectively delivered services while in office, they may be able to claim the organizations they work for have (Cloward and Weghorst 2018). In other words, civic activism could provide a means of developing a performance record absent actually being in government. Relatedly, opposition candidates with civic activism experience can demonstrate their values – ideological positions, goals in politics – to voters through their work in the public sphere. A civic activism background may provide prospective candidates with skills they can use on the campaign trail. Organizational capacity, public-speaking ability, budget management, and planning skills are all useful for conducting an effective campaign and are attributes that can be developed through careers in the civil society sector. The remainder of the chapter sheds light on why civic activists are successful as opposition candidates.

Evidence regarding campaign spending points to one reason why opposition candidates anchored in civic organizations are more likely to win election contests. From previous discussions, we know that opposition winners spent more on campaigns than losers did, suggesting the unsurprising intuition that electoral success is driven by spending. But not all shillings are equal and the funds of civic activists go further, paving the way for their success. At very low levels of activism, campaign expenditure has little impact on the chances of success; at increasing levels of civic group membership and leadership, campaign spending has a large impact on the probability of winning an election contest. Figure 7.5 visualizes this interactive effect, whereby higher levels of campaign cost translate into opposition victory, but only at higher levels of civic activism.[10] The figure presents profiles of opposition candidates at various levels civic association membership captured by the civic activism index measure and shows the predicted rate of opposition victory based on expenditures at varying

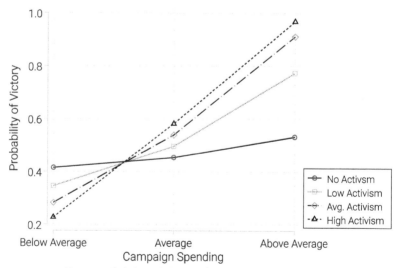

FIGURE 7.5 Impact of civic activism and campaign expenditure on opposition victory

[10] Analysis includes controls for age, gender, and education and is found in Appendix B.5.

levels derived from self-reported expenditure data. For opposition candidates who lack any activism background, throwing extra funds at their campaigns can do little to help them win. As candidate's level of engagement in civil society organizations grows in leadership and in breadth across various sectors, so does the impact of each additional shilling spent on the campaign on victory.

Activist candidates also spent more on their campaigns. The greater expenditure of activist candidates and that the impact of expenditure on opposition victory is conditional on civic activism point to the role of activism in enhancing mobilization capacity (LeBas 2011). Candidates with links to civic organizations are able to draw upon those organizations for logistical support in the form of campaign infrastructure in a way that oppositions candidates and their parties cannot do alone. Further disaggregating activism into specific organization types affirms this intuition – across student government, religious groups, professional organizations, and trade associations, membership and leadership map onto higher campaign expenditure. The notable exception to this pattern is found among grassroots activists: candidates with grassroots membership and leadership, and also more years of grassroots experience, had less expensive campaigns on average. Grassroots, community organizations in Tanzania are highly localized and often specialize in soft skills like empowerment (e.g., representation, education). These resources can be mobilized politically but are not institutionally resource rich in the ways that other civic organizations in Tanzania are (Mushi 2001).

Civic activism also changes candidate strategy in terms of winning over new voters and mobilizing supporters to turn out to vote. Earlier, in comparing ruling party versus opposition candidates, we noted that CCM winners relied more heavily on elite targeting and less on door-to-door canvassing. Seeing a CCM presidential campaign through the eyes of January Makamba showed that focusing on elite targeting was a tactic that worked effectively for the ruling party; with its extensively localized party branch structure, the party has elite nodes down to the ten-cell level that can be activated in service of electoral goals to both get their partisans to the polls and win over new voters. In comparison to CCM candidates, opposition candidates drew upon door-to-door canvassing to ensure their voters showed up at the polls. This approach allows candidates to connect supporters who may fear disclosing political preferences. It also allows them to compensate for lack of financial resources through sheer outpouring of personal effort.

Opposition candidates who have civic activism experience differ from other opposition candidates, primarily in terms of how they target new voters. Civic activists in the opposition report they use elite targeting to win over new voters at greater rates than non-activist opposition candidates, while they allocate less of their personal effort to door-to-door canvassing to win over CCM supporters. The reasons for this tie back to opposition party disadvantages that are constitutive of electoral authoritarian regimes: massive resource asymmetries between the ruling party and opposition parties and coordination problems among voters who fear supporting the opposition. As stated before, elite targeting could be an effective technique for opposition candidates if elites and potential supporters in their networks did not fear punishment from the ruling party for divulging willingness to support the opposition. Civic activist organizations are a medium through which this kind of information can travel – leaders in organizations like student governments and grassroots groups are well known and networked among local communities, giving them the kind of local know-how on where people stand politically in a way similar to how CCM's ten-cell structure operates. Cooperation between civic activists and other social actors facilitates regular interaction that takes place between these actors outside the context of electoral politics, which is the very type of relationship and trust-building activity that underlies effective coordination of potential opposition supporters. Statistical evidence showing this difference is found in Figure 7.6.[11]

Figure 7.6 also highlights how civic activists direct less of their own efforts to door-to-door canvassing because they can rely on the mobilization capacity of their organizations to assist in this. Indeed, the benefit of coalitions that form between opposition parties and civic actors around election time is the alignment of their goals and the mutually beneficial assets they offer each other. Opposition candidates and parties serve as political outlets for ambitions of social change, and civic organizations have infrastructural and institutional capacity that can be mobilized for election campaigns. In other words, civic connections can be used so that opposition candidates can benefit from canvassing performed on their behalf by civil society actors.

Earlier, Ismail Jussa showed us the value of canvassing for opposition candidates in connecting with voters, listening to their needs, and delivering important information about what the opposition had to offer. Yet, the canvassing was ultimately performed by loosely organized groups of

---

[11] Analysis includes controls for age, gender, and education and is found in Appendix B.5.

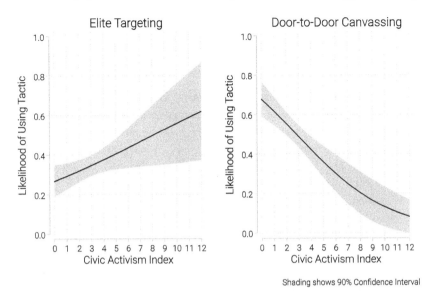

FIGURE 7.6 Impact of civic activism on campaign strategy

youth activists. Even to this day around Stone Town, you can find Jussa's 2010 campaign posters hanging on the aging coral and mortar walls throughout city. And yet, he was not responsible for them: "The same young people who pushed me to stand were the ones who were doing much of the work." In detailing his canvassing effort, he noted that teams of canvasser volunteers were operating in parallel to his own activities:

I would go with them sometimes just to give moral support, to show that I appreciate what they are doing. ... I would meet them, for example, once a week just to check as to how the progress was and they will let me know which areas they thought needed my opinion. I would then go with them to certain localities to canvas door-to-door just to enhance the campaign, especially whenever they saw [CCM candidate] Simai come to a certain area. ... to try to convince them to vote for him.

In terms of allocating campaign funds, opposition candidates with civic activism experience are broadly similar to those who do not have that background. They differ on two dimensions: opposition candidates who are activists use fewer resources on speakers and more on campaign materials like *fulana*. The speaker category includes audio and video equipment for promoting the messaging of the party, including "campaign on wheels" vehicles where candidates ride through towns and villages loudly speaking on policies and seeking voter support. This is consistent with the notion that civic organizations have infrastructure that opposition candidates and parties can draw upon. From religious services to health information and advocacy campaigns, civil society organizations need amplification systems and can loan them to candidates on the campaign trail. The observation that opposition candidates who are more active across civic organizational sectors spend comparably more on *fulana* than their non-activist counterparts is driven primarily by members of professional organizations and trade associations. It is possible that this phenomenon is sector specific and that branding is more commonly used for such organizations. Groups like legal aid organizations give out pens and pads of paper with the company logo as a form of advertising for their business rather than corruption; candidates from these backgrounds may draw upon the repertoire of the civic organizations they come from without the political baggage that more obviously surrounds corrupt forms of electoral handouts like vote buying. Campaign-branded items can address voter coordination challenges if public displays of support for a candidate in the form of a hat or a t-shirt can convince other potential supporters that the candidate is viable, thus solving problems that constrain opposition candidates.

CONCLUSION

This chapter has reaffirmed that opposition candidates face structural conditions that impact their electoral performance. However, it also demonstrated that opposition candidates use campaign tactics that can enhance their prospects of success, including door-to-door mobilization and broadcasting campaign messages widely. I showed that civic activism is associated with election success for opposition candidates and offered insight into the mechanisms that underlie victory: civic activists are able to translate campaign expenditure into greater success and they use their resources differently, drawing upon their networks and organizational backgrounds to overcome many of the structural disadvantages they face.

8

Benefits of Winning (and Losing) Elections

Cha wenyewe huliwa na wenyewe
What is theirs is consumed by them

Washindwapo ndipo washindapo.
Where there are losers there also are winners.

There is one thing that is true for most Tanzanian legislators, no matter their party: entering the Parliament and the House of Representatives after being elected for the very first time is a special and meaningful moment, one that marks the completion of the journey to office and the beginning of a career as a legislator. You see that in the way Ismail Jussa and January Makamba relay their experiences. Jussa had come to politics though advocacy for a stronger, more independent, and peaceful Zanzibar. When he entered the House of Representatives there, he was a part of a new power-sharing government where CUF had an equal hand in shaping policy and development in the isles; one Jussa had helped create through his activism:

When you go there having won a popular mandate, you feel very special. You see yourself as being honored to be given the trust of your fellow citizens in your constituency to represent them. Especially for me, because I never wanted the position for myself. I remember when I was called to be sworn in by the speaker, I really felt like this was a very special moment and the feeling inside is something that I cannot explain to this day. You really feel like you are there to make laws on behalf of the citizens. It's like a symbol of what a country should be if it were governed democratically. It's an honor that you've won from your fellow constituents and a feeling of service to your country. In 2010, it was especially unique because we were full of hope that Zanzibar was going into a different era.

We didn't accomplish everything, but I think the feeling that particular House that was elected in 2010 would mark history by restoring to Zanzibar its past glory was always there in me.[1]

January Makamba's first day on the job was marked by a similar sense of excitement and mission to get started:

There is euphoria. Some people who go into parliament already have national name recognition and I was fortunate in that way. There [are] people you know that had been there before you, you've seen them on TV and are excited to meet them. There are new people who know you. ... [W]e have three days of swearing-in, where it's families there to see you sworn in as an MP. Another dimension is you wait for the Parliament to be inaugurated by the president, also a momentous ceremonial time. You wait for the nomination of the cabinet. It's a hectic week of hopes, new friends, and new future. The new Parliament time is always a very exciting time. For me it was interesting because I went there knowing that I have to work my way up to prominence and relevance in the Parliament.[2]

This chapter focuses on the experiences of legislators when they enter into office and the benefits of candidacy. I begin by reviewing what we have learned from studies of legislators in democracies about what they want from office: they are primarily motivated by material benefits of officeholding. Legislatures in electoral authoritarian regimes differ from these settings in important ways; the chapter shows, using survey data and qualitative interviews, that opposition candidates in Tanzania do not want the same things ruling party candidates do. The heterogeneity in terms of what candidates want when they run for office does not just arise over partisan differences. The final section of the chapter shows that civic activism and career partisanship experiences impact the benefits aspirants seek when running for office. While the accounts that opened this chapter suggest similar beginnings for January Makamba and Ismail Jussa and while their trajectories have since differed, both remain active and committed legislators. It will become clear from this chapter that the experiences of other opposition and ruling party legislators diverge quickly: what they seek from office has been conditioned by their experiences leading into politics. Moreover, expectations that constituents place on them as a consequence of their party reinforce those differences, further propelling them apart.

[1] Drawn from in-person interview with Ismail Jussa.
[2] Drawn from in-person interview with January Makamba.

8.1 BENEFITS OF CANDIDACY IN ELECTORAL AUTHORITARIAN REGIMES

In Chapter 2, I introduced four benefit ideal-types that corresponded with what legislators seek in electoral authoritarian regimes – material goods, prestige, pursuing ideological/policy goals, and career opportunism. Drawing on existing insight about legislators in advanced democracies and across sub-Saharan Africa, I noted the strong material drive for running for office, particularly for those who represent the party in power. Authoritarian elections are characterized by "competitive clientelism," through which aspirants vie for positions in government in exchange for access to resources to consume and distribute among supporters, as well as to get the material perks of officeholding and potential links to promote careers after leaving office (Lust-Okar 2009). I also discussed how expressive benefits that come from standing up for one's principles, policies, and values can be especially appealing for members of the opposition, who are not muzzled by their party in the same way as ruling party MPs.

Considering the shared wisdom in the literature on legislators in Africa, democracies, and electoral authoritarian regimes, the benefits of office-holding in Africa's electoral authoritarian regime fall into the broad categories of material goods, prestige, pursuing ideological/policy goals, and career opportunism, and these benefits are offered heterogeneously by ruling parties versus the opposition. Specifically, *hyper-incumbency* advantages combined with the *punishment regime* employed by electoral authoritarian governments suggest both material and career opportunism benefits are skewed heavily toward the ruling party; the latter has been demonstrated empirically in other nondemocratic settings (e.g., Treux (2014)). While opposition legislators are constrained in terms of actually passing laws – given they often face ruling party supermajorities – they nonetheless can meaningfully pursue ideological goals in ways that ruling party legislators cannot. Both ruling party and opposition legislators may derive prestige benefits from legislative activities. That is, while ruling party legislator may be constrained in their influence over policy, they nonetheless interact with prominent international actors, travel abroad for their duties and for networking in political party federations, and enjoy heightened status within their constituency and among family and friends as a consequence of their position. The same is true for prestige of opposition legislators, particularly insofar as they are vocal spokespersons for their constituents in parliamentary proceedings (which are commonly broadcast live on TV) and elevated by pro-democracy international actors wishing to bring attention to conditions of the regime.

In addition to benefits of officeholding and performing legislative duties, the theory introduced in Chapter 2 stands out from existing literature that portrays these benefits as contingent on electoral victory. Rather, this book joins a minority of work that posits that benefits of legislative candidacy may be delivered even in defeat on election day or in nomination contests.

Opposition challengers who face little competition in the nomination stage but significant barriers to electoral success may nonetheless benefit from losing election contests. Greene (2007, 129) introduces the concept of "message-seeking" politicians who "want to change political interests in society in order to win elections. ... message seekers seek transformation." Such individuals gain less from obtaining office as an end than conventional understandings of "ambitious politicians" anticipate. They derive additional utility from being activists, promoting system change, and other nonmaterial benefits that accrue from officeseeking. With this consideration, the chapter now moves on to review evidence identifying the benefits of officeseeking in Tanzania with survey data.

Benefits of Running for Office

The preceding discussion highlighted that ruling party and opposition candidates are heterogeneous in the benefits desired from running for office and, further, that ruling parties versus opposition parties differ in their ability to offer candidates such benefits in electoral authoritarian settings. For example, it may be the case that winning an office by the opposition is not meaningful at all to a prospective candidate because their primary goal in winning office is to protect an industry in their constituency (e.g., car production). For this individual, elected office serves them only insofar as they may implement laws that protect that business. An opposition politician where the ruling party has a supermajority in the legislature has little hope of realizing such benefits of office. Thus, benefits of office are both individually specific in that individuals want different things out of seeking office and party specific in that different parties offer their candidates the promise of different benefits of winning office.

I first address the matter of what candidates want when they decide to run for office and analyze survey data to do so. Designing a survey to study this topic has a number of difficulties, especially when asking about motivations to run for office that might not be especially acceptable to

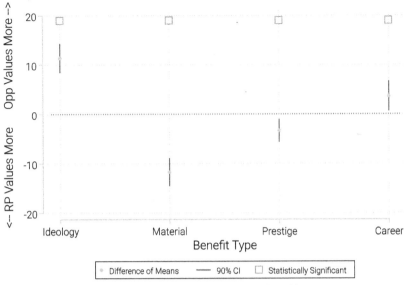

FIGURE 8.1 Benefits of running for office

divulge honestly. Who would want to admit the real reason they wanted to be an MP is that it pays well and comes with government-provided benefits? Or who would say that, actually, improving government oversight is not important? I discussed ways the survey was crafted to alleviate many of these concerns in Chapter 3. To review, I determine how important a given benefit type was to an individual by presenting a series of lists containing a mixture of motivations that fall under the categories of material, ideology, prestige, and career benefits of office and asking which benefits are the most important of those on a given list. This forces the respondent to prioritize and choose which matters the most to them.

Figure 8.1 summarizes statistical analyses that test whether opposition aspirants want different things from running for office than their CCM counterparts.[3] Each benefit type listed in the figure corresponds with a measure that indicates how often that benefit was identified as the most important on a given list of reasons to run for office, with the highest values typically being 75 and indicating a given benefit was identified as most important 75 percent of the time.[4] The figure depicts the difference

---

[3] Appendix B.6 contains the underlying analyses presented in the figure.

[4] It ranges in principle from 0 to 100, but because of the nature of the survey instrument, responses are generally 75 or below. A value of 75 for a benefit category corresponds with the respondents (1) allocating all "most important" reasons to that benefit category, (2) the "second most important" for the list where two benefits from that category appear,

between the average importance of a benefit for opposition nomination seekers compared with CCM legislators. It shows that the benefits that motivate the opposition are completely different from what drives the ruling party.

What are the most important reasons for running for office according to the opposition? Opposition nominees and candidates prioritize ideological goals like aiming to enhance government oversight, shape economic policy, improve the protection of rights for minorities, and mitigate deficiencies in public service delivery. By contrast, CCM legislators' motivations lie more in the material and prestige benefits of office. Additional analyses in the Appendix detailing what discourages people from running for office show the same pattern: decisions for opposition aspirants are driven by ideological motivations, while the ruling party is shaped by material and prestige concerns.

Seeing that material benefits appeal to CCM legislators more (and conversely, that opposition legislators care about material benefits less) is central to the narrative that shapes opposition politics in Tanzania and electoral authoritarian regimes around the world. Electoral authoritarian regimes are "winner take all" politics to the extreme, and thus the material benefits of office disproportionately accrue to legislators from the party in power. While originally established under principles of social and economic equality, it is clear that the face of modern CCM rule is steeped in this materialist tradition, coupled with a desire for the prestige that comes with representing the world's second longest-lasting ruling party.

This prominence of material gains for CCM legislators reflects, according to some observers, the evolution of CCM's economic image under multiparty rule. Indeed, this underlies the critical platform upon which the opposition positions itself: the claim that material desire, rather than drive to address citizen demands for economic and political change, has rotted CCM from the inside. According to Julius Nyerere's former economic advisor, "the CCM of Mwalimu Julius Kambarage Nyerere had undergone complete metamorphosis, and [under] Ali Hassan Mwinyi and Benjamin Mpaka it was no longer the part of the downtrodden. It was now a Party of the 'filthy rich,' backed by unscrupulous, corrupt international capitalist tycoons masquerading as pro-development envoys under

and (3) providing the remaining three "second most important" responses. Since the measure is calculated as the prioritization of a given benefit relative to total responses, item nonresponse means this measure could be, but rarely is, as high as 100.

the umbrella of globalisation" (Mtei 2009, 215). CCM saw the rise to prominence in Parliament and the party of business magnates like Rostam Aziz, Iddi Simba, and Mo Dewji, who played the role of financiers in exchange for access to government resources. Rostam Aziz reportedly ran for office because "political leverage is good for business" (Collard 2019, 217). Collard (2019) deftly illustrates how material demands of CCM MPs now follow a regular cycle in which they agree to push through controversial legislation ahead of elections in exchange for financial resources. In 2015, CCM MPs even threatened to prevent President Kikwete from delivering closing remarks at the final legislative session of his presidency unless they received ancillary "gratuity" payments due before the end of the legislative terms.

The reasons for the material ambition of CCM aspirants may in part arise from the expectations voters place on candidates. January Makamba notes this as one of his own key sources of frustration: "People have a wrong expectation of the role of MP. They believe that somehow you are loaded all the time, you're going to solve problems instantly, even personal problems. They say 'My kids are not going to school. I'm building my house and I've roofed one side but there's one side left.' You can't do it because you can't fix everybody's problem. You are constantly pressed do to it." Indeed, as Gandhi and Lust-Okar (2009) have established, the dependencies of voters on electoral authoritarian regimes keeps supporters loyal to the regime but only insofar as representatives of the party deliver on the goods voters have come to expect.

That opposition aspirants are less motivated by material benefits also helps inform what it means to achieve benefits along ideological dimensions in an electoral authoritarian setting like Tanzania. The legislatures are dominated by CCM; they have held a supermajority in Parliament since 1995 and in Zanzibar either a majority or supermajority. The only cabinet positions that the opposition has held were those in Zanzibar's Government of National Unity (GNU) from 2010 to 2015; with the opposition's boycott of the rescheduled 2015 polls, the GNU no longer exists and CCM controls all of government there. Any policy that comes to the floor in Tanzania and is passed into law is written by CCM and the opposition can do little to stamp its name on the policy outcome. The policy and ideology they can stand behind are about influencing the law of the land and reforming how it impacts opposition parties' ability to compete. Schedler (2006) captures this concept as a "nested game" in which a lower-level political game surrounding elections is one in which the opposition may regularly lose, while simultaneously trying to shift the balance of power over the rules that govern that game. The opposition may have little power over the policy that comes out of the Parliament, but it can wield its influence to shape the overall dynamics of power and function of democratic institutions within the regime.

This can be seen in various parliamentary activities, from wielding standing orders to disrupt proceedings to vocally criticizing the government on the floor while constituents watch live broadcasts of the sessions at home – that is, before live broadcasts were unsuccessfully banned in 2013 and successfully in 2016 (Mutiga 2016). Most would point to ACT-Wazalendo Chair (former CHADEMA elite) Zitto Kabwe, a parliamentary wizard who has skillfully navigated the institution to maximize the power opposition can wield in the chambers. As chair of a parliamentary committee established in 2007 to oversee government-owned enterprises – the Public Organizations and Accounts Committee (POAC) – he repeatedly exposed the government for corruption and mismanagement. The committee publicized reports that brought down eight cabinet ministers and even threatened the prime minister with impeachment, leading the committee to be abolished after a short-lived six years. Kabwe secured leadership of the Public Accounts Committee (PAC) after the POAC was shuttered and through that brought attention to one of the most prominent corruption scandals in twenty-first century Tanzania, known as the IPTL or escrow scandal. IPTL was a troubled private electricity provider that Tanesco, Tanzania's state-run electrical company, had taken to court over excessive fees. As the case continued on, funds Tanesco paid into an escrow account were diverted to finance the sale of IPTL to a foreign company; so when the court rule in favor of Tanesco more than \$100 million of escrow funds due from IPTL to Tanesco were already gone. Then NCCR-Mageuzi MP David Kafulia – a vocal anti-corruption critic in his own right – was also credited with shedding light on the scandal. After delivering blistering a critique of Attorney General Judge Frederick Werema on the floor of the *Bunge*, even more attention was drawn to the escrow scandal when Werema physically attacked Kafulia outside the *Bunge* during a recess (Lugongo 2014). In 2018, opposition MPs identified a 1.5 trillion shilling gap in reported government revenue and expenditure data and an additional trillion shillings of improperly managed and misallocated funds (equivalent to \$640 million and \$1.03 billion dollars, respectively). In response, the Parliament's speaker halted all activities of its oversight committees and scuttled the auditor's report that tipped the MPs off (Anonymous 2018).

Perhaps the most notable contemporary example of the importance of policy and ideology to the opposition was the role of opposition legislators in the unsuccessful effort to ratify a new, modern constitution in Tanzania and the consequences it had for opposition unity and coordination in the 2015 elections. In advance of completing his term-limited tenure in office, Jakaya Kikwete launched a constitutional reform process that promised to transform the country's legal framework, a constitution ratified in 1977 that had last been reformed significantly in 1985. In Kikwete's eyes, it offered an opportunity to cement his legacy as a president who succeeded where both his predecessors Ali Hassan Mwinyi and Benjamin Mkapa had tried and failed. He appointed Joseph Warioba to lead the Constitutional Review Commission (CRC). Warioba is a highly respected statesman who chaired Mpaka's anti-corruption commission and served as vice-president and prime minister under previous regimes. This CRC's work was widely participatory, the commission held thousands of in-person meetings, and more than one million Tanzanians presented input to the commission in person or by phone, email, or text. The draft produced from the commission had several promising reforms that could address underlying issues in Tanzania: term-limiting MPs, requiring financial disclosures, boosting gender equity in political representation, legalizing nonparty/independent candidates and legislators, and introducing a constituency-level process to recall legislators.

Perhaps unsurprisingly, the Warioba-led commission would come to the same conclusion as Mkapa's 1998 constitutional reform report and the so-called G55 group of 55 MPs during the reintroduction of multipartyism in the 1990s: Tanzania needed a three-government structure in which matters of the Union shrunk to shift greater legal authority to the Zanzibar and a yet-to-be created Tanganyikan government. The majority of citizens in both mainland Tanzania and Zanzibar supported the change. In spite of this, CCM leadership followed its own past precedent and quickly moved to reject a Union restructuring. A change to the shape of the Union that afforded greater autonomy for Zanzibar meant turning back the clock on Union relations to 1964, when Tanzania was created. Fearing such a reform was an irreversible step toward the future dissolution of the Tanzanian Union altogether, Kikwete's legacy-building effort yielded real risk of the worst-possible legacy in the eyes of CCM leaders: starting to break apart the nation and the Union that founding father Julius Nyerere built. By the time the 640-member Constituent Assembly – made up of all 439 legislators from Tanzania's Parliament and the Zanzibar House of Representatives and about 200 leaders from civil society – met to debate and revise the draft constitution to create a document to put to a popular referendum, it was clear the three-government structure, reforms aimed at curbing presidential power, and amendments that gave anti-corruption efforts real teeth would never make it to the final draft; CCM leadership instead proposed an alternative draft with few meaningful changes.

CHADEMA, CUF, and NCCR-Mageuzi banded together to form UKAWA (*Umoja wa Katiba ya Wananchi*, the Coalition of Defenders of the People's Constitution) and collectively boycotted the proceedings, a sufficiently large enough group to prevent the CCM draft from being approved and put to a citizen referendum. Their effort to block the alternative draft ultimately failed due to various actions of the ruling party: ballot secrecy rules were removed to make sure CCM members supported the adulterated draft, opposition accused CCM of winning over delegates with vote buying, approval votes were recorded for members who claimed they did not vote, and government officials who supported three governments were dismissed (Branson 2015).

While the "people's constitution" did not emerge from the constitutional reform process, what did was a unified commitment among major opposition players to fight together against the ruling party. They found common ground related to the constitutional reform and its goals to reduce corruption; improve democratic safeguards; and, especially a Zanzibari faction emboldened by the original draft, greater sovereignty for the archipelago. UKAWA faced the 2015 elections unified behind one presidential candidate and generally a single parliamentary candidate in each constituency, in a show of cooperation that had never before taken place in Tanzania's multiparty history. Indeed, while there is a difference in the overall positioning of opposition parties on standard left-right issues – CHADEMA is pro-business and generally center-right on economic policy, while CUF is conversely a member of Liberal International and promotes redistributive social development policies – they share in common a goal to change the laws of the land to improve their standing and to hold the government to account in the eyes of the public.

This mission – improving Zanzibar through increasing its role in the Union – is the single most important issue that drove Jussa to run for office and still does to this day. In his words,

I don't believe Zanzibar deserves to be what it is today. I believe that Zanzibar can be better and should be better in many ways. Politically, economically, socially, culturally. I believe just like the way it was during this old glorious past when it became such an important player in the world politics in the Indian Ocean, I think it can still do that. It has been manifested by the many writings that have been there showing that Zanzibar can change its position but it needs the right people at the position of government to steer their way to its rightful place in the world. I don't regret. I believe I made very positive contribution in getting Zanzibar to where it is today, and I still believe that the future is bright. One day we'll achieve what we've been fighting for all these years.

Parties Offer Different Benefits

Legislators and prospective candidates have heterogeneous preferences, which may influence whether or not they seek a nomination for office in a given year. Parties themselves differ greatly as well, in terms of the kind of public exposure they provide for their members, their policy and governance priorities, and the perks they offer to party elites. This has been established in terms of the congruence between party and voter positions (Luna and Zechmeister 2005, van Eerd 2011) and has clear extensions to candidate-party coherence.

Ruling parties in electoral authoritarian regimes have been demonstrated to hold weaker policy commitments outside of vote and seat-maximizing goals (Greene 2007, Greene 2002). On the other hand, when there are established opposition parties that can survive across multiple elections, they can develop meaningful policy positions (van Eerd 2011) and sometimes niche or extreme ones (Greene 2007). The mechanism by which voter–party ideological coherence is developed in these settings is through party activists and electoral candidates, who translate voter preferences into parties. As such, the ability of individuals in opposition parties to appeal to the policy goals and aims of its candidates is more substantial. The literature thus anticipates the opposition's appeal to ideologists is in their comparative advantage in offering ideological benefits to their candidates.

Similar benefits may be gained from the opposition through prestige. With fewer members to make official statements to the press; to be quoted in the newspaper; to stand out and deliver speeches at rallies; the opportunities to be visible to one's friends, family, home community, and others are more common. However, on the other side of this is that other sorts of prestige, such as traveling with the cabinet abroad and attending statehouse dinners with world leaders are opportunities restricted to the ruling party only. Thus, one might expect that legislators experience the prestige benefits of both opposition and ruling parties compared with non-legislators, but the ability of the party to deliver benefits offered to legislators by those parties are similar (even if the benefits themselves are different). There are risks of government interference in businesses whose leaders stand against the ruling regime and government controls employment in the civil service sector as well as other types of patronage jobs within the administration. It is therefore anticipated the ruling party is better positioned to provide its members and legislators with material benefits related to employment. Authoritarian parties also have access to the financial assets of the state and can direct resources away from public accounts to its members and activists. Thus, ruling party members are more likely to evaluate their party's ability to deliver material goods more favorably than opposition party activists view their own parties' ability to deliver material benefits derived from employment, preferntial treatment, and physical goods.

To assess how prospective candidates evaluated their party's ability to provide candidates and legislators with the four ideal-type benefits associated with holding office – prestige, career opportunism, material gains, and ideological/policy goals – respondents for the Legislator Survey and Candidate/Noncandidate Survey were asked to rate how well their own party performed a number of tasks for their members and activists. Items were designed to capture these four attributes. Figure 8.2 visualizes the results from analyses of these survey data.

It is first worth highlighting that respondents almost universally offered positive responses, with the average for almost all responses and sample subgroups being rated as above the "Average" response category. This is unsurprising, as self-reported evaluations of a party are likely to provide a flattering position of them. The most substantial advantages for the opposition party are in terms of how individuals assess its ability to meet the ideological goals of its activists and candidates. In fact, the evaluation of opposition parties in delivering ideology/policy benefits is the only category that is rated above "well" for any of the benefits. January Makamba – by all accounts an elected representative who is skilled and driven to improve policy outcomes – shares the difficulty CCM MPs face on this dimension, even for those motivated to do so because of the control the party exercises over their actions:

When you are in parliament, ruling party MP, you are expected to defend the ruling party, the government's position as an MP of CCM because it is CCM government. Often, the government is not doing well. ... As a CCM MP, everybody – the party leadership – expects you to endorse the budget. Always, you are caught in a very tough spot as a ruling party MP. Sometimes you have a challenge, conflicts between backbenchers and the government, because it gets to a point

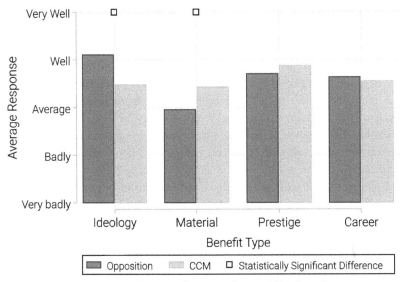

FIGURE 8.2 Party performance in providing benefits

where that support costs you but the national government says your support is necessary for us to pass the budget.

So far, this chapter has illustrated that opposition candidates want different things from holding office than those from CCM. Specifically, they value ideological and policy-related benefits and value material ones less. If they are driven by the ability of parties to facilitate these benefits, then it appears they are making the right choice: opposition parties are better at delivering these benefits to their members. By contrast, CCM excels at offering their aspirants material benefits, which they highly prioritize.

8.2 BENEFITS OF LOSING ELECTIONS

The motivating puzzle of opposition candidacy under a strategic framework centers on the idea that aspirants are driven to gain benefits from doing so. In electoral authoritarian regimes, certain types of benefits can only come from the ruling party: it excels in offering material benefit. But those who run for the opposition are driven by what challenger parties best offer: emphasis on nonmaterial, ideological goals like holding a poor performing government to account and fighting corruption. Still, the barriers to victory for opposition candidates loom large. We saw from the previous chapter that elections are stacked dramatically against the opposition and that even victory can be taken away by the ruling party, which controls whether or not election outcomes will be respected. Thus, even if being a legislator for the opposition is more desirable because it allows one to hold government to account and to fight for constituents, this does not change the difficulties of getting there. This section addresses this question: is there anything to be gained from losing elections? If so, then the benefit of candidacy may not rest solely on prospects of winning. The answer will be a resounding yes: fighting and losing a hard contest may ultimately deliver meaningful benefit to an opposition candidate.

CCM candidates do see benefit in defeat, but only at the nomination stage. For the ruling party, candidacy may offer far superior electoral prospects compared with the opposition but intraparty competition is significant. Given that intraparty cohesion is critical for the longevity of electoral authoritarian regimes, well fought but unsuccessful nomination contests may deliver the very goods that motivate legislators, especially material benefits to contain potential resulting dissent, greater prestige and notability among party members and leaders and voters, as well as potential benefits to a nonpolitical career as a consequence of the nomination outcome.[5] One CCM parliamentarian describes how losing a nomination contest can help prepare one for a subsequent attempt. He notes,

I set out to become an MP by displacing the [CCM] incumbent. In 2005, I stood against him in the internal candidate selection for CCM but was unsuccessful. I was disappointed but accepted the outcome. Although I had lost the contest, I earned a lot of respect from the constituency and became viewed as the MP in waiting. Opposition parties came to me and offered me the chance to compete in the elections if I would join their ticket. But at this point, I thought I was too young to already leave CCM over not getting an opportunity to compete. It was the party that I had supported for a long time, and the party that I had technical knowledge of its policies and so on. I resolved to set aside politics till later [the next election]. I knew that to best the old man, I needed to work hard in the constituency. So I started an agricultural development project to improve the cotton sector of Ngeza. I brought new technology to the cotton farms–like tractors, better quality fertilizers, high-quality seeds and so on in order to help modernize the sector. I also made a lot of promotional materials for the project, like calendars with pictures of the project, pictures of me, explanations of how the projects were benefiting the constituency. When it came around to 2010,

---

[5] Analysis of perceived benefits of losing nominations is not included in the main text but is found in Appendix B.6. It shows that CCM candidates see some benefits in losing nominations, while opposition candidates do not.

folks in the constituency saw what I had to offer and chose me to be their CCM candidate.[6]

January Makamba offers a similar perspective – perhaps a message of inspiration for young CCM hopefuls who do not win CCM nomination contests;

Kura za maoni (Primaries): you go to a branch, you speak. ... As a young person, as anybody, if you go through the process for a month. If you went through every village, every branch to say who you are, what are you going to do, and to receive questions. If you're good, even if you don't win, you will have a chance because already members know you. Also, you'll come out with a perspective. There's a saying that "No election is ever lost." Even if you lose the primary, the lessons are a victory.

There is little to be gained for the opposition losing nomination contests, particularly when they are not very competitive. But opposition candidates may gain from an unsuccessful elections – in terms of honing their skills on the campaign trail and in gaining popularity among voters. Outperforming expectations of their party may also increase popularity for that party, demonstrating a capacity suited for skilled work in the party secretariat. Given opposition candidates are "message seekers," simply getting the word out about criticisms of the party in power may be worth something. Recall from Chapter 7 that this is where they allocate significant effort in messaging on the campaign trail.

Evidence from legislative aspirants in Tanzania supports this view. Presented with a list of reasons of what might be gained from losing an election contest, survey participants were asked to identify up to two benefits of the unfortunate outcome of defeat or if they instead thought there was nothing to gain from losing. In answering the questions, many were drawing on their own experiences, as a substantial number of the opposition aspirants had experienced electoral defeat at some point in their political careers. How Tanzanian aspirants view the fruits of election defeat is visualized in Figure 8.3. Of the six possible responses, opposition candidates differ from CCM legislators in four ways.

First, and most critically, opposition candidates who lose election campaigns note the experiential benefits of planning and executing one. As documented in Chapter 7, opposition parties face infrastructural and

---

[6] Interview carried out with MP Hamisi Kigwangalla, February 6, 2013, in the Parliament of Tanzania.

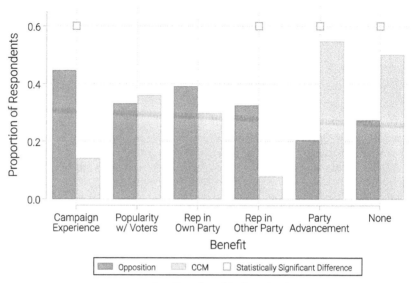

FIGURE 8.3 Benefits of losing elections

organizational challenges in electoral authoritarian settings. This means they may lack the infrastructure to train members in how to carry out elections and the resources to finance campaigns that prominently place the face, name, and policies of candidates in voters' minds. It appears that losing an election may be one of the best ways to overcome such challenges to be successful in subsequent elections.

CHADEMA youth-wing leader Deogratis Siale Munishi points to how experience in elections can be one of the best ways to accelerate a candidate to electoral success: "In the youth wing [BAVICHA], we hold seminars to learn policies and the party stances, but the best way they can learn campaign skills to experience them. That helps them learn how to campaign and how to win support."[7] This sentiment is further echoed by a local councilor who considered candidacy for legislative office but instead opted to run for mayor in a northern municipality: "Without being patriotic, you cannot run for the position. ...You must sacrifice. This is because you will struggle to get support the first time around and only after showing the voters what you can offer in an election will they come around to listen to your message in the future."[8]

---

[7] Interviewed carried out at CHADEMA Headquarters, Kidondoni, Dar es Salaam. February 1, 2013.
[8] Interview with Moshi Municipal Council Leader Raphael Japhary Michael, December 12, 2012.

Running in elections not only gives opposition candidates experience running campaigns; many of them ultimately go on to win elections. Ismail Jussa relays several examples in the Zanzibar House of Representatives elections, including that of Nassor Ahmed Mazrui, who first stood for elections in 2005 and lost. In addition to the common barrier of electoral manipulation, in the aftermath of the unsuccessful campaign "he used that experience and he worked tirelessly for five years from 2005. He said one thing that he learned is that in constituencies like [Mtoni], you could not win just by going there during the election time. You have to go to do a long-term campaign and that's what he did. ... He used those lessons that he learned in 2005 and won handsomely in 2010. He won I think almost by 65 percent." In addition to his lessons on the campaign trail in 2005, he also served on the bipartisan "Committee of Six" that negotiated the structure of the Government of National Unity established in Zanzibar ahead of the 2010 elections. Like Jussa, his role as an activist in working toward peace in and autonomy of Zanzibar likely also enhanced his elections prospects by demonstrating his ideological commitment in the eyes of voters. In other constituencies, candidates ran and lost more than once.

The analysis depicted in Figure 8.3 also shows that opposition candidates who lost elections see a benefit of improving their reputation among other parties. The wording of the question leaves open the possibility that co-optation is a credible motivation for competing in elections when losing: by demonstrating that one is a viable candidate who can win some support – even if not enough to win an electoral contest – one's appeal in the eyes of other political parties rises. However, there is good reason to think it means something else. My first interpretation points to how electoral contests might impact one's reputation in other opposition parties. One factor that holds challenger parties back in electoral authoritarian regimes is coordination problems voters face, including which opposition candidate to support in a given constituency. Indeed, Tanzania's legislatures are filled with a number of CCM MPs who won not because they secured a majority of voters in their constituency but because multiple opposition candidates split the vote. Maximizing opposition performance requires coordination among parties over who runs where, a strategic negotiation brokered by opposition leaders based at least in part on candidate viability. Indeed, the agreement under UKAWA was that a single opposition candidate would be fielded in each constituency to maximize seats gained from voter support. As an opposition candidate, the better one performs in losing an election is likely to improve chances of being fielded as a jointly supported opposition candidate in future elections. There is also volatility in the performance of opposition parties over time; while opposition parties do have their geographical anchors, there is still some flux in their comparable fortunes over time. Picking the "right" opposition party, particularly in mainland Tanzania, can be difficult if one is projecting forward multiple elections. Fracturing of CUF between mainland and Zanizbari camps led to the wholesale movement of CUF's entire presence in Zanzibar, including candidates, officers, and members into ACT-Wazalendo, the party Zitto Kabwe founded after CHADEMA kicked him out. Under those circumstances, one's reputation in the eyes of ACT leaders might matter for CUF candidates who lost previous elections.

A second interpretation suggests that opposition candidates might actually value their reputations in the eyes of CCM legislators and leaders for the sake of achieving some policy goals. There are definitely opportunities for collaboration between the opposition and CCM, if not publicly then behind the scenes to achieve the benefits that opposition candidates truly seek. The opening passage of the book noted that Ismail Jussa and January Makamba first formally interacted brokering *MWAFAKA*, an agreement that marked the steps required to resolve the Zanzibari political impasse and to pave the road for the Government of National Unity there. Zanzibar's peace and strength are core to Ismail Jussa's driving ideology and why he cares about being in the legislature. Zitto Kabwe's work fighting corruption through the Public Organizations and Accounts Committee (POAC) and later the Public Accounts Committee (PAC) was possible in part because CCM MP Deo Filikunjombe, his co-chair, was willing to work with Zitto and use the committee to punish government actors who were engaging in malfeasance (Collard 2019, 181). January ascended quickly in Parliament in part because Zitto sought him out upon his arrival at Parliament and helped him become chair of the Energy and Minerals Committee even before committee assignments were known to other members. Zitto is, according to Makamba, a "master of parliamentary politics." His help let January get a head start on potential rival leaders on the committee, who would only find out their assignments an hour before the committees met for the first time. New legislators relegated to back-benching by default may align with one another to gain collective influence over more senior members, even if it means reaching across party lines. New members may achieve positions of importance more quickly if they have demonstrated a record of close misses on election performance. Abdallah Jihad Hassan lost twice in the contest for a

House of Representative's seat in Magogoni, but when he won in 2010, his persistence and popularity translated into a cabinet post in Zanzibar's power-sharing government in the ministries that govern tourism and subsequently fishing and livestock, both of which are critical portfolios for Zanzibar's economy. These accounts all suggest that reputation matters among legislators, even those from different parties. The extent to which losing elections but fighting hard in them can boost one's reputation among political allies and rivals may facilitate achieving benefits related to policy and ideological outcomes down the road.

Nearly 60 percent of CCM legislators state that they see nothing to gain from losing elections, at a rate about twice that of opposition aspirants. For CCM legislators, where winning office means access to the government mandate and membership in a legislative supermajority, overcoming the hurdles of nomination but failing to win a seat simply is not that valuable. Those who run and lose may never have a chance to run again and instead will be replaced by a more attractive nominee who can deliver in the next election. A little more than half of CCM respondents do, however, see losing an election as an opportunity to gain an alternate position within the political party: members who lose elections but are nonetheless important to the legacy of the party can be retained in offices of prestige in the party organization.

8.3 ORIGINS OF BENEFITS: LIFE HISTORIES AND SOCIALIZATION

The literature on candidacy has mostly argued that decisions to act on political ambition and run for office are driven by cost-benefit considerations of what a potential candidate wants from winning, the chances they will win, and the costs of winning. When conceived of in its conventional form where benefits are primarily material and are derived from office-holding, the framework cannot account for the high rate of opposition candidacy in electoral authoritarian regimes. This chapter has shown that the framework can nonetheless be adapted to operate in those settings. I have presented evidence that opposition candidates choose whether or not to run for office on the basis of policy and ideological benefits. These benefits can be achieved in the legislature in spite of facing ruling party supermajorities and even in the face of electoral defeat.

The goal of this book, however, is not to simply take the existing account of strategic candidacy choice suitable for advanced democracies and make it applicable to the electoral authoritarian contexts that predominate in Africa and other regions of the world. I want to address *why* opposition candidates care about expressive benefits like exposing government malfeasance and highlighting the importance of human rights protections. To do this, I return to the origins of candidacy paths and trace the impact of civic activism versus career partisanship on the benefits that aspirants seek when running for office. What is the impact of civic activism and career partisanship on candidacy decisions? The analysis will show that those who spend their pre-political careers engaged in grassroots activism and work in civil society organizations value the policy and ideological benefits that come from office, while career partisans go on to desire the material benefits of office.

I conduct a multivariate statistical analysis where the outcome of interest is the importance one places on a type of benefit when deciding to run for office. These are the same four indicators used in Section 8.1, which generally range between 0 and 75 and positive values on each of the ideology, material, prestige, and career measures correspond with thinking they are more important in guiding the choice to run. I use the same independent variables to capture civic activism – the associational membership index and years of grassroots mobilization experience – and career partisanship – five dichotomous variables associated with service at five party office levels and a variable of years since officially joining a political party and include control variables that could also account for placing varying value on each benefit type. The most important conclusions from the statistical analysis, which is provided in Appendix B.6, are visualized in Figure 8.4.

Figure 8.4 focuses on the two most critical differences in benefits that were highlighted in the previous section: the ideological and policy drivers of opposition candidacy and the material ones that underlie ruling party ambition. The left panel of the figure plots the impact of civic activism on the importance of ideological/policy benefits, while the right panel shows the relationship between civic activism and career partisanship and valuing material benefits of candidacy. The results suggest that civic activism – in particular, in the form of membership and leadership in distinctive types of civic associations – underlies desire for obtaining ideological benefits associated with candidacy, while eschewing material ones. This points to the potential socialization effect that civic activism can have on candidacy ambition. Emerging research on candidacy pipelines in Africa points to the role that NGO and CSO work can play in promoting political ambition: individuals may enter into such organizations absent a particular desire to run for office but through those groups come

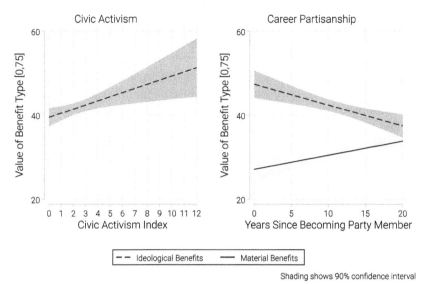

FIGURE 8.4 How civic activism and career partisanship impact benefits preferences

to care deeply about issues that are inherently political and over time learn that those goals can be better achieved through political office (Cloward and Weghorst 2019). This is what Trejo (2014) ultimately taps into when he writes about "socio-electoral coalitions" between opposition parties and civic activists: while they may be symbiotic in exchanging mobilization capacity for political representation, more fundamentally they value the same things because the mission of civic organizations that drives its activities also shapes what individual candidates want when they transition from activism to candidacy. The measure of civic activism derived from the life history calendar – years of grassroots mobilization experience – is not correlated with benefit preferences, pointing to the role of civic organizations as institutions that shape preferences of candidates.

This also helps make sense of the negative relationship between civic activism and valuing material benefits of office. Opposition leaders in Tanzania whose political careers have shaped this narrative and many others passed through civic organizations and associations en route to office in ways that shaped why they ultimately ran. By the time Tundu Lissu ran for office, he had already been charged by the government for sedition related to his work with LEAT to expose extrajudicial killings carried out by the government at the Bulyanhulu mine. He researched and coauthored the *Orodha ya Mafisadi* or "List of Shame" that detailed financial scandals of CCM's government and brought down the prime minister and several other cabinet members. It should come as no surprise that someone like him – who could have pursued a productive, profitable career as a private attorney engaged in benign legal activities but instead focused his legal acumen on government corruption and misconduct – would not be compelled to run for office for the formal financial perks of being an MP or to steer government funds to his own benefit. Rather, the desire for material gain grows from career partisanship, measured as years of formal party membership.[9]

To be clear, the claim here is not that all CCM MPs are corrupt: there are many who are dedicated toward reform and dutifully improving the lives of everyday Tanzanians. Indeed, there has historically been and remains an ongoing struggle within the party to sanction members for corruption because it ultimately is an electoral liability. Part of President Magufuli's ability to wrestle for and consolidate control within CCM while simultaneously cracking down on the opposition from his election in 2015 till his death in 2021 was driven by voter fatigue with corruption and his overtures to root it out. The point is that career partisanship is an investment of political capital in a political party. The ruling party is best positioned to offer material benefits to its legislators and as investment in that party increases, so do expectations of material returns on that investment.

These results suggest that not only do ruling party and opposition candidates differ on the benefits they expect from running for office. In fact, differences in civic activism and career partisanship experiences partially explain *why* individuals vary in terms of what they want from office. This work thus offers empirical evidence of the origins of political ambition and how the motivations to run for office are heterogeneous and based on personal background experiences.

CONCLUSION

This chapter has demonstrated in greater detail what parties offer legislative aspirants and what those aspirants want from parties. First, I explored what shapes the benefits of office for opposition and ruling party members who consider running for office and showed opposition candidates placed greater emphasis on ideology and prestige. Parties were

---

[9] Regional-level party leadership is also positively correlated with valuing material benefits and negatively with ideological ones.

viewed distinctly in terms of what benefits they provided for their candi-dates and once again, opposition versus ruling party candidacy maps onto differences over ideological versus material benefits provided by those parties. What should now be clear from this is that candidacy decisions for the opposition seem much more rational when viewed through the lens of choice-specificity – it appears that opposition parties delver what opposition candidates want, and the same holds for the ruling party side of things. I concluded the chapter by exploring origins of the desires for various benefits, linking civic activism to ideological benefits and career partisanship to material ones. The next chapter will look at the costs associated with candidacy conceptualized as costs outside of campaign expenditure undertaken when running for office in electoral authoritarian regimes.

9

Costs of Competing in Authoritarian Elections

Mpemba hakimbii mvua ndogo
A Pemban does not run away from a small shower.

Mstahimilivu hula mbivu
A patient man will eat ripe fruits.

This chapter explores the final term of the strategic candidacy framework: costs of competition. In advanced democracies, where candidates are primarily studied, the costs of candidacy are the amount spent on campaigns. Campaign finance is important in shaping candidacy motivations. When clientelism and "hyper-incumbency" advantages prevail, however, such costs are more optimally embedded within election prospects.

This chapter, instead, focuses on the costs of political competition outside of campaign financial expenditures that distinguish electoral authoritarian regimes from democracies, particularly those the opposition disproportionately bears. The chapter will characterize costs as perspectives toward risk associated with political actions and time horizons associated with political goals. In this chapter, I first review the types of nonfinancial costs and costs outside of campaigns that prospective candidates face in electoral authoritarian regimes. I then discuss measuring attitudes toward risk and time perspectives, focusing on challenges and solutions for retrospectively assessing such attitudes with regard to candidacy decisions. I compare the risk and time horizon attitudes of prospective legislators, showing contrasts between ruling party and opposition aspirants. The subsequent section of the chapter builds on the narratives of civic activism and career partisanship weaving through the preceding chapters, showing through the perspectives of Tanzanian politicians and with statistical analysis how backgrounds in these two trajectories shape attitudes toward risk and time perspectives. The chapter then concludes.

9.1 VIOLENCE AND REPRESSION IN TANZANIA

Tanzania features both a capacity to engage in coercion (Levitsky and Way 2010a, 254) and a willingness to use it for political ends. This threat of repression is particularly credible in Zanzibar, where political competition is robust and "has been intense, deadly, and zero-sum" (Killian 2008, 99). In the events surrounding elections in Zanzibar in 1995, an election in which the opposition allegedly beat CCM outright and thus the party resorted to fraud to maintain power, "many *maskani* youths on election day were given police uniforms, guns, and instructions – probably by Salim and his hard-line supporters – that, if CCM lost, they were to go on a rampage, attacking CUF supporters, especially those from Pemba" (Burgess 2009, 283). The period of protest following the October 2000 elections featured similar forms of repression and greater violence in both Zanzibar and mainland Tanzania. As CUF's candidate from the Zanzibar Presidency notes,

Throughout Tanzania on January 25 and 26, the police arrested many of our active leaders, including district chairmen, secretaries, and rank-and-file activists. …as people were leaving the Mwembetanga mosque in Zanzibar town, the police came and shot the imam dead and injured some of the people who happened to be there. They did this to intimidate the opposition, that people would not come out the following day. …The worst situation was in Pemba, especially in the Micheweni and Wete districts. People came out in the thousands. The police were unable to cope, so the officers used live bullets against the demonstrators. In all, they killed more than forty-five people, but there were also so many other atrocities. They broke into people's homes and stole anything they could. Many people were afraid that they would be arrested and tortured so they abandoned their homes to live in the bush. Police officers broke into our party branches and took all they could, destroying our files, party flags, and office furniture, even pulling down doors and windows. Much worse, they raped women and young girls and forced more than 2000 people to take refuge in Mombasa [Kenya]. It was as if a foreign army had invaded the island of Pemba. It was hard to believe that Tanzanian men in uniform could be so inhuman and cruel. (Burgess 2009, 294–295)

Human Rights Watch estimated that over 600 people were injured in violence led by state security forces and informal militia of the ruling party in the 2000 elections (Arnold, McKim, Rawlence, and Tate 2002).

Such repression is also present in the mainland. Former Civic United Front leader Ibrahim Lipumba relays this is the case, even in off-cycle years when smaller-scale by-elections take place. In describing a 2008 election in Ruvuma, he states:

The condition for us to campaign became impossible. Our supporters when they heard that we were there they were waiting for us. The police told them to disperse. When they did not do that they were tear-gassed and when we arrived there we found that police surrounded the whole place. And many of our supporters had been taken to prison. We had to go to the District Commissioner and negotiate the release of our supporters from prison. So there were as lot of use of police force. ... What was even worse was we found that very few voters actually voted during the Election Day and when we investigated with our supporters we were told that they had been threatened severely. We saw that there were very few people at the polling stations. We found out that representatives of CCM were buying identity cards from voters. The ten cell leaders of CCM also threatened people particularly people in vulnerable positions that they would register the numbers of the identity cards of the voters and that they had their way to know everyone who voted for CUF. (Ewald 2013, 229)

Party leaders and candidates too fall under additional scrutiny from and abuse by the government. For example, describing efforts of establishing CHADEMA ahead of the 1995 multiparty elections, party founder Edwin Mtei recounts: "At this time I also became aware of the fact that the National Security Service was following my movements closely, and especially trying to identify those who were visiting me – either at home in Arusha, or in my hotel if I happened to be in Dar es Salaam. This surveillance did not bother me, or any of my friends" (Mtei 2009, 196). He later recounts that during international travel to link with Tanzanian expats and similarly minded foreign parties, he was erroneously identified as a *persona non grata* in the United States by the Tanzanian Embassy, and Tanzania's ambassador to the United States was recalled as a punishment for meeting with Mtei (Mtei 2009, 201). Perennial candidate for the Civic United Front Maalim Seif notes similar patterns on the eve of multiparty rule: "[The government] began to post security officers around my house to question and intimidate my guests. They kept track of everyone who came there" (Burgess 2009, 258). Ewald (2013, 238) finds that even smaller opposition parties had these experiences, including the chairman of the United Democratic Party in Tanzania:

The police have been harassing the opposition parties in campaign especially when opposition party candidates have exceeded even a second in their campaigning hours. The opposition parties' candidates are fiercely ordered to step down [from] the pulpit. The police have never dared to do the same practice to the ruling party (CCM) candidates. This act is undemocratic and the favouritism to the ruling party can be viewed as a threat to the democratization processes in Tanzania. The IGP [Inspector General of Police] Mr Omary Mahita has been offering threatening statements to opposition parties, and protecting the ruling party CCM and its government.

It is documented that "the police and the TPDF [Tanzania People's Defense Forces] do indeed periodically and detain opposition party leaders, deploy excessive force for breaking-up opposition rallies, and commit seeming random acts of violence against citizens for unclear reasons" (Whitehead 2009, 87).

In addition to police harassment surrounding elections, administrators of Tanzania's decentralized government who are political appointees and expected to be nonpartisan – particularly regional commissioners (RCs) and district commissioners (DCs) – are also instruments of government repression against the opposition. As McLellan (2018) establishes, RCs and DCs are CCM stalwarts and often have military backgrounds and are particularly repressive in areas where opposition controls the local government and, thus, could develop a record of credible performance in government. This fits a broader pattern of threat and imbalance under which opposition supporters leaders live, including

having tax collectors target opposition supporters as well as business owners who fail to support or vote for CCM; threatening to revoke the licenses of business owners who do not support CCM; ordering police to shut down business during CCM rallies to boost attendance; telling public school teachers to encourage their students to attend CCM rallies and to discourage them from going to opposition gatherings; telling citizens that basic services are contingent on a ruling-party victory in their area; threatening civil servants with firing if they fail to mobilize the electorate for CCM. (Makulilo 2012, 38)

Threats toward civil servants and government employees over exercising their right to vote are documented elsewhere as well: "The ballot papers in 1995 carried serial numbers, so after, CCM conducted an investigation and connected individuals' names with serial numbers, and those in government employment who voted for CUF were often demoted or sacked" (Burgess 2009, 283).

For their own part, opposition parties have created paramilitary security forces charged with the protection of their leaders. The stated purpose of the Blue Guards of the Civic United Front is "the responsibility of protecting party leaders and property and on maintaining security at public rallies" (Burgess 2009, 286), particularly given concerns that the ruling party could use unrest at opposition rallies to justify government intervention. CHADEMA's so-called Red Brigade was created under its 2006 party constitution.[1] Such organizations have been publicly criticized by government officials as responsible for inciting conflict.[2]

As noted in Chapter 3, the capacity of the Tanzanian government to engage in repression has been a constant throughout its rule. The willingness of the regime to use its repressive abilities increased substantially from 2015 through 2020 under the first term of President John Pombe Magufuli, including more direct and overt efforts to harass, intimidate, attack and sometimes kill opposition activists and party leaders. The potential costs of violence and repression for opposition candidacy are thus significant in electoral authoritarian regimes and these dynamics are found in Tanzania.

At the same time, the impact of these potential costs on prospective opposition candidates may be mitigated by two potential factors: willingness to bear risks of potential costs and willingness to wait for the slow-moving, long-term political change opposition figures seek.

9.2 RISK AND TIME PERSPECTIVES THROUGH *Methali*

Survey questions assessing risk and time horizons presented two counterposed *methali*. After being read each of the *methali*, respondents for the Candidate/Noncandidate Survey and the Legislator Survey were asked to identify which was truer to their views of life at the time when they first considered seeking legislative candidacy. Respondents were then probed for the strength of this attitude. Two counterposed proverbs were used to allow an individual to think about the trade-offs of one over the other, which is truer to behavioral game designs that seek to explore risk through paired decisions regarding lotteries.

The first pair of *methali* tapped into attitudes toward risk aversion. Behavioral game designs capture risk aversion by presenting respondents with two lotteries: one where the benefits are high but the risk that one will not obtain them is high also, the other with lower benefits and lower risk. As noted earlier, a proverb-based risk assessment would capture

---

[1] As noted in Kweka (2015), its constitution states "There shall be a security system for the party's assets, leaders and interests which shall be known as Red Brigade."
[2] See, for example, statements from police commissioners in Arusha surrounding the 2012 by-elections there (Nkwame 2012).

these same trade-offs but also introduce a broader, nonfinancial sense of risk. Thus, the *methali* associated with risk tolerance was *Mla mla uchungu na tamu*, which translates to "She/He who eats bitter things also gets sweet ones." Noting that this resonated with an individual meant that to obtain things of value, there are costs and risks of doing so and that the individual was willing to accept that trade-off. The other proverb was associated with making decisions that are guided by caution and fear of consequences. This is "The timid crow withdraws its wings from harm," translated from *Kunguru mwoga hukimbiza ubawa wake*.[3]

If opposition activists – candidates and noncandidates alike – put themselves at substantial risk for standing against the incumbent government, one would expect to see opposition individuals demonstrating higher levels of risk tolerance, or conersely, lower levels of risk aversion. This means identifying more with the first *methali* rather than the second.

A second pair of proverbs looks at risk attitudes in the context of retrospection versus prospection. Recall that research finds that the policies and ideology of opposition parties can help candidates win offices when they emphasize retrospective evaluation of government performance, but that the politicians themselves are expected to have forward-looking dispositions. In other words, risk tolerance and risk aversion also relate to the idea of whether one should "learn from risk" and make progressively less risky decisions, particularly when they are associated with negative outcomes. On the other hand, it could be that politicians are willing to accept risk and also willing to suffer the consequences of that risk without fear or attitude change regarding risk in the future.

These attitudes are represented by two *methali*. The first one *Mwenye kuumwa na nyoka akiona nyasi zinasikitisha hushtuka* is tied to the idea of risk aversion formed from bad experiences in the past – that an individual may have taken risks at some prior point, but they should know now to not undertake such risks. The lessons of this expression are similar to the English language expression "Once bitten, twice shy." An individual who has been bitten by a snake before is now afraid even of movement in the grass. This *methali* is commonly used in social interaction and has a number of variations that point to this message.[4] The counterposed proverb is *Mla mla leo mla jana kala nini?*. It intends a meaning that

---

[3] It should be noted here that the language of this proverb does not imply negativity toward such a decision, which would suggest something other than risk aversion.

[4] For example, *Mwenye kuumwa na nyoka hamaliziki uboka* ("A person bitten by a snake does not finish being afraid.") See Swahili Proverbs (2014).

retrospective evaluation of personal action or experience is unimportant: it does not matter what you ate yesterday, but what you will eat today. In comparison to the first proverb, where individuals cannot move past the things that have affected them and cause them to fear risk, the second proverb promotes an attitude that decisions about risk in the present should not be conditioned based on what happened before.

To assess perspectives of ruling party versus opposition supporters toward time and the realization of political outcomes, the same strategy as before is utilized. Here, the first proverb – *Kawia Ufike* – is associated with longer-term time perspectives and translates to "Better to delay but arrive." This expression and variations of its message are perhaps the most common cultural lessons reinforced through *methali* in Tanzania. Many *methali* speak to this lesson of patience and longer-term views toward goals. The mantra of *pole pole* (slowly, slowly) that permeates the public discourse in Tanzania is present in many such proverbs: *Pole pole ndio mwendo* ("Slow, slow is the way to go"), *Haraka haraka haina baraka* ("Hurry, hurry has no blessings"), *Bandu bandu huisha gogo* ("Chip, chip, finishes the log"). Each promotes a message of patience, but the selected proverb also is unambiguously outcome oriented: there is a place where one is headed and it will take time to arrive there, but it is better to accept the longer-term perspective for the pursuit of such goals.

The second proverb is *Ngoja? Ngoja huumiza matumbo* and emphasizes that outcomes (here, filling the stomach) unrealized cause harm. In other words, it is time to eat now, not in the future. The selection of a *methali* that is oriented toward eating is no mistake: the idea of "eating" or "filling the stomach" is one commonly used in many African countries to refer to consumption, particularly the consumption of power and resources. Lindberg (2003) points out that a "chop" refers to small cash or material handouts (i.e., "chop money") and its meaning is established in relation to consuming food: "chops" or quick snacks. Iconic works on African postcolonial politics also invoke the metaphor of eating, as does Bayart (1993) in his *L'Etat en Afrique: La Politique du Ventre* ("The State in Africa: Politics of the Belly"), among others (Cheeseman, Branch, and Gardener 2010).

The metaphor of consumption is also important because it helps clarify that the meaning of *methali* in the survey is to be interpreted in the context of political outcomes, rather than personal ones. If there were ambiguity about the role of time horizons in terms of personal outcomes (e.g., whether or not one were to win a nomination in the ruling party versus the opposition), then one might expect to observe the opposition

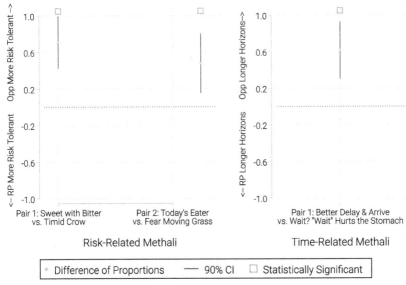

FIGURE 9.1 Risk and time perspectives with *methali*

pattern: potential candidates who choose a party with more accessible nomination spots could, outside of purely strategic behavior, have different perspectives toward time. By using proverbs that resonate with ideas of consumption, respondents had the unambiguous referent of power in government and the ability to enact political and ideological goals.

Results which compare the average responses of opposition and ruling party aspirants' attitudes toward these three pairs of methali are summarized in Figure 9.1. As with a number of preceding analyses, the figure plots the differences in views between the two groups of survey respondents. Values above the dotted line indicate the opposition on average identifies more with the *methali* in a given pair that is associated with more risk-tolerance/longer-time horizons. It illustrates that across the board, opposition activists are more risk tolerant. Among the opposition, legislators and candidates hold the attitudes most strongly – with 57.4 percent and 46.7 percent of respondents strongly agreeing that sweet things come with bitter ones. This makes sense, given their choice to run for office and those who won seats have likely faced many bitter consequences of doing so. The most frequent response for ruling party members was oriented "strongly" toward the risk-tolerant attitude, with a bit under half of respondents identifying this response (44 percent).[5]

[5] Disaggregated responses by group and strength of attitude are found in Appendix B.7.

For the second *methali* pair, differences between the ruling party and opposition members again indicate higher rates of risk tolerance of opposition candidates. In this case, CCM respondents are roughly split between the two *methali*, with the most common response being "strong" agreement with the risk-tolerant proverb, followed by "strong" agreement with the risk-averse attitude. "Strong" agreement is higher for opposition legislators, with almost two-thirds of respondents indicating this response and three-quarters of opposition legislators identifying with the the real eater being "today's" not yesterday's. Patterns similar to those found with the previous pair of proverbs are also present: opposition legislators demonstrate the highest levels of risk tolerance, and the views toward risk softens slightly for other groups of opposition respondents, particularly for noncandidates. While the aggregate total agreement with the risk-tolerant proverb is slightly lower for other opposition groups it is still significantly greater than the risk tolerance of CCM.[6]

Figure 9.1 also demonstrates that, as anticipated, opposition supporters held views more aligned with longer-term time horizons than did ruling party members at the time of seeking candidacy. About 70 percent of opposition legislators indicated at that time a message of being in for the long haul. By comparison, about 55 percent of ruling party respondents found the shorter time horizons more appealing. This resonates with a common joke opposition supporters make about the acronym of the ruling party that points to a desire for material goods and haste in getting them: "CCM: Chakua Chako Mapema" ("CCM: Take yours early!") (Wisjen and Tanner 2002, 111). The greatest prevalence of long-term time horizons is for opposition nomination seekers who were not selected as candidates, with just a shade under 80 percent of respondents agreeing with this attitude. Similar to how taking on the most risk held the risk attitude at highest rates, those individuals who sought nominations and were told by their party to wait are those who held longer-term time perspectives.

This section has demonstrated two main findings. First, respondents who are in opposition parties are more risk tolerant and this is especially the case for the most visible members of the opposition: candidates for office. Moreover, opposition members hold time perspectives that are compatible with the long-term effort needed to realize policy objections and potentially government turnover in an electoral authoritarian regime.

---

[6] Analyses of disaggregated responses by group and strength of attitude are found in Appendix B.7.

The final empirical section of this chapter moves to address the potential link between risk and time attitudes whereby lifelong experiences in civic activism versus career partisanship influence views about risk and time.

9.3 HOW CIVIC ACTIVISM AND CAREER PARTISANSHIP SHAPE CANDIDACY COSTS AND RISK ATTITUDES

How do backgrounds of civic activism versus career partisanship shape candidacy decisions? A growing empirical literature suggests activism begets activism: participation in protest, rallies, and anti-government demonstrations forges downstream cycles of protest activity through the channel of risk. In this view, exposure to risks, repression, and violence can enhance risk tolerance, reducing the barriers to higher-risk, higher-visibility actions against an electoral authoritarian regime. This path of civic activism thus impacts candidacy decisions by providing a route to opposition candidacy. By contrast, career partisanship may induce a sort of conservatism. After all, party recruitment and grooming procedures in electoral authoritarian regimes exist in service of the party – to manage internal dissent and to ensure members follow party positions and protocol. With regard to time perspectives, there are arguments for why either civic activism or career partisanship would be associated with longer-time horizons. On one hand, the goals of civic activists center on long-term political objectives, like deepening the rule of law and respecting human rights. The alignment of these goals with the stated objectives of the opposition makes them ideal complements. Even less explicitly political civic organizations nonetheless pursue long-term objectives: economic development, transforming attitudes toward women in the public realm. On the other hand, career partisanship is a long and grueling path through a political organization with a potential but uncertain candidacy opportunity. Earlier in the book, I argued that time horizons with regard to decisions to run for office are best understood in terms of prospects for government, following Shefter (1994) and others.

To further understand the relationship between risk and time attitudes and civic activism, I again draw upon a cross-sectional analysis of the Legislator Survey and Candidate/Noncandidate Survey data. The independent variable specification follows previous chapters, whereby civic activism is the additive measure of membership and leadership in several potential civic and grassroots organizations. Positions associated with career partisanship are captured as dichotomous variables indicating whether an individual held that position prior to running for office. I also use the two variables derived from the life history calendar – the number of years between having first engaged in civic activism (grassroots organizing) or in career partisanship (joining a party).

The dependent variables are created from the questions analyzed descriptively in Section 9.2. Each of these three questions is analyzed as a dichotomous variable where agreement or strong agreement with a risk attitude or time perspective is recoded as 1 and agreement or strong agreement for the opposition *methali* is coded as 0.[7] For the risk *methali*, these variables are coded such that regressions estimate the probability of a respondent identifying the *risk-tolerant* attitude, fitting a logistic regression model. Thus, independent variables indicate the impact of a given indicator of civic activism and career partisanship on the probability of agreement or strong agreement with the risk tolerant *methali – Mla mla uchungu na tamu* and *Mla mla leo mla jana kala nini?*. For the time perspectives measure, values of 1 indicate strong agreement or agreement with the longer time horizons *methali* – better delay but arrive, or *Kawia Ufike*. Analysis includes non-legislator respondents and thus has a higher number of observations.[8] The fully-specified regression results are found in Appendix B.7.

The analysis reveals no systematic pattern between either pathway to candidacy and time perspectives. Earlier in the chapter, we saw that opposition candidates hold longer-term perspectives toward time, but it does not appear that civic activism impacts opposition candidacy by shaping time perspectives. It may be that the concepts competing in this model are long-term paths: through political parties versus long-term paths in the civic sector. Thus, when analyzing such paths without the lens of partisan differences that undergird the structure of political competition in electoral authoritarian regimes, the role of civic activism versus career partisanship on time perspectives is not apparent. I review results from the two other pairs of *methali* now.

The first *methali* associated with risk tolerance was *Mla mla uchungu na tamu*, which translates to "She/He who eats bitter things also gets sweet ones." Noting that this resonated with an individual meant that to

---

[7] These questions presented interviewees with four possible response options (agreement or strong agreement with one of the two statements), as well as a fifth nonresponse/refused option that was not read out loud. Responses of this fifth type are treated as missing data.

[8] Findings are robust to the smaller legislator sample. Note regressions also include controls for gender, education, and age.

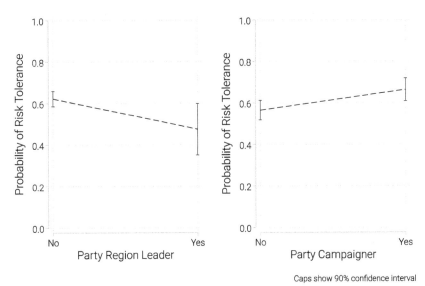

FIGURE 9.2 Risk tolerance, *methali* Pair 1

obtain things of value, there are costs and risks of doing so and that the individual was willing to accept that trade-off. The other proverb was associated with making decisions that are guided by caution and fear of consequences of making decisions. This is "The timid crow withdraws its wings from harm," translated from *Kunguru mwoga hukimbiza ubawa wake*. The results of this analysis are visualized in Figure 9.2. It indicates that career partisanship experiences have consequences for attitude toward risk. Specifically, individuals who served in regional party offices are less likely to identify with the risk-tolerant *methali*. Chapter 4 showed that career partisanship in the form of regional-level party service careers was significantly more likely to be found in ruling party candidates. Thus, risk attitudes may be a channel through which opposition versus ruling party decisions are charted.

Interestingly, we see the inverse is true for working for parties on the campaign trail: those who worked for a candidate or party on the campaign trail prior to running for office are less likely to identify with risk-averse attitudes and, instead, find resonance with *Mla mla uchungu na tamu*, that bitterness is accompanied by sweet things. In a broader view, this result coheres with empirical findings from previous chapters.

First, this chapter has documented well that participation in election campaigns for the opposition involves risk. Candidates themselves, as well as their supporters and staff, may be imprisoned, attacked, or beaten on the campaign trail. So, the extent to which campaign team-work is something demonstrated by opposition candidates, it would be unsurprising to see such experiences align with greater risk tolerance. Second, excepting perhaps higher-level campaign management activities (e.g., Ismail Jussa and January Makamba managed campaigns of pres-idential candidates for CUF and CCM, respectively), campaign work is viewed as a "young man's game." Workers try to mobilize voters to attend rallies, spread enthusiasm about a candidates and ultimately turn out vot-ers to the polls. Thus, it is a job that is the domain of the youth. Recall from Chapter 4 that opposition youth wing members identify the pri-mary activity of such youth wings as vehicles for party recruitment (25.5 percent of opposition youth wing members said the primary activity was recruiting new partisans; 16.6 percent said poaching members of other parties; 7.6 percent specifically said participating in rallies). Viewed as a form of mobilization and recruitment, campaign team activity may be characterized as youth-driven mobilization and recruitment, a tactic specifically used by risk-tolerant opposition actors. Chapter 8 provided evidence that prospective opposition candidates believe involvement in election campaigns (as candidates) is experientially beneficial – including boosting voter valence and gaining experience with election campaigns. It stands to reason that prospective opposition candidates may derive simi-lar benefits from simply participating in campaigns. While one might best learn the job of candidacy by being a candidate, opposition members may also improve their skills and abilities through campaign activism. I also showed that campaign work was associated with greater preference for ideological benefits, which may be another way these factors are related. It is for these reasons we see the correlation of risk tolerance and experience with campaign activism.

Moving to the second set of counterposed *methali*, we observe even more directly that career partisanship and civic activism experiences have consequences for attitudes toward risk. On the right panel of Figure 9.3, we see that career partisanship in the form of duration of party member-ship is negatively correlated with risk tolerance. On the left, by contrast, civic activism is positively associated with risk tolerance. Specifically, membership in civic organizations – from student and youth organiza-tions to women's advocacy groups and local, grassroots movements – is associated with a lower likelihood of identifying with a view of timidly withdrawing when facing potential harm. For each additional civic organ-ization membership or shift from membership to leadership, a prospective

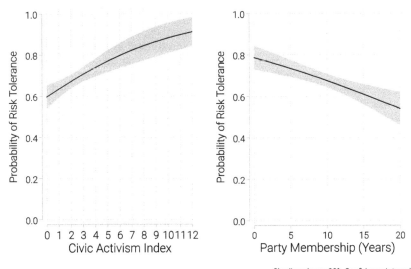

FIGURE 9.3 Risk tolerance, *methali* Pair 2

candidate is roughly 4 percent more likely to to choose this attitude, though the effect levels off with very high activism. Stated differently, those who are active in civic organizations and, in particular, across many types of organizations are more willing to accept consequences associated with "sweet things." This finding lends support to a literature arguing that activism begets further activism and suggests it might operate through risk aversion. If the risks of civic participation in electoral authoritarian regimes conditions individuals to accept further, increasing risks, then this may explain why individuals engage in the riskiest of such activities: running on opposition tickets in these settings.

Considering the narratives of political leaders in Tanzania reinforces the message borne out by the preceding regression analyses: participation in civic activism and lower-stakes political actions has consequences for attitudes toward risk, unlocking pathways to engage in a campaign against an authoritarian regime as an opposition candidate. Ismail Jussa describes his view on the movement from civil society to opposition as, in part, an opportunity structure problem in which civic organizations will not bear the risks that their members are willing to regarding anti-government activities. Thus, individuals in civil society who aspire to such activism must seek out the opposition to achieve those goals. From civil society groups like religious organizations, Jussa says there is support for the aspirations of opposition parties:

There's support. As recently said, I think it was Tundu Lissu who said, "You guys [in civil society organizations] who keep on talking there in the corridors and nobody is bold enough to come out and say something." In Tanzania, this whole struggle has been left to political parties. Even the political parties themselves have to face so many challenges including being infiltrated upon. I said it is so difficult because everything has to be fought by political parties.The civil societies are waiting for any man to follow, then for them to go and have their piece or share of that meat. They really want to be part of that struggle.

This echoes the experiences of his mentor – CUF's perennial candidate for president of Zanzibar Maalim Seif – who served the single-party government as a legislator, Minister of Education, and ultimately the Chief Minister of Zanzibar by the mid-1980s. He was sacked from this position for being branded as an agitator and a "liberator" – an activist for the cause of greater Zanzibari autonomy. After he was removed from his position, he carried on grassroots activities aimed at forming unity among Zanzibaris over this issue. It was at this time his risks related to civic activism transformed from career costs to more significant, personal security ones:

On May 9, I got wind while in Chake Chake [Pemba] that the police wanted to arrest me, so my bodyguards hid me in a safe house. I thought if the authorities arrested me in Pemba, it would lead to bloodshed, so better to be arrested in Unguja. My bodyguards chartered a plane, and we flew out about 6:30 the next morning. ... The same day two Land Rovers full of police arrive with a warrant to search my house. At the end of the search, the authorities arrested me and took me to the Mwembe Madema police station. After formalities, I was taken, barefoot, to a very dirty and wet cell that smelled of urine, with concrete benches around the room. ... The magistrate had been instructed not to give me bail, so I was sent straight to the central prison at Kilimani, under heavy escort. I was sent to a special area called "Cottage for Children" set aside for offenders under the age of eighteen. The prison officials reserved a special room for me alone, with a mattress but no bed. I was kept there as a sort of psychological torture, surrounded by children, with no adults to talk to. ... To isolate me further, they transferred me from the juvenile section to a room very close to the kitchen, where all the smoke tended to concentrate. I protested to my lawyers, so they transferred me to the cells on death row.

The role civic activism played in shaping risk attitudes is highlighted by Seif's response to this dire situation. An international actor became involved in advocating for Seif's release as his trial dragged on. Then Zanzibari President Salmin Amour agreed to release Seif from prison "on the condition that I refrain from politics. When she came to me with this news, I told the ambassador that I would never forsake this right, even if it meant staying in prison all my life" (Burgess 2009, 263). As Paget (2017) notes, the opposition has made the willingness of the government to engage in publicized repression a critical point in undermining the ruling party's credibility.

The use of this strategy requires its candidates and leaders to be willing to pay high costs of bearing such repression; one opposition MP protesting police intervention on the floor of Parliament recently said, "I won't leave this chamber. You can kill me. I'm ready."[9]

In his first public statements after being abducted by the police in the 2020 elections, Ismail Jussa called called to international actors and allies to support the opposition's struggle, saying "we ourselves have tried our best and are ready to make any sacrifice needed" for the sake of democracy. He further downplayed the costs he has paid: "In the end, I want to say when you seek justice, there is always a price, and this is the price we pay for fighting for national sovereignty. We want to have a state that respects the rule of law, human rights, and the foundations of democracy. We want a nation where all citizens will be treated equally. That will be the basis of the legitimacy of government in the country."

CONCLUSION

The main contribution of this chapter was an exploration of attitudes toward costs of candidacy and risk and time horizons. Using cultural proverbs called *methali*, this chapter demonstrated that opposition activists and candidates have attitudes more tolerant of risk and have longer-term orientation toward achieving outcomes The chapter pointed to contemporary successes of opposition in challenging government repression by working at the grassroots level, where existing structures of civic activism and resistance can be mobilized against the ruling party.

---

[9] Paget (2017, 161), citing Godbless Lema as quoted in *The Citizen*.

10

Testing the Argument across Africa

Mwanzi hauvunjwi na upepo
A reed is not broken by the wind.

Tembea ukaone
Travel and look. Travel and learn.

10.1 OPPOSITION CANDIDACY IN SUB-SAHARAN AFRICA

What explains the decision to run on opposition tickets in legislative elections held by authoritarian regimes? While opposition candidacy is incredibly common in these settings, our prevailing understanding of candidacy decisions predicts it should not be. There are significant risks of anti-regime activism in electoral authoritarian contexts. The party in power is also all but guaranteed to win big and continue to control the government. This renders the predominant explanation of candidacy in advanced democracies – a strategic framework whereby aspirants decide to run (or not) based on assessments of chances of winning, candidacy costs, and benefits of office – inadequate to make sense of candidacy choices in the nondemocratic regimes that predominate in sub-Saharan Africa and much of the rest of the world. Existing alternative accounts primarily emphasize instrumental and materially driven motivations underlying candidacy. Such approaches are theoretically useful, but incomplete.

Key Insights

In this book, I have evaluated three new insights that address gaps in our current understanding of legislative ambition and shed light upon opposition candidacy in electoral authoritarian regimes. First, candidacy decisions reflect more than a simple, strategic calculus legislative aspirants engage in at the moment of choosing to run or not. The decision is reflective of personal experiences that shape perspectives toward politics and impose a path dependence on political ambition. Just as there are career and social pipelines to political office in advanced democracies, I established that the decision to run for office in electoral authoritarian regimes – and doing so on opposition tickets rather than with the ruling party – can be attributed to previous experiences in activism. Chapter 4 presented an empirical analysis of survey data collected from aspirants for legislative office in Tanzania. The analysis illustrated that greater civic activism in the form of community organizing and associational membership activity was associated with opposition candidacy. Conversely, ruling party candidacy is linked to career partisanship, a process whereby political capital of potential candidates is cultivated in the lower rungs of the party. Some opposition candidates contributed to their parties, but in ways that differed significantly from those of ruling party aspirants. Such service was narrowly tailored to the needs of the opposition: filling critical vacancies in skilled positions at the highest levels of the party and in youth mobilization are activities core to the voter recruitment strategy of the opposition. Sequence analyses of the vocational and political careers of current and former Tanzanian legislators in Chapter 5 further affirmed this pattern. Working in the NGO and CSO sector propelled individuals toward the opposition, while ruling party trajectories into office reflect slow, incremental credential building in low-prestige, local and regional party offices prior to candidacy as well as political party and government employment.

Second, I argued that the elements that shape the strategic candidacy framework – chances to win, benefits of victory, and the costs of competing – required innovation to adequately capture the realities of candidacy outside advanced democracies. Chapter 6 emphasized that political competition is highly asymmetrical in electoral authoritarian settings, where odds are stacked against opposition candidates. Yet, equating prospects of victory as resting solely on election day overlooks a prior political obstacle all aspirants must overcome before election day: winning a party endorsement. Winning nomination contests for the ruling party is much more difficult. Together, Chapters 6 and 7 concluded that higher chances of making it onto an electoral ballot for the opposition versus ruling party offset some electoral disadvantages opposition candidates face. Chapter 8 established that anticipated benefits of running for office are choice-specific in that opposition parties have comparative advantages in drawing candidates who are motivated by boosting public visibility and promoting ideological/policy goals, especially because these can be earned even without winning an election. Costs of candidacy in the existing literature are generally viewed as out-of-pocket campaign expenses; Chapter 9 made clear the significant non-campaign costs present in authoritarian elections and the willingness of opposition candidates to bear those costs.

Third, I linked these two ideas. Each chapter showed that experiences in civic activism versus career partisanship not only accounted for differences in opposition versus ruling party candidacy decisions; the distinctive paths into politics an aspirant traveled down prior to candidacy impacted how they evaluated election prospects, benefits of candidacy, and costs and risks of running. More experience with civic activism is associated with greater electoral success among opposition candidates. Civic activists report greater tolerance of personal and political risk, are motivated by policy and ideological benefits, see benefits in losing well-fought election contests, and are more likely to win nominations and elections. Candidates with career partisanship backgrounds, by contrast, place a high premium on material benefits of office and see little to gain by losing elections.

The book has tested a theory regarding opposition candidacy in great detail in Tanzania. The goal of this chapter is to assess how well the theory extends to other regimes in sub-Saharan Africa. The analysis in this chapter offers three primary insights. First, the core findings of the book are supported in other electoral authoritarian regimes in Africa with regard to the role of civic activism in promoting opposition candidacy and how career partisanship drives ambition for the ruling party. Moreover, I show that opposition legislators place much greater emphasis on policy goals regarding the legislature than do ruling party MPs. This contrasts with a robust literature suggesting African candidates and parties do not differ on policy grounds. Second, much of the theory this book offers applies to "dominant" or "hegemonic" party democracies. In these regimes, civic activism does not serve the critical role for opposition candidacy because parties themselves are permitted more room to operate independently. Patterns of career partisanship remain a pathway to power in the ruling party. Ideological differences between ruling party and opposition legislators are also present in dominant party settings. In these environments, policy conflict emerges regarding the role of the legislature and in the "nested game" in which ruling parties and challengers compete over the structure of political competition.

Finally, I show that candidacy in competitive democracies in Africa differs greatly from these other two regime types. When change in the party in power is possible, there is less to differentiate the prospects of candidacy between parties. Parties in these settings are often organizationally weak and ephemeral. This leads to entrepreneurial politicians who have little incentive to invest in a political party and are less committed to lofty political ideals. Under these circumstances, the conventional approach toward theorizing legislative candidacy – rather than my account emphasizing long-term pathways to politics, intraparty competition, heterogeneous benefits preferences, and life and death risks of political participation – is better suited for explaining patterns of candidacy in Africa's competitive democracies.

The chapter begins by introducing the African Legislatures Project (ALP), a data resource equipped to test the external validity of my theory. In the section that follows, I categorize the regimes included in the dataset and describe how ALP can be leveraged to examine pieces of the theory guiding the book. Each of the subsequent three sections of chapter is dedicated to one of the regime types represented in the ALP: electoral authoritarian regimes, dominant party democracies, and democracies with robust interparty competition. For each of these regime types, I focus the empirical investigation on two aspects of the theory: (1) the impact of career partisanship versus civic activism on ruling party versus opposition candidacy and (2) differences between opposition and ruling party legislators over policy positions and perceived benefits of running for office. The chapter concludes by reflecting on what testing this theory with ALP data has taught us about opposition candidacy in electoral authoritarian regimes and about electoral politics in Africa.

10.2 DATA RESOURCE: AFRICAN LEGISLATURES PROJECT

Data used in this chapter are from the African Legislatures Project (ALP). ALP grew out of recognition of the importance of legislatures in elections, representation, and accountability in Africa. Scholars studying these phenomena have access to a wealth of citizen-level data, but there is a dearth of information about the role of candidates and legislators in linking citizens to government and serving as stewards of development.

To rectify this deficiency, pioneering scholars of African legislatures and public opinion surveys in Africa – Joel Barkan, Robert Mattes, Shaheen Mozaffar, and Kimberly Smiddy – collected surveys from legislators in eighteen African countries from 2008 through 2012. ALP is the most extensive effort to study African parliaments in the history of the institutions. The countries are a mixture of competitive democracies, dominant party democracies, and electoral authoritarian regimes. In my analysis, I include sixteen countries.[1] Table 10.1 shows the sixteen countries that I use categorized by regime type.[2]

The survey was primarily designed to study the function of African legislatures and their role in democratization. Much of the questionnaire focuses on formal aspects of the institution (e.g., committee structure, staff provisions, salary) and legislator activities (e.g., the nature of constituency service and voter linkage, party discipline and voting). The data thus do not permit a comprehensive test of each element of the theory and do not have directly comparable survey items. The resource nonetheless does include a number of established survey questions regarding legislator background and motivations that speak to the concepts underlying the theory presented in this book, particularly career partisanship versus civic activism and differences over the benefits of running for office. Those measures are described in the subsections that immediately follow. The gap between growing scholarly interest in African legislatures and data more specifically tailored to pathways into the legislature points to important opportunities for future researchers to contribute to this growing and significant literature.

Career Partisanship versus Civic Activism

I use the African Legislatures Project to test whether career partisanship covaries with ruling party candidacy across regime type and if civic activism is associated more with opposition candidacy. The primary way I capture career partisanship versus civic activism is through a demographic question asked at the beginning of the ALP survey: the "main occupation" of the respondent prior to entering the legislature.

---

[1] I drop Mali because of the 2012 coup that occurred after the collection of the ALP data. Cape Verde is also dropped because data coverage is not complete for the subset of questions I study in this chapter.

[2] Electoral authoritarianism versus single-party dominance is classified consistent with Morse (2019), with the exception of Nigeria.

TABLE 10.1 *Classifying African Legislatures Project regimes*

Regime Type	Cases
Electoral Authoritarian	Tanzania, Uganda, Zimbabwe, Mozambique, Burkina Faso
Dominant Party Democracy	Botswana, South Africa, Namibia, Nigeria,† Lesotho‡
Competitive Democracy	Benin, Ghana, Kenya, Malawi, Senegal, Zambia

†: Nigeria's People's Democratic Party (PDP) won four successive presidential elections from 1999 through 2011, a majority of the upper house in this period, and a majority in the lower house for the first three elections. The PDP lost power in 2015 but is considered a dominant party in reference to the African Legislatures Project data, which was collected prior to the defeat of the PDP in 2015.
‡: Lesotho Congress for Democracy (LCD) won elections in 1998, 2002, and 2007; it was a splinter from the Basotho Congress Party, which won 1993 elections that were the first competitive elections since 1970. Like Nigeria, the ruling party LCD has lost an election between the completion of the ALP data collection effort and the time of writing. In 2012, the Democratic Congress – a party that was formed when LCD's 2007–2012 prime minister left the party – defeated LCD, which finished third. LCD remained in government through 2017. From 2012-2015, it was in a coalition with the All Basotho Convention, a party that splintered from LCD in 2006 and placed second in the 2012 elections. From 2015–2017, it was in a coalition with the Democratic Congress.

The variable is transformed into binary indicators of career partisanship (one's "main occupation" was in a political party), civic activism (a "civil society/NGO" occupational background), or the pathway common to advanced democracies (work in government and/or civil service).[3] There are limitations of this measure. In evaluating my theory in earlier chapters, civic activism and career partisanship were operationalized richly, inclusive of non-occupational experiences as they unfold over time: grassroots organization; publicly pledging support to a political party;

---

[3] This variable is drawn from an open-ended question after which responses were coded into roughly fifty response categories by the ALP. I then further simplified the coding into categories that included civil society, political party, government, and other conventional legislator career backgrounds (e.g., business, law, teaching). Coding details are found in Appendix B.8.

years of side work performed in a party office; mobilization activity proximate to an election; and civic and party leadership falling outside of formal career commitments. The ALP measure is specific to formal employment and occupation and captures a specific, fixed point in time. This less comprehensive measure is therefore likely to underestimate the true prevalence and variability of civic activism and career partisanship among ALP respondents but is nonetheless the best available option to test for them in a broad set of African regimes.

I use two additional measures for examining the relationship between party service and party choice across different regimes. Observed heterogeneity between opposition and ruling party legislators suggested that the latter group develop party capital through lower-rank "grunt work" in the party. Opposition legislators who demonstrated party service held high-prominence, skilled positions – as Ismail Jussa and James Mbatia showed. To evaluate the role of party service of different type and intensity across African electoral regimes, I use a survey item that asked legislators about party positions held before becoming an MP. The question categorized positions as national, subnational (e.g., district, region, province), or local.

A second measure captures career partisanship as a vehicle to reinforce party loyalty and compliance, whereby accrued political capital becomes inextricably tied to the ruling party. If career partisanship is pronounced in this way for ruling party legislators and is not for opposition legislators, then ruling party legislators should exhibit greater party loyalty and greater willingness to put the priorities and views of the party first, above their own view, those of citizens, and the national interest broadly. ALP asked respondents whether the views of the party should take primacy if they come in conflict with these three alternative viewpoints.

All measures of career partisanship and civic activism described here are dichotomous. Analysis is presented in the text visually and corresponds with statistical tests found in Appendix B.8.

Benefits of Candidacy

Previous chapters highlight how opposition aspirants in electoral authoritarian regimes simply want different things than their ruling party adversaries: they are motivated to "fight the good fight" to strengthen human rights, boost service delivery and government accountability, support marginalized groups and improve development outcomes. Relatedly, these benefits can even be obtained by opposition legislators in the face of electoral defeat. By contrast, ruling party legislators seek out material benefits at much higher rates. Using information from the African Legislatures Project, I aim to determine how well these patterns travel to other authoritarian regimes and to democracies in Africa.

ALP data permit a general assessment of the significance of ideology to legislators and the role of the legislature in policy making – evidence of the significance legislators assign to ideological benefits of office. ALP participants were asked whether the legislature exercised too much or too little control over a total of ten duties that include oversight, legislation, and constituency development. Respondents reported if the legislative body had "Far too little," "Too little," "About right," or "Too much" control over policy making. Demanding more policy-making power of the legislature aligns with seeking ideological benefits of officeholding.

10.3 TESTING THE THEORY IN OTHER ELECTORAL AUTHORITARIAN REGIMES

The first empirical effort in this chapter is to consider whether the findings presented in the previous chapters are supported in other electoral authoritarian regimes in Africa. The African Legislatures Project dataset includes five electoral authoritarian regimes: Uganda, Zimbabwe, Mozambique, and Burkina Faso, as well as Tanzania.

Morse (2019) categorizes both Burkina Faso and Mozambique in the same electoral authoritarian subtype as Tanzania for the time period in which ALP study participants have served as MPs: "tolerant hegemony". In them, legislative supermajorities or similar presidential vote margins are obtained across multiple elections and there is some minimum threshold of restraint in exercising the "menu of manipulation" available to autocrats across domains of use of physical violence, conduct of elections, freedom of association, and freedom of assembly.[4]

Burkina Faso

In Upper Volta – renamed Burkina Faso by military leader and President Thomas Sankara – multiparty elections were reintroduced by President Blaise Compaoré at the close of 1991. Since assuming power leading by a

---

[4] See pages 72–89 of Morse (2019) for more information on coding.

coup against Sankara in 1987, these presidential elections were boycotted by opposition challengers and marked the first of twenty-three years Compaoré would govern under regular multiparty electoral competition. He remained in power until he was forced out in the Burkinabè uprising, in which a coalition of formal opposition, political activists, and citizens protested a proposed referendum to remove term limits that would have required Compaoré to step down in 2015. His party – Organisation pour la Démocratie Populaire - Mouvement du Travail (ODP/MT) – won parliamentary elections in 1992 with nearly 75 percent of seats and, after forming Congrès pour la Démocratie et le Progrès (CDP) by merging ODP/MT with several smaller pro-regime parties, would go on to win legislative majorities across the four elections before Compaoré resigned. CDP's rule under Compaoré was less institutionalized than its ruling party counterparts in Tanzania and Mozambique, a "catch-all" party that emphasized the centrality of Compaoré while managing factionalism from rival elites within the party (Elischer 2013, 208). It notably lacked meaningful programmatic positions in campaigns (Bleck and van de Walle 2013).

Opposition candidates regularly faced a risk of arrest and imprisonment and government responses to evidence of political crimes focused on quelling dissent rather than significant reform (Santiso and Loada 2003, 400–402).[5] The ideological focus of the opposition under Compaoré's presidency was "surprisingly precise" (Elischer 2013, 209). The repression faced by opposition activists became a focal point around which the opposition organized its policy orientation: the murder of Norbert Zongo. A journalist who was investigating the mysterious death of the driver of Compaoré's brother, Zongo's death led to the creation of the *Collectif des Organisations Démocratiques de Masse et de Partis Politiques* (the Collective of Democratic Mass Organizations and Political Parties, CODMPP), a formal alliance between opposition parties and students, unions, civic activists, and human rights organizations over political and economic policy goals (Engels 2015, 97–98).

Compaoré's ousting in 2014 is attributed to student activists, trade unions, and *Le Balai Citoyen* (The Citizen's Broom), a grassroots movement led by musicians Sams'K Le Jah (Sama Karim) and Smockey (Serge Bambara), who worked in collaboration with opposition parties to force

---

[5] As Santiso and Loada (2003) note, the government nonetheless was compelled to implement modest electoral reforms that boosted opposition prospects through a more proportional electoral system and heightened electoral commission independence.

Compaoré from power. While the analysis of legislator viewpoints will focus on electoral authoritarianism under the Compaoré regime, the events that occurred subsequently affirm the role of civic activism and political opposition pathways identified in this book.

Uganda

Uganda has been governed by Yoweri Museveni since 1986, when the National Resistance Movement's (NRM) military wing removed President Tito Okello in a coup d'état. The NRM held subnational elections through the first decade of Museveni's tenure in power and its first quasi-parliamentary and Constituent Assembly polls were held in 1989 and 1994, respectively. Political parties were not banned; opposition parties were brought into coalition with the NRM. In 1996, the no-party "movement system" came into force. Under it, presidential and parliamentary candidates competed in regular elections and both party endorsements of candidates and single-party rule were constitutionally prohibited, while the NRM increasingly operated organizationally like a political party (Kasfir 1998).

Uganda's introduction of multiparty competition resembled the actions of many autocratic ruling parties that survived to compete under multiparty rule. First, they were a concession to preserve the rule of those in power. As Tripp (2010) notes, Museveni was term limited under the 1995 constitution and permitting multiparty elections was offered as a *quid pro quo* in exchange for lifting presidential term limits. Second, the change entrenched the NRM's hold on power because separating from the state meant it inherited credibility, experience, resources, and power that no challenger party could hope to amass in the two years between the proposed reforms and the 2006 national elections (Tripp 2020, 85–86).

The NRM as a party is institutionally weaker than Burkina Faso's CDP was and Tanzania's Chama Cha Mapinduzi is. However, it excels in the sustaining its rule through a combination of patronage distribution and repression from various state and parastatal channels, including organizations that engage in torture and executions (Tripp 2010, 135–141). Like many autocratic regimes in Africa, Uganda has introduced a number of laws that restrict political activity and can be harnessed to punish the opposition. The Anti-Terrorism Act of 2002, for example, was used to threaten radio station deejays with imprisonment or hanging for engaging with the leader of opposition party Forum for Democratic Change (FDC) Dr. Col. Kissa Besigye (Tripp 2004). In the 2016 elections, the government specifically targeted social media use to manage the role that civil society actors could play in mobilizing for democratic policies (Tripp 2017).

Given the comparably shorter period of formal opposition in Uganda, many prominent leaders in the contemporary opposition defected from the ruling party and prominent defections primarily occurred from NRM into the opposition (consistent with my expectations regarding co-optation). The main opposition party FDC is led by a former NRM/NRA leader and a new splinter party formed in 2016 by former prime minister Amama Mbabazi (Khisa 2016). There is, however, a long-documented relationship between student activism and anti-government political activism since independence (Byaruhanga 2006); former leaders from Makerere University's Guild are current MPs for opposition parties or independents (Wesonga 2018). Women's associational autonomy and the resulting landscape for women's organizations in Uganda have promoted high levels of political engagement(Tripp 2012), including several prominent legislators in the opposition. Under no-party and multiparty rule, Uganda's trade unions have been formally represented in parliament and they have maintained an alliance with Museveni (Webster 2007).

In the 2021 elections there, Museveni's main challenger was musician turned politician parliamentarian Bobi Wine of the National Unity Platform. When he first ran for the legislature in 2017, he drew from his popularity as the "Ghetto President" of Karmwoyka, the slum where we grew up and honed his musical craft, in order to mobilize urban youth behind his campaign. Bobi Wine's political credibility is also rooted in the focus of his music on issues aligned with the goals of Uganda's opposition. His songs have criticized government public health services, highlighted crackdowns on digital and social media, and promoted youth activism during election campaign periods. Wine is far from the first musician to run for office in an electoral authoritarian regime, but there may be a contemporary alignment between young musicians and their ability to mobilize constituencies that support the opposition. Tanzanian hip-hop artist turned MP Joseph Mbilinyi followed a similar path in gaining fame performing as Sugu and Mr. II, turning to political messaging in music, and running for parliament on the CHADEMA ticket. Like Bobi Wine, a number of Mbilinyi's songs explicitly criticize government performance and have been publicly banned for this reason, leading to their further spread through digital and social networks that are also used to organize resistance against authoritarian governments.

Zimbabwe

Zimbabwe is unique among the autocratic cases included in the ALP dataset in that it has been an electoral authoritarian regime since its recognization as an independent state: its liberation struggle resulted in the dissolution of white rule and the introduction of multiparty elections in 1980 that were won by the Zimbabwean African National Union (ZANU) without interruption through 2008. While it narrowly lost its legislative majority to the Movement for Democratic Change (MDC) in 2008, ZANU-Patriotic Front (ZANU-PF) remained in power and re-entrenched its hold over the legislature in the subsequent two national elections.

With its origins in military insurgency, ZANU was an organizationally competent political party that inherited a state that was itself strong, with an especially high capacity for repression and a robust military force (Levitsky and Way 2010*a*, 238–239). ZANU's origins as an insurgency that mobilized local support networks means that, like Burkina Faso and Tanzania, Zimbabwe's ruling party had local party presence that extended from the national government, through regional and district headquarters, to local branches at the cell level. ZANU incorporated its electoral rival Zimbabwe African People's Union (ZAPU) to become ZANU-PF following a series of attacks by Zimbabwe's national army that killed ZAPU supporters and dissidents in Matabeleland (Mashingaidze 2005). The resulting consolidation of political power and a reform to introduce-presidential rule ensured Robert Mugabe and ZANU-PF would not face credible political rivals in the foreseeable future.

The primary sources of political opposition came from student activists, religious and civil society groups, and labor organizations in response to political and economic crises in the late 1990s. Structural adjustment reforms adopted had wide-ranging consequences for Zimbabweans, and the Zimbabwe Congress of Trade Unions (ZCTU) organized demonstrations, protests, and strikes regarding these economic consequences in response (LeBas 2011, 118–121). Civil society actors – including the Catholic Church, tenants' associations, grassroots movements, student governments – also protested the consequences of the structural adjustment reforms (LeBas 2011, 124–129). However, no broad-based or credible political organization existed through which these grievances could be channeled.

These disparate forces were catalyzed by the ZCTU's creating of the National Constitutional Assembly (NCA) as an umbrella organization pursuing constitutional reform, as it simultaneously developed a local, diffuse presence of the organization in anticipation of supporting a new, unified political opposition (LeBas 2011, 139). It subsequently launched as the Movement for Democratic Change (MDC) in September 1999. It quickly coalesced into a formidable political force by drawing extensively on the existing organizational structure of the ZCTU and including leaders drawn from organized labor, student movements, and human rights activism, "since these individuals had skills, expertise, and, occasionally, ties to some popular constituencies that labor lacked" (LeBas 2011, 181; 185). The origins of Zimbabwe's contemporary political opposition echoes the overall message of my book: civic activism forges a pathway to the political opposition for both push and pull reasons. Activists have goals that align with those of the political opposition and can find avenues to pursue those goals through political participation; opposition parties facing autocratic rivals need all the help they can get in their struggle against the party in power.

Zimbabwe also stands out among the electoral authoritarian regimes included in the African Legislatures Project in that it is the most repressive. According to Morse's (2019) figures, Zimbabwe's political tolerance is rated about 10 out of 100, compared with roughly 25 for Uganda, 40 for Tanzania and Mozambique, and 50 for Burkina Faso.[6] It is particularly pronounced on dimensions of violence (risks/costs of candidacy) and electoral manipulation. In the 2002 Zimbabwean elections, the MDC "declared 49 out of the 120 [parliamentary] constituencies too violent to campaign at all" (Kurebwa 2001, 49); the party's presidential candidate Morgan Tsvangirari was arrested over charges of plotting to assassinate Mugabe (Raftopoulos 2002); after the election, the government repressed protests and attacked MDC activists (LeBas 2006). It is also widely acknowledged that election results were fraudulent in 2002 and that in 2008, MDC presidential candidate may have actually won the first round of voting with an outright majority. He went on to lose in the runoff after a campaign of violence against the MDC (Hill 2003, Levitsky and Way 2010*a*, 246)

Mozambique

Mozambique's FRELIMO has governed since Mozambique attained its colonial independence from Portugal in 1975. Its current period of rule

---

[6] See Appendix A in Morse's (2019) book.

under multiparty politics began with elections in 1994 that followed the resolution of a protracted civil war against its contemporary political rival and former insurgency RENAMO in 1992. Like Tanzania's ruling party, FRELIMO invested significantly in building party infrastructure and institutionalizing recruitment and training mechanisms for youth, women, and workers (Manning 2005) and upon liberalizing political competition nonetheless maintained party control over many state institutions (Carbone 2003). Opposition activists face repression (Manning 2002), the government physically and financially punishes opposition supporters and elections feature fraud, financial malfeasance, and limited violence carried out by the incumbent regime (Carter Center 2005). FRELIMO's efficacy as a political party arises in part from its legacy as a liberation movement and military organization (Levitsky and Way 2010*a*).

Expectations

Career Partisanship and Civic Activism

Generally speaking, the claims advanced in this book regarding career partisanship versus civic activism and ruling party versus opposition candidacy should be supported in other electoral authoritarian regimes, particularly those in Africa. There is nothing so unique about Tanzania or party dynamics there such that empirical findings would not be valid in other electoral authoritarian settings.

Recall from Chapter 2 that civic activism captured the journey by which individuals who engage in grassroots activism, work for NGOs, and run civil society organizations become invested in goals that align with opposition parties. This foments political ambition which, when realized, funnels them to run with the opposition. The concept of career partisanship encompasses the relative importance of party service and experience in deeming prospective candidates fit to run for office in an electoral authoritarian regime. Unlike democratic settings, where political experience is a critical marker of candidate preparation and quality, "career politicians" commonly dominate electoral ballots party positions provide opportunities for prospective candidates to develop political capital and prove loyalty to the ruling party. The longevity of electoral authoritarian governments hinges on their ability to maintain cohesion and to punish noncompliance and factionalism. Career partisanship serves this function. It also channels political ambition toward the ruling party for individuals along this pathway.

This leads to a pair of strong empirical expectations that should be affirmed in electoral authoritarian regimes in sub-Saharan Africa. Most importantly, the theory is externally valid if civic activism pathways to the opposition are found in other electoral authoritarian regimes in Africa. LeBas's (2011) account of Zimbabwean opposition party building certainly points in this direction. She convincingly demonstrates that civil society organizations provide organizational capacity and institutionalized linkages to grassroots movements and illustrates how such pro-democracy forces can be transformed into political party mobilization. The nature and source of civic activism are likely to differ by case – trade unions shaped the Zimbabwean experience, and in other settings women's groups, religious organizations, student government, grassroots movements, or transnational movements may play the key role. Thus, the first testable implication of the theory is whether opposition legislators have more background experience in civic activism than do their ruling party counterparts.

The second empirical expectation regards career partisanship. Ruling party candidates feature party service at greater rates, and this service should be concentrated in lower-level, unskilled positions. If opposition candidates have background party experience, it should be found in national-level party duties.

A related implication of the theory regards the role of government employment, which is viewed as a pathway to office and a key characteristic of career politicians in advanced democracies. Chapter 4 portrayed career partisanship as a substitute for this formal political experience: having worked in government – even though it is controlled almost entirely by the ruling party – does not distinguish ruling party candidates from opposition challengers. Chapter 5 showed that political positions in government work may be useful for ruling party candidacy. This does not provide clear expectations with regard to government work.

Strategic Candidacy Framework: Benefits and Costs

Chapter 8 argued that benefits of office under electoral authoritarianism are heterogeneous in terms of (1) what candidates want, (2) what parties are capable of or have comparative advantages in facilitating, and (3) whether those benefits can be obtained even in electoral or nomination defeat.

With regard to the first point, I theorized that opposition candidacy facilitates ideological benefits, particularly in terms of how candidacy delivers expressive benefits associated with visible and vocal political

TABLE 10.2 *External validity in Africa's electoral authoritarian regimes*

Component of Theory	Expectations
Pathways to Office	Career Partisanship ⇒ RP Civic Activism ⇒ Opp Govt Exp ⇒ RP (?)
Benefits of Candidacy	Material: RP>Opp Ideology: RP<Opp

action. Ruling party candidates are motivated by the material benefits of office, along with the ways in which serving in office can serve private sector career advancement and goals. Empirical analysis in preceding chapters strongly supported the intuitions regarding material and ideological benefits. For the electoral authoritarian regimes considered in this chapter – Mozambique, Burkina Faso, Zimbabwe, and Uganda (along with Tanzania) – I anticipate similar empirical patterns, although the ALP data are limited in how effectively I can test this.

Expectations that should be verified for the theory to be externally valid are summarized in Table 10.2. The section that immediately follows tests these expectations.

Career Partisanship and Civic Activism in Electoral Authoritarian Regimes

Do we observe career partisanship pathways among ruling party legislators and civic activism among parliamentarians from the opposition? I first test this expectation across five electoral authoritarian regimes in Africa using the demographic question from the African Legislatures Project: a respondent's occupation prior to becoming an MP. Figure 10.1 shows the proportion of respondents who fall into one of three categories: civic activism, career partisanship, and a third more conventional path to office in advanced democracies: government service.

The figure shows the African Legislators Project data support the theory advanced in this book with regard to respondents' reported occupation prior to running for office. First, 15.5 percent of opposition legislators from electoral authoritarian regimes had occupations in the civil society (CS) sector, compared with about a third as many ruling party legislators. The opposition-ruling party gaps found in this subset of countries are largest in Zimbabwe (roughly 14 percent of opposition legislators

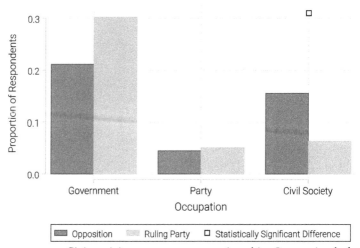

FIGURE 10.1 Civic activism versus career partisanship: Occupation before becoming MP

had CS occupations versus no ruling party legislators), Mozambique (15 percent versus none for the ruling party), and Burkina Faso (28 percent of opposition legislators versus 9 percent for the ruling party). Given the limitations of this measure, the finding here speaks to the importance of the book's core conclusion regarding how opposition candidacy in electoral authoritarian regimes is driven by histories of civic activism.

This limited measure does not offer evidence of career partisanship, but this should not be surprising: career partisanship as a concept includes the possibility of deriving income from performing party duties but envisions this resource accumulation as supplementary to core earning activities. Holding party positions is commonly revenue neutral or comes at a financial cost. For this reason, I delve into more detailed measures of career partisanship.

One more comprehensive measure of career partisanship I employ is derived from the question of whether individuals held a "senior" position in a political party prior to becoming a parliamentarian. Responses to this survey question are summarized in Figure 10.2.

It may initially seem counterintuitive that we observe that the proportion of opposition legislators in electoral authoritarian regimes who held such positions is significantly greater than that of ruling party legislators. Recall, however, that this finding is consistent with the theory the book develops and the narratives and evidence supporting it. Ismail Jussa's path to office began in civic activism – as a young, passionate student activist

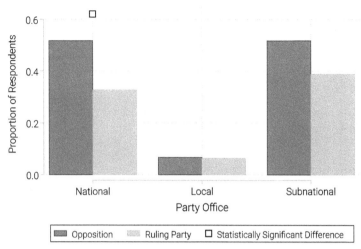

FIGURE 10.2 Evidence of career partisanship through party service

in Zanzibar who forged a path to politics through activities that began in secondary school. That activism and his public support for a jailed political leader led him to serve that leader – Maalim Seif, the Zanzibari presidential candidate for the opposition party Civic United Front – as his assistant in the secretariat of the party. In other words, respondents who report having held "senior" positions in "national" party offices prior to becoming an MP much more resemble the way civic activism translates into offering critical skills that opposition party needs in the "socio-electoral coalitions" (Trejo 2014). Further note that Chapter 4 demonstrated the significance of youth wing mobilization as an opposition party recruitment strategy. Youth wings are appendages of national party organs; thus, this variable captures youth activism among the opposition. The narrative of career partisanship, by contrast, is a slog through low-profile political positions in local party offices, followed by advancement within an office and vertically through a party hierarchy, a process by which party loyalty is cultivated with the ruling cadre. The current measure is not nuanced enough to unpack these complexities.

Another measure comes close to capturing the path dependent socialization mechanism of career partisanship, whereby party primacy shapes political decision making. It represents compliance and prioritization of party positions over personal conviction and local and national political interests. Do ruling party legislators place party first in political decisions, even when that comes in conflict with their own beliefs or desires? Figure 10.3 shows results derived from the African Legislatures Project data.

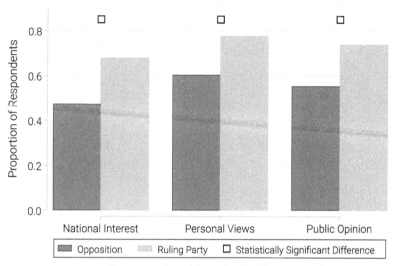

FIGURE 10.3 Career partisanship and prioritizing party interests

The patterns displayed in this figure are striking: ruling parties in electoral authoritarian regime reflect high rates of party compliance among their members. About 70 percent of respondents in those regimes take the position of the political party over what is in the national interest (68 percent), their own views (78 percent), and the views and needs of their constituents (74 percent). These are significantly greater than opposition legislators in electoral authoritarian regimes. As evidenced in the appendix, ruling party compliance is also much higher in electoral authoritarian regimes than it is for ruling parties in any other regime type.

These three pieces of evidence considered together offer support for the applicability of the book's theory on career partisanship and civic activism to Africa's electoral authoritarian regimes. Opposition legislators in electoral authoritarian regimes worked in civil society occupations at significantly higher rates prior to running for office. They also held senior positions in the national party organization, which reflects the patterns of party service for ruling party versus opposition legislators in electoral authoritarian regimes: ruling party legislators' paths through career partisanship feature long stints of low-status party work during which mutual dependencies between party and prospective candidate are forged. By contrast, opposition candidates who do serve their party occupy high-status positions on the eve of entering the legislature.

Strategic Candidacy Decisions in Electoral Authoritarian Regimes

The theory advanced in this book argues that legislators are heterogeneous in the benefits they seek when running for office, that parties differ in their capacity to deliver those benefits, and some prospective candidates may benefit from unsuccessful nomination and election contests. The African Legislatures Project data permit evaluating the first claim. I proceed by first assessing core ideological views about the duties of being a legislator and the role the legislature plays in a regime. I then take a broader perspective toward motivations to be in the legislature.

ALP asked legislators how they viewed the strength of the legislature in performing various duties. The interest and willingness of MPs to empower the legislature to carry out these responsibilities is how I gauge policy and ideological motivation. Study participants considered nine policy-making instruments available to legislators that broadly fall under the four roles of legislatures: oversight, lawmaking, representation, and constituency service (Mattes and Mozzaffar 2018). For each item, I evaluate whether the responses from ruling party and opposition legislators are different and, specifically, if opposition legislators report more policy-driven attitudes. Figure 10.4 summarizes the results of this assessment. The figure presents the difference between opposition and ruling party respondents' preferences for strengthening the legislature's role in performing each function. The horizontal line graph found at 0 on the y-axis represents a hypothetical response distribution whereby ruling party and opposition legislators hold identical views regarding that policy domain. Points above that line indicate that opposition legislators support greater policy-making power for the legislature; below the line captures when ruling party legislators place more emphasis on growing policy-making capacity with respect to a given duty.

The literature on politics in Africa has long held that parties are not differentiated by policy dimensions; this is echoed by work on legislatures in electoral authoritarian regimes that argues such institutions are vehicles of co-optation and "rubber stamp" institutions. Figure 10.4 suggests the story is more complicated. The figure shows that the views of opposition MPs differ significantly from their ruling party counterparts regarding the strength and activities of the legislature. We see almost universally across policies that fall under oversight, lawmaking, representation, and constituency service that opposition legislators promote a more powerful and policy-driven parliament. Bleck and van de Walle (2018, 196) note that opposition parties commonly use rhetoric of constitutionalism and

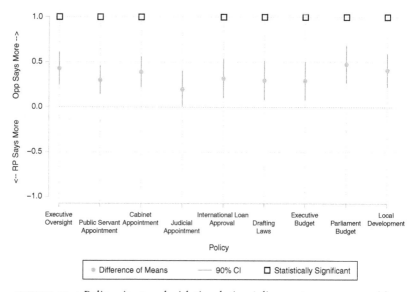

FIGURE 10.4 Policy views on legislative duties, ruling party versus opposition

democracy in campaign messaging, "fram[ing] themselves as defenders of democracy and criticiz[ing] incumbents for actions that can be portrayed as limiting freedoms or consolidating the incumbent's own power." These positions come in conflict with the ruling party because they threaten to dilute their power. Like the concept of a "nested game" (Lindberg 2007, Schedler 2006) the fight over policy on the campaign trail and on election day is part of a broader policy goal of reshaping the political landscape.

Opposition MPs even emphasize legislative policy on domains where the ruling party stands to disproportionately benefit materially (e.g., setting the legislature's budget, enhancing the role of the legislature in local development). The one category where opposition legislators did not hold significantly different policy views regards the appointment of justices. On the one hand, impartiality of the judiciary is a considerable concern, given authoritarian courts can be used to validate the ruling regime and punish trangressions against them. However, it also is the case that the courts are the weakest of the tripartite government structure in electoral authoritarian regimes and, thus, perhaps not where opposition legislators most prefer to invest policy efforts. On the whole, policy differences are present and significant in Africa's electoral authoritarian regimes, a result that challenges much of the existing knowledge of electoral politics in sub-Saharan Africa.

10.4 SCOPE CONDITIONS: DOMINANT PARTY DEMOCRACIES

The dynamics of political competition in dominant party democracies share much with electoral authoritarian regimes. Like electoral authoritarian regimes, regular multiparty elections in which opposition faces significant disadvantages yield reliable victories for the party in power. While Pempel (1990) noted that such democracies were "uncommon" in the twentieth century, many late-twentieth and twenty-first democratizers fall into this category, especially in sub-Saharan Africa. The competitive disadvantages opposition parties face due to material resources afforded by incumbency and the "winner-take-all" nature of electoral contests are similar in both contexts. Africa's longest-standing democracy – Botswana – also features one of the world's longest-ruling parties. Botswana's Democratic Party (BDP) has governed since 1965, during which it has won twelve legislative majorities in twelve consecutive elections. South Africa's African National Congress (ANC) has not lost a national election since democratizing in 1994 at the end of apartheid; Namibia's elections since its transition from South African occupation in 1989–1990 are marked by seven electoral victories by SWAPO (South West Africa People's Organisation). In Lesotho, the Basotho Congress Party and a splinter Lesotho Congress Party were elected from 1993 through 2007, winning four consecutive elections. Nigeria's People's Democratic Party similarly won four elections in a row until defeat in 2015. By most criteria of single-party dominance, the periods of rule in the latter two cases constitute a sufficiently "substantial" time of governance (Pempel 1990) and sustained electoral success meeting conditions of "dominance" (Blondel 1968, Bogaards 2004, Greene 2007, Sartori 1976, Ware 1996).

Expectations

Dominant party democracies do differ from electoral authoritarian regimes in important ways. As discussed in Chapter 2, they stand apart primarily in terms of the costs – in the form of risk and repression – that regime opponents face. Ruling party victory may be sustained through undemocratic practices like personalizing state resources to reinforce hyper-incumbency advantages but not through the use of the state to intimidate, harass, and attack the opposition.[7] Thus, many of the lessons

---

[7] There is some debate whether regimes like South Africa and Botswana – where the ruling party has never lost – should be considered democracies until an election loser willingly concedes defeat (e.g., Przeworski, Alvarez, Cheibub, and Limongi (2000)) but few

regarding opposition candidacy in electoral authoritarian regimes should be applicable to understanding the decision to run for office on opposition tickets in dominant party democracies.

Career Partisanship and Civic Activism

Electoral authoritarian regimes permit a restricted form of political and economic pluralism, where those who engage in public, visible displays of anti-government activity through formal political institutions like parties face significant risks. Governments can threaten the economic livelihoods of business and citizens who wish to support the opposition, ensuring challenger parties will remain financially and therefore institutionally weak (Arriola 2013). Social pluralism is more widespread and less controlled by the government. The confluence of these factors pushes nascent political activism in electoral authoritarian regimes into the civic sphere, accounting for a pathway from civic activism leading to opposition party candidacy. Absent the space to develop their own institutions for recruitment and training and mobilization capacity, opposition parties must draw on resources – including supporters and candidates – from the civil society realm to offset their own deficiencies.

Dominant party democracies, by contrast, have more permissive environments where the political sphere is less tightly controlled and regulated. Opposition parties may still perform poorly in elections but not because they face the constant threat of government infiltration and interference: their headquarters are not ransacked by state security forces, their leaders are not subject to regular detainment, and they do not face existential threats of being deregistered or banned. Indeed, democratic dominant party systems are less volatile than other African regimes (Bogaards 2008); this is attributed to their democratic nature (van Eerd 2010). In these settings, opposition parties are able to develop their own infrastructure to carry out basic functions (e.g., office keeping, accounting, and so on) and create party pipelines to candidacy, meaning they need to rely less on external resources from the civic sector. For this reason, the civic activism pathway to opposition candidacy *is not likely* to be found in dominant party democracies.

Career partisanship, however, may still shape candidacy pathways in dominant party regimes. Dominant parties face the same challenges of managing intraparty factionalism that commitment and loyalty in the form of party service help address and, given a backlog of aspirants and

Africanists dispute that the two countries meet minimal thresholds of democracy aside from this criterion.

a finite number of candidacy opportunities, party service in the dominant party can help legislator hopefuls make it onto the party's legislative ballots.

There are two reasons, however, why career partisanship may not be a pathway to office in dominant party democracies. First, candidates may have candidacy options outside the ruling party that are not in the opposition. Electoral authoritarian regimes incentivize sticky legislator attachments to party; 60 percent of Africa's electoral authoritarian regimes punish party disloyalty by forcing legislators who change parties to resign their seats. By comparison, only about 14 percent of democracies in the world have such laws. Four of the five dominant parties in the ALP sample also permit independent candidates, meaning candidates have pro-government alternatives to the ruling party that may nonetheless be aligned with the government. Both factors reduce control of the ruling party over access to power and enhance portability of political capital developed in the party, thus undermining the value of party service as a pathway to office. This is particularly the case for service in the form of low-status, party grunt work that is otherwise immediately unrewarding and also in terms of the loyalty that ruling parties are able to extract from prospective candidates.

Second, government service may be more useful political capital for legislative aspirants in dominant party democracies than electoral authoritarian regimes. The narrative of citizen–state relationships in African democracies generally characterizes linkages as operating through the state via access to the government bureaucracy, whereby government officials capture state resources and redirect them from the state to deliver patronage goods. The ruling party in electoral authoritarian regimes operates in lockstep with and sometimes "as" the state but may serve a more diminished brokerage function in democratic regimes where state actors enjoy more autonomy. Nonparty sources of capital diminish the value of career partisanship, allowing legislative aspirants to successfully achieve ruling party ambition via government service pathways. This leads to the expectation that government careers can serve as a pathway to ruling party office in dominant party democracies, unlike what is observed in electoral authoritarian regimes.

Strategic Candidacy Framework: Benefits and Costs

The prevailing models of candidacy decisions emphasize election prospects, benefits of office, and the costs of competing. The critical difference between the strategic environment facing opposition hopefuls in dominant party democracies versus electoral authoritarian regimes lies in the regime's use of repression, violence, and intimidation against its opponents; the potential costs of candidacy are much higher in electoral authoritarian regimes. On the other two parameters, though, they are largely the same. Opposition candidates face poor election prospects due to incumbency advantages of ruling party access to massive campaign war chests.

Benefits sought for prospective legislators in dominant party democracies are heterogeneous in ways similar to electoral authoritarian regimes: material and career benefits should be associated with ruling party candidacy and ideological and policy benefits with opposition candidacy. Greene (2007), for example, showed that opposition candidates who challenged the *Partido Revolucionario Institucional*'s (PRI) seventy-plus period of uninterrupted rule in Mexico during the twentieth century were "value rational" and benefited from criticizing the government, even in the face of electoral defeat. Notably, Greene (2007) classifies PRI's tenure as a dominant/hegemonic party regime, while other scholars have categorized this regime as electoral authoritarian. That candidacy can be understood in a case that ambiguously fits between the two regime types suggests the motivations of candidates to run for and win office should not differ much between the two categories. Table 10.3 summarizes expectations regarding scope conditions in dominant party democracies.

Before testing these hypotheses regarding dominant party democracies in Africa, I offer an important caveat. The electoral logic underlying my theory best applies under majoritarianism, where opposition candidates compete head to head with ruling party adversaries over the only seat available in a constituency. Of the five dominant party democracies in ALP, three are proportional systems (South Africa, Botswana, Namibia). Additionally, South Africa and Botswana are parliamentary regimes, meaning the relationship between legislative and executive branches differs. This introduces additional factors that I cannot control for in assessing the external validity of the theory. Thus, evaluating the external validity of the theory to dominant party regimes with this particular set of cases is a "hard" test of the theory; if it generalizes to these cases, then it would possibly be even more strongly supported in dominant party democracies that are majoritarian.

Career Partisanship and Civic Activism in Dominant Party Democracies

How well does the theory of career partisanship and civic activism capture dynamics of dominant party democracy, where patterns of political

TABLE 10.3 *Scope conditions for Africa's dominant party democracies*

Component of Theory	Expectations
Pathways to Office	Career Partisanship $\Rightarrow$ RP Civic Activism $\nRightarrow$ RP/Opp Govt Exp $\Rightarrow$ RP
Benefits of Candidacy	Material RP>Opp Ideology RP<Opp

competition resemble electoral authoritarianism but the rights and freedom enjoyed in those settings differ? I first address this question by comparing occupational backgrounds of opposition versus ruling party legislators in Africa's dominant party democracies. Figure 10.5 summarizes the patterns revealed by the ALP data. As expected, there is no evidence of a civic activism path to opposition candidacy in dominant party regimes. In regimes where formal political channels of competition are less constrained, opposition parties are able to develop without existential barriers imposed by the ruling party. Their activists do not face the same risks of regular harassment and abuse suffered under electoral authoritarianism. In this environment, civic activism does not play the same role in cultivating political ambition even if civic organizations work in complementary ways with opposition parties to pursue shared goals.

The figure does, however, suggest career partisanship, in that legislators from dominant parties reported careers in the party at significantly higher rates than their opposition counterparts. There are also some similarities in the nature of party service in electoral authoritarian and dominant party regimes: those from opposition parties that do perform duties for political parties commonly do so in higher-profile and skilled national positions, rather than the kinds of low-status positions performed "in the trenches" by ruling party hopefuls. This is depicted in Figure 10.6.

In the ALP sample of electoral authoritarian regimes in Africa, we observed that the consequences of party allegiance were severe for ruling party legislators. From the perspective of the ruling party, demonstrations of political loyalty are more important than technical skills or job proficiency, as cutting off in-fighting and achieving cohesion are important for the longevity of the party. In democracies – including dominant party democracies – laws that constrain movement of political capital

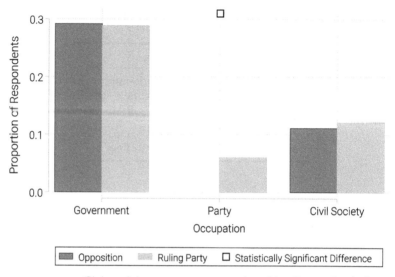

FIGURE 10.5 Civic activism versus career partisanship: Occupation before becoming MP in dominant party democracies

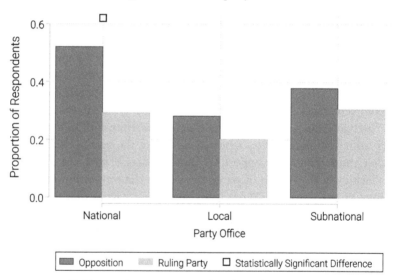

FIGURE 10.6 Evidence of career partisanship through party service in dominant party democracies

from party to party are less common, meaning the ruling party exercises less control over legislators and can less effectively control how they perform their duties. It is perhaps for this reason that ruling party legislators do not put party views at the forefront of their decision making

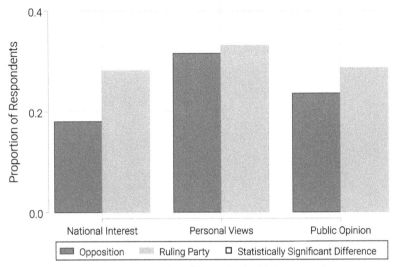

FIGURE 10.7 Career partisanship and prioritizing party interests

in dominant party democracies. This is shown in Figure 10.7, where ruling party and opposition legislators make decisions at similar rates based on national interest, personal views, and public opinion versus their political party's views. The differences that do exist between the two groups are not statistically significant.

Together, this points to evidence that the concept of career partisanship extends to dominant party democracies but in ways that are somewhat different. Most importantly, career partisanship as a compliance mechanism appears to be weaker in these settings. Ruling party legislators simply have more options for how to utilize their political capital, reducing the ability of the party to root out disobedience. As expected, the path of civic activism to the opposition is not found in dominant party democracies, where opposition party activity is not vigorously punished. Absent the repressive environment of electoral authoritarianism, opposition activism is not forced outside of the political realm and into more pluralistic civic spaces; it can exist on its own merit within opposition parties.

Strategic Candidacy Decisions in Dominant Party Democracies

The literature on electoral politics in Africa has long argued that due to a combination of centralized, presidential power (van de Walle 2003) and long-held expectations of patronage exchange between legislator and voter (Barkan 1979, Lindberg 2003), there exists little space for intensive

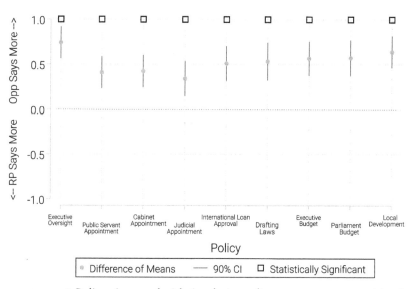

FIGURE 10.8 Policy views on legislative duties, ruling party versus opposition in dominant party democracies

policy debate. I provided evidence that opposition legislators in electoral authoritarian settings are, in fact, motivated by broad and transformative ideological goals and thus should hold policy views that differ greatly from those of their ruling party counterparts. I also noted political aspirants faced similar strategic considerations in dominant party democracies, as the ruling party dominates political competition and the legislative mandate in both regime types.

To assess whether or not opposition legislators hold different policy views from ruling party MPs, I return to the ALP survey data regarding policy-making instruments of the legislature. Following the approach found in Figure 10.4 earlier in the chapter, Figure 10.8 compares the views of legislators across duties of oversight, lawmaking, representation, and constituency service. The horizontal line represents where opposition and ruling party legislators hold the same views and points above that line indicate opposition legislators more strongly believe in enhancing policy-making capacity of the legislature.

The patterns presented in the figure are nearly identical to those found in electoral authoritarian regimes: in electoral authoritarian regimes, opposition legislators were more policy motivated than ruling party members on eight of the nine policy dimensions. In dominant party regimes, the opposition is more policy driven on all nine of them, including the appointment of the judges. In dominant party democracies, the judiciary may enjoy more power, autonomy, or prestige, in comparison with electoral authoritarian regimes, where the judiciary is often the weakest of a tripartite government structure. Showing that significant policy differences exist among legislators in both electoral authoritarian regimes and dominant party democracies deserves further attention, as it provides evidence that contradicts much of the inherited wisdom of electoral politics in sub-Saharan Africa.

On the whole, the theory offered in this book can help shed light on candidacy decisions in dominant party democracies. The comparably more open environments mean that pathways into politics are less dependent on long-term life trajectories that predate candidacy ambitions. Civil society does not play the critical role in fomenting opposition candidacy ambition as it does in electoral authoritarian regimes because opposition parties do not face regular existential threats that push activism outside of the political sphere. Careers in the ruling party are still viable ways to office and opportunities to accrue material resources and ruling party capital. However, more diverse forms of political capital are found in these regimes, meaning ruling party aspirants can marshal alternative resources to low-level party service and the ruling party cannot extract the level of compliance or loyalty found in electoral authoritarian regimes. There is evidence that opposition candidates in dominant party systems value policies regarding the legislature and governance, in contrast with the prevailing view on electoral politics in Africa casting parties as similar along policy dimensions. Perhaps because the positions evaluated relate to the overall distribution of power within a regime, rather than taxation, international finance, social programs, or other more detailed, technical issues, these important differences are not captured in conventional campaign materials like manifestos, rally speeches, and media ads. Indeed, as Schedler (2006) notes, the primary opposition–ruling party cleavage in electoral authoritarian regimes is about the "rules of the game" of the political system and competition within it. This appears to be equally applicable to dominant party democracies in Africa.

10.5 SCOPE CONDITIONS: COMPETITIVE DEMOCRACIES

While many of Africa's best democratic performers feature single-party dominance, there are also notable democracies that feature robust competition between political parties. Elections may yield divided governments and, in some cases, turnovers in the party in power. For the purposes of candidacy decisions, Africa's competitive democracies can be differentiated into two groups. The first group features competition between established political parties that are well institutionalized, run effective national campaigns, and are coalitions of multiple social groups. Levitsky and Way (2010*a*) characterize such parties as possessing high "organizational power."

Among the countries where the African Legislatures Project collected data, Ghana best represents this dynamic. When voters head into the polling station in any given election year, the party choices they face are familiar. Candidates are known and frequently chosen through internal participatory contests like primaries (Ichino and Nathan 2012). Parties compete to maintain their reliable bases of support from core voters and to win over swing voters without firm allegiances (Weghorst and Lindberg 2013). Between elections, volatility – measured as the percentage of legislative seats changing hands between parties – is low and volatility driven by the collapse of existing parties or victories of new, ephemeral party organizations is rare (Weghorst and Bernhard 2015).

The second type of regime features more case-by-case variability but is characterized by weak party institutionalization. In settings like Kenya, voting patterns of several key social groups are regularized in that prominent ethnic groups commonly vote as a "block" and thus can be thought of as "core" voters (Horowitz 2019). However, for any number of reasons, the parties themselves are not well established. Ferree (2010) notes that while ethnicity undergirds the support base in many party systems, conflict over the cleavage around which to organize a party – ethnicity or language group – can lead to weak parties. The constituent social groups that form a party's support base is consistent, but the parties or coalitions in which they compete may dissolve after a single election.

In other democracies, the authoritarian regimes that preceded them neutralized or eliminated political rivals, leading to dramatic, rather than managed, democratic transitions. This resulted in a widely opened political space complemented by weakened social institutions for parties to build upon. Together these factors yielded poorly institutionalized political parties in settings like Benin and Zambia (Riedl 2014). Some democracies have also transitioned from single-party dominance to less institutionalized systems upon the defeat of the long-ruling party (as in Senegal), where parties, candidates, and voters are still learning to navigate the new political terrain. In these types of settings, parties are more personal vehicles of self-promotion than institutional actors (Kelly 2019).

Expectations

Civic Activism and Career Partisanship

The more predominant vocational pathway to office in competitive democracies is from public employment and other lucrative sectors like business. The work on legislative careers in Africa shows political leaders in democracies overwhelmingly come from careers in government, law, and business (Koter 2016, Pinkston 2016). Those with civil society backgrounds are commonly "outsiders" (Cloward and Weghorst 2019). Civic activism should thus not be a common pathway to legislative office and should not differentiate opposition from ruling party legislators. Competitive democracies in Africa are not likely to feature patterns of career partisanship, especially in settings characterized by weak party institutionalization. Parties themselves can have lives far shorter than the careers of politicians, so there is little value in cultivating party loyalty or making significant investments in party service. It may be far more common for highly institutionalized political parties if party capital provides resources to compete for party nominations and to win over support from party leaders, but such parties are not the norm.

Robust competition in elections also suggests that the higher prevalence of public sector employment and lower frequency of civic activism and career partisanship should not differentiate opposition and ruling party candidates. Turnover in power means the parties have previously switched roles and that a current opposition party may have been in government only a year or two before. The relationship between career background and candidacy is better thought of as differences *between* competitive democracies and other regime types regardless of party rather than differences between ruling party and opposition legislators *within* competitive democracies.[8]

Strategic Candidacy Framework: Benefits and Costs

Chapter 2 recounted how the dominant narrative regarding electoral politics in Africa is the "politics of the belly" (Bayart 1993), a system of accruing public resources which are both consumed by officeholders and redistributed to their supporters. The literature has extensively documented how this translates into material motivations for political

---

[8] I leave analyses comparing ruling parties and opposition parties across regime type out of the main text, but these are found in Appendix B.8. and support this view.

TABLE 10.4 *Scope conditions for Africa's competitive democracies*

Component of Theory	Expectations for Competitive Democracies (CDs)
Pathways to Office in CDs	Career Partisanship $\not\Rightarrow$ RP/Opp Civic Activism $\not\Rightarrow$ RP/Opp Govt Exp $\Rightarrow$ RP/Opp
Benefits of Candidacy in CDs	Material $\Rightarrow$ RP/Opp Ideology $\not\Rightarrow$ RP/Opp

office as an avenue for extraction of public resources. Other formal benefits of officeholding attract materially motivated aspirants, including salary and fringe benefits, access to executive positions, and discretionary development funds. These goods are obtained by holding office and controlling government. Thus, under conditions of robust competition between political parties (e.g., "winner-take-all" politics where candidates and their parties take turns doing the winning), both candidates who are in the current government and those in the opposition should be motivated.

The applicability of other expectations of differences found among legislators in Africa's competitive democracies regarding benefits is more ambiguous. It is certainly the case that the literature sees little nonmaterial benefit in being a legislator or performing legislative duties and, further, argues that parties in African democracies are motivated primarily by valence issues. Absent a pro-competition or pro-democratic cleavage present in electoral authoritarian and dominant party regimes, ideological benefits are not likely to appeal to ruling party or opposition legislators. Similarly, while officeholding may offer prestige, it is not clear that the prestige associated with it is distinct from the material implications of officeholding. Careers could also be advanced by officeholding or, alternately, it could be that officeholding is among the best possible careers (especially for those selected into ministries). Differences between legislators based on whether their party is currently in government or is the opposition are minimized because those parties might or have already switched roles. Differences in the relative salience of ideological, career, and prestige benefits are more likely to be found in comparison with other regimes: legislators in competitive democracies value them less than do legislators in other regimes. These expectations are summarized in Table 10.4.

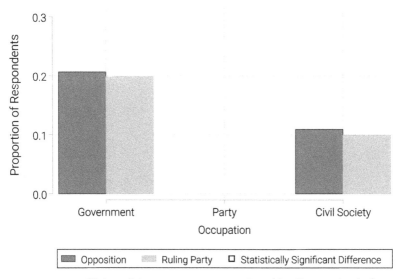

FIGURE 10.9 Civic activism versus career partisanship: Occupation before becoming MP in competitive democracies

Civic Activism and Career Partisanship in Competitive Democracies

Do paths to opposition versus ruling party candidacy follow the patterns of civic activism versus career partisanship discovered in electoral authoritarian regimes or, instead, do those differences between parties disappear in environments with more political pluralism, higher rates of government turnover, and frequently ephemeral or volatile party systems? Figure 10.9 offers an answer to that question by summarizing the occupational background of legislators in competitive democracies in Africa. What it shows is consistent with expectations. Ruling party and opposition MPs in these settings are not differentiated by political party careers and occupational experience in the civil society sector. Confirming that party service offers much less value to prospective legislators in competitive democracies – especially where the organizational power of parties is weak – the figure illustrates that no MP from Benin, Ghana, Kenya, Malawi, Senegal, or Zambia included in the ALP study identified party work as their primary occupation prior to entering the legislature. About 10 percent of legislators had career backgrounds in civil society, following emergent evidence that legislators in African democracies working in the nongovernmental and civil society organizations are political outsiders who constitute a small, but growing proportion of legislators in Africa. Such experience does not distinguish opposition versus ruling party pathways to power.

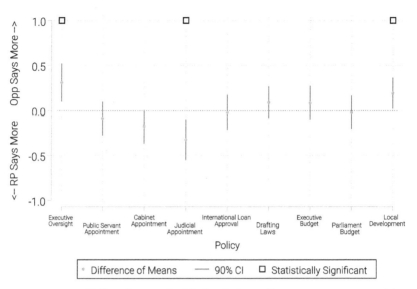

FIGURE 10.10 Policy views on legislative duties, ruling party versus opposition in competitive democracies

Mostly prominently, more than 20 percent of legislators in competitive democracies came from careers in government, regardless of whether they represented the party in power or its challenger.

Strategic Candidacy Decisions in Competitive Democracies

Earlier sections of this chapter showed that the general consensus regarding policy and ideology in Africa's electoral politics – namely, that it does not play a significant role – does not cohere with insight from legislators in Africa's electoral authoritarian regimes and dominant party democracies. For both types of regimes, opposition legislators held views that differ from those of the ruling party, systematically supporting empowering the legislature to shape monetary policy, development strategy, laws, and international engagement. The legislature is the staging ground for conflict over the rules of political competition. Unable to check executive power, opposition directs efforts to wield political influence to the legislative arena.

What then accounts for this gap between expectations derived from the literature and what is observed in the regimes discussed so far? The answer lies in understanding policy views for ruling party and opposition legislators in competitive democracies. Shown in Figure 10.10, legislators in competitive democracies held mostly similar views across these policy dimensions. As before, this figure compares the average positions of opposition versus ruling party legislators on policies related to legislative duties and influence. Points above the solid line indicate differences in policy where the opposition places greater emphasis; below the line the ruling party does. The gaps that do exist are substantively smaller than those found in electoral authoritarian regimes and dominant party democracies. Unsurprisingly, opposition legislators in competitive democracies want more executive oversight, likely to limit the efficacy or performance of the incumbent party; they also report demands for greater influence over development outcomes. Ruling party legislators, on the other hand, prioritize policies about strengthening legislative control over judicial appointments.

Competitive democracies in Africa thus feature much less differentiated positions between ruling party and opposition legislators. In addition to fewer and smaller gaps, legislators in competitive democracies also care less about policy in absolute terms – compared with electoral authoritarian regimes and dominant party democracies' legislators emphasize issues regarding legislative policy less.[9]

This section has demonstrated that many of the intuitions of my theory of opposition candidacy do operate as well in competitive democracies. This is what should be expected: the key difference between advanced democracies where the strategic candidacy model thrives and electoral authoritarian settings relates to the costs of competition and the chances of victory. Further, when pathways to power are blocked by restrictive political space or through rigorous party vetting and service contribution requirements, civic activism funnels aspirants to the opposition and career partisanship to the ruling party. Absent these constraints, however, neither pre-candidacy pathway influences the decision to run for office. The candidates who result from this process do not look the same in terms of their motivations: ruling party legislators emphasize various policy priorities as much as their opposition counterparts.

10.6 CONCLUSIONS FOR AFRICAN POLITICS AND AUTHORITARIAN REGIMES

This chapter has aimed to assess external validity and scope conditions of my theory of opposition candidacy using a survey of MPs in sixteen

---

[9] A more detailed analysis across regime type is found in Appendix B.8.

African electoral regimes. I affirmed my findings with a different set of Tanzanian legislators with surveys collected prior to my study, tested my theory in other electoral authoritarian regimes in Africa, and addressed what the theory can teach us about candidacy in dominant party and competitive democracies.

The chapter offered three important insights. First, paths of civic activism and career partisanship are externally valid to Africa's electoral authoritarian regimes. The association between civil society work and opposition candidacy is actually stronger among non-Tanzanian electoral authoritarian regimes in the sample. The measure was not ideal for capturing how career partisanship develops slowly and hierarchically over time for ruling party aspirants. Still, career partisanship patterns echoed the narratives of Tanzania's legislators, whereby opposition legislators occupied high-prestige, national positions and ruling party legislators demonstrated deep loyalty and socialized partisanship. As anticipated, there was some evidence of career partisanship for ruling parties in dominant party democracies and no evidence of either civic activism or career partisanship in competitive democracies.

Second, the preceding pages challenged a predominant narrative of African politics decrying the absence of meaningful political differences between parties. Opposition parties in electoral authoritarian regimes and dominant party democracies have significantly different policy priorities than their ruling party counterparts in the legislature. Analysis of the African Legislatures Project showed that ideological goals are important to opposition legislators in these settings and, further, that the opposition is least driven by ideological benefits in competitive democracies. This presents an important challenge to research on party policy in Africa's electoral regimes: scholars must further explore whether the apparent lack of policy differences between parties and candidates identified in existing research may be, in part, a consequences of the overwhelming focus of African politics scholarship on a subset of countries that are democracies featuring robust interparty competition.

Third, the chapter showed that there are real differences among African regimes that appear to be less about the type of regime on dimensions of democracy versus authoritarianism. Insofar as what distinguishes Botswana or Namibia from Tanzania and Burkina Faso is the level of toleration shown to opposition forces, civil society, and everyday citizens, this provides a different pathway into politics but does not dilute the prominence of ideological goals. The greatest differences among legislators in regimes in Africa lays along dimensions of hegemony; the more the ruling party dominates political competition in democracies, the more similar legislators' experiences and attitudes are to their counterparts in electoral authoritarian regimes.

Elections and Authoritarianism in the Twenty-first Century

Asiyejua kitu, hawezi kujua thamani yake
A person who does not know an object cannot know its value.

What drives individuals to run for legislative office in electoral authoritarian regimes? And why, when they run, do they choose to run on opposition tickets instead of for the ruling party? Scholars and policy makers have long acknowledged that contestation is essential to governance and accountability and a formidable opposition is necessary if citizens living under authoritarianism can ever hope to experience democracy. But in authoritarian settings, the opposition has little chance of winning and undertakes significant risks by standing against the government. The answer scholars have offered to date is deeply unsatisfying: the prevailing cost-benefit framework that predominates in the study of candidacy would anticipate no opposition would ever run in electoral authoritarian regimes. Alternative explanations rooted in electoral authoritarian contexts claim that all political actors are driven by aspirations to extract as many resources as possible from the state, including those in the opposition. What distinguishes opposition candidates from ruling party rivals is that, for whatever reason, a pathway to government resources that is unlocked through service in the ruling party is unavailable. Their next best option is to run in the opposition and hope to bring home something for it – co-optation benefits from government or at least formal salaries, government pensions, and so on. Even if there are aspirants unique enough to value policy-making priorities, opposition parties cannot offer much on this front because they have little chance of breaking ruling party majorities and supermajorities in parliament.

This book has demonstrated that the decision to run for legislative office on opposition tickets in electoral authoritarian regimes is explained by unique political ambitions that set opposition candidates apart from ruling party candidates and that pre-candidacy life experiences outside of politics explain why they differ so much. While my book also offers a modified version of the strategic candidacy approach that can account for opposition candidacy, I ultimately conclude that these early life experiences not only shape whether candidacy ambition emerges, they also determine how individuals weigh their options when it comes time to make candidacy decisions. In this final chapter, I review the main arguments and findings from each of the preceding chapters. I bring attention to limitations of this volume, with hopes that other scholars interested in the dynamics of political competition under electoral authoritarianism in Tanzania, Africa, and globally will work toward those issues I have left unresolved. I also speak to the contributions of my work to the communities of scholars working on electoral authoritarianism, African politics, and legislatures and candidacy broadly. I conclude by highlighting what I believe to be important, real-world policy implications of this book for domestic and international actors who engage in democracy promotion around the world.

11.1 MAIN FINDINGS

My book has offered a theory of opposition candidacy under electoral authoritarianism that emphasized the role played by early life activism in beginning journeys that later turn into candidacy ambition for challenger parties. Chapter 2 established that civic activism and participation in civil society organizations are the central features of the theorized pathways to opposition. Civil society organizations play a critical role overseeing authoritarian governments and holding them accountable in their own right, especially when nascent political opposition is weak. Ruling party candidates experience a process of training within political parties whereby they demonstrate loyalty to the party while accruing political capital to be cashed in to support legislative ambition. Under a modified version of the strategic candidacy framework, the superior nomination prospects, preferences for different benefits of candidacy – ones that can be obtained in spite of electoral loss – and a greater willingness to bear the nonmaterial, non-campaign costs of candidacy together make running for challenger parties more appealing than it appears at first glance. In developing my theory, I argued the origins of these different preferences point back to civic activism: civil society feeds opposition ambition and yields candidates who value long-term struggles for ideological and policy goals and can effectively transform their organizational capital and mobilization capacity into election victory. Showing that civil society activism feeds directly into organized political opposition and opposition candidacy underscores how important a robust civil society sector is for the promise of democratic futures in today's authoritarian regimes.

The third chapter of the book grounded Tanzania in the broader context of electoral authoritarianism in Africa and other regions of the world. Tanzania is often regarded as unique in ways that make it difficult to compare with other African cases. Chapter 3 showed that this view is mistaken. It is true that features like relatively low political salience of ethnic group cleavages, a well-institutionalized and credible ruling party in Chama Cha Mapinduzi (CCM), and a shrewd opposition that has consolidated gains over time do to some extent differentiate Tanzania from other countries. Yet, on dimensions of authoritarian toleration and electoral hegemony, Tanzania fits very well among electoral authoritarian contemporaries and well-known cases from the past. The chapter recognized that the level of ruling party credibility in the form of local institutionalization is especially high in Tanzania but also presented evidence that local party development is the norm across authoritarian ruling parties. In other words, it is best to think about CCM as a particularly successful example of what autocratic parties strive to do. With regard to the opposition, I admit that weak, rent-seeking opposition candidates and parties are not the types of individuals and organizations my book is concerned with, but that focusing instead on capable and organized opposition with national ambitions does not limit the relevance of the theory to the case of Tanzania and a handful of others. Rather, the opposition parties that field candidates in the case of Tanzania look much like others found in electoral authoritarian regimes. This chapter also laid out the extensive empirical strategy that leveraged multiple sources and types of data used to evaluate this theory.

Chapters 4 and 5 drew upon several of the empirical resources I collected to test the first element of my theory. My analysis showed opposition candidacy is preceded by experiences with activism in the form of civic organization membership and "grassroots" mobilization, whereas various forms of career partisanship were significantly more common among ruling party legislators. The core statistical evidence of this chapter was supported extensively by interviews with Tanzanian politicians and in-depth engagement with the Tanzanian case. I also employed sequence analysis of vocational and political career data with a broader set of Tanzanian political leaders to further illustrate the significance of the trajectories on candidacy decisions.

The subsequent empirical chapters shed light on candidacy calculations in electoral authoritarian regimes. Drawing upon scholarly insights from advanced democracies, the inspiration for these chapters began with this literature's intuitively appealing, parsimonious framework of costs and benefits of candidacy. Recognizing, however, that without modification this framework could not explain opposition candidacy, each chapter added depth to one of the parameters of the ambitious politics calculus.

The first parameter I studied was party nomination processes, a critical yet largely overlooked aspect of candidacy. In regimes where ruling parties have defection problems and reproducing rule and party cohesion is accomplished through elected representatives, intraparty processes that determine who runs for office are important. And, in these processes, the chances of being chosen as a ruling party nominee are inversely related to that party's dominance in the general election. Prospects of being nominated to election ballots are much poorer for ruling party aspirants than for the opposition. Through analyses that included election losers, unsuccessful nomination seekers, and prospective "noncandidates" from Tanzania, I studied the structure of party nomination in Tanzania. Using statistical analysis, this chapter contrasted relatively easy nomination processes for the opposition with the poor prospects of ruling party nominations. I concluded the discussion of nominations by linking these experiences to long-term candidate trajectories: opposition aspirants with civic activism experiences are more likely to seek and win nominations; CCM partisans lacking career partisanship are more likely to defect to the opposition to run.

I focused on the next stage of political competition in Chapter 7: elections. Opposition candidates in electoral authoritarian regimes face a political environment that constrains their chances of success, but we also know the probability of winning a given legislative contest is greater than zero. Thus, Chapter 7 shed light on what challenger candidates can do to enhance their election prospects. Comparing ruling party and opposition candidates, I showed that campaign expenditures differ between parties, with ruling party aspirants commanding much larger resource pools, including their own, personal contributions. However, opposition challengers who employ campaign techniques that adapt to underlying disadvantages they face can make the difference on election day. I show this by comparing winning and losing opposition candidates. I also trace opposition election outcomes to civic activism, showing that activist backgrounds drive perceived chances of victory and actual election success. More critically, the chapter shows that civic activism underlies the efficacy of running bigger and better campaigns. For opposition candidates without grassroots experience and lacking civic association networks, no amount of additional spending can help them win their contests.

Having captured the chances of winning in the two preceding chapters, the subsequent two chapters of the book looked to how opposition candidates stand out in terms of what they want from running and what they are willing to endure to get it. Chapter 8 offered evidence that candidates are heterogeneous in the benefits they want from office, how well they view parties' abilities to deliver those benefits, and whether those benefits can be obtained in spite of defeat. Following Greene (2007), I showed opposition candidates are driven by nonmaterial motivations, including ideological/policy and prestige benefits. Being blocked from accessing material benefits of office – what drives ruling party candidates – does not discourage opposition candidates. A desire for ideological/policy benefits is linked to civic activism, while material benefits can be traced back to the career partisanship process. Chapter 9 studied the nonmaterial costs of candidacy outside of campaign expenditure and showed that while the costs of opposition candidacy are high, opposition candidates are willing to bear those costs. Drawing insights from scholarship on social movements, I argue this arises from experiences in civic activism, whereby early decisions to accept moderate risks of activism under electoral authoritarianism set off cycles of repeated activism with increasing risks. This chapter introduces a first-of-its-kind method of measuring risk attitudes and time horizons with cultural proverbs (*methali*), anchored with important meanings applicable to decision making. Views of opposition figures who have taken on such risks due to their civic activism ground the statistical analysis. Chapter 10 tests the theory I advance outside the context of Tanzania. It supports the book's theory in four other electoral authoritarian regimes in Africa and provides insight on scope conditions and the external validity of the theory in twelve other regimes in the subcontinent. Civic activism is a pathway to office in other authoritarian regimes in Africa and the role of career partisanship in cultivating party loyalty and grooming future ruling party aspirants appears in dominant party regimes as well. There is also evidence that opposition candidates share policy ambitions across multiple domains.

11.2 LIMITATIONS

Many of the limitations of this volume arise from the empirical strategy employed. At its core, this book is a story about the politics of Tanzania and with that comes concerns about theory testing in a setting that is regarded by some as exceptional. It is my hope that readers are convinced Tanzania is a case that is broadly comparable to other electoral authoritarian regimes on the most important dimensions. Tanzania does stand out from its peers in other ways, but even these ultimately make it a harder setting for testing my theory. First, opposition candidates today are running against a party that is strong and has governed for fifty years. These realities heighten the challenges of winning; drive down some benefits of running for the opposition; and increase the nonmaterial, non-campaign costs of standing against the ruling party. Second, Tanzania is a setting where civil society was flattened under single-party rule, meaning civic associations and civil society organizations emerging in the reform period of the 1990s were especially weak and faced significant onset challenges. Electoral authoritarian regimes where one or both of these conditions are absent may offer even stronger evidence of how civic activism establishes pathways to opposition candidacy.

I also evaluated components of my theory in the context of sixteen other regimes in sub-Saharan Africa, including four other electoral authoritarian settings. The data support my central conclusions regarding the role of civic activism in opposition candidacy, policy and ideological motivations of opposition legislators, and the role of career partisanship in dominant party and electoral authoritarian regimes. The African Legislatures Project (ALP) data, however, are limited in how directly they can test my theory. No other data sources are available currently to allow systematic assessment of the theory and the kinds of measures I used – life history calendars to ease retrospective data collection, *methali* for capturing risk attitudes, benefit measures that account for different benefit types and different preferences for them – are highly specific to the Tanzanian context. I believe this to be a strength with regard to the analytical rigor of this book. It is my hope other scholars will employ these approaches elsewhere to generate insight on their applicability to other settings.

A second limitation also comes from the use of these survey data. Like many political and social phenomena where the central question relates to why someone engages in a high-stakes decision, it is much easier to identify individuals who made the decision to act on their motivation than those who did not. For the study of candidacy, who belongs to the population of prospective aspirants who select out of candidacy is fundamentally unknowable. For opposition candidates in Tanzania, I drew a sample of prospective aspirants who did not run for office from within opposition parties and surveyed members of opposition party youth and women's wings who collected forms to begin the administrative process of entering into nomination contests, a credible and observable sign of ambition. However, it is also undeniable that an unknown but potentially large number of those who aspire to run for office never try. It could be the case that these individuals are different from other noncandidates included in the study. During fieldwork, I administered a citizen-level survey that had a branch for candidacy questions conditional on the respondent divulging having considered running for office but no respondent expressed this motivation.[1] This exercise showed that prevalence of candidate ambition among representative citizen surveys is low enough that this strategy would be a cost-prohibitive solution.

While this book is focused on opposition candidacy, the greatest limitation of the sample is that all CCM participants are legislators, and I do not have data from losing candidates, unsuccessful nomination seekers, and prospective noncandidates. This was not for lack of trying. My research permits in mainland Tanzania and Zanzibar helped me work with the legislatures to carry out research at *Bunge* and *Baraza la Wawakilishi*, but surveying non-legislators required earning cooperation and buy-in from political parties. In the end, CCM party leadership in mainland Tanzania and Zanzibar approved of carrying out my research at regional and district party branches but were unwilling to provide a written endorsement to do so. Formal, top-down notification and endorsements are the norm for research in Tanzania from elite interviewing to citizen-level surveys and they were key for carrying out interviews with CHADEMA and Civic United Front (CUF). Without this, interviewing non-legislators from CCM was not possible. This limits the conclusions I can derive about career partisanship, particularly with regard to how career partisanship impacts the strategic candidacy framework for ruling party career partisans who choose to not run. Government transparency and engagement with international academic and policy-making communities has declined since I completed data collection and even more sharply since Magufuli became

---

[1] With Sterling Roop, I co-directed *Wasemavyo Wazanzibari*, which was a three-year, monthly mobile phone-based panel survey carried out in Zanzibar. One participant included in our ∼500 person sample was a member of the Zanzibari House of Representatives at the time but having already completed the candidacy survey, we did not administer those questions again.

Tanzania's president in 2015. While Magufuli's premature death in 2021 has introduced uncertainty into Tanzania's future trajectory, there remains little hope such data could be gathered in Tanzania in the foreseeable future. Insight on career partisanship among ruling party hopefuls who decide not to run is an opportunity area for future studies of candidacy in other electoral authoritarian settings.

11.3 IMPLICATIONS

The findings of my book speak to four audiences in academic and policy circles: those who study electoral authoritarianism, African politics, candidacy and legislative careers, and civil society and democratization in the world. I discuss the first three in sequence and conclude the book by tying lessons on civil society and democratization to concrete policy implications for the contemporary era of authoritarian resurgence around the world.

Implications for Electoral Authoritarianism

The existing literature on electoral authoritarianism has long focused on authoritarian leaders, durability, and the diffusion of power through elections as the phenomena of interest. The resulting outcome is a narrow focus on the mechanizations of authoritarian rule, where opposition players are afforded little or no agency. Reflecting on such an orientation, Morse (2012, 186) notes that "the role of alternative variables is not always given a fair chance, even when they have theoretical value to add." Others have noted that in contrast to the study of ruling parties in places like Africa, studies of opposition parties are few (Lindberg 2006*b*). Research that does pay attention to the opposition is commonly less interested in what they do and instead focuses on what they are: fragmented (Bogaards 2008), pulverized (van Eerd 2010), or coordinated (Wahman 2013). The literature offers very little on how the opposition works internally in electoral authoritarian regimes.

First, focusing on the norms and institutions within political parties that influence candidacy outcomes shapes lessons about the opposition. While ruling parties may use candidate selection procedures to manage intraparty conflict against difficult selectorate odds, the opposition can win over prospective candidates by appealing odds of becoming a nominee. The appeal of the opposition due to intraparty dynamics means that less electorally popular parties may court prospective candidates, compared with ruling parties where a nomination is unlikely.

Second, the book demonstrates that parties manage and plan campaigns differently. Clever, efficient use of campaign resources can help opposition candidates get elected in spite of resource shortages. Specifically, campaign tactics that create public information about the viability of the opposition win over voters. This represents just one of many ways the opposition is able to compete in an "uneven playing field" and improve their prospects in spite of the ruling party's efforts to entrench its power through elections.

Third, my work suggests the choices that actors regarding candidacy link to variable risk and benefit profiles. While the literature has heretofore assumed a homogeneity in the individual drivers of behavior and, thus, that actions are determined by the environment in which any individual is placed, my book offers that opposition candidates simply have different perspectives toward risks and benefits associated with running. Opposition activists noted that running for office could provide benefits to them, even if winning an election was out of the question. Such benefits represent nonmaterial gains associated with running for office. These are what others have called "expressive" rather than "instrumental" benefits (Greene 2007). Even if one anticipates winning and acts strategically to obtain office, in losing office one nonetheless reaps utility from "fighting the good fight." Considering non-instrumental benefits offers potential directions of development for other theories of strategic actor behavior where outcomes of failure are likely.

Fourth, and most critically, I showed that candidacy in electoral authoritarian regimes is a path dependent outcome. It is in shedding light on what sows the seeds of interest in candidacy that determines why and when prospective opposition candidates seek office. Civic activism offers a channel to opposition candidacy where both party-sided and candidate-sided explanations cohere under this framework. Career partisanship as a commitment over time that exposes an individual to potential interests in candidacy is relevant to understanding electoral authoritarian regimes. Experiences in these paths have important consequences not only for the decisions aspirants make but also for the very way in which they evaluate their prospects.

Implications for African Politics

To the scholarship on African politics broadly, my work contributes to four key topic areas: (1) the importance of policy dimensions in competition, (2) the nature of party building in Africa, (3) significance of legislatures and legislators, and (4) novel measurement approaches suited for the subcontinent.

Scholarship on African politics has long argued that political behavior is motivated by the pursuit of material goods. Thus, at the level of interparty competition, platforms and campaigns are not differentiable along dimensions of ideology or policy. This book challenges that view and points to the insufficiency of treating political parties as vacant of policy. The book offered evidence that ruling parties and the opposition take different stances on meaningful political issues and use positions on salient policies to win over voters. Further, opposition candidates are wooed by ideological benefits and prestige associated with being the public face of an opposition movement. Opposition parties can use the ideological packages to their advantage as an opportunity to project an image of unity alongside sometimes haphazard and contradictory policy records accrued by the ruling party in government. The book pointed to reformist policy synergy among opposition parties in both electoral authoritarian regimes and dominant party democracies in Africa. In this way, the opposition can compete in the "game of institutional reform" by emphasizing policies that further pro-democratic change. Showing differences in ideology across parties points to an important direction for future research in African electoral regimes and echoes an emerging view that parties may couch campaigns in valence appeals but do actually offer differences, including on dimensions of democracy and constitutionalism (Bleck and van de Walle 2018, 195–205).

My book also offers insights on opposition party building. As Riedl (2014) shows, Africa's postcolonial leaders faced a choice over whether to incorporate local elites into the state or to instead engage in "state substitution" by building structures to rival the power of these local elites. The historical legacies of state substitution under multiparty rule include lower barriers to creating new parties and fewer incentives for coordination among opposition actors. State substitution also impacted today's opposition parties indirectly by diminishing civil society and dampening its mobilization capacity. This makes it less viable for opposition parties to develop around powerful civic organizations with broad appeal in the way that, for example, Zimbabwe's Movement for Democratic Change drew from the existing strength of trade organizations (LeBas 2011).

My account suggests that even in environments with more fragile and diffuse civil society, these structures can play a powerful role in opposition party development. While they may lack broad enough appeal to shape the foundations of a party, smaller-scale civic organizations like faith-based groups, student movements, and rights-based NGOs can form "socio-electoral coalitions" with opposition parties and support them during elections (Trejo 2014). These groups provide training and resources to activists who can later use them to win seats if they decide to run as opposition candidates. When opposition legislators use parliaments to pursue institutional reforms that promote democratic change, they further empower the civil society sector. This points to ways opposition parties and civil society actors can strengthen each other over time in spite of legacies of postcolonial rule that hinder their contemporary growth.

Empirical research on elections and accountability in Africa has overwhelmingly focused on voters, supported by a wealth of individual-level data on the decisions and views of everyday citizens. Theorizing the exercise of power has narrowed in on the executive, given the significance of presidential power in African regimes (van de Walle 2003). The volume joins a growing stream of literature focused on the elite politics of national legislative elections in Africa. Legislatures play a critical role as stewards of development and its members are responsible for passing laws, overseeing the executive, and serving as the primary link between citizens and the state. My work has identified sources of candidates for legislative office and how candidates seek election, allowing us to distinguish what makes aspirants decide to run for office (versus not running) and what kinds of promises and appeals candidates make to voters. Future research will do well to build upon these contributions by studying how candidate backgrounds and campaign tactics impact the quality of representation.

Finally, my book offers several novel data collection and analytical techniques with particular appeal for the empirical study of African politics. I investigated risk attitudes and offered alternative approaches to measuring risk. By using novel cultural lessons taught to individuals in the form of proverbs known as *methali*, the empirical strategy was able to tap into risk and time attitudes that resonated with respondents. Elsewhere, I have validated the use of *methali* as measures of risk. It is likely in many African settings, where modern political institutions remain attached to traditional structures of social organization, that expressions similar to *methali* offer a powerful way to study political choices. My book joins a select few in political science who have employed the life history calendar (Cloward and Weghorst 2019, Zeria 2019) to collect retrospective data about paths to political candidacy. This represents one of many promising uses of the life history calendar technique for the purposes of studying decision making when the relevant population of interest (in this case, legislators) is only visible months, years, or decades after these decisions were made. As detailed in the book, the life history calendar has been shown to accurately collect factual data about past events. Life history calendars would be particularly useful in sub-Saharan Africa; the use of visual modes of communicating political and social information is commonly used by political actors (e.g., parties and candidates) and other civic organizations (e.g., posters regarding health practices). I hope scholars of African politics will explore the applicability of these data collection techniques across other settings.

Implications for Candidacy and Legislatures

The main contributions to the literature on candidacy and more broadly on political competition are threefold. First, in showing the applicability of a general candidacy theory to the context of an electoral authoritarian regime in sub-Saharan Africa, the book has claimed that political behavior is not so idiosyncratic to require entirely new or different theories to account for decisions to seek office. Instead, the approach introduced modifications to well-established theories so that they fit in contexts outside of advanced democracies. Demonstrating that parsimonious models of political behavior are adaptable to an array of contexts is a fruitful way to understand elite actions in politics. This book encourages scholars of candidacy in electoral authoritarian regimes to look to the extant literature from advanced democracies as a valuable theoretical building block.

Second, adapting a parsimonious model of candidacy to an authoritarian context feeds back lessons for candidacy outside of those settings. Specifically, it offers several contributions to the broad scholarship on candidacy that has mostly focused on advanced democracies. Candidacy decisions in a multiparty environment must take into account differences between political parties. Work built from Black (1972), for example, models a candidacy decision as a binary one of running or not running with some party. This book has demonstrated that depending on the party at hand, candidacy may or may not be appealing. Candidate preferences are choice specific, depending on what candidates want and what parties offer. Losing an election or nomination may offer some benefit to a prospective candidate, depending on the circumstances. Candidate selectorates matter substantially in candidacy decision making. This work has offered a number of ways in which the framework of strategic candidacy decisions can be enhanced in advanced democracies.

Third, this work extended our understanding of so-called "ambitious politics." This literature has been most focused on two lines of inquiry: ambition as a single-shot decision to enter political office and "progressive ambition," seeking out higher-prestige elected office, such as moving from a state to a national legislature. Strategic calculations in this view are made at the moment of seeking nomination and candidacy. My research has established this approach is not tenable. This book joined recent scholarship in applying the concept of "nascent ambition" to candidacy decisions (Lawless 2012, Fox and Lawless 2005, 2004, Bernhard, Shames, and Teele 2021). The research demonstrated that paths to candidacy are frequently initiated long before the actual decision of candidacy was even under consideration. They begin instead in meaningful early events in an individual's life. Civic activism and career partisanship fit alongside nascent ambition, which portrays running for office as the first stage along a path to "expressive ambition" (e.g., seeking candidacy). My work showed that paths into candidacy not only matter for understanding this sort of nascent ambition, but further that this can account for the very values prospective candidates assign to the parameter of strategic candidacy decision making. It also offered new applications of analytical techniques like sequence analysis that show promise for empirical research embracing this longer term view toward political ambition.

Policy Implications for Authoritarianism and Democratization

The hope for democracy seen at the beginning of the third wave of democratization and in Africa's transitions in the late twentieth century has largely turned to pessimism two decades into the twenty-first century. There is disagreement among scholars and policy actors regarding the magnitude of its severity, but it is clear that democracy and democratic institutions are under attack. Freedom House notes that 2019 marked the fourteenth consecutive year of global democratic decline. 2020 saw that trend accelerate, with seventy-three countries – together containing three-quarters of the world's population – ending the year less democratic than they started (Freedom House 2021). 2019 was the first time in nearly twenty years that the majority of countries in the world were ruled by autocratic governments (Lührmann and Lindberg 2019) and global decline in democracy in 2020 left the world at levels of democracy similar to those at the end of the Cold War (Alizada et al. 2021)). Much of the decline has squarely focused on the forces of political change I study in this book: leaders who govern electoral autocracies in Africa and around the globe have targeted political opposition and cracked down on civic space.

Many governments in developing countries that once saw NGOs as potential allies (Brass 2018) have turned against them. Regulating, restricting, and repressing the NGO sector have been increasingly common in Africa in recent years. Autocracies in Africa that have succeeded, are trying, or have tried and failed to pass restrictive NGO legislation include Tanzania, Uganda, Rwanda, Ethiopia, Mozambique, and Zimbabwe, the very types of regimes where civic activism pathways to political opposition are most likely to emerge (Musila 2019). These regulations include extensive government oversight into organization registration, limiting international financial support, and prohibiting activities that are deemed political. Crippling the institutional strength of NGOs and civil society, limiting the domains they work in to things seen as explicitly apolitical, and cutting off international funding streams how civil society channels activism into political ambition.

In spite of these discouraging patterns, my book offer reasons for domestic and international actors to hold cautious optimism about future democratic prospects in today's electoral authoritarian regimes. *Foreign Policy* deemed 2019 the "Year of Global Protest" (Johnson 2019) and nearly half of the countries in the world experienced pro-democracy protests in 2019 (Lührmann et al. 2020). The rates of mass mobilization in autocracies were the highest in recorded history. While the global COVID-19 pandemic meant 2020 saw the lowest levels of mass mobilization in more than ten years, experts believe the dip will be followed by another year of widespread citizen demonstration and protest (Alizada et al. 2021). For the sake of pressuring autocrats to relent or curtail the speed at which they are peeling away gains toward democracy, such widespread engagement suggests that citizens can force governments to concede reforms or to retreat on efforts to close down civic space. In Uganda and Ethiopia, civil society actors negotiated with governments to strike down many of the most restrictive components of anti-NGO/CSO regulations; in other settings, courts, legacy advocacy groups, and international human rights and civil rights organizations have succeeded in substantially reducing the impact of these restrictions or even defeating them. There is significant opportunity for international actors to stand up for NGOs and civil society in sub-Saharan Africa. Among some thirty international organizations working to protect civil society against government efforts to constrain them, few are providing direct financial support for NGOs in Africa (Baldus, Poppe, and Wolff 2017, Musila 2019).

When facing closing political space, international actors can shift democracy support resources to other settings or they often look to pivot their focus to civil society engagement. This book suggests that upping investments in civil society can yield compounding returns for the sake of democracy. It is clear from the widespread level of citizen resistance against autocratization and the role of civil society and NGOs that under-lying capacity and interest in activism are high and efforts by policy makers to feed them can boost civic space in the short run, but also political competition in the longer term. Strengthening membership-based nongovernment organizations and civic associations of today can lay the foundations of opposition that is strong and capable. From these institu-tions can also emerge the future candidates of opposition parties who are committed to fighting for democratic reform and political change.

Appendix A

Qualitative and Survey Interviews: Sample Design, Response Rates, and Representativeness

A.1 LEGISLATOR SURVEY

The discussion begins by considering surveys carried out in Tanzania's legislatures.

Data Collection

Legislators were recruited to participate during legislative sessions that are held quarterly. Specifically, the surveys were administered during the annual budget sessions, as these are typically the longest and best attended meetings of the legislatures. For the Parliament of Tanzania, interviews were conducted in April–June of 2013 and for the Zanzibar House of Representatives during June through August of the same year.

Respondents were sought out by a team of enumerators, four individuals for the Parliament and two for the House of Representatives. Recruitment began with a brief description of the project, its goals and outputs, as well as the informed consent script approved by the University of Florida's Institutional Review Board. If requested, enumerators also provided interviewees with digital copies of the various permissions required to administer the project. For the Parliament, this included letters from the Tanzania Commission for Science and Technology (COSTECH, Ref. No. 2012-478-NA-2012-158), the Office of the Clerk of the Parliament of Tanzania (Ref. No. EB.155/297/01/185), as well as background verifications of the enumerators' good standing (Ref. No. EB.155/297/01/41). Enumerators also had digital copies of permission letters provided by leaders of political parties endorsing and encouraging participation in the project. In Zanzibar, enumerators carried digitized copies of a government-issued research permit (issued by the Zanzibar Research Committee in the Second Vice-President's Office) and party endorsement letters.

To further boost participation, several efforts to publicize the ongoing research project took place. The day prior to and on the first day of data collection, the parliament's information technology office sent out a text blast to the parliament members' cell phones to alert them the research was being conducted. This was to inform members that they would be approached in the coming days regarding the research project about their decisions to run for office and, more generally, about their personal political histories and interaction with constituents.[1] In the case of the Zanzibar House of Representatives, the Speaker of the House made an announcement regarding the project that carried a similar message. I made additional efforts to boost respondent participation by recruiting respondents outside of sessions to schedule interviews with enumerators in subsequent days. These primarily took place in the evening at local restaurants, bars, and the handful of hotels where MPs tend to stay in Dodoma. It is common for them to meet with fellow members, party leaders, and visiting constituents in these settings during the evenings, particularly because Dodoma is a small town located several hundred kilometers from Tanzania's largest cities. In the Parliament, interviews were carried out either in public areas such as the cafeteria or sitting areas outside of the main chambers during the day. Enumerators were allowed some discretion in choosing alternate interview locations. For the House of Representatives, whose legislative grounds have far fewer amenities and meeting spaces outside the chambers, the library, research rooms, and vacant committee meeting rooms were used.

The data collection effort yielded an overall response rate of 30.5 percent of legislators in Tanzania. Further breakdowns of participation across legislatures and parties can be found in Table A.1. These participation rates are comparably higher than the most substantial effort to survey African legislators, which is the African Legislatures Project. While the sampling strategies are not directly comparable, the African Legislatures Project captured about 14 percent of Tanzania MPs compared to

---

[1] Initially, it was requested to have the Speaker of the Parliament make an announcement about the project. Citing concerns of setting precedents of doing such things or prioritizing one research project over another, the text message effort was proposed as an alternative.

TABLE A.1 *Distribution of respondents*

	Total Members	Ruling Party	Opposition
Sample, Both Legislatures	132	64	68
Population, Both Legislatures	433	308	125
AAPOR Response Rate	30.5%	20.8%	54.4%
Sample, Parliament	67	32	35
Population, Parliament	349	259	90
AAPOR Response Rate	19.2%	12.4%	38.9%
Sample, House of Representatives	65	32	33
Population, House of Representatives	84	49	35
AAPOR Response Rate	77.4%	65.3%	94.3%

Note: Response rates are calculated based on the American Association for Public Opinion Research (AAPOR) Standard Definitions.

19 percent in this project.[2] These response rates are, however, lower than some other single-country studies of legislators.[3]

Most notably, the opposition participated at substantially higher rates than did the ruling party. In the Parliament, the response rates of the opposition are more than three times greater than ruling party members. In the House of Representatives, all but two opposition members took part in the project. The reasons for this are sensible, as the perceived benefit of research about party members, candidacy, and the like is greater for parties that have yet to take control of the government. In general, cooperation with parties was more constructive with the opposition. In the section of the survey designed for internal-party usage, the opposition was more proactive in suggesting items that they wished to know and assess about their performance.[4]

For a number of research questions, this imbalance of opposition versus ruling party participation could present analytical problems. For this study, however, overrepresenting opposition respondents is actually desirable to ensure the number of respondents permits meaningful

---

[2] The African Legislatures Project did not include Zanzibar's legislature, as it was concerned with national legislatures.

[3] Lindberg's (2010) work in Ghana obtained roughly 50 percent response rates, while work in Uganda has obtained closer to 70 percent participation in some studies.

[4] Surveys included internal assessments specific to each party to encourage greater cooperation and participation; this is detailed in Chapter 3, Section 3.3.

comparisons between the ruling party and the opposition. It is further important because the ruling party is not disaggregated in analyses, while comparisons between members of various opposition parties are analytically important in some chapters. With a smaller number of opposition participants, one would encounter statistical power issues upon disaggregating the opposition into political parties. Because analyses in the book compare ruling party to the opposition and candidates and non-candidates *among* the opposition, the higher opposition participation rates do not present inferential issues. Rather, possible issues related to inference arise from whether or not the sample is representative of the legislature more broadly. Discussion now moves to address this issue.

Sample Representativeness

The sampling goal of this research was not, in fact, to capture a sample of legislators. Setting practical considerations aside, the aim was to collect a census of all members of the current Parliament of Tanzania and the House of Representatives of Zanzibar. Thus, the differences between members captured in the sample and those in the population who were not included in the research study cannot be understood through conventional sampling practices where randomized recruitment ensures representativeness of the sample. Participation and nonparticipation in this study are nonrandom, in that respondents themselves determined whether or not they were a part of the study.[5] Given the comparably lower participation rates of members of Tanzania's Parliament highlighted in the preceding discussion, it is important to establish the representativeness of the sample.

To do so, one must begin with considering what is known about the legislature and its members broadly and how this compares with that information for the respondent sample. The book's inclusion of the legislator biographies permits such comparisons. While the database contains less comprehensive and rich data compared with the survey, it allows one to establish a background picture of members of the legislatures. Discussion focuses on variables related to demographics, education, constituency competitiveness, and professional and political experience.

---

[5] This includes personal constraints, such as extended leave from legislative duties due to health problems or other governance responsibilities taking priority over attending parliamentary sessions.

TABLE A.2 *Sample representativeness*

Variable	Parliament		Difference	House of Representatives		Difference
	Sample	Population	Significant?	Sample	Population	Significant?
Percent Female	29.8%	36.1%	Yes	36.9%	42.6%	Yes
Mean Birth Year	1963	1961	No	1963	1961	No
Percent with Bachelor's Degree	35.8%	39.2%	No	16.9%	17.0%	No
Years Worked in Education Sector	2.15	2.54	No	3.54	2.90	No
Years Worked in Government Sector	1.97	1.94	No	0.90	1.25	No
2010 CCM Vote Share in Constituency	53.8%	58.9%	No	43.5%	45.6%	No

If the sample of legislators differs significantly from the population of Tanzanian legislators broadly, this would raise concern about the extent to which conclusions advanced in the book speak to more general dynamics in Tanzania. Table A.2 evaluates these concerns, using tests that compare whether the average tendencies of the legislator samples and populations are different across a number of indicators. Sampling bias is assessed at conventional levels of statistical significance ($p < .05$) and established using either difference of means or difference of proportion tests that compare the sample and population.

On the whole, the samples of legislators from the Parliament of Tanzania and Zanzibar's House of Representatives mirror the whole of their legislative bodies. There is one exception. Women are underrepresented by a 5 percent to 6 percent margin for both legislative bodies. The reasons for this may be an artifact of the data collection strategy, where the gender distribution of enumerator teams was uneven (with four male and two female enumerators). Male enumerators actually interviewed a higher proportion of female legislators than did female enumerators, casting some doubt on this possibility. It may also be that legislators who come to the legislature through party-appointed quota seats see less value in participating in a survey that emphasized its goal as learning about how individuals become legislators and their personal political histories. Project descriptions also spoke to enhancing the way in which legislators dialogue with constituents to improve democratic representation. The latter reason for participation may have garnered less appeal with individuals whose "constituency" was a party-based one, rather than a district's electorate. Across the other variables, the samples are statistically similar to the legislative bodies. This holds for demographic factors, like age and education, as well as other substantively important variables like political experience, career background, and constituency competitiveness. These latter factors would point to potential biases that could more directly damage inferences about the qualities of candidates that drive them to run for office.

A.2 CANDIDATES AND NONCANDIDATE SURVEYS

Dialogue now turns to the comparably more complex effort to collect data through party-based surveys.

Data Collection Strategy

The data collection strategy for the research was developed in collaboration with the two major opposition parties in Tanzania. Some of these procedures are already discussed in Section 3.3. After the questionnaire was vetted with the parties, the geographic sampling plan was devised. Due to expense of transporting research teams across Tanzania and the sparse support for opposition in Tanzania's hinterlands, a profile of regions where each party has a strong support base was developed. Regions for each party's surveys were selected from these regions to limit the geographic scope of the project. Regions of Tanzania in which surveys were administered for CUF were Dar es salaam, Lindi, Mwanza, Mtwara, Pwani, Shinyanga, Simiyu, and Tabora. For CHADEMA, the regions included were Arusha, Kilimanjaro, Mara, and Tanga. From this list of regions, districts were identified as being accessible through motor transportation (located a practical distance from a trunk road, where a local minibus could transport the research team further into rural areas). From this list, districts were randomly selected.

Once districts were selected, a research timeline was developed such that a research assistant traveled in a single path to visit district offices for proximate regions. Each district convened members of the three respondent groups – losing candidates from the 2010 elections, unsuccessful nomination seekers, and prospective candidates who considered running (drawn from members of the youth and women's wings of the party who took but did not submit nomination forms). Party leaders located in central offices notified each district of the day the research team would arrive in the district. They also tasked district and regional officials with informing party members meeting participation criteria to report to the district office in the morning. When en route to a district the day prior, the research assistant verified the reporting date and time for that particular district. For the most part, this strategy was successful in yielding high participation rates. Locating unsuccessful candidates sometimes took additional effort, including telephoning former campaign staff and other notables. The CUF surveys took a total of seventeen days, while the CHADEMA surveys presented less challenging travel conditions and lasted nine days. Both were carried out in July 2013.

Respondents received instructions about how to complete the survey and were provided with a pen and envelope to submit their completed self-administered questionnaire. The packet also contained the informed consent script. Prior to receiving the actual questionnaire, each individual was asked to verify that they, in fact, did fit the description of the respondent group for which they were taking the survey. At the completion of the survey, respondents gave the questionnaire to a research assistant in the sealed envelope. In more sparsely populated districts, research assistants had a discretionary transportation allowance to organize a *dala dala* (minibus) for transporting respondents back to their homes and villages.[6] After travel for survey administration was completed, the author held a debrief session with research assistants to collect survey materials.

Sample Representativeness

Showing the representativeness of the candidate and noncandidate samples is more challenging. It may be possible to establish some parameters

---

[6] Due to concerns over potentially violating campaign and party finance laws regarding financial contributions to a political party, all transactions were documented by specific expense receipts.

of the population of 2010's losing candidates but, the logistical barriers to doing so in such a large, infrastructure-poor country render this task impossible in practice. While the members of this population can be identified based on registering to run for office with Tanzania and Zanzibar's electoral bodies, information like age and education of that population is not publicly known or made available.

To further complicate matters, the population of "prospective, noncandidates" is unobserved and, hence, cannot be known. The sampling design for candidates and noncandidates alike was by definition not intended to give all individuals an equal or known chance of being selected. By targeting areas where the opposition parties have modest or strong support, the sampling strategy focused where respondents of substantive importance were most likely to be found while excluding others in low-support regions.

In spite of these challenges, it is nonetheless valuable to get a sense of how participants in these surveys would compare with the population from which the sample is drawn. Since one cannot collect such information about the target population, an alternative is to draw upon the data resources collected through this project and make cautious assessments about how these individuals should compare with other respondent groups like successful legislative candidates and average citizens.

Table A.3 addresses whether or not the background characteristics of survey respondents suggest a picture of representativeness. The discussion here focuses on variables that are either (1) demographic and lack strong prior expectations in the text or (2) useful for comparison with population-based surveys, such as social group membership. Citizen data are drawn from data collection efforts that ultimately were not included in this volume but will appear in other research outputs.

Beginning with demographic data, the strongest anticipated similarities are between election winners and losers. These individuals passed the greatest number of hurdles on the path to candidacy and met whatever expectations existed for parties in terms of "what a candidate looks like." Moving down the first two columns of Table A.3, one sees that, for the most part, this expectation holds. In terms of age, marital status, and number of children, legislators and unsuccessful candidates are statistically indistinguishable. There are differences between legislators and losing candidates in terms of education, but they are modest compared with other respondent groups and still substantially greater than the average educational attainment of Tanzanians broadly (the final column of the table). Perhaps unsurprisingly, youth and women's wing members

TABLE A.3 *Opposition sample representativeness*

	Legislator	Election Loser	Nomination Loser	Women's Wing	Youth Wing	Citizen Surveys
Age (in 2010)	40.9	42.3	42.2	37.7	31.2	35.5
Significant vs. Legislator?		No	No	Yes	Yes	Yes
Married with One Spouse	83.8%	84.6%	66.9%	69.3%	63.6%	53.0%
Significant vs. Legislator?		No	Yes	Yes	Yes	Yes
Children	5.0	4.3	3.6	2.9	1.8	3.6
Significant vs. Legislator?		No	Yes	Yes	Yes	Yes
Education Level	5.6	4.6	4.1	3.8	4.4	3.8
Significant vs. Legislator?		Yes	Yes	Yes	Yes	Yes
Member: Union	30.9%	25.0%	15.7%	8.4%	16.2%	5.2%
Significant vs. Legislator?		No	Yes	Yes	Yes	Yes
Member: Student Government	45.6%	30.7%	16.9%	23.6%	29.8%	9.1%
Significant vs. Legislator?		Yes	Yes	Yes	Yes	Yes
Member: Professional Association	23.5%	25.0%	14.4%	14.2%	19.4	12.4%
Significant vs. Legislator?		No	Yes	Yes	Yes	Yes

Note: Education is represented by an ordinal variable, with the following values: 1 (None), 2 (Partial Primary), 3 (Completed Primary), 4 (Partial Secondary), 5 (Completed Secondary), and 6 (Partial or Completed Tertiary).

who considered candidacy but decided not to run are younger and in earlier life stages with respect to marriage, children, and education. Maybe an awareness that they are not quite ready to undertake the responsibilities of running an election campaign or that they are not of the "right age" discourages seeking nominations. In most cases, they are nonetheless older, married at higher rates, and more educated than average citizens.

Nomination seekers fall mostly between candidates and noncandidates on demographic dimensions. Given that most legislators are married, it could be that the social status of marriage is important in obtaining a party nomination and the lower rates of marriage of this group contribute to not being selected to run for office. If voters view marriage as a short-cut for assessing social maturity and status, then unmarried nomination seekers are not likely to appeal to political parties.

In the lower half of the table, the differences between the prospective candidate sample and the average Tanzanian become clear. Across a number of social organizations, one views that the general rate of civic participation in Tanzania is quite low. Even though party activism can impose an opportunity cost on an individual's activity in other civic organizations, study participants are significantly more active in trade unions, student governments, and other professional associations (e.g., NGO boards). Importantly, social membership of legislators and losing candidates is similar, which points to further comparability of these groups. One also observes that nomination losers have lower rates of participation in civic organizations, perhaps pointing to the way in which low social valence can contribute to poor nomination prospects. Finally, the pattern of lower rates of women's participation in the public sphere holds across these social organizations as well. Women are the least active of respondents who participated in the party-based surveys.

Considered together, these results suggest that the sample of candidates and noncandidates who were recruited through party-based procedures meet plausible expectations regarding representativeness of the population of potential candidates for office in Tanzania. While the population of prospective, noncandidates is truly not observable and that of losing candidates and nomination seekers unobservable in practical terms, analysis of background survey data demonstrates three points. First, the more election-related hurdles a party-based survey respondent has crossed, the more they resemble the most elite sample considered (Tanzanian legislators). Second, this is most pronounced with election losers, whose differences from legislators are more likely to be observed in what determines election outcomes – campaign strategy and other substantively important variables. Third, all groups are considerably more "elite" than the average Tanzanian, suggesting that the group of individuals included in this survey were truly "likely" candidates for legislative office and look to be in future elections.

Appendix B

Statistical Results, Analysis Details, and Robustness

B.1 SUPPORTING MATERIAL FOR CHAPTER 2

In Chapter 2, I claim that opposition parties in Africa use more inclusive candidate selection procedures compared with ruling parties. This is based on descriptive data from Ohman (2004) as well as analysis of a Varieties of Democracy (V-Dem)'s February 2022 version of the V-Party dataset, which codes party characteristics over time and includes all forty-nine countries in sub-Saharan Africa. The candidate nomination questions regard who is in the selectorate where higher values indicator a more inclusive selectorate, ranging from a party leader's unilateral decision to all registered voters being eligible. The unit of analysis in Table B.1 is a party-election year; parties appear multiple times in the analysis to capture variation in party procedures over time. The responses are aggregated and rescaled by V-Dem using a proprietary measurement model and generally range between -5 and 5. Differences between ruling party and opposition when transformed back to their original coding are also significant. I compared the two groups using a simple difference of means test.

B.2 SUPPORTING MATERIAL FOR CHAPTER 4

Main Analysis

Table B.2 presents the fully-specified regression that underlies the main analysis presented and discussed in Section 4.2.

Civic Activism Measurement and Robustness

The measure of civic activism that appears in the analysis of the cross-sectional survey presented in Figure 4.1 is an index ranging from 0 to

TABLE B.1 *Analysis of V-Dem party-level data regarding candidate selection*

	Average	P-Value
Opposition Parties	0.079	–
N	502	
Parties in Government	−0.214	–
N	559	
Difference	−0.293	<.01
N	1061	

TABLE B.2 *Regression corresponding with Figures 4.1 and 4.2*

	Opposition Legislator	Opposition Legislator
Civic Activism Index	0.20*	
	(0.108)	
Local Govt Experience	−0.33	
	(0.608)	
Party, Campaign Team	−0.25	
	(0.567)	
Party Leader: Secretariat	0.49	
	(0.456)	
Party Leader: Region	−2.59***	
	(0.547)	
Party Leader: Local	−0.51	
	(0.791)	
Party, Youth Leader	1.55***	
	(0.593)	
Years of Party Membership		−0.25***
		(0.054)
Years of Grassroots Organizing		0.08*
		(0.043)
Age Quintile	−0.30**	0.18
	(0.148)	(0.172)
Education	−0.32*	−0.12
	(0.167)	(0.151)
Male	0.31	−0.10
	(0.491)	(0.436)
Constant	2.79**	2.76***
	(1.303)	(1.057)
N	132	132

Notes: * $p<0.10$, ** $p<0.05$, *** $p<0.01$.

12 and is the sum of activism level across six domains of civic association: religion, women's, student, professional associational, union, and grassroots. I use this measure because it best captures the breadth of civic engagement and allows for heterogeneity in which particular organizations may be more important in a given context. For example, religious associations may be especially important in priming opposition candidacy in areas where minority religious communities are marginalized by the government or if there are historical links between certain religious denominations and a locally popular challenger party – both of these scenarios are true for the case of Tanzania. The disadvantage of such a measure is that it risks undervaluing the impact of significant investment in a single leadership outlet while elevating activists who have low-intensity engagement across multiple sectors. I think this downside is conceptually appropriate but nonetheless consider alternative measures. Findings almost universally point in the same direction as in the text and a number of the disaggregated organizational findings are independently statistically significant. I describe each alternative measure and present the related statistical result in Table B.3.

Civic Activism Index: This is the measure used in the main text. Each of six organization types (religion, women's, student, professional associational, union, and grassroots) is coded as 0 if the individual was not a member of such an organization before or at the time they ran for office, 1 if they were a member and 2 if they were a leader. The index is the sum of the six measures. Because the measure captures organizational sector, not specific organizations, the index and its sub-components would not represent a scenario where an individual is a member of multiple organizations within the same organization type. As discussed in the text, I think this is appropriate.

Leader in Any Organization: A dichotomous variable that is coded as 1 if an individual held a leadership position in any of the six organizational domains/types included in the survey.

Total Leadership Positions: An ordinal variable ranging from 0 to 6; each 1 point increase in this variable corresponds with having been the leader one of the six organizational domains/types included in the survey.

Highest Activism: An ordinal variable ranging from 0 to 3 that corresponds with the original variable coding (0=not a member, 1=unofficial member, 2=official member, 3=leader). This variable takes on the highest value observed across any of the six organizational types, corresponding with the highest level of activism present across any of the six types. In other words, someone who was a leader in student government and a member of three other organization types would be coded as "3" for this variable.

Leader: *Org Type*: A dichotomous variable that is coded as 1 if an individual held a leadership position in a given organizational sector, 0 if they did not. In these analyses, other organization types are not included in the statistical analysis, meaning each results row in the table corresponds with a distinctive statistical analysis and that analysis does not control for leadership in the other five organizational types.

Leader: *Org Type,* **Other Orgs Incl:** The same as the immediately prior, except all six leadership variables are included in a single analysis meaning the findings control for leadership in other organizational types.

Member: *Org Type*: A dichotomous variable that is coded as 1 if an individual was a member in a given organizational sector, 0 if they were not. In these analyses, other organization types are not included in the statistical analysis, meaning each results row in the table corresponds with a distinctive statistical analysis and that analysis does not control for membership in the other five organizational types.

Member: *Org Type,* **Other Orgs Incl:** The same as the immediately prior, except all six membership variables are included in a single analysis meaning the findings control for membership in other organizational types.

Member Type: *Org Type*: An ordinal variable that is coded as 0 if an individual was not a member, 1 if the individual was an unofficial member, 2 if the individual was an official member, and 3 if the individual was a leader in the given organization type. In these analyses, other organization types are not included in the statistical analysis, meaning each results row in the table corresponds with a distinctive statistical analysis and that analysis does not control for membership in the other five organizational types.

Member Type: *Org Type,* **Other Orgs Incl.:** The same as the immediately prior, except all six membership variables are included in a single analysis meaning the findings control for membership in other organizational types.

TABLE B.3 *Robustness of alternative civic activism measures for analysis corresponding with Table B.2*

	Coefficient Sign (DV Opp=1, CCM=0)	P-Value
Civic Activism Index (Table B.2)	+	.066
Leader in Any Organization	+	.156
Total Leadership Positions	+	.192
Highest Activism	+	.043
Leader, *Religion*	+	.081
Leader, *Women's Org*	+	.612
Leader, *Prof Org*	+	.954
Leader, *Union*	+	.943
Leader, *Student Gov*	-	.967
Leader, *Grassroots*	+	.243
Leader, *Religion*, Other Orgs Incl.	+	.056
Leader, *Women's Org*, Other Orgs Incl.	-	.894
Leader, *Prof Org*, Other Orgs Incl.	+	.534
Leader, *Union*, Other Orgs Incl.	+	.920
Leader, *Student Gov*, Other Orgs Incl.	-	.549
Leader, *Grassroots*, Other Orgs Incl.	+	.191
Member, *Religion*	+	.295
Member, *Women's Org*	+	.097
Member, *Prof Org*	+	.685
Member, *Union*	-	.942
Member, *Student Gov*	+	.864
Member, *Grassroots*	+	.090
Member, *Religion*, Other Orgs Incl.	+	.509
Member, *Women's Org*, Other Orgs Incl.	+	.101
Member, *Prof Org*, Other Orgs Incl.	-	.905
Member, *Union*, Other Orgs Incl.	+	.944
Member, *Student Gov*, Other Orgs Incl.	+	.738
Member, *Grassroots*, Other Orgs Incl.	+	.182
Member Type, *Religion*	+	.149
Member Type, *Women's Org*	+	.098
Member Type, *Prof Org*	+	.732
Member Type, *Union*	-	.999
Member Type, *Student Gov*	+	.914
Member Type, *Grassroots*	+	.119
Member Type, *Religion*, Other Orgs Incl.	+	.240
Member Type, *Women's Org*, Other Orgs Incl.	+	.132
Member Type, *Prof Org*, Other Orgs Incl.	+	.985
Member Type, *Union*, Other Orgs Incl.	+	.980
Member Type, *Student Gov*, Other Orgs Incl.	+	.901
Member Type, *Grassroots*, Other Orgs Incl.	+	.240

B.3 SUPPORTING MATERIAL FOR CHAPTER 5

Analyses of Vocational Careers

Table B.4 provides the fully-specified regression model associated with Figure 5.2, derived from the coding of the vocational careers of legislators' CVs derived from the POLIS database and collecting them from the Zanzibar House of Representatives clerk. Observations that were completely missing career data are not included in this analysis. The age variable used with this data is slightly different from analyses of survey data using age quintile, as it is anchored at the start of legal adulthood in Tanzania and includes age by year rather than collapsing into quintiles. The age spread of successful legislative candidates is smaller than the survey dataset which includes unsuccessful aspirants and non-candidates.

Sequence Analysis

Originally developed to analyze patterns in DNA and compare DNA sequences, sequence analysis shares in common some features with time-series, cross-sectional approaches where multiple observations come from the same unit and are ordered systematically. Unlike conventional time-series, cross-sectional analyses where an observation-year (e.g., a person in a given year) is treated as the unit of analysis, the concept of a sequence considers the entirety of a respondent's or case's related events/states together as a single observation (a sequence). Sequence analysis is ideal for studying phenomena where a given piece of information is best understood in relation to others in its sequence and when comparing the trajectories of one observation with another is theoretically appropriate. Applications of sequence methods in the social sciences include the study of pathways through schooling (Brzinsky-Fay 2007, Dietrich, Andersson, and Salmela-Aro 2014, McVicar and Anyadike-Danes n.d.), life course and family development (Martin, Schoon, and Ross 2008, Oris and Ritschard 2014), and vocational careers (Abbott and Hrycak 1990, Blair-Loy 1999, Pollock, Antcliff, and Ralphs 2002). While not commonly used in political science, sequence analysis has promise for studying political phenomena featuring path and temporal dependence (Gryzmala-Busse 2011). Sequences methods have been used to study legislatures (Borghetto 2014) and legislative output (Abbott and DeViney 1992), as well as activism (Fillieule and Blanchard 2011) and democratic transitions (Wilson 2014).

TABLE B.4 *Regressions corresponding with Figure 5.1*

	Opposition Legislator
Percentage of Career in CSO/NGO	2.04**
	(0.429)
Percentage of Career in Party	−2.71***
	(1.161)
Percentage of Career in Government	−1.35***
	(0.310)
Age (Adult Years)	−0.12
	(0.013)
Education	0.05
	(0.052)
Female	0.64***
	(0.239)
Constant	−1.21
	(0.532)
N	542
Pseudo R^2	0.16

Note: * $p<0.10$, ** $p<0.05$, *** $p<0.01$.

Sequence data are structured in a way that resembles cross-sectional, time-series data in long format. Each sequence is uniquely identified with one variable (e.g., a person, a country); a second variable orders a sequence, generally with a discrete time unit (e.g., years, development stages, position number in a genome, etc.); a third variable contains the sequence attribute – the substantive information of interest (e.g., employment status, regime type, family size, an event, and so on etc. (Blanchard 2013)). Each sequence contains two types of information. First, an *element* represents the value or state of a sequence in a single time unit. Second, sequences contain *episodes*. Episodes describe each group of consecutive, identical elements. The totality of episodes together form a sequence. Figure B.1 provides a visual overview of how elements and episodes characterize sequences, largely adapted from Brzinsky-Fay, Kohler, and Luniak (2006).

Each individual legislator has a career partisanship sequence, ordered in discrete time units of the number of years from reaching adulthood (eighteen years of age) to the year they aspired to run for office. The sequence variable contains elements that represent different positions that individuals held in a political party in a given time period. Career partisanship is a sequence variable that is first categorized on the basis of the level

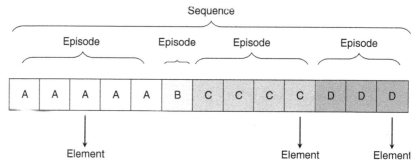

FIGURE B.1 Components of a sequence

of the office where a given position is located. There are six possible levels: ward (sub-constituency), constituency, district, region, secretariat, and central committee.[1] Within each of the six office levels, positions are further divided based on whether they are low- or high-prestige positions. On the first dimension, low-prestige positions are functional, low-visibility ones – serving as an administrative assistant, secretary, accountant, and so on. Positions are coded as high prestige if they are leadership positions within an office, including executive directors, managers, and leaders. This includes leaders of sub-party wings, like serving as a women's wing leader.

When an individual held multiple positions at different levels in a given year, the position at the less-centralized party office is recorded. If holding multiple positions within a party office, the position of higher prestige is documented. For example, someone who was the chair of a ward party office and a treasurer of a district office would be categorized as holding a high-prestige, ward-level party position in that year. The reason for coding the lower-level office over the higher one is that the duration of the lower-level service more accurately captures the notion of low-status "grunt work" performed to gain the favor and experience that facilitate later running for office.

---

[1] District and region are treated as distinctive offices. This distinction is most important for CCM because the party structure was developed identically to the administrative structure of the state, where regional and district governments are separate (Ewald 2013). There is some functional overlap between district and regional CCM offices and they often share office space or are located on the same plot of land, particularly in rural areas. Opposition parties sometimes do not have distinctive regional and district offices in practice, especially in areas where they are weak, but organizationally the offices are separate. CHADEMA in particular has succeeded in building the administrative reach of the subnational party apparatus (Paget 2017, 59).

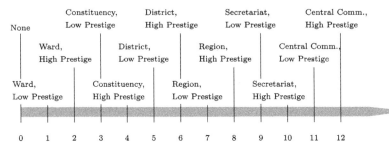

FIGURE B.2 Possible elements in career partisanship sequences

Together, this means an individual element could take on thirteen possible states in any given year; these elements are visualized in Figure B.2. Analyses in the main text simplify this measure by collapsing it into four categories: a local position, a subnational (district/region) position, a national position, or no position.

As described in the main text, data for these sequences are drawn from CVs I collected and combined with additional primary source documents from party and public records. Analyses presented in this book do not include profiles for those with significant political information missing that could not be augmented in a systematic or accurate manner, e.g., politicians who are widely known to have served a significant time in CCM's secretariat under single-party rule and later held office, but the specific years for that party service are not documented in reputable source documents.

Describing Career Partisanship Sequences

Figure B.3 provides a visual representation career partisanship sequences for Tanzanian legislators, with the left panel showing patterns for the ruling party and the right panel for the opposition. To simplify the figure, positions are not differentiated by prestige and central committee positions are represented in the same category as the broader secretariat. Each row in the figure corresponds with an individual; sequences are sorted and ordered by the first element that appears in a sequence, with lower-value elements (e.g., low prestige, ward-level service) higher along the y-axis in the figure. The opposition panel has fewer sequences, accounting for the vertical gaps in the right panel of the figure. Sequences where an individual never held any party position are not shown. In the figure, there are

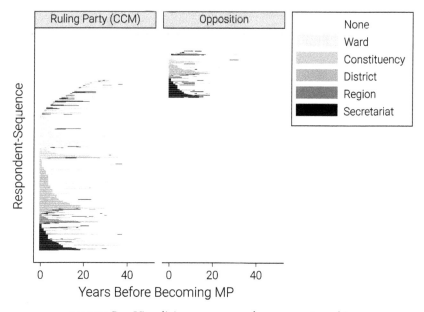

FIGURE B.3 Visualizing sequences of career partisanship

others who held party offices some time prior to running for office but did not in the period immediately before doing so. The measure of "Year of Sequence" begins at 0, indicating when an individual turned eighteen.

There are important differences between partisanship patterns for ruling party versus opposition legislators. For the opposition, party service is concentrated in one of two offices: the secretariat and, to a lesser extent, district-level offices. The most common type of party service for opposition legislators is low-prestige positions in the secretariat, consistent with the idea that opposition candidates bring organizational skills and capacity that such parties often lack – serving as accountants, public affairs staff, and in other administrative positions that keep the offices running. Such low-prestige service is also common at the district level. In part, this is an artifact of party institutionalization and structure with weak downward penetration outside of competitive areas. Opposition legislators have little experience in ward, constituency, or regional offices. Also of note for opposition candidates is that individual service records are fairly unvaried – individuals who do hold positions tend to work in the same position or position type at the same level of centralization. Ruling party service records are different in three ways: they are (1) more varied, (2) longer, and (3) feature more lower-level positions.

Sequence analysis is a means of comparing individual sequences by estimating their similarity to one another (Abbott and Tsay 2000). The sequences of two individuals are most similar when they are identical – they share the same element (for this study, holding a particular party position, holding no position at all) at a given time period (e.g., year 12 of the sequence) and this is true for all time periods within the sequence. For the sequence to be identical, it must also be of the same in duration. For the present analysis, this would mean the number of years between becoming eligible to run (eighteen years of age) and doing so is the same. For most applications, two sequences are seldom identical; sequence methods provide a means by which this qualitative distinction ("not-identical") can be quantified in terms of degree of dissimilarity.

Optimal Matching

Dissimilarity between the sequences of two given observations is conceptualized as the "distance" between them – the number of operations that must be performed to make one of the sequences identical to the other "reference" sequence (Levenshtein 1966). These operations include substitution, which refers to changing a given element within the existing structure of the sequence and insertion and deletion of elements (*indel* in the literature), which transforms the length of the sequence itself by adding or removing elements (Gautheir, Buhlmann, and Blanchard 2014). The primary sequence analysis method is Optimal Matching (OM), whereby each operation required (substitution; *indel*) is associated with a given cost. Substitutions are conventionally regarded as costlier because they combine both insertion and deletion operations.[2] A measure of "distance" of a sequence is thus determined by the total cost of operations to make a sequence identical to another reference sequence or a series of reference sequences with the minimum possible distance, as derived from the Needleman-Wunsch algorithm (Needleman and Wunsch 1970). The reference sequence used for OM calculations is often the

---

[2] For two sequences of equal length, for example, one substitution would be identically accomplished by a deletion *and* insertion, meaning a substitution is treated as twice as costly as an insertion *or* deletion. There is some debate regarding assigning costs to OM operations, particularly with regard to theoretical-driven reasons why substitution costs would be more than twice *indel* costs (Gautheir, Widmer, Bucher, and Notredame 2009), especially if the structure of sequences vary substantially (Macindoe and Abbott 2004).

TABLE B.5 *Substitution matrix*

	None	Local	Subnational	National
None	0	1	3	5
Local	1	0	2	4
Subnational	3	2	0	2
National	5	4	2	0

most common sequence found in the data but other times is a sequence of theoretical importance.[3]

Social scientific research often aspires to truly capture underlying concepts of theoretical interest but struggles to do so because few examples in reality conform to these core concepts. One advantage of sequence analysis is that it allows us to populate our dataset with hypothetical examples that we think best represent those concepts – ideal-types – and evaluate how real-world observations compare with these theoretical ideal-types. This is the strategy I use to perform sequence analysis.

Optimal matching is performed with the TraMineR package in R. Generally speaking, sequence analyses use constant substitution and *indel* costs of 2 and 1, respectively. Under this approach, any substitution between two given states would have an identical cost. However, we know that moving from no party position to serving in a local party office is conceptually "less different" from moving from no party service to a national role or from a local party position to the party's central committee. For this reason, it is more appropriate to specify a substitution matrix that captures the distinctive nature of each state change. The corresponding substitution costs are found in Table B.5.[4] The substitution matrix is symmetrical in that a change between two given positions is identical, regardless of the direction of the change. The specification of costs in the substitution matrix follows with the idea that party positions are hierarchies in which movement into the upper levels of the hierarchy is increasingly difficult and thus costlier. Moreover, leaping from no party service to a party's central committee is much more challenging than taking on a local position. The values

---

[3] An alternative approach is performing OM for each sequence against each other sequence in a dataset (Brzinsky-Fay, Kohler, and Luniak 2006).

[4] Findings are robust to alternative specifications of the substitution matrix that are conceptually similar (where larger position jumps correspond with higher substitution costs).

TABLE B.6 *Alternate Matrix 1*

	None	Local	Subnational	National
None	0	1	2	3
Local	1	0	1	2
Subnational	2	1	0	1
National	3	2	1	0

TABLE B.7 *Alternate Matrix 2*

	None	Local	Subnational	National
None	0	3	5	7
Local	3	0	2	4
Subnational	5	2	0	2
National	7	4	2	0

reflect this intuition, echoing ideas about advancing in political office from the scholarship on "progressive ambition." *Indel* costs are set arbitrarily high (at the maximum observed *indel* cost operation in the dataset), to minimize the likelihood that the optimal matching results are unduly influenced by the variable length of a given sequence. Missing values are ignored in calculating sequence dissimilarity as well. This is critical because sequences are right-censored due to when individuals entered Parliament.

Optimal matching produces a measure of dissimilarity for each observation in the dataset relative to each other observation in the dataset; I utilize optimal matching scores computed in comparison with the three ideal-types described earlier: twenty-nine years of local-level party service; twenty-nine years in party service progressive climbing from local to subnational to national service; and twenty-nine years in national-level party duties.

Findings are robust to a range of alternative specifications of the substitution matrix. I describe two in the text that immediately follows in Tables B.6 and B.7; I present these two because they are conceptually closest to how I theorize career partisanship in the form of party service operates. The consistency in findings shown in Table B.8 is observed across an array of substitution matrices not included in this appendix.

Alternate Matrix 1: This matrix, like the one used in the main analysis in the book is symmetric. It differs from that analysis in that it assesses

TABLE B.8 *Alternative specifications and robustness of career partisanship sequence analysis*

Local party service ideal type	Coefficient	p-value
Substitution Matrix in Table B.5	0.013**	0.021
Alternate Matrix 1	0.023**	0.015
Alternate Matrix 2	0.010**	0.013

Ladder climber ideal type	Coefficient	p-value
Substitution Matrix in Table B.5	0.011**	0.037
Alternate Matrix 1	0.016*	0.058
Alternate Matrix 2	0.006*	0.063

National party service ideal type	Coefficient	p-value
Substitution Matrix in Table B.5	0.013**	0.012
Alternate Matrix 1	0.020**	0.026
Alternate Matrix 2	0.007*	0.050

Note: * $p<0.10$, ** $p<0.05$, *** $p<0.01$. Analyses include controls for gender, age, and education.

all changes from one position in the hierarchy of party offices to be identical. Thus, moving from a local office to a subnational office position is equivalent to moving from no position to a local office and from a subnational office to a national one.

Alternate Matrix 2: Like the previous two approaches, this matrix is symmetric. The assumptions represented in this specification is that the biggest difference in career partisanship sequences is between holding no party position and holding a local position (a substitution cost of 3). The other three columns in the substitution matrix are similar to the one used in the main analysis in the book.

Table B.8 shows the robustness of the relationship between each career partisanship ideal type and the odds of a legislator being in the opposition varying the substitution matrix that is used to calculate optimal matching scores.

B.4 SUPPORTING MATERIAL FOR CHAPTER 6

Table B.9 presents robustness checks for alternative measures of civic activism and its relationship with opposition nomination prospects.

TABLE B.9 *Robustness of alternative civic activism measures for analysis corresponding with Table 6.5*

	+/- Diff Seek vs Not	P-Value	+/- Diff Win Win Nom vs Lose	P-Value
Index (Table 6.5)	+	.001	+	.001
Index w/ Women's Org	+	.155	+	.000
Leader in Any Organization	+	.072	+	.001
Total Leadership Positions	+	.002	+	.007
Highest Activism	-	.810	+	.000
Leader, *Religion*	+	.123	+	.442
Leader, *Women's Org*	-	.671	+	.007
Leader, *Prof Org*	+	.012	-	.637
Leader, *Union*	+	.243	+	.090
Leader, *Student Gov*	+	.014	+	.000
Leader, *Grassroots*	+	.431	+	.003
Member, *Religion*	-	.429	-	.844
Member, *Women's Org*	-	.000	+	.640
Member, *Prof Org*	+	.318	+	.004
Member, *Union*	+	.256	+	.031
Member, *Student Gov*	+	.675	+	.000
Member, *Grassroots*	-	.844	+	.000
Member Type, *Religion*	+	.808	+	.534
Member Type, *Women's Org*	-	.001	+	.002
Member Type, *Prof Org*	+	.035	+	.084
Member Type, *Union*	+	.032	+	.000
Member Type, *Student Gov*	+	.219	+	.000
Member Type, *Grassroots*	+	.840	+	.000

Note: The measure in the main text is an index that does not include women's organizations. The analysis suggests that women's organization membership is negatively correlated with nomination seeking and winning nominations. This I believe is an artifact of the coding.

B.5 SUPPORTING MATERIAL FOR CHAPTER 7

Table B.10 shows descriptive statistics that are visually represented in Figure 7.2 as difference of proportions tests.

Table B.11 shows descriptive statistics that are visually represented in Figure 7.3 as difference of proportions tests.

Table B.12 presents the statistical analysis which is visually represented in Figure 7.4 in the main text.

TABLE B.10 *Descriptive statistics corresponding with Figure 7.2*

Strategy		Turnout Supporters	Win Over Opponents
Rallies	Ruling Party	0.69	0.45
	Opposition	0.54	0.44
Door to Door	Ruling Party	0.45	0.44
	Opposition	0.59	0.52
Elite Targeting	Ruling Party	0.39	0.44
	Opposition	0.21	0.31
Development	Ruling Party	0.36	0.38
	Opposition	0.23	0.26
Criticism	Ruling Party	0.06	0.22
	Opposition	0.19	0.24
Cash	Ruling Party	0.02	0.02
	Opposition	0.02	0.04

Table B.13 presents the statistical analysis which is visually represented in Figure 7.5 in the main text.

Table B.14 presents the statistical analysis which is visually represented in Figure 7.6 in the main text.

B.6 SUPPORTING MATERIAL FOR CHAPTER 8

The analysis presented in Table B.15 corresponds with Figure 8.1 in main text. Findings presented there are robust to inclusion of noncandidate respondents but only include respondents represented in the first four rows represented in Table B.15, as this is the more appropriate group of comparison on theoretical grounds.

Reasons to Not Run for Office

In addition to considering reasons why an individual would seek office, I sought to understand what reasons would push them away from seeking elected office. Using an approach similar to the one used to ask about benefits of candidacy, respondents were asked to consider the importance

TABLE B.11 *Descriptive statistics corresponding with Figure 7.3*

Strategy		Proportion
Speakers	Opposition Winner	0.41
	Opposition Loser	0.44
Transport	Opposition Winner	0.43
	Opposition Loser	0.94
Fulana	Opposition Winner	0.46
	Opposition Loser	0.30
Handouts	Opposition Winner	0.16
	Opposition Loser	0.05
Development	Opposition Winner	0.10
	Opposition Loser	0.00
Ilani	Opposition Winner	0.03
	Opposition Loser	0.00
Staff	Opposition Winner	0.02
	Opposition Loser	0.02
Malazi	Opposition Winner	0.09
	Opposition Loser	0.07
Other	Opposition Winner	0.00
	Opposition Loser	0.10

TABLE B.12 *Regressions corresponding with Figure 7.4*

	Odds	Odds	Victory	Victory
Civic Activism Index		0.17***		0.17**
		(0.058)		(0.072)
Years Since	0.02		0.01	
"Grassroots" Organizing	(0.0022)		(0.025)	
Constant	4.142***	3.82***	−0.54**	−0.88***
	(0.210)	(0.207)	(0.243)	(0.257)
N	154	154	172	172
Pseudo R^2	0.00	0.04	0.00	0.04

Note: * p<0.10, ** p<0.05, *** p<0.01.

TABLE B.13 *Regressions corresponding with Figure 7.5*

	Winning Election
Activism & Cost Interaction	0.23**
	(0.100)
Campaign Cost Total	0.16
	(0.224)
Civic Activism Index	−0.38**
	(0.181)
Age Quintile	−0.80***
	(0.199)
Education	0.33**
	(0.128)
Male	−0.91**
	(0.454)
Constant	1.16
	(1.093)
N	160
Pseudo R^2	0.26

Note: * $p<0.10$, ** $p<0.05$, *** $p<0.01$.

TABLE B.14 *Regressions corresponding with Figure 7.6*

	Elite Targeting	Door-to-Door Canvassing
Civic Activism Index	0.12*	−0.26***
	(0.068)	(0.073)
Age Quintile	−0.09	0.16
	(0.123)	(0.124)
Education	0.06	0.10
	(0.089)	(0.089)
Male	0.15	−0.50
	(0.337)	(0.333)
Constant	−1.15	0.04
	(0.705)	(0.694)
N	228	228
Pseudo R^2	0.02	0.05

Note: * $p<0.10$, ** $p<0.05$, *** $p<0.01$.

of various reasons for not seeking office from lists that included items related to prestige, career, ideology, and material benefits, as well as a fifth item regarding risk. English-language translations of the items that

TABLE B.15 *Benefits of running for office*

	Prestige	Career	Ideology	Material	N
Ruling Party, Winners	13.6%	13.3%	32.6%	40.4%	64
Opposition, Winners	16.4%	11.6%	42.9%	29.1%	68
Opposition, Elec Loser	7.9%	16.8%	48.4%	26.9%	97
Opposition, Nom Loser	8.8%	20.3%	40.9%	30.0%	116
Opposition, Noncandidate	8.8%	21.4%	42.9%	26.8%	261

Table shows percentage of total responses to each category. P-value for two-tailed t-test vs. CCM in table in order for Prestige [.11, .00, .00, .00], Career [.41, .08, .00, .00], Ideology [.00, .00, .00, .00], and Material [.00, .00, .00, .00]

TABLE B.16 *Survey items capturing reasons to not run for office*

Benefit type	Statement
Material	Not having enough money
	Constituents depend on candidates for money, things
	Unwanted attention/investigations of private life
Prestige	Opponent is more popular/well liked
	My personal shortcomings
	Damaging my reputation in party
Career Opportunism	Candidates have to leave careers
	Not enough experience as leader
	Not enough free time for politics
Ideology	Party too weak to impact Parliament/House of Representatives
	Inability to influence policy
	Needing to compromise over political views
Risk	Running and losing is embarrassing
	Party could just appoint someone else
	Fear some people might (physically) hurt you

were included in these lists are shown in Table B.16. The results from this exercise are found in Table B.17.

As in Table B.15, ideology is important for opposition figures when considering seeking office. While it is not the strongest reason for individuals who did not seek nominations (16.8 percent of important reasons), ideology is the driver for the other three opposition response groups, roughly netting between 25 percent and 40 percent of important reasons. CCM allocates the least of any group to ideology (10.7 percent), which

TABLE B.17 *Reasons to not run for office*

	Prestige	Career	Ideology	Material	Risk	N
Ruling Party, Winners	27.1%	21.7%	10.7%	27.7%	12.9%	64
Opposition, Winners	16.7%	14.3%	37.9%	19.6%	11.5%	68
Opposition, Elec Loser	11.9%	21.6%	31.2%	20.1%	15.1%	97
Opposition, Nom Loser	21.6%	21.1%	26.5%	17.2%	13.5%	116
Opposition, Noncandidate	17.4%	22.1%	16.8%	25.9%	17.7%	254

Table shows percentage of total priorities allocated to each category, totaling to 100% across rows. P-value for two-tailed t-test vs. CCM in table in order for Prestige [.00, .00, .04, .00], Career [.00, .97, .80, .83], Ideology [.00, .00, .00, .00], Material [.01, .01, .00, .48], and Risk [.49, .58, .32, .71, .02].

is significantly lower than that for the three opposition groups. The items associated with policy were core to the goal of implementing meaningful political change, with reasons including (1) not wielding enough power in parliament to promote change, (2) not being able to influence policies, and (3) having to compromise on ideological positions. These captured both symbolic roles of ideological attachments and practical policy concerns related to formal legislative duties.

Material considerations, in contrast, push ruling party members away from seeking office (about 28 percent of reasons). The three concerns related to material reasons discouraging candidacy – (1) worrying about community members depending on them for money and other material resources, (2) not having enough funds to run a campaign, and (3) drawing unwanted attention from others into an individual's private life and affairs – are associated with a greater proportion of responses from the ruling party than all but the noncandidate opposition group (roughly 20 percent for legislators and election losers, 17 percent for nomination losers, and 26 percent for non-seekers).

Along career and risk dimensions, the ruling party and opposition respondent subgroups are not very different. Most respondent groups allocated about one-fifth of their reasons to run as career related. Loss of prestige is a more important reason for ruling party legislators than for opposition subgroups (27.1 percent), differences that are statistically significant. Election losers are least concerned about prestige-related reasons, only netting about 12 percent of responses.

TABLE B.18 *Party performance in providing benefits*

	Prestige	Career	Ideology	Material	N
Ruling Party, Winners	3.88	3.55	3.48	3.43	64
Opposition, Winners	3.96	3.72	4.12	2.89	67
Opposition, Elec Loser	3.58	3.60	4.12	2.94	93
Opposition, Nom Loser	3.66	3.62	4.08	3.01	115
Opposition, Noncandidate	3.57	3.61	4.13	2.97	240

Table shows the average evaluation by party, of the five value scale 1-5 corresponding with [Very Badly, Badly, Average, Well, Very Well]. P-value for two-tailed t-test vs. CCM in table in order for Prestige [.62, .06, .14, .02], Career [.32, .75, .59, .62], Ideology [.00, .00, .00, .00], and Material [.00, .02, .05, .00].

TABLE B.19 *Benefits of losing election contests*

	Party Rep	Other Party Rep	Popularity w/ Voters	Party Advancement	Campaign Experience	No Benefit
Ruling Party, Winners	21.9%	7.8%	31.3%	54.6%	14.1%	60.9%
N	14	5	20	35	9	39
Opposition, Winners	30.9%	17.6%	57.4%	19.1%	51.5%	4.4%
N	21	12	39	13	35	3
Opposition, Elec Loser	35.6%	31.7%	40.4%	10.6%	55.8%	5.8%
N	37	33	42	11	58	6
Opposition, Nom Loser	39.8%	22.0%	28.0%	21.1%	55.2%	21.2%
N	47	26	33	25	65	25
Opposition, Noncandidate	43.8%	33.8%	39.5%	21.7%	36.3%	7.7%
N	123	95	111	61	102	20

Since respondents were given the opportunity to provide two answers, rows total to 200% and the number of observations twice the number of respondents. In instances where they do not, this is the result of (1) respondents indicating the same item twice for emphasis, (2) item nonresponse, and (3) data read or recording errors. P-value for two-tailed t-test vs. CCM in table in order for Party Rep [.24, .06, .01, .00], Other Party Rep [.09, .00, .01, .00], Popularity w/ Voters [.00, .24, .64, .22], Party Advancement [.00, .00, .00, .00], Campaign Experience [.00, .00, .00, .00], and No Benefit [.00, .00, .00, .00].

Table B.18 corresponds with Figure 8.2 in main text.

Data summarized in Table B.19 correspond with Figure 8.3 in main text.

Benefits of Losing Nominations

In advanced democracies, the "divisive primary hypothesis" suggests that parties suffer electoral consequences for intraparty contests where one camp's supporters are alienated from the party when their preferred candidate is not selected (Makse and Sokhey 2010). For this reason, one might expect that nomination losers could obtain conciliatory positions in the government administration in exchange for bringing their supporters back into the fold of the election.

The logic fits the politics of presidential nominations in Tanzania. After later President Jakaya Kikwete lost CCM's presidential nomination contest to Benjamin Mkapa in 1995, Mkapa appointed him as to his cabinet and raised "an intriguing and open question as to whether the foreign ministry was a consolation prize for JK" (Nyan'goro 2011, 113). A similar pattern can observed when Zanzibari's preferences for Dr. Mohammed Bilal as CCM Zanzibar's presidential candidate were ignored by the national party in 2010, when they instead chose Dr. Ali Mohammed Shein. Dr. Bilal had already been passed up in lieu of another candidate in 2000 in spite of then being the most popular nomination seeker (Fjeldstad et al. 2010a, Fjeldstad, Moss, Roop, and Weghorst 2010b). Needing Bilal's support in Zanzibari in the 2010 elections, he was selected as the vice-presidential candidate for Tanzania to "pacify Dr. Gharib Bilal and his camp, which could become spoilers of the current conciliatory initiatives in politically turbulent Isles, if their anchorman were to be left out in the political cold" (Guardian Staff 2010).

Implicit in theories of opposition co-optation is the idea that losing elections can have benefits. An opposition candidate who gives the ruling party a "run for their money" according to these theories is likely to garner the attention of the ruling party and perhaps obtain a privileged position in the local administration, which offers both the prestige of holding government office as well as a living stipend and other perks of working in the bureaucracy. They also may gain a party-based position that can afford different kinds of benefits to the candidate. Thus, one would suppose there to be some nonzero benefit for each stage along the path to candidacy and the benefits to grow as one makes it further along the path; thus, the benefits of winning an office are greater than those for winning a nomination and losing an election and those benefits are greater than what comes with entering and losing a nomination contest.

The benefits of running for office and losing, as with the benefits of winning office, are both individually specific and party specific. For example, with rare exception does a CCM candidate lose an election bid and ever have the chance to run for office again: given the tremendous advantages CCM politicians have on the campaign trail, being ousted by an opposition challenger is like a "kiss of death." Those individuals rarely win subsequent primaries or even put their name in for a nomination.

To assess the types of benefits one obtains from losing election and primary contests, respondents were provided a list of six items and asked to identify the most significant gain and second-most significant gain from losing a primary contest. Because there is only one question list, the results are presented as the percentages of groups selected a given reason as the most or second-greatest benefit. Table B.20, consequently, totals sum to 200 percent across rows and the number of responses is two times the number of respondents.

The list for what might be gained from losing a nomination contest is as follows. Small language changes were used for the specific procedures used by each party to select its nominees.

- Improves your reputation as a leader
- Becoming more popular politically
- To get another opportunity within your party
- To get experience with nomination campaigns
- Helps with winning a nomination in the future
- No benefit to losing a nomination contest

Chapter 6 indicated that nomination contests for the ruling party are highly competitive. The number of competitors and their quality are greater compared with the opposition. This means ruling party members might use primaries to shore up support within the political party. Also, because ruling party defections loom large in intraparty decision making, ruling party members might be able to obtain other positions in the party as consolation for losing the primary. Importantly, this logic pertains to decisions to seek candidacy – losing a primary contest after holding a seat for decades and serving in the cabinet would have very different consequences. Finally, research demonstrates that primary campaigns may reduce the popularity of candidates for the ruling party, as the divisive nature of highly competitive ruling parties can hurt nomination seekers in the election stage (Ichino and Nathan 2013).

From the perspective of the opposition, who suffer from both deficits of quality and of information – about their own popularity within the

TABLE B.20 *Benefits of losing nomination contests*

	Leader Rep	Pol. Popularity	Party Advancement	Nom Exp	Nom Odds	No Benefit
Ruling Party, Winners	21.9%	43.8%	45.3%	26.5%	56.3%	6.3%
N	14	28	29	17	36	4
Opposition, Winners	32.3%	54.4%	14.7%	47.1%	38.2%	4.4%
N	22	37	10	32	26	3
Opposition, Elec Loser	67.3%	51.0%	12.5%	33.6%	25.0%	6.7%
N	70	53	13	35	26	7
Opposition, Nom Loser	51.7%	29.7%	22.9%	33.8%	46.6%	5.1%
N	61	35	27	40	55	6
Opposition, Noncandidate	48.0%	22.0%	20.6%	29.9%	41.9%	24.2%
N	135	62	58	84	118	68

Since respondents were given the opportunity to provide two answers, rows total to 200% and the number of observations twice the number of respondents. In instances where they do not, this is the result of (1) respondents indicating the same item twice for emphasis, (2) item nonresponse, and (3) data read or recording errors. P-value for two-tailed t-test vs. CCM in table in order for Leader Rep [.18, .00, .00, .00], Pol Popularity [.22, .37, .06, .00], Party Advancement [.00, .00, .00, .00], Nom Exp [.00, .33, .31, .60], Nom Odds [.04, .00, .22, .04], and No Benefit [.64, .90, .74, .00].

party and among the electorate – they should benefit experientially from the nomination contest, learning more about how to compete in the nomination campaign. Further, it has been observed that opposition parties when holding nomination contests obtain spillover benefits of popularity that translate into electoral gains (Ichino and Nathan 2013). Thus, benefits obtained by losing nominations might translate into greater chances in an election down the road and, further, more qualifications as a legislative candidate.

In addition to opposition versus ruling party comparisons, individuals who generally see no benefit in losing a primary contest would be those most likely to stay away from them. Further, opposition actors sharing most in common with ruling party legislators will be opposition MPs, who also succeeded in winning nominations and elections. Table B.20 reports descriptive comparisons of the different election subgroups.

TABLE B.21 *Regression corresponding with Figure 8.4*

	Material	Ideology	Prestige	Career
	β/ (SE)	β/ (SE)	β/ (SE)	β/ (SE)
Party, Youth Leader	−0.82 (1.972)	−1.12 (2.346)	0.96 (1.368)	0.98 (1.844)
Party Leader: Local Office	−2.47 (2.212)	1.92 (2.632)	−0.67 (1.535)	1.23 (2.069)
Party, Campaign Team	0.17 (1.573)	1.57 (1.872)	1.11 (1.091)	−2.86* (1.471)
Party Leader: Region Office	5.23** (2.108)	−6.49** (2.508)	0.80 (1.462)	0.46 (1.972)
Party Leader: Secretariat	0.85 (1.844)	0.67 (2.195)	1.99 (1.280)	−3.50** (1.725)
Local Govt Experience	−0.40 (1.899)	2.31 (2.259)	−1.27 (1.317)	−0.64 (1.776)
Civic Activism	−0.35 (0.360)	0.98** (0.428)	−0.25 (0.250)	−0.38 (0.336)
Years Since Joined Party	0.33** (0.137)	−0.49*** (0.163)	−0.07 (0.095)	0.23* (0.128)
Years Since "Grassroots" Organizing	0.04 (0.124)	−0.03 (0.148)	0.12 (0.086)	−0.13 (0.116)
N	345	345	345	345
R^2	0.07	0.11	0.08	0.11

Notes: * p<0.10, ** p<0.05, *** p<0.01.
Constant and controls for gender, education, and age not shown.

Stark contrasts emerge ruling between party legislators to opposition challengers in terms of the potential benefits of losing primaries. More than 55 percent of CCM members a primary loss as an opportunity to enhance their chances of winning a primary down the road. Potential conciliatory positions in the party are one potential appeal of losing a primary contest for ruling party members (45.3 percent), which is more than twice as much as any opposition respondent group. The message here is that losses in primaries – particularly when putting forth a good showing in those contests – are not very costly for ruling party candidates. By contrast, the main benefit opposition aspirants see in losing nomination contests are ones that boost later election chances: campaign experience and popularity with voters. Those who lost nomination contests are the opposition respondents who most prominently hold the

view that there is little gained from doing so. A special seats nomination seeker from CHADEMA who lost highlighted difficulties about
the transparency of the primary process and its outcome. As a party
mobilizer for gaining financial support abroad while studying for an
advanced degree outside Tanzania and also being from the village of the
party's chairperson and former presidential candidate Freeman Mbowe,
she viewed her prospects as favorable. After she was not selected, she
noted, "No one reached out to me after the results became public. Not
on how I could improve, not the criteria by which others were chosen
instead."[5]

Table B.21 shows the statistical analysis that is represented visually in
Figure 8.4.

B.7 SUPPORTING MATERIAL FOR CHAPTER 9

Table B.22 shows the disaggregated distribution of risk attitudes corresponding with the first survey item represented in Figure 9.1. For stylistic
purposes, the analysis Figure 9.1 represents a difference of proportions
test that simplifies this distribution in two ways: (1) it combines "Strongly
Agree" and "Agree" into a single category representing agreement with
an item and (2) combines opposition respondents into a single group.
Difference of means tests in Table B.22 correspond with analyses of the
further disaggregated and yield results that are substantively the same as
those presented in the text.

Table B.23 shows the disaggregated distribution of risk attitudes corresponding with the second survey item represented in Figure 9.1. The
presentational differences between the analysis represented in Figure 9.1
and the data here are the same as those for Table B.22. Statistical results
here are substantively the same as those presented in the text.

Table B.24 shows the disaggregated distribution of time-horizon attitudes corresponding with the third survey item represented in Figure 9.1.
The presentational differences between the analysis represented in Figure
9.1 and the data here are the same as those for Table B.22. Statistical
results here are substantively the same as those presented in the text.

Table B.25 presents the fully specified regression models that are
visually represented in Figures 9.2 and 9.3 in the main text.

---

[5] Interview with Kilimanjaro region nomination seeker, conducted in Dar es Salaam,
January 14, 2013.

TABLE B.22 *Risk attitudes and proverbs*

| | Methali 1
(S)He who eats bitter things
also gets sweet ones. | | | Methali 2
The timid crow withdraws
its wings from harm. | | |
	Strongly Agree Methali 1	Agree Methali 1	Agree Methali 2	Strongly Agree Methali 2	T-test vs. CCM
Ruling Party, Winners	23.8%	17.5%	14.3%	44.4%	
N	15	11	9	28	
Opposition, Winners	57.4%	8.8%	7.4%	26.5%	p<.01
N	39	6	5	18	
Opposition, Elec Loser	46.7%	19.6%	17.4%	17.4%	p<.01
N	42	18	16	16	
Opposition, Nom Loser	37.7%	25.4%	21.9%	14.9%	p<.01
N	43	29	25	17	
Opposition, Noncandidate	28.0%	32.2%	22.2%	17.6%	p<.01
N	67	77	53	42	

Methali 1 translated from *Mla cha uchungu na tamu*
Methali 2 translated from *Kunguru muoga hukimbiza mbawa zake*

TABLE B.23 *Risk and retrospection through proverbs*

	Methali 1 (S)He who has been bitten by a snake is afraid when seeing grass move. [Once bitten, twice shy].		Methali 2 The real eater is today's not yesterday's.		T-test vs. CCM
	Strongly Agree Methali 1	Agree Methali 1	Agree Methali 2	Strongly Agree Methali 2	
Ruling Party, Winners	40.3%	8.1%	3.2%	48.4%	
N	25	5	2	30	
Opposition, Winners	20.0%	6.2%	9.2%	64.6%	p<.01
N	13	4	6	42	
Opposition, Elec Loser	17.4%	12.0%	16.3%	54.4%	p<.02
N	16	11	15	50	
Opposition, Nom Loser	20.7%	7.8%	21.6%	50.0%	p<.03
N	24	9	25	58	
Opposition, Noncandidate	21.2%	12.0%	22.4%	44.4%	p<.05
N	51	29	54	107	

Methali 1 translated from *Mwenye kuumwa na nyoka akiona nyasi zinasikitisha hushtuka*
Methali 2 translated from *Mla mla leo mla jana kala nini?*

TABLE B.24 *Time horizons through proverbs*

	Methali 1 Better delay but arrive		Methali 2 Wait? "Wait" hurts the stomach		T-test vs. CCM
	Strongly Agree Methali 1	Agree Methali 1	Agree Methali 2	Strongly Agree Methali 2	
Ruling Party, Winners	34.5%	11.3%	8.1%	45.2%	
N	22	7	5	28	
Opposition, Winners	61.5%	7.7%	9.2%	21.5%	p<.01
N	40	5	6	14	
Opposition, Elec Loser	47.4%	16.8%	12.6%	23.2%	p<.01
N	45	16	12	22	
Opposition, Nom Loser	44.0%	25.9%	17.2%	12.9%	p<.01
N	51	30	20	15	
Opposition, Noncandidate	34.2%	24.2%	19.6%	22.1%	p<.03
N	82	58	47	53	

Methali 1 translated from *Kawaia Ufike*.
Methali 2 translated from *Ngoja? Ngoja huumiza matumbo*.

TABLE B.25 Partisan and civic activism and risk and time attitudes

	Risk Tolerance: Sweet Things		Risk Tolerance: Today's Eater		Time Horizons: Better Arrive	
Party, Youth Leader	−0.07 (0.257)		0.09 (0.240)		−0.18 (0.244)	
Party Leader: Local Office	−0.14 (0.318)		−0.15 (0.290)		0.00 (0.297)	
Party, Campaign Team	0.17 (0.204)		−0.42** (0.198)		0.24 (0.202)	
Party Leader: Region	0.39 (0.342)		0.60* (0.328)		−0.28 (0.333)	
Party Leader: Secretariat	0.50* (0.279)		−0.26 (0.278)		0.12 (0.281)	
Local Govt Experience	−0.34 (0.274)		0.01 (0.248)		−0.35 (0.253)	
Civic Activism Index	−0.16*** (0.054)		0.05 (0.048)		0.01 (0.049)	
Years Since Joined Party		0.06*** (0.018)		−0.00 (0.017)		0.03* (0.018)
Years Since "Grassroots" Organizing		−0.01 (0.017)		0.00 (0.016)		−0.00 (0.017)
Age	0.07 (0.126)	−0.08 (0.129)	−0.06 (0.119)	−0.06 (0.120)	0.15 (0.127)	0.19 (0.124)
Age Flag for Imputed	0.13 (0.221)	0.25 (0.225)	0.27 (0.213)	0.30 (0.216)	−0.60*** (0.226)	−0.74*** (0.223)
Education	−0.06 (0.057)	−0.07 (0.053)	0.14*** (0.053)	0.15*** (0.049)	−0.31*** (0.053)	−0.33*** (0.057)
Male	0.09 (0.207)	0.12 (0.202)	0.42* (0.198)	0.36* (0.193)	−0.27 (0.199)	−0.26 (0.203)
constant	−0.58 (0.539)	−0.82 (0.536)	−1.23** (0.515)	−1.29** (0.503)	1.54*** (0.523)	1.79*** (0.534)
N	574	574	574	574	576	576

TABLE B.26 *Policy views on legislative duties*

Policy Issue	Regime		
Exec	Ruling Party	2.12	2.67
Oversight	Opposition	2.55	1.93
Pub Serv	Ruling Party	1.68	1.87
Appt	Opposition	1.38	1.46
Cabinet	Ruling Party	1.80	1.88
Appt	Opposition	1.40	1.45
Judges	Ruling Party	1.71	1.89
Appt	Opposition	1.51	1.55
Int Loan	Ruling Party	2.19	2.16
Approval	Opposition	1.88	1.65
Drafting	Ruling Party	2.65	2.92
Laws	Opposition	2.35	2.39
Gov	Ruling Party	2.53	2.40
Budget	Opposition	2.23	1.83
Own	Ruling Party	2.53	2.57
Budget	Opposition	2.06	2.00
Local	Ruling Party	2.16	2.18
Dev	Opposition	1.75	1.53

B.8 SUPPORTING MATERIAL FOR CHAPTER 10

Table B.26 presents descriptive statistics visualized as difference of means in Figure 10.4.

Comparing Competitive Democracies to EA and DP Democracies

Comparably low prevalence of career partisanship in competitive democracies is evident when comparing across regime types. Party service is less common for both ruling party and opposition legislators in competitive democracies, compared with their counterparts in dominant party democracies and electoral authoritarian regimes. This is depicted in Figure B.4. This figure shows the proportion of ALP respondents in

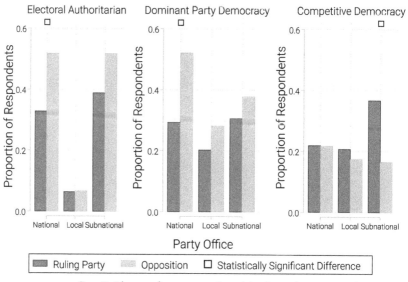

FIGURE B.4 Evidence of career partisanship through party service

competitive democracies who reported holding positions in local, district, and national offices before entering the legislature, found on the left-most panel of the figure. It also includes the patterns previously analyzed in electoral authoritarian regimes and dominant party democracies, as comparable references. Looking across regime types, electoral authoritarian regimes feature significantly higher rates of party service across both national- and district-level offices than those in competitive democracies. The same is true for national-level party service in dominant party democracies versus competitive ones.[6] Among competitive democracies, there is one observed difference between ruling party and opposition legislators, where ruling party parliamentarians have more experience in district-level party service. Benin and Ghana account for this finding, where both feature substantial gaps in experience in this capacity across party (roughly 14 percent and 21 percent of opposition legislators (respectively) versus 33 percent and 50 percent for ruling party MPs).

---

[6] Difference of proportions tests comparing all respondents in electoral authoritarian regimes versus competitive democracies for national and district-level offices are statistically significant at p<.01. Difference of proportions tests comparing all respondents in dominant party democracies versus competitive democracies for national-level offices is statistically significant at p<.01.

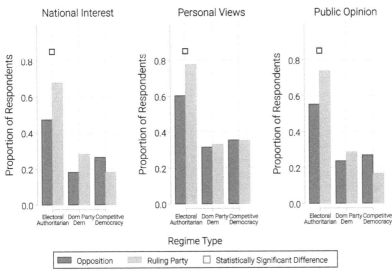

FIGURE B.5 Career partisanship and prioritizing party interests

The different consequences of career partisanship across regimes is even more starkly illustrated when considering the implications of party service for how legislators balance competing demands from different interest groups over policy. For ruling party legislators in electoral author- itarian regimes, the priorities of the ruling party supersede the views of citizens, the national interest, and even their own disposition. Figure B.5 shows the opposite is the case in competitive democracies: ruling party and opposition legislators report prioritizing party priorities over the national interest, their own views, and those of citizens at similar rates. This is evident in the third panel of the figure. Strikingly, the propor- tion of legislators siding with party views when they conflict with the national interest, their personal opinions, and the views of citizens is between two and three times higher in electoral authoritarian regimes than in competitive democracies.[7]

In addition to fewer and smaller gaps, legislators in competitive democ- racies also care less about policy in absolute terms. Figure B.6 provides visual evidence of this insight. This figure differs from previous ones on

---

[7] Difference of proportions tests comparing all respondents in electoral authoritarian regimes versus competitive democracies are statistically significant at p<.01 for all three survey questions.

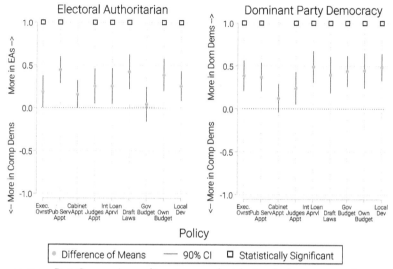

FIGURE B.6 Comparing policy views on legislative duties across regimes

policy positions in this chapter. It highlights how much legislators empha-size legislative policy power in competitive democracies versus other regimes. The left panel of the figure compares positions of all legislators in competitive democracies versus opposition legislators in electoral author-itarian regimes. The right panel does so for all legislators in competitive democracies versus opposition MPs in dominant party democracies.[8] In both figures, points above the solid line indicate legislators emphasize those issues in competitive democracies *less* than legislators in the other regime type. Compared with electoral authoritarian regimes and domi-nant party democracies, MPs in Africa's competitive democracies simply care about policy less.

[8] Findings are similar when considering only opposition legislators for competitive democ-racies; all MPs are included because the ruling party versus opposition distinction in competitive democracies means something different than it does in the less competitive regime types.

References

Abbott, Andrew, and Stanley DeViney. 1992. "The Welfare State as Transnational Event: Evidence from Sequences of Policy Adoption." *Social Science History* 16(2):245–274.

Abbott, Andrew, and Alexandra Hrycak. 1990. "Measuring Resemblance in Sequence Data: An Optimal Matching Analysis of Musicians' Careers." *American Journal of Sociology* 96(1):144–185.

Abbott, Andrew, and Angela Tsay. 2000. "Sequence Analysis and Optimal Matching Methods in Sociology: Review and Impact." *Sociological Methods & Research* 29(1):3–33.

Adams, James, and Samuel Merrill III. 2008. "Candidate and Party Strategies in Two-Stage Elections Beginning with a Primary." *American Journal of Political Science* 52(2):344–359.

Ake, Claude. 1996. *Democracy and Development in Africa*. Washington, DC: Brookings Institution Press.

Aldrich, John H. 2011. *Why Parties? A Second Look*. Chicago, IL: University of Chicago Press.

Alizada, Nazifa, Rowan Cole, Lisa Gastaldi, et al. 2021. *Autocratization Turns Viral. Democracy Report 2021*. University of Gothenburg: V-Dem Institute.

Alvarez, Michael, Jose Antonio Cheibub, Fernando Limongi, and Adam Przeworski. 1996. "Classifying Political Regimes." *Studies in Comparative International Development* 31(2):3–36.

Aid Management and Accountability Programme (AMAP). 1997. "Tanzania NGOs." Report of the Workshop on the Formation of an NGOs Apex Body, Ministry of Finance, Tanzania.

Andreoni, Antonio. 2017. "Anti-Corruption in Tanzania: A Political Settlements Analysis." *Anti-Corruption Evidence* (1):1–59.

Anonymous. 2018. "Tanzania Search for Missing Millions Raises Questions over 1 Billion." Available at https://africanarguments.org/2019/02/tanzania-search-missing-millions-reveals-missing-billion/.

Arian, Asher. 1994. Incumbency in Israel's Knesset. In *The Victorious Incumbent: A Threat to Democracy?*, ed. Albert Somit, Rudolf Wildenmann, Bernhard Boll, and Andrea Rommele. Burlington, VT: Dartmouth Publishing Company, pp. 77–102.

Arnold, Nathalie, Bruce McKim, Ben Rawlence, and Tony Tate. 2002. "The Bullets Were Raining: The January 2001 Attack on Peaceful Demonstrations in Zanzibar." Available at www.hrw.org/reports/2002/tanzania/zanzo402.pdf.

Arriola, Leonardo. 2013. *Multi-Ethnic Coalitions in Africa: Business Financing of Opposition Election Campaigns*. Cambridge: Cambridge University Press.

Arriola, Leonardo. 2009. "Patronage and Political Stability in Africa." *Comparative Political Studies* 42(10):1339–1362.

Arriola, Leonardo, Donghyun Danny Choi, and Staffan I. Lindberg. 2018. "The Rejection of Election Results in Africa." *African Affairs*.

Ash, Konstantin. 2015. "The Election Trap: The Cycle of Post-electoral Repression and Opposition Fragmentation in Lukashenko's Belarus." *Democratization* 22(6):1030–1053.

Ashly, Jaclynn. 2020. "Tanzania's Firebrand Tundu Lissu." Available at www.newframe.com/tanzanias-firebrand-tundu-lissu/.

Askew, Kelly M. 2002. *Performing the Nation: Swahili Music and Cultural Politics in Tanzania*. Chicago, IL: University of Chicago Press.

Axinn, William G., Lisa D. Pearce, and Dirgha Ghimire. 1999. "Innovations in Life History Calendar Applications." *Social Science Research* 28:243–264.

Bakari, Mohammed A. 2001. *The Democratization Process in Zanzibar: A Retarded Transition*. Hamburg: Institut für Afrika-Kunde.

Bakari, Mohammed A. 2012. "Religion, Secularism, and Political Discourse in Tanzania: Competing Perspectives by Religious Organizations." *Interdisciplinary Journal of Research on Religion* 8(1):3–34.

Baldus, Jana, Annika Elena Poppe, and Jonas Wolff. 2017. "An Overview of Global Initiatives on Countering Closing Space for Civil Society." Center for Strategic and International Studies (CSIS). Available at www.jstor.org/stable/resrep23289.

Baldwin, Kate A., and John D. Huber. 2010. "Economic versus Cultural Differences: Forms of Ethnic Diversity and Public Goods Provision." *American Political Science Review* 104(4):644–662.

Barkan, Joel D. 1979. Legislators, Elections, and Political Linkage. In *Politics and Public Policy in Kenya and Tanzania*, ed. Joel D. Barkan and John J. Okumu. New York: Praeger, pp. 62–92.

Barkan, Joel D. 1994. *Beyond Capitalism vs. Socialism in Kenya and Tanzania*. Boulder, CO: Lynne Rienner Publishers.

Barkan, Joel D., ed. 2009. *Legislatures in Emerging African Democracies*. Boulder, CO: Lynne Rienner Publishers.

Barkan, Joel D., and Robert Mattes. 2014. "Why CDFs in Africa? Representation vs. Constituency Service." In *Distributive Politics in Developing Countries: Almost Pork*, ed. Mark Baskin and Michael L. Mezey. Lexington, KY: Lexington Books, pp. 31–48.

Baroin, Catherine. 1996. "Religious Conflict in 1990–1993 among the Rwa: Secession in a Lutheran Diocese in Northern Tanzania." *African Affairs* 95(381):529–554.

Barro, Robert J. 1973. "The Control of Politicians: An Economic Model." *Public Choice* 14(1):19–42.

Barz, Gregory F. 2003. *Performing Religion: Negotiating Past and Present in Kwaya Music of Tanzania*. Kerk en theologie in context. Amsterdam: Rodopi.

Basedau, Matthias, Gero Erdmann, and Andreas Mehler. 2007. *Votes, Money and Violence: Political Parties and Elections in Sub-Saharan Africa*. Uppsala, Sweden: The Nordic Africa Institute.

Baskin, Mark. 2014. "Constituency Development Funds (CDFs) as a Tool of Decentralized Development." In *Distributive Politics in Developing Countries: Almost Pork*, ed. Mark Baskin and Michael L. Mezey. Lexington, KY: Lexington Books, pp. 182–186.

Bauer, Gretchen. 2001. "Namibia in the First Decade of Independence: How Democratic?" *Journal of Southern African Studies* 27(1):33–55.

Bauer, Gretchen. 2008. "Fifty/Fifty by 2020." *International Feminist Journal of Politics* 10(3):348–368.

Bayart, Jean-Francois. 1993. *The State in Africa: The Politics of the Belly*. New York: Longman.

Beck, Rose Marie. 2005. "Texts on Textiles: Proverbialty as Characteristic of Equivocal Communication at the East African Coast (Swahili)." *Journal of African Cultural Studies* 17(2):131–160.

Beck, Thorsten, George Clarke, Alberto Groff, Phillip Keefer, and Patrick Walsh. 2001. "New Tools in Comparative Political Economy." *The World Bank Economic Review* 15(1):165–176.

Beissinger, Mark R. 2007. "Structure and Example in Modular Political Phenomena: The Diffusion of Bulldozer/Rose/Orange/Tulip Revolutions." *Perspectives on Politics* 5(2):259–276.

Bekoe, Dorina, ed. 2012. *Voting in Fear: Electoral Violence in Sub-Saharan Africa*. United States Institute of Peace: Washington, DC.

Belli, Robert F., William L. Shay, and Frank P. Stafford. 2001. "Event History Calendars and Question List Surveys: A Direct Comparison of Interviewing Methods." *Public Opinion Quarterly* 65(1):45–75.

Bendor, Jonathan, and Dilip Mookherjee. 1987. "Institutional Structure and the Logic of Ongoing Collective Action." *American Political Science Review* 81(1):129–154.

Benstead, Lindsay J. 2008. "Does Casework Build Support for a Strong Parliament? Legislative Representative and Public Opinion in Morocco and Algeria" PhD thesis University of Michigan. Ann Arbor.

Bermeo, Nancy G. 2003. *Ordinary People in Extraordinary Times: The Citizenry and the Breakdown of Democracy*. Princeton, NJ: Princeton University Press.

Bernhard, Rachel, Shauna Shames, and Dawn Langan Teele. 2021. "To Emerge? Breadwinning, Motherhood, and Women's Decisions to Run for Office." *American Political Science Review* 115(2):379–394.

Bhasin, Tavishi, and Jennifer Gandhi. 2013. "Timing and Targeting of State Repression in Authoritarian Regimes." *Electoral Studies* 32:620–631.

Bienen, Henry. 1967. *Tanzania: Party Transformation and Economic Development*. Princeton, NJ: Princeton University Press.

Birch, Sarah. 2007. *Electoral Malpractice*. Oxford: Oxford University Press.

Bishop, Sylvia, and Anke Hoeffler. 2014. "Free and Fair Elections: A New Database." *Journal of Peace Research* 53(4):608–616.

Black, Gordon S. 1972. "A Theory of Political Ambition: Career Choices and the Role of Structural Incentives." *The American Political Science Review* 66(1):144–159.

Blair-Loy, Mary. 1999. "Career Patterns of Executive Women in Finance: An Optimal Matching Analysis." *American Journal of Sociology* 104(5): 1346–1397.

Blanchard, Phillippe. 2013. "What Is Time for Sequence Analysis?" *Newsletter of the American Political Science Association Organized Section for Qualitative and Multi-Method Research* 11(2):17–21.

Blaydes, Lisa. 2013. *Competition without Democracy: Elections and Distributive Politics in Mubarak's Egypt.* Cambridge: Cambridge University Press.

Bleck, Jaimie, and Nicolas van de Walle. 2010. "Political Issues in French West African Electoral Democracies: An Exercise in Theoretical Brush Clearing." *Democratization* Vol 18, pp. 1125–1145.

Bleck, Jaimie, and Nicolas van de Walle. 2013. "Valence Issues in African Elections: Navigating Uncertainty and the Weight of the Past." *Comparative Political Studies* 46(11):1394–1421.

Bleck, Jaimie, and Nicolas van de Walle. 2018. *Electoral Politics in Africa since 1990: Continuity in Change.* New York: Cambridge University Press.

Blondel, Jean. 1968. "Party Systems and Patterns of Government in Western Democracies." *Canadian Journal of Political Science* 1(2):180–203.

Bloom, David, David Canning, and Kevin Chan. 2005. *Higher Education and Economic Development in Africa.* Washington, DC: World Bank.

Bobo, Lawrence D., and Franklin D. Gilliam. 1990. "Race, Sociopolitical Participation, and Black Empowerment." *American Political Science Review* 84(2):377–393.

Bogaards, Matthijs. 2004. "Counting Parties and Identifying Dominant Party Systems in Africa." *European Journal of Political Research* 43:173–197.

Bogaards, Matthijs. 2008. "Dominant Party Systems and Electoral Volatility in Africa." *Party Politics* 14(1):113–130.

Boix, Carles. 2007. The Emergence of Parties and Party Systems. In *The Oxford Handbook of Comparative Politics*, ed. Carles Boix and Susan C. Stokes. Oxford: Oxford University Press, pp. 499–521.

Boix, Carles, and Milan Svolik. 2013. "The Foundations of Limited Authoritarian Government: Institutions and Power-sharing in Dictatorships." *Journal of Politics* 75(2):300–316.

Boll, Bernhard. 1994. Parliamentary Incumbents in Germany: No Matter of Choice? In *The Victorious Incumbent: A Threat to Democracy?*, ed. Albert Somit, Rudolf Wildenmann, Bernhard Boll, and Andrea Rommele. Brookfield, VT: Dartmouth Publishing Company, pp. 150–189.

Bordignon, Massimo, Tommaso Nannicini, and Guido Tabellini. 2016. "Moderating Political Extremism: Single Round versus Runoff Elections under Plurality Rule." *American Economic Review* 106(8):2349–2370.

Borghetto, Enrico. 2014. "Legislative Processes as Sequences: Exploring the Temporal Dimensions of Lawmaking by Means of Sequence Analysis." *International Review of Administrative Sciences* 80(3):554–576.

Bouton, Laurent. 2013. "A Theory of Strategic Voting in Runoff Elections." *American Economic Review* 103(4):1248–1288.

Bouton, Laurent, and Gabriele Gratton. 2015. "Majority Runoff Elections: Strategic Voting and Duverger's Hypothesis." *Theoretical Economics* 10(2): 283–314.

Branson, Nick. 2015. "Party Rules: Consolidating Power through Constitutional Reform in Tanzania." African Research Institute. Available at https://media .africaportal.org/documents/ARI_Tanzania_Briefing_Notes_download.pdf.

Brass, Jennifer N. 2018. *Allies or Adversaries? NGOs and the State in Africa.* Cambridge: Cambridge University Press.

Brass, Paul R. 2003. *The Production of Hindu–Muslim Violence in Contemporary India.* Seattle University of Washington Press.

Bratton, Michael, and Nicolas van de Walle. 1997. *Democratic Experiments in Africa: Regime Transitions in Africa.* Cambridge: Cambridge University Press.

Bratton, Michael, Ravi Bhavnani, and Tse-Hsin Chen. 2011. "Voting Intentions in Africa: Ethnic, Economic or Partisan?" *Afrobarometer Working Paper Series* 127:1–25.

Brehm, John, and Wendy Rahn. 1997. "Individual-Level Evidence for the Causes and Consequences of Social Capital." *American Journal of Political Science* 41(3):999–1023.

Brierley, Sarah, and Eric Kramon. 2020. "Party Campaign Strategies in Ghana: Rallies, Canvassing and Handouts." *African Affairs* 119(477):587–603.

Brockett, Charles D. 1991. "The Structure of Political Opportunities and Peasant Mobilization in Central America." *Comparative Politics* 23:253–274.

Brown, Andrea M. 2001. "Democratization and the Tanzanian State: Emerging Opportunities for Achieving Women's Empowerment." *Canadian Journal of African Studies* 35(1):67–98.

Brown, Nathan J. 2012. *When Victory Is Not an Option: Islamist Movements in Arab Politics.* Ithaca, NY: Cornell University Press.

Brown, Ryan, Verónica Montalva, Duncan Thomas, and Andrea Velásquez. 2019. "Impact of Violent Crime on Risk Aversion: Evidence from the Mexican Drug War." *The Review of Economics and Statistics* 101(5):892–904.

Brownlee, Jason. 2007. *Authoritarianism in an Age of Democratization.* Oxford: Oxford University Press.

Bruhn, Kathleen. 2012. The PRD and the Mexican Left. In *Oxford Handbook of Mexican Politics,* ed. Roderic Ai Camp. Oxford: Oxford University Press, pp. 113–131.

Brzinsky-Fay, Christian. 2007. "Lost in Transition? Labour Market Entry Sequences of School Leavers in Europe." *European Sociological Review* 23(4):409–422.

Brzinsky-Fay, Christian, and Ulrich Kohler. 2010. "New Developments in Sequence Analysis." *Sociological Research Methods* 38(3):359–364.

Brzinsky-Fay, Christian, Ulrich Kohler, and Magdalena Luniak. 2006. "Sequence Analysis with Stata." *The Stata Journal* 6(4):435–460.

Buckles, Grant T. 2019. "Internal Opposition Dynamics and Restraints on Authoritarian Control." *British Journal of Political Science* 49(3):883–900.

Bunce, Valerie, and Sharon Wolchik. 2011. *Defeating Authoritarian Leaders in Postcommunist Countries*. Cambridge: Cambridge University Press.

Burgess, Gary Thomas. 2009. *Race, Revolution, and the Struggle for Human Rights in Zanzibar*. Athens, OH: Ohio University Press.

Burke, Jason. 2020. "Tanzanian Government Cracks Down on Opposition after Disputed Election." The Guardian, November 2. Available at www .theguardian.com/world/2020/nov/02/tanzanian-opposition-figures-arrested-after-disputed-election.

Bush, Sarah S. 2011. "International Politics and the Spread of Quotas for Women in Legislatures." *International Organization* 65(1):103–137.

Byaruhanga, Frederick K. 2006. *Student Power in Africa's Higher Education : A Case of Makerere University*. New York: Routledge.

Byrd, Robert O. 1963. "Characteristics of Candidates for Election in a Country Approaching Independence: The Case of Uganda." *Midwest Journal of Political Science* 7(1):1–27.

Calhoun, Craig. 1993. "New Social Movements of the Early Nineteenth Century." *Social Science History* 17(3):385–427.

Carbone, Giovanni M. 2003. "Emerging Pluralist Politics in Mozambique: The Frelimo-Renamo Party System." *Crisis States Research Centre Working Papers Series* 1(23):1–26.

Carey, John M., and John Polga-Hecimovich. 2006. "Primary Elections and Candidate Strength in Latin America." *Journal of Politics* 68:530–543.

Carey, Sean, and Matthew Lebo. 2006. "Election Cycles and the Economic Voter." *Political Research Quarterly* 59:543–558.

Carlitz, Ruth. 2017. "Money Flows, Water Trickles: Understanding Patterns of Decentralized Water Provision in Tanzania." *World Development* 94: 16–30.

Carlitz, Ruth, and Rachael McLellan. 2021. "Open Data from Authoritarian Regimes: New Opportunities, New Challenges." *Perspectives on Politics* 19(1):160–170.

Carnes, Nicholas, and Noam Lupu. 2015. "Rethinking the Comparative Perspective on Class and Representation: Evidence from Latin America." *American Journal of Political Science* 59(1):1–18.

Carter Center. 2005. *Observing the 2004 Mozambique Elections*. Atlanta, GA: The Carter Center.

Chabal, Patrick, and Jean-Pascal Daloz. 1999. *Africa Works: Disorder as a Political Instrument*. Oxford: James Curry.

Chacón, Mario, James A. Robinson, and Ragnar Torvik. 2011. "When Is Democracy an Equilibrium? Theory and Evidence from Colombia's La Violencia." *Journal of Conflict Resolution* 55(3):366–396.

Chaligha, Amon, Robert Mattes, Michael Bratton, and Yul Derek Davids. 2002. "'Uncritical Citizens' or 'Patient Trustees': Tanzanian's Views of Political and Economic Reform." *Afrobarometer Working Paper Series* 18.

Charurvedi, Asish. 2005. "Rigging Elections with Violence." *Public Choice* 125(1/2):189–202.

Cheeseman, Nic, Daniel Branch, and Leight Gardener. 2010. *Our Turn to Eat: Politics in Kenya Since 1950*. Berlin, Germany: Lit Verlag.

Chwe, Michael. 2001. *Rational Ritual: Culture, Coordination, and Common Knowledge*. Princeton, NJ: Princeton University Press.

Chwe, Michael Suk-Young. 2009. "Rational Choice and Humanities: Excerpts and Folktakes." *Occasion: Interdisciplinary Studies in the Humanities* 1.

Cloward, Karisa, and Keith Weghorst. 2018. "Candidacy and Careers in Africa's New Democracies: Insiders, Outsiders, and Political Ambition." Presented at the Annual Meeting of the American Political Science Association.

Cloward, Karisa, and Keith Weghorst. 2019. "Career Background and Electoral Campaign Strategy in African Democracies." Working paper.

Collard, Michaela. 2019. "The Political Economy of Institutions in Africa: Comparing Authoritarian Parties and Parliaments in Tanzania and Uganda." PhD thesis University of Oxford.

Collier, Paul and Pedro Vicente. 2014. "Votes and Violence: Evidence from a Field Experiment in Nigeria." *The Economic Journal* 124(574):327–355.

Congleton, Roger D. 2002. The Median Voter Theorem. In *The Encyclopedia of Public Choice*, ed. Charles Rowley and Frederick Schneider. New York: Springer, pp. 702–712.

Cornwall, Andrea and Vera Schattan Coelho. 2007. Introduction. In *Spaces for Change? The Politics of Participation in New Democratic Arenas*, ed. Andrea Cornwall and Vera Schattan Coelho. New York: Zed Books, pp. 1–29.

Corstange, D. 2010. "Vote Buying under Competition and Monopsony: Evidence from a List Experiment in Lebanon." Presented at the Annual Meeting of the American Political Science Association.

Cox, Gary W. 2009. "Authoritarian Elections and Leadership Succession, 1975–2000." Unpublished manuscript.

Cox, Gary W., and Matthew D. McCubbins. 1986. "Electoral Politics as a Redistributive Game." *Journal of Politics* 48(2):370–389.

Cox, James C., and Glenn W. Harrison. 2008. Risk Aversion in Experiments: An Introduction. In *Risk Aversion in Experiments*, ed. James C. Cox and Glenn W. Harrison. Bradford, UK: Emerald Publishing Group Limited chapter 1, pp. 1–7.

Croke, Kevin. 2017. "Tools of Single Party Hegemony in Tanzania: Evidence from Surveys and Survey Experiments." *Democratization* 24(2):189–208.

Dahl, Robert. 1971. *Polyarchy: Participation and Opposition*. New Haven, CT: Yale University Press.

d'Anieri, Paul, Clarie Ernst, and Elizabeth Kier. 1990. "New Social Movements in Historical Perspective." *Comparative Politics* 22:445–458.

Diamond, Larry. 1994. "Rethinking Civil Society: Toward Democratic Consolidation." *Journal of Democracy* 5(3):4–17.

Diamond, Larry. 1999. *Developing Democracy: Towards Consolidation*. Baltimore, MD: Johns Hopkins University Press.

Diamond, Larry. 2002. "Thinking About Hybrid Regimes." *Journal of Democracy* 13(2):21–35.

Dietrich, Julia, Hakan Andersson, and Katariina Salmela-Aro. 2014. Development Psychologists' Perspective on Pathways Through School and Beyond. In *Advances in Sequence Analysis: Theory, Method, Applications*, ed. Jacques-Antoine Gautheir, Felix Buhlmann, and Phillippe Blanchard. Springer, pp. 129–150.

Dionne, Kim. 2011. "The Role of Executive Time Horizons in State Responses to AIDS in Africa." *Comparative Political Studies* 44(1):55–77.

Donno, Daniela. 2013. "Elections and Democratization in Authoritarian Regimes." *American Journal of Political Science* 57(3):703–716.

Downie, Richard. 2015. Evolving Attitudes toward Secularism in Tanzania. In *Religious Authority and the State in Africa*. Rowman and Littlefield Publishers, Inc., pp. 100–115.

Downs, Anthony. 1957. *An Economic Theory of Democracy*. New York: Harper and Row.

Dunning, Thad. 2011. "Fighting and Voting: Violent Conflict and Electoral Politics." *Journal of Conflict Resolution* 55(3):327–339.

Duverger, Maurice. 1954. *Political Parties: Their Organization and Activity in the Modern state*. Third ed. New York: Routledge Kegan and Paul.

Edmonson, Laura. 2007. *Performance and Politics in Tanzania: The Nation on Stage*. Bloomington: Indiana University Press.

Eggers, Andrew C. and Jens Hainmueller. 2009. "MPs for Sale? Returns to Office in Postwar British Politics." *American Political Science Review* 103(4): 513–533.

EISA. 2005. "Election Update 2005: Tanzania." Available at www.eisa.org/pdf/eutz200502.pdf.

Eisenstadt, Todd. 2000. "Eddies in the Third Wave: Protracted Transitions and Theories of Democratization." *Democratization* 7(3):3–24.

Eisenstadt, Todd. 2003. *Courting Democracy in Mexico: Party Strategies and Electoral Institutions*. Cambridge: Cambridge University Press.

Ekeh, Peter P. 1975. "Colonialism and the Two Publics in Africa: A Theoretical Statement." *Comparative Studies in Society and History* 17:91–112.

Elischer, Sebastian. 2013. *Political Parties in Africa: Ethnicity and Party Formation*. Cambridge: Cambridge University Press.

Ellis, Erin. 2014. "A Vote of Confidence: Retrospective Voting in Africa." *Afrobarometer Working Paper Series* 147:1–30.

Engels, Bettina. 2015. "Different Means of Protest, Same Causes: Popular Struggles in Burkina Faso." *Review of African Political Economy* 42(143): 92–106.

Ewald, Jonas. 2013. *Challenges to the Democratisation Process in Tanzania: Moving towards Consolidation Years after Independence?* Dar es Salaam, Tanzania: Mkuku na Nyota Publishers.

Fabricus, Peter. 2016. "Panama Papers: No Huge Fish but a Huge Haul." Available at https://issafrica.org/iss-today/panama-papers-no-huge-fish-but-a-huge-haul.

Fafchamps, Marcel, and Flore Gubert. 2007. "The Formation of Risk Sharing Networks." *Journal of Development Economics* 83(2):326–350.

Fenno, Richard F. 1973. *Congressmen in Committees*. Berkeley: University of California Press.

Fenno, Richard F. 1978. *Home Style: House Members in Their Districts*. London: Longman.

Ferejohn, John A. 1986. "Incumbent Performance and Electoral Control." *Public Choice* 50(1):5–25.

Ferree, Karen E. 2010. "The Social Origins of Electoral Volatility in Africa." *British Journal of Political Science* 40:759–479.

Field, Bonnie N., and Peter M. Siavelis. 2008. "Candidate Selection Procedures in Transitional Polities: A Research Note." *Party Politics* 14(5):620–639.

Fillieule, Olivier, and Phillippe Blanchard. 2011. "Fighting Together: Assessing Continuity and Change in Social Movement Organizations Through the Study of Constituencies' Heterogeneity." Working paper, University of Lausanne.

Firth, David. 1993. "Bias Reduction in Maximum Likelihood Estimates." *Biometrika* 80(1):27–38.

Fish, M. Steven. 2006. Creative Constitutions: How Do Parliamentary Powers Shape the Electoral Arena? In *Electoral Authoritarianism: The Dynamics of Unfree Competition*, ed. Andreas Schedler. Boulder, CO: Lynne Rienner Publishers, pp. 181–198.

Fisman, Raymond, Florian Schulz and Vikrant Vig. 2014. "The Private Returns to Public Office." *Journal of Political Economy* 122(4):806–862.

Fjeldstad, Eivind, Sigrun Marie Moss, Sterling Roop, and Keith R. Weghorst. 2010a. "CCM's Primary Elections: New Protocols and a More Democratic CCM." *Zanzibar Special Reports* 22:1–14.

Fjeldstad, Eivind, Sigrun Marie Moss, Sterling Roop, and Keith R. Weghorst. 2010b. "Mending Fences: Introducing the CCM Candidates and a First Attempt at Uniting the Party." *Zanzibar Special Reports* 19:1–10.

Fombad, Charles Manga. 2004. The Dynamics of Record-Breaking Endemic Corruption and Political Opportunism in Cameroon. In *The Leadership Challenge in Africa: Cameroon underl Paul Biya*, ed. Jpohn M. Mbaku and Joseph Takougang. Trenton, NJ: African World Press, Inc.

Fowler, James, and Cindy D. Kam. 2007. "Beyond the Self: Social Identity, Altruism, and Political Participation." *American Journal of Political Science* 69(3):813–827.

Fox, Richard A., and Jennifer L. Lawless. 2005. "To Run or Not to Run for Office: Explaining Nascent Political Ambition." *American Journal of Political Science* 49(3):642–659.

Fox, Richard A. and Jennifer L. Lawless. 2004. "Entering the Arena? Gender and the Decision to Run for Office." *American Journal of Political Science* 48(2):264–280.

Frantz, Erica, and Andrea Kendall-Tayler. 2014. "A Dictator's Toolkit: Understanding how Co-optation Affects Repression in Autocracies." *Journal of Peace Research* 51(3):322–346.

Fredrickson, George. 1996. *Black Liberation: A Comparative History of Black Ideologies in the United States and South Africa*. New York: Oxford University Press.

Freedman, Deborah, Arland Thornton, Donald Camburn, Duane Alwin, and Linda Young-DeMarco. 1988. "The Life History Calendar: A Technique for Collecting Retrospective Data." *Sociological Methodology* 18:37–68.

Freedom House. 2020. *A Leaderless Struggle for Democracy*. Washington, DC: Freedom House.

Freedom House. 2021. *Democracy under Siege*. Washington, DC: Freedom House.

Gallagher, Michael. 1988. Introduction. In *Candidate Selection in Comparative Perspective: The Secret Garden of Politics*, ed. Michael Gallagher and Michael Marsh. London: Sage Publications, pp. 1–19.

Galvan, Dennis. 2001. "Political Turnover and Social Change in Senegal." *Journal of Democracy* 12(3):50–62.

Gandhi, Jennifer. 2008. *Political Institutions Under Dictatorship*. Cambridge: Cambridge University Press.

Gandhi, Jennifer and Adam Przeworski. 2007. "Authoritarian Institutions and the Survival of Autocrats." *Comparative Political Studies* 40(11): 1279–1301.

Gandhi, Jennifer and Ellen Lust-Okar. 2009. "Elections Under Authoritarianism." *Annual Review of Political Science* 12:403–422.

Gautheir, Jacques-Antoine, Felix Buhlmann, and Phillippe Blanchard. 2014. Introduction: Sequence Analysis in 2014. In *Advances in Sequence Analysis: Theory, Method, Applications*, ed. Jacques-Antoine Gautheir, Felix Buhlmann, and Phillippe Blanchard. Springer, pp. 1–17.

Gauthier, Jacques-Antoine, Eric D. Widmer, Philipp Bucher, and Cédric Notredame. 2009. "How Much Does It Cost?: Optimization of Costs in Sequence Analysis of Social Science Data." *Sociological Methods & Research* 38(1):197–231.

Geddes, Barbara. 1999. "What Do We Know about Democratization after Twenty Years?" *Annual Review of Political Science* 2:115–144.

Geddes, Barbara. 2005. "Why Parties and Elections in Authoritarian Regimes?" Presented at the Annual Meeting of the American Political Science Association, Washington DC.

Giollabhui, Shane Mac. 2013. "How Things Fall Apart: Candidate Selection and the Cohesion of Dominant Parties in South Africa and Namibia." *Party Politics* 19(4):577–600.

Goeke, Martin and Christof Hartmann. 2011. "The Regulation of Party-Switching in Africa." *Journal of Contemporary African Studies* 29(3): 263–280.

Goldberg. 2018. "Tanzania and Israel Sign Military Training and Intelligence Gathering-Sharing Agreement." *Strategic Intelligence*.

Goldfrank, Benjamin. 2007. "The Politics of Deepening Local Democracy: Decentralization, Party Institutionalization, and Participation." *Comparative Politics* 39(2):147–168.

Goldman, Mara J., and Jani S. Little. 2015. "Innovative Grassroots NGOS and the Complex Processes of Women's Empowerment: An Empirical Investigation from Northern Tanzania." *World Development* 66:762–777.

Gonzalez-Ocantos, E., C.K. de Jonge, C. Meléndez, J. Osorio, and D.W. Nickerson. 2011. "Vote Buying and Social Desirability Bias: Experimental Evidence from Nicaragua." *American Journal of Political Science* 56(1):202–217.

Green, Donald P., and Alan S. Gerber. 2004. *Get Out the Vote: How to Increase Voter Turnout*. Washington, DC: Brookings Institution Press.

Green, Donald P., Alan S. Gerber, and David W. Nickerson. 2003. "Getting Out the Vote in Local Elections: Results from Six Door-to-Door Canvassing Experiments." *Journal of Politics* 65(4):1038–1096.

Greene, Elliott D. 2008. "Decentralization and Conflict in Uganda." *Conflict, Security, and Development* 8(4):427–450.

Greene, Kenneth F. 2002. "Opposition Party Strategy and Spatial Competition in Dominant Party Regimes." *Comparative Political Studies* 35(7):755–783.

Greene, Kenneth F. 2007. *Why Dominant Parties Lose: Mexico's Democratization in Comparative Perspective*. New York: Cambridge University Press.

Greene, Kenneth F. 2010. A Resource Theory of Single-Party Dominance: The PRI in Mexico. In *Dominant Political Parties and Democracy: Concepts, Measures, Cases, and Comparisons*, ed. Francoise Bogaards, Matthijs and Boucek. New York: Routledge, pp. 173–192.

Grossman, Guy, and Kristin Michelitch. 2018. "Information Dissemination, Competitive Pressure and Politician Performance between Elections: A Field Experiment in Uganda." *Amerircan Political Science Review* 112(2):280–301.

Gryzmala-Busse, Anna. 2011. "Time Will Tell? Temporality and the Analysis of Causal Mechanisms and Processes." *Comparative Political Studies* 44(9): 1267–1297.

Guardian Staff. 2010. "Nation Awaits New VP." *Guardian on Sunday* July 11, 2010.

Gurr, Ted Robert. 1970. *Why Men Rebel*. Princeton, NJ: Princeton University Press.

Gyimah-Boadi, Emmanuel. 1996. "Civil Society in Africa." *Journal of Democracy* 7(2):118–132.

Hanaoka, Chie, Hitoshi Shigeoka, and Yasutora Watanabe. 2015. "Do Risk Preferences Change? Evidence from Panel Data before and after the Great East Japan Earthquake." *NBER Working Paper Series* (21400).

Heilman, Bruce E., and Paul J. Kaiser. 2002. "Religion, Identity and Politics in Tanzania." *Third World Quarterly* 23(4):691–709.

Heller, Patrick. 2001. "Moving the State: The Politics of Democratic Decentralization in Kerala, South Africa and Porto Alegre." *Politics and Society* 29(1):131–163.

Herbst, Jeffery. 2000. *States and Power in Africa: Comparative Lessons in Authority and Control*. Princeton, NJ: Princeton University Press.

Heß, Moritz, Christian von Scheve, Jürgen Schupp and Gert G. Wagner. 2013. "Members of German Federal Parliament More Risk-Loving Than General Population." *DIW Economic Bulletin* 4:20–24.

Hibbing, John R. 1999. "Legislative Careers: Why and How We Should Study Them." *Legislative Studies Quarterly* 24(2): 149–171.

Hicken, Allen. 2011. "Clientelism." *Annual Review of Political Science* 14: 289–310.

Hill, Geoff. 2003. *The Battle for Zimbabwe: The Final Countdown*. Cape Town, South Africa: Zebra Press.

Hinton, S. 2002. *University Student Protests and Political Change in Sierra Leone*. New York: Edwin Mellen Press.

Holbrook, Allyson L., and Jon A. Krosnick. 2010. "Social Desirability Bias in Voter Turnout Reports." *Public Opinion Quarterly* 74(1):37–67.

Holt, Charles A., and Susan K. Laury. 2002. "Risk Aversion and Incentive Effects." *American Economic Review* 92(5):1644–1655.

Holt, Charles A., and Susan K. Laury. 2005. "Risk Aversion and Incentive Effects: New Date without Order Effects." *American Economic Review* 95(3): 902–904.

Hopkins, Raymond F. 1970. "The Role of the M.P. in Tanzania." *American Political Science Review* 64(3):754–771.

Horowitz, Jeremy. 2015. "Ethnicity and Campaign Effects in Africa's Multiethnic Democracies: Evidence from Kenya." Presented at the Annual Meeting of the American Political Science Association.

Horowitz, Jeremy. 2019. "Ethnicity and the Swing Vote in Africa's Emerging Democracies: Evidence from Kenya." *British Journal of Political Science* 49(3):901–921.

Howard, Marc Morje, and Phillip G. Roessler. 2006. "Liberalizing Electoral Outcomes in Competitive Authoritarian Regimes." *American Journal of Political Science* 50(2):365–381.

Huddy, Leonie, Lilliana Mason and Lene Aaroe. 2015. "Expressive Partisanship: Campaign Involvement, Political Emotion, and Partisan Identity." *American Political Science Review* 109(1):1–17.

Hyden, Goran. 1980. *Beyond Ujamaa in Tanzania: Underdevelopment and an Uncaptured Peasantry*. Berkeley: University of California Press.

Hyden, Goran. 1983. *No Shortcuts to Progress: African Development Management in Perspective*. Berkeley: University of California Press.

Hyden, Goran. 1999. "Top Down Democratization in Tanzania." *Journal of Democracy* 10(4):142–155.

Hyden, Goran and Colin Leys. 1972. "Elections and Politics in Single-Party Systems: The Case of Kenya and Tanzania." *British Journal of Political Science* 2(4):389–420.

Hymes, Dell. 1962. The Ethnography of Speaking. In *Anthropology and Human Behaviour*, ed. William C. Sturtevant and Thomas Gladwin. Anthropological Society of Washington.

Ichino, Nahomi, and Noah L. Nathan. 2012. "Primaries on Demand? Intra-Party Politics and Nominations in Ghana." *British Journal of Political Science* 42(4):769–791.

Ichino, Nahomi, and Noah L. Nathan. 2013. "Do Primaries Improve Electoral Performance? Evidence from Ghana." *American Journal of Political Science* 57(2):428–441.

Iida, Takeshi. 2013. "The Consequences of Risk-taking Voting Behavior: An Analysis of the 2012 General Election in Japan." Presented at the Annual Meeting of the Western Political Science Association.

Indridason, Indridi, and Gunnar Helgi Kristinsson. 2015. "Primary Consequences: The Effects of Candidate Selection through Party Primaries in Iceland." *Party Politics* 21(4):565–576.

Jackson, John S. 1994*a*. Incumbency in the United States. In *The Victorious Incumbent: A Threat to Democracy?*, ed. Albert Somit, Rudolf Wildenmann, Bernhard Boll, and Andrea Rommele. Brookfield, VT: Dartmouth Publishing Company, pp. 29–70.

Jackson, Keith. 1994*b*. Stability and Renewal Incumbency and Parliamentary Composition. In *The Victorious Incumbent: A Threat to Democracy?*, ed.

Albert Somit, Rudolf Wildenmann, Bernhard Boll and Andrea Rommele. Brookfield, VT: Dartmouth Publishing Company, pp. 251–277.

Jacobson, Gary C. 1986. *Money in Congressional Elections*. New Haven, CT: Yale University Press.

Jacobson, Sarah, and Ragan Petrie. 2007. "Inconsistent Choices in Lottery Experiments: Evidence from Rwanda." Working paper.

Jakiela, Pamela and Owen Ozier. 2018. "The Impact of Violence on Individual Risk Preferences: Evidence from a Natural Experiment." *The Review of Economics and Statistics*.

James, Bernard. 2015. "Our 10-cell Leadership to Thwart Ukawa Dreams." Available at www.thecitizen.co.tz/news.Our-10-cell-leadership-to-thwart-Ukawa-dreams/1840406-2837014-127ho2/index.html.

Janda, Kenneth. 2009. "Laws against Party Switching, Defecting, or Floor-Crossing in National Parliaments." Paper presented at the 2009 World Congress on the International Political Science Association, Santiago.

Jiang, Junyan, and Dali L. Yang. 2016. "Lying or Believing? Measuring Preference Falsification from a Political Purge in China." *Comparative Political Studies* 49(5):600–634.

Johnson, Keith. 2019. "2019: A Year of Global Protest." *Foreign Policy*. Available at https://foreignpolicy.com/2019/12/23/2019-a-year-of-global-protest/.

Joseph, Richard. 1987. *Democracy and Prebendal Politics in Nigeria*. Cambridge: Cambridge University Press.

Joseph, Richard. 1998. "African Ambiguities: Africa 1900–1997 – From Abertura to Closure" *Journal of Democracy* 9(2):3–17.

Kabendera, Erick. 2019a. "Electoral Body Now Moves to Seal the Fate of Lissu." *The East African*. Available at www.theeastafrican.co.ke/tea/news/east-africa/electoral-body-now-moves-to-seal-the-fate-of-lissu-1421876.

Kabendera, Erick. 2019b. "How Hamad's Defection Alters Zanzibar Vote." *The East African*. Available at www.theeastafrican.co.ke/tea/news/east-africa/how-hamad-s-defection-alters-zanzibar-vote-1414820.

Kalugila, Leonidas, and Abdulaziz Y. Lodhi. 1980. *More Swahili Proverbs from East Africa*. Uppsala, Sweden: Scandinavian Institute of African Studies.

Kalyvas, Stathis N. 1996. *The Rise of Christian Democracy in Europe*. Ithaca, NY: Cornell University Press.

Kam, Cindy D. 2012. "Risk Attitudes and Political Participation." *American Journal of Political Science* 56(4):817–836.

Kam, Cindy D., and Elizabeth N. Simas. 2012. "Risk Attitudes, Candidate Characteristics, and Vote Choice." *Public Opinion Quarterly* 76(4):747–760.

Kamagai, Deogratius. 2018. "Dr Slaa: I resigned from Chadema because of Lowassa." *The Citizen*.

Kane, James G., Stephen C. Craig and Kenneth D. Wald. 2004. "Religion and Presidential Politics in Florida: A List Experiment." *Social Science Quarterly* 85:281–293.

Karombo, Tawanda. 2020. "Tanzania has Blocked Social Media, Bulk SMS as Its Election Polls Open." *Quartz Africa*.

Karugendo, Privatus. 2015. *Maswali 40 majibu 40: Mazungumzo na January Makamba kuhusu Tanzania mpya*. Dar es Salaam: Privatus Karugendo.

Kasara, Kimuli. 2006. "Ethnic Beachheads and Vote Buying: Explaining the Creation of new Administrative Districts in Kenya 1963–2001." Paper presented at the annual meeting of the American Political Science Association, Marriott, Loews Philadelphia, and the Pennsylvania Convention Center, Philadelphia, PA.

Kasfir, Nelson. 1998. "'No-party Democracy' in Uganda." *Journal of Democracy* 9(2):49–63.

Kavasoglu, Berker. 2021. Opposition Parties and Elite Co-Optation in Electoral Autocracies. Working Paper 120, Varieties of Democracy (V-Dem) Institute.

Kaya, Hassan O. 2004. "Electoral Violence, Political Stability, and the Union in Tanzania." *African Journal of Conflict Resolution* 4(2):145–169.

Kaya, Ruchan, and Michael Bernhard. 2013. "Are Elections Mechanisms of Authoritarian Stability or Democratization? Evidence from Postcommunist Eurasia." *Perspectives on Politics* 11(3):734–752.

Kazee, Thomas A. 1980. "The Decision to Run for the U.S. Congress: Challenger Attitudes in 1970s." *Legislative Studies Quarterly* 5(1):79–100.

Keck, Margaret E., and Kathryn Sikkink. 1998. *Activists Beyond Borders: Advocacy Networks in International Politics*. Ithaca, NY: Cornell University Press.

Kelly, Catherine Lena. 2019. *Party Proliferation and Political Contestation in Africa: Senegal in Comparative Perspective*. London: Palgrave MacMillan.

Kelsall, Tim. 2004. *Contentious Politics, Local Governance, and the Self: A Tanzanian Case Study*. Uppsala, Sweden: Nordiska Africaninstitutet.

Kelsall, Tim, Siri Lange, Simeon Mesaki, and Max Mmuya. 2005. Understanding Patterns of Accountability in Tanzania: Component 2, the Bottom-Up Perspective. Technical report REPOA Dar es Salaam, Tanzania.

Key, Vladmir O. 1964. *Politics, Parties, and Pressure Groups*. 5th ed. New York: Cromwell.

Khisa, Moses. 2016. "Managing Elite Defection in Museveni's Uganda: The 2016 Elections in Perspective." *Journal of Eastern African Studies* 10(4): 729–748.

Killian, Bernadeta. 2008. "The State and Identity Politics in Zanzibar: Challenges to Democratic Consolidation in Tanzania." *African Identities* 6(2):99–125.

Kitschelt, Herbert. 2013. Democratic Accountability and Linkages Project. Technical report Duke University Durham, NC. Dataset.

Klesner, Joseph A. 2007. "Social Capital and Political Participation in Latin America: Evidence from Argentina, Chile, and Peru." *Latin American Research Review* 42(2):1–32.

Konings, Piet J.J. 2003. "Organised Labour and Neo-Liberal Economic and Political Reforms in West and Central Africa." *Journal of Contemporary African Studies* 21(3):447–471.

Kosterina, Svetlana. 2017. "Why Vote for a Co-opted Party? Endogenous Government Power Increases and Control of Opposition Politicians in Authoritarian Regimes." *Comparative Political Studies* 50(9):1155–1185.

Koter, Dominika. 2016. *Beyond Ethnic Politics in Africa*. Cambridge: Cambridge University Press.

Kramon, Eric. 2011. "Is Vote-Buying Effective? Survey Experimental Evidence from Kenya." Unpublished manuscript.

Kramon, Eric. 2017. *Money for Votes: The Causes and Consequences of Electoral Clientelism in Africa.* Cambridge University Press.

Kramon, Eric, and Keith Weghorst. 2019. "(Mis)Measuring Sensitive Attitudes with the List Experiment: Solutions to List Experiment Breakdown in Kenya." *Public Opinion Quarterly* 83(1):236–263.

Kricheli, Ruth, Yair Livine, and Beatriz Magaloni. 2011. "Taking to the Streets: Theory and Evidence on Protests under Authoritarianism." Unpublished paper.

Krook, Mona Lena. 2010. *Quotas for Women in Politics: Gender and Candidate Selection Reform Worldwide.* Oxford: Oxford University Press.

Krosnick, Jon A. 1991. "Response Strategies for Coping with the Cognitive Demands of Attitude Measures in Surveys." *Applied Cognitive Psychology* 5:213–236.

Kuklinski, James, Michael D. Cobb and Martin Gilens. 1997. "Racial Attitudes and the 'New South'." *Journal of Politics* 59:323–349.

Kuran, Timur. 1989. "Sparks and Prairie Fires: A Theory of Unanticipated Political Revolution." *Public Choice* 61(1):41–74.

Kuran, Timur. 1991. "Now Out of Never: The Element of Surprise in the Eastern European Revolution of 1989." *World Politics* 44(1):7–48.

Kuran, Timur. 1995. *Private Truths, Public Lies: The Social Consequences of Preference Falsification.* Cambridge, MA: Harvard University Press.

Kurebwa, Jospeh. 2001. Crisis of Governance: A Report on Political Violence in Zimbabwe: Volume 1. Technical report Catholic Commission for Justice and Peace in Zimbabwe Harare, Zimbabwe.

Kwayu, Aikande. 2015. A Touchstone For Legitimacy in Tanzania. In *Remembering Julius Nyerere in Tanzania: History, Memory, Legacy*, ed. Marie-Aude Fouere. Mkuki na Nyota Publishers, pp. 127–140.

Kweka, Dastan. 2015. "Party Militias and Election-related Violence in Tanzania."

Laitin, David. 1994. "The Tower of Babel as a Coordination Game: Political Linguistics in Ghana." *American Political Science Review* 88(3):622–634.

Lange, Peter, Cynthia Irvin and Sidney Tarrow. 1989. "Phases of Mobilization: Social Movements and the Italian Communist Party since the 1960s." *British Journal of Political Science* 22:15–42.

Langston, Joy. 2006. "The Changing Party of the Institutional Revolution: Electoral Competition and Decentralized Candidate Selection." *Party Politics* 12(3):395–413.

Larmer, Miles. 2006. "'The Hour Has Come at the Pit': The Mineworkers' Union of Zambia and the Movement for Multi-Party Democracy 1982–1991." *Journal of Southern African Studies* 32(2):293–312.

Larner, Jennifer S. and Dacher Keltner. 2001. "Fear, Anger, and Risk." *Journal of Personality and Social Psychology* 81(1):146–159.

Lawless, Jennifer L. 2012. *Becoming a Candidate: Political Ambition and the Decision to Run for Office.* Cambridge: Cambridge University Press.

LeBas, Adrienne. 2006. "Polarization as Craft: Party Formation and State Violence in Zimbabwe." *Comparative Politics* 38(4):419–438.

LeBas, Adrienne. 2011. *From Protest to Parties: Party-Building & Democratization in Africa.* Oxford: Oxford University Press.

Lemarchand, Rene. 1972. "Political Clientelism and Ethnicity in Tropical Africa: Competing Solidarities in Nation-Building." *The American Political Science Review* 66(1):68–90.

Levenshtein, V. 1966. "Binary Codes Capable of Correcting Deletions, Insertions, and Reversals." *Social Physics Doklady* 10:707–710.

Levitsky, Steven, and Lucan A. Way. 2002. "The Rise of Competitive Authoritarianism." *Journal of Democracy* 13(2):51–65.

Levitsky, Steven, and Lucan A. Way. 2005. "International Linkage and Democratization." *Journal of Democracy* 16(3):20–34.

Levitsky, Steven, and Lucan A. Way. 2010a. *Competitive Authoritarianism: Hybrid Regimes After the Cold War*. Cambridge: Cambridge University Press.

Levitsky, Steven, and Lucan A. Way. 2010b. "Why Democracy Needs a Level Playing Field." *Journal of Democracy* 21(1):57–68.

Levy, Yagil. 2010. "How the Military's Social Composition Affects Political Protest: The Case of Israel." *Peace and Change* 35(1):123–145.

Lindberg, Staffan. 2003. "It's Our Time to "Chop": Do Elections in Africa Feed Neopatrimonialism Rather than Counteract It?" *Democratization* 10(2): 121–140.

Lindberg, Staffan I. 2006a. *Democracy and Elections in Africa*. Baltimore, MD: Johns Hopkins University Press.

Lindberg, Staffan I. 2006b. Tragic Protest: Why Do Opposition Parties Boycott Elections? In *Electoral Authoritarianism: The Dynamics of Unfree Competition*, ed. Andreas Schedler. Boulder, CO: Lynne Rienner Publishers.

Lindberg, Staffan I. 2007. "Institutionalization in African Party Systems? Stability and Fluidity Among Legislative Parties in Africa's Democracies." *Government and Opposition* 42(2):215–241.

Lindberg, Staffan I. 2009. A Theory of Elections as a Mode of Transition. In *Democratization by Elections: A New Mode of Transition?*, ed. Staffan I. Lindberg. Baltimore, MD: Johns Hopkins University Press, pp. 1–21.

Lindberg, Staffan I. 2010. "What Accountability Pressures Do MPs in Africa Face and How Do They Respond?" *Journal of Modern African Studies* 48(1): 117–42.

Lindberg, Staffan I. 2012. "Have the Cake and Eat It: The Rational Voter in Africa." *Party Politics* 19(5):945–961.

Linz, Juan J., and Alfred C. Stepan. 1996. *Problems of Democratic Transition and Consolidation: Southern Europe, South America, and Post-communist Europe*. Baltimore, MD: Johns Hopkins University Press.

Lipset, Seymour Martin, and Stein Rokkan. 1967. *Party Systems and Voter Alignments: Cross-National Perspectives*. New York: The Free Press.

Little, Andrew T. 2014. "An Informational Theory of Noncompetitive Elections." Unpublished manuscript, http://andrewtlittle.com/papers/.

Lohmann, Susanne. 1994. "The Dynamics of Informational Cascades: The Monday Demonstrations in Leipzig, East Germany, 1989–1991." *World Politics* 47(1):42–101.

Love, Roy. 2006. "Religion, Ideology and Conflict in Africa." *Review of African Political Economy* 33(110):619–634.

Loveman, Mara. 1998. "High-Risk Collective Action: Defending Human Rights in Chile, Uruguay, and Argentina." *American Journal of Sociology* 104(2): 477–425.

Lovenduski, Joni, and Pippa Norris. 1993. *Gender and Party Politics*. Thousand Oaks, CA: Sage Publications.

Loxton, James. 2015. "Authoritarian Successor Parties." *Journal of Democracy* 26(3):157–170.

Lucardi, Adrian. 2015. "Making Authoritarian Elections Competitive: The Origins of Ruling Party Defections and Opposition Coalitions in Competitive Authoritarian Regimes." Working paper.

Luescher-Mamashela, Thierry. 2005. *Student Governance in Africa: A Thematic Review of Literature on African Student Politics*. Unpublished paper. Cape Town: Centre for Higher Education Transformation.

Lugongo, Bernard. 2014. "Kafulia Asks President Kikwete to Intervene in IPTL Sale Saga." *The Citizen* (Tanzania). Available at www.thecitizen.co.tz/ tanzania/news/kafulila-asks-president-kikwete-to-intervene-in-iptl-sale-saga-2511868.

Lugongo, Bernard. 2017. "Dar, Seoul Team up against Rising Cases of Cybercrimes." *Daily News* (Tanzania). Available at https://allafrica.com/ stories/201704200305.html.

Luhanga, Matthew Laban. 2009. *The Courage for Change: Re-Engineering the University of Dar es Salaam*. Dar es Salaam, Tanzania: Dar es Salaam University Press.

Lührmann, Anna, Nils Düpont, Masaaki Higashijima, Yaman Berker Kavasoglu, Kyle L. Marquardt, Michael Bernhard, Holger Doring, Allen Hicken, Melis Laebens, Staffan I. Lindberg, Anja Neundorf, Ora John Reuter, Saskia Ruth-Lovell, Keith Weghorst, Nina Wiesehomeier, Joseph Wright, Nazifa Alizada, Paul Bederke, Lisa Gastaldi, Sandra Grahn, Garry Hindle, Nina Ilchenko, Johannes von Rümer, Daniel Pemstein, and Brigitte Seim. 2020. "Varieties of Party Identity and Organization (V–Party) Dataset V1." *Varieties of Democracy (V-Dem) Project*.

Lührmann, Anna, Seraphine F. Mearz, Sandra Grahn, Nazifa Alizada, Lisa Gastaldi, Sebastian Hellmeier, Gary Hindle and Staffan I. Lindberg. 2020. *Autocratization Surges – Resistance Grows. Democracy Report 2020*. Gothenburg, Sweden: Varieties of Democracy (V-Dem).

Lührmann, Anna, and Staffan I. Lindberg. 2019. "A Third Wave of Autocratization Is Here: What Is New about It?" *Democratization* 26(7):1095–1113.

Luna, Juan P. and Elizabeth J. Zechmeister. 2005. "Political Representation in Latin America: A Study of Elite-Mass Congruence in Nine Countries." *Comparative Political Studies* 38(4):388–416.

Lust-Okar, Ellen. 2005. *Structuring Conflict in the Arab World: Incumbents, Opponents, and Institutions*. Cambridge: Cambridge University Press.

Lust-Okar, Ellen. 2008. The Politics of Jordanian Elections: Competitive Clientelism. In *Political Participation in the Middle East and North Africa*, ed. Ellen Lust-Okar and S. Zerhouni. Boulder, CO: Lynne Rienner Publishers, pp. 75–94.

Lust-Okar, Ellen. 2009. Legislative Elections in Hegemonic Authoritarian Regimes. In *Democratization by Elections: A New Mode of Transition?*, ed. Staffan I. Lindberg. Baltimore, MD: Johns Hopkins University Press, pp. 226–245.

Lyons, Terrence. 2016. "From Victorious Rebels to Strong Authoritarian Parties: Prospects for Post-war Democratization." *Democratization* 23(6):1026–1041.

Macindoe, H., and A. Abbott. 2004. Sequence Analysis Methods and Optimal Matching Techniques for Social Science Data. In *Handbook of Data Analysis*, ed. M. Hardy and A. Bryman. Sage Publications, pp. 387–406.

MacKenzie, Scott Alan. 2015. "Life before Congress: Using Precongressional Experience to Assess Competing Explanations for Political Professionalism." *The Journal of Politics* 77(2):505–518.

Mackenzie, William, and Kenneth Robinson. 1960. *Five Elections in Africa*. Oxford: Clarendon Press.

Maestas, Cherie D., Sarah Fulton, Sandy L. Maisel and Walter J. Stone. 2006. "When to Risk It? Institutions, Ambitions, and the Decision to Run for the U.S. House." *American Political Science Review* 100(2):195–208.

Magaloni, Beatriz. 2006. *Voting for Autocracy: Hegemonic Party Survival and Its Demise in Mexico*. Cambridge: Cambridge University Press.

Mahoney, James. 2000. "Path Dependence in Historical Sociology." *Theory and Society* 29:507–548.

Makse, Todd, and Anand E. Sokhey. 2010. "Revisiting the Divisive Primary Hypothesis: 2008 and the Clinton–Obama Nomination Battle." *American Politics Research* 38(2):233–265.

Makulilo, Alexander Boniface. 2012. "Where Have All the Researchers Gone? Use and Abuse of Polls for the 2010 Elections in Tanzania." *International Journal of Peace and Development Studies* 3(3):33–56.

Maliyamkoko, T.L. 2002. *Nani Hupiga Kura Tanzania na Kwa Nini?* Dar es Salaam, Tanzania: Tema Publishers Company, Ltd.

Manin, Bernard. 1997. *The Principles of Representative Government*. Cambridge: Cambridge University Press.

Manning, Carrie. 2002. *The Politics of Peace in Mozambique: Post-Conflict Democratization, 1992–2000*. Westport, Connecticut: Praeger.

Manning, Carrie. 2005. "Assessing African Party Systems after the Third Wave." *Party Politics* 11(6):707–727.

Mares, Isabela and Lauren Young. 2016. "Buying, Expropriating, and Stealing Votes." *Annual Review of Political Science* 19:267–288.

Martin, Peter, Ingrid Schoon, and Andy Ross. 2008. "Beyond Transitions: Applying Optimal Matching Analysis to Life Course Research." *International Journal of Social Research Methodology* 11(3):179–199.

Mashingaidze, Terence. 2005. The 1987 Zimbabwe National Unity Accord and its Aftermath: A Case of Peace without Reconciliation. In *From National Liberation to Democratic Renaissance in Southern Africa*, ed. Cheryl Hendricks and Lwazi Lushaba. Dakar, Senegal: Council for the Development of Social Science Research in Africa, pp. 82–92.

Mattes, Robert and Shaheen Mozzaffar. 2018. "Legislatures and Democratic Development in Africa." *African Studies Review* 59(3):201–215.

Matthews, Donald R. 1984. "Legislative Recruitment and Legislative Careers." *Legislative Studies Quarterly* 9(4):547–585.

Mattozzi, Andrea, and Antonio Merlo. 2008. "Political Careers or Career Politicians?" *Journal of Public Economics* 92(3-4):597–608.

McAdam, Douglas. 1990. *Freedom Summer*. Oxford: Oxford University Press.

McAdam, Douglas, John D. McCarthy, and Mayer N. Zald. 1996. *Comparative Perspectives on Social Movements*. Cambridge: Cambridge University Press.

McAdam, Douglas, Sidney Tarrow, and Charles Tilly. 2001. *Dynamics of Contention*. Cambridge: Cambridge University Press.

McClurg, Scott D. 2003. "Social Networks and Political Participation: The Role of Social Interaction in Explaining Political Participation." *Political Research Quarterly* 56(4):449–464.

McGlinchey, Eric. 2011. *Chaos, Violence, Dynasty: Politics and Islam in Central Asia*. Pittsburg: University of Pittsburgh Press.

McGowan, Patrick, and Patrick. Bolland. 1971. "The Political and Social Elite of Tanzania: An Analysis of Social Background Factors." *Program of East African Studies*.

McLellan, Rachael. 2018. "Why Is Once-peaceful Tanzania Detaining Journalists, Arresting Schoolgirls and Killing Opposition Leaders?" *Washington Post*. Available at www.washingtonpost.com/news/monkey-cage/wp/2018/11/30/why-is-once-peaceful-tanzania-detaining-journalists-arresting-schoolgirls-and-killing-opposition-leaders/?utm_term=.3f2dc748a646.

McVicar, Duncan and Michael Anyadike-Danes. 2002. "Predicting Successful and Unsuccessful Transitions from School to Work by Using Sequence Methods." *Journal of the Royal Statistical Society: Series A (Statistics in Society)*. 165(2):317–334.

Meng, Anne. 2020. *Constraining Dictatorship: From Personalized Rule to Institutionalized Regimes*. Cambridge: Cambridge University Press.

Mercer, Claire. 1999. "Reconceptualizing State-Society Relations in Tanzania: Are NGOs 'Making a Difference'?" *Area* 31(3):247–258.

Mesomapya, Janeth. 2017. "Hamad Says He Can't Sit with Lipumba." *Citizen* (Tanzania). Available at www.thecitizen.co.tz/tanzania/news/hamad-says-cant-sit-with-lipumba-2587714.

Michelson, Melissa R., Lisa Garcia Bedolla, and Margaret A. McConnell. 2009. "Heeding the Call: The Effect of Targeted Two-Round Phone Banks on Voter Turnout." *Journal of Politics* 71(4):1549–1563.

Miguel, Edward. 2004. "Tribe or Nation? Nation Building and Public Goods in Kenya versus Tanzania." *World Politics* 56(3):327–362.

Miller, Michael K. 2015. "Electoral Authoritarianism and Human Development." *Comparative Political Studies* 48(12): 1526–1562.

Miller, Michael K. 2020. "The Autocratic Ruling Parties Dataset: Origins, Durability, and Death." *Journal of Conflict Resolution* 64(4):756–782.

Mishler, William. 1978. "Nomination Attractive Candidates for Parliament: Recruitment to the Canadian House of Commons." *Legislative Studies Quarterly* 3(4):581–599.

Mishra, Sandeep, and Dallas Novakowski. 2016. "Personal Relative Deprivation and Risk: An Examination of Individual Differences in Personality, Attitudes, and Behavioral Outcomes." *Personality and Individual Differences* 90:22–26.

Mmuya, Max, and Amon Chaligha. 1994. *Political Parties and Democracy in Tanzania*. Dar es Salaam, Tanzania: Dar es Salaam University Press.

Mohammed, Omar. 2015. "Tanzania's ex-PM Is Running for President with the Party that Once Called Him Corrupt." *Quartz*. Available at https://qz.com/africa/467729/tanzania-s-ex-pm-is-running-for-president-with-the-party-that-once-called-him-corrupt/.

Moncrief, Gary F., Pervill Squire, and Malcom E. Jewell. 2000. *Who Runs for the Legislature?* Bergen County, New Jersey: Prentice Hall.

Moore, Michael K., and John R. Hibbing. 1998. "Situational Dissatisfaction in Congress: Explaining Voluntary Departures." *The Journal of Politics* 60: 1088–1107.

Morgenstern, Scott, and Elizabeth Zechmeister. 2001. "Better the Devil You Know Than the Saint You Don't? Risk Propensity and Vote Choice in Mexico." *The Journal of Politics* 63(1):93–119.

Morse, Yonatan L. 2012. "The Era of Electoral Authoritarianism." *World Politics* 64(1):161–198.

Morse, Yonatan L. 2015. "From Single-Party to Electoral Authoritarian Regimes: The Institutional Origins of Competitiveness in Post-Cold War Africa." *Comparative Politics* 48(1):126–143.

Morse, Yonatan L. 2019. *How Autocrats Compete: Parties, Patrons, and Unfair Elections in Africa*. Cambridge University Press.

Morton, Rebecca B., and Kenneth C. Williams. 2010. *Experimentation in Political Science and the Study of Causality: From Nature to the Lab*. Cambridge: Cambridge University Press.

Moya, Andrés. 2018. "Violence, Psychological Trauma, and Risk Attitudes: Evidence from Victims of Violence in Colombia." *Journal of Development Economics* 131(C):15–27.

Msekwa, Pius. 2006. *Reflections on the First Decade of Multiparty Politics in Tanzania*. Dar es Salaam, Tanzania: Hanns Seidel Foundation.

Msuya, Elias. 2012. "James Mapalala: Mwanzilishi wa mageuzi aliyeishia kwenye mikosi." *Mwananchi* (Tanzania). Available at www.mwananchi.co.tz/mw/habari/makala/siasa/james-mapalala-mwanzilishi-wa-mageuzi-aliyeishia-kwenye-mikosi-2739196.

Mtei, Edwin. 2009. *From Goatherd to Governor: The Autobiography of Edwin Mtei*. Dar es Salaam, Tanzania: Mkuki na Nyota Publishers.

Muchena, Deprose. 2020. "Tanzania: Killings, Arbitrary Detention and Torture of Opposition Members in Aftermath of Elections." Amnesty International Report. Available at www.amnesty,org/en/latest/news/2020/11/tanzania-killings-arbitrary-detention-and-torture-of-opposition-members-in-aftermath-of-elections/.

Muller, Edward N., and Mitch A. Seligson. 1987. "Inequality and Insurgency." *American Political Science Review* 81(2):425–452.

Mushi, Samuel S. 2001. *Development and Democratisation in Tanzania: A Study of Rural Grassroots Politics*. Dar es Salaam: Fountain Publishers.

Musila, Godfrey M. 2019. *Freedoms Under Threat: The Spread of Anti-NGO Measures in Africa*. Freedom House.

Mutembei, Aldin K. 2011. "Ukimwishaji wa Utanzu wa Fashihi: Mifano kutoka Methali za Tanzania." *Jarida la Kiswahili*, pp. 76–89.

Mutiga, Murithi. 2016. "Tanzania Cuts Live Parliamentary Coverage, Ending Vital News Source for Citizens." Technical Report Committee to Protect Journalists. Available at https://cpj.org/2016/05/tanzania-cuts-live-parliamentary-coverage-ending-v/.

Mwakyusa, Alvar. 2015. "Lipumba Resigns from CUF Leadership." *Tanzania Daily News*.

Mwiti, Lee. 2017. "Factsheet: How Much Do Kenyan Members of Parliament Earn – and Are They Overpaid?" Africa Check. Available at https://africacheck.org/fact-checks/factsheet-how-much-do-kenyan-members-parliament-earn-and-are-they-overpaid.

Mwollo-Ntallima, Angolwisye Malaisyo. 2011. Higher Education and Democracy: A Study of Students' and Student Leaders' Attitudes towards Democracy in Africa. Master's in Education: University of Western Cape Western Cape, South Africa.

Namkwahe, John. 2020. "Shuffling Act as CCM Unveils Final List." *The Citizen* (Tanzania). Available at www.thecitizen.co.tz/tanzania/news/shuffling-act-as-ccm-unveils-final-list-2714868.

Ndegwa, Stephen N. 1996. *The Two Faces of Civil Society*. West Hartford, CT: Kumarian Press.

Needleman, S. and C. Wunsch. 1970. "A General Method Applicable to the Search for Similarities in the Amino Acid Sequence of Two Proteins." *Journal of Molecular Biology* 48:443–453.

Netzer, Nick. 2009. "Evolution of Time Preferences and Attitudes toward Risk." *American Economic Review* 99(3):937–955.

Ng'Wanakilala, Fumbuka. 2020. "Tanzania Opposition Leader Backs Lissu as Presidential Candidate." *Bloomberg*. Available at www.bloomberg.com/news/articles/2020-10-17/tanzania-opposition-leader-backs-lissu-as-presidential-candidate.

Nikolenyi, Csaba. 2011. "Constitutional Sources of Party Cohesion: Anti-Defection Laws Around the World." Paper delivered at the Oslo-Rome International Workshop on Democracy, Rome, Italy.

Nkwame, Marc. 2012. "Police Ban Political Party "Armies". Daily News (Tanzania). Available at www.dailynews.co.tz/news/police-ban-political-party-armies.aspx.

Norris, Pippa. 1997. Introduction: Theories of Recruitment. In *Passages to Power: Legislative Recruitment in Advanced Democracies*. Cambridge: Cambridge University Press.

Nyan'goro, Julius E. 2011. *JK: A Political Biography of Jakaya Mrisho Kikwete, President of the United Republic of Tanzania*. Trenton, NJ: African World Press, Inc.

Nyanto, Salvatory S. 2020. "Ujamaa, Small Christian Communities, and Moral Reform in Western Tanzania, 1960s–1990." *The Catholic Historical Review* 106(2):312–334.

Obangome, Gerauds Wilfried. 2016. "Over 1,000 Arrested as Post-election Riots Rage in Gabon." Reuters. Available at www.reuters.com/article/us-gabon-idUSKCN1160DT.

O'Brien, Diana and Yael Shomer. 2013. "A Cross-National Analysis of Party Switching." *Legislative Studies Quarterly* 38(1):111–141.

O'Donnell, Guillermo A. and Philippe C. Schmitter. 1986. *Transitions from Authoritarian Rule: Tentative Conclusions about Uncertain Democracies*. Baltimore, MD: Johns Hopkins University Press.

Odula, Tom. 2020. "Observers Say Tanzania's Presidential Vote Is Already Flawed." *Associated Press*.

Ohman, Magnus. 2004. *The Heart and Soul of the Party: Candidate Selection in Ghana and in Africa*. Uppsala, Sweden: Universitatis Upsaliensis.

Olson, Mancur. 1993. "Dictatorship, Democracy, and Development." *The American Political Science Review* 87(3):567–576.

Opalo, Ken Ochieng'. 2019. *Legislative Development in Africa: Politics and Postcolonial Legacies*. Cambridge: Cambridge University Press.

Oris, Michel, and Gilbert Ritschard. 2014. Sequence Analysis and Transition to Adulthood: An Exploration of the Access to Reproduction in Nineteenth-century East Belgium. In *Advances in Sequence Analysis: Theory, Method, Applications*, ed. Phillippe Blanchard, Felix Buhlmann and Jacques-Antoine Gautheir. New York: Springer-Verlag, pp. 151–167.

Ostrom, Elinor. 1990. *Governing the Commons: The Evolution of Institutions for Collective Action*. Cambridge: Cambridge University Press.

Othman, Haroub, and Chris Maina Peter. 2006. *Zanzibar and the Union Question*. Zanzibar, Tanzania: Zanzibar Legal Services Center.

Paget, Dan. 2017. "Tanzania: Shrinking Space and Opposition Protest." *Journal of Democracy* 28(3):153–167.

Paget, Dan. 2018. "The Authoritarian Origins of Well-organized Opposition Parties: The Rise of Chadema in Tanzania." *African Affairs* 118 (473): 692–711.

Paget, Dan. 2019. "The Rally-Intensive Campaign: A Distinct Form of Electioneering in Sub-Saharan Africa and Beyond." *The International Journal of Press/Politics* 24(5):444–464.

Paget, Dan. 2020. "Campaign Modernization without Mediatization: Capitalizing Rallies and Parties in Tanzania." Working paper.

Palmer, Barbara, and Dennis Simon. 2003. "Political Ambition and Women in the U.S. House of Representatives, 1916–2000." *Political Research Quarterly* 56(2):127–138.

Payne, James L., and Oliver H. Woshinsky. 1972. "Incentives for Political Participation." *World Politics* 24:518–546.

Pedersen, Mogens N. 1994. Incumbency Success and Defeat in Times of Electoral Turbulences: Patterns of Legislative Recruitment in Denmark 1945–1990. In *The Victorious Incumbent: A Threat to Democracy?*, ed. Albert Somit, Rudolf Wildenmann, Bernhard Boll, and Andrea Rommele. Brookfield, VT: Dartmouth Publishing Company, pp. 218–250.

Pempel, T.J. 1990. *Uncommon Democracies: The One-Party Dominant Regimes*. Ithaca, NY: Cornell University Press.

Pepinsky, Thomas. 2007. "Autocracies, Elections, and Fiscal Policy in Malaysia." *Studies in Comparative International Development* 42(1-2):136–163.

Pepinsky, Thomas. 2014. "The Institutional Turn in Comparative Authoritarianism." *British Journal of Political Science* 44(3):631–653.

Pierson, Paul. 2000. "Increasing Returns, Path Dependence, and the Study of Politics." *American Political Science Review* 94:251–267.

Pinkston, Amanda Leigh. 2016. Insider Democracy: Private Sector Weakness and the Closed Political Class in Democratic Africa. PhD Thesis Harvard University, Graduate School of Arts & Sciences: Cambridge, MA.

Pollock, Gary, Valerie Antcliff, and Rob Ralphs. 2002. "Work Orders: Analysing Employment Histories Using Sequence Data." *International Journal of Social Research Methodology* 5(2):91–105.

Powell, G. Bingham Jr. 2000. *Elections as Instruments of Democracy*. New Haven, CT: Yale University Press.

Przeworski, Adam. 1991. *Democracy and the Market: Political and Economic Reforms in Eastern Europe and Latin America*. Studies in Rationality and Social Change Cambridge: Cambridge University Press.

Przeworski, Adam. 2015. "Acquiring the Habit of Changing Governments Through Elections." *Comparative Political Studies* 48(1):101–129.

Przeworski, Adam et al. 2011. "Political Institutions and Political Events (PIPE) Data Set." Department of Politics, New York University.

Przeworski, Adam, and J. Sprague. 1986. *Paper Stones: A History of Electoral Socialism*. Chicago, IL: University of Chicago Press.

Przeworski, Adam, Michael Alvarez, Jose Antonio Cheibub, and Fernando Limongi. 2000. *Democracy and Development: Political Institutions and Well-Being in the World, 1950–1990*. Cambridge: Cambridge University Press.

Przeworski, Adam, Susan Stokes, and Bernard Manin. 2000. *Democracy, Accountability, and Representation*. Cambridge: Cambridge University Press.

Putnam, Robert D. 1993. *Making Democracy Work: Civic Traditions in Modern Italy*. London: Penguin Press.

Quintelier, Ellen. 2008. "Who is Politically Active: The Athlete, the Scout Member or the Environmental Activist? Young People, Voluntary Engagement and Political Participation." *Acta Sociologica* 51(4):355–370.

Raftopoulos, Brian. 2002. "Briefing: Zimbabwe's 2002 Presidential Election." *African Affairs* 101: 413–426.

Rahat, Gideon, and Reuven Y. Hazan. 2001. "Candidate Selection Methods: An Analytical Framework." *Party Politics* 7(3):297–322.

Rainey, Carlisle. 2016. "Dealing with Separation in Logistic Regression Models." *Political Analysis* 24(3):339–355.

Rakner, Lise, and Nicolas van de Walle. 2009*a*. Opposition Parties and Incumbent Presidents: The New Dynamics of Electoral Competition in Africa. In *Democratization by Elections: A New Mode of Transition?*, ed. Staffan I. Lindberg. Baltimore, MD: Johns Hopkins University Press, pp. 202–225.

Rakner, Lise, and Nicolas van de Walle. 2009*b*. "Opposition Weakness in Africa." *Journal of Democracy* 20(3):108–121.

Randall, Vicky, and Lars Svasand. 2002. "Political Parties and Democratic Consolidation in Africa." *Democratization* 9(3):30–52.

Ranger, Terence O. 1975. *Dance and Society in Eastern Africa, 1890–1970: The Beni Ngoma*. London: Heinemann.

Reed, Steven R. 1994. The Incumbency Advantage in Japan. In *The Victorious Incumbent: A Threat to Democracy?*, ed. Albert Somit, Rudolf Wildenmann, Bernhard Boll and Andrea Rommele. Brookfield, VT: Dartmouth Publishing Company, pp. 278–303.

Reuter, Ora John, and Graeme Robertson. 2012. "Subnational Appointments in Authoritarian Regimes: Evidence from Russian Gubernational Appointments." *Journal of Politics* 74(4):1023–1037.

Reuter, Ora John, and Graeme Robertson. 2015. "Legislatures, Cooptation, and Social Protest in Contemporary Authoritarian Regimes." *Journal of Politics* 77(1):235–248.

Reuter, Ora John, and Jennifer Gandhi. 2011. "Economic Performance and Elite Defection from Hegemonic Parties." *British Journal of Political Science* 41(1):83–110.

Reuter, Ora John, and Rotislav Turvosky. 2014. "Dominant Party Rule and Legislative Leadership in Authoritarian Regimes." *Party Politics* 20(5):664–674.

Riedl, Rachel B. 2014. *Authoritarian Origins of Democratic Party Systems*. Cambridge: Cambridge University Press.

Rogers, Alan R. 1994. "Evolution of Time Preference by Natural Selection." *American Economic Review* 84(3):460–481.

Rogoff, Kenneth. 1990. "Equilibrium Political Budget Cycles." *American Economic Review* 80:21–36.

Rohde, David W. 1979. "Risk-Bearing and Progressive Ambition: The Case of Members of the United States House of Representatives." *American Journal of Political Science* 23(1):1–26.

Roop, Sterling, and Keith Weghorst. 2016. "The 2015 National Elections in Tanzania." *Electoral Studies* 100(43):190–194.

Rosenzweig, Leah R. 2018. "Community Carrots and Social Sticks: Why the Poor Vote in a Dominant-Party System." PhD dissertation, MIT.

Rotberg, Robert I., and Jennifer Erin Salahub. 2013. "African Legislative Effectiveness." The North–South Institute: Available at www.nis.ins.ca/wp-content/uploads/2013/10/2013-African-Legislative-Effectiveness1.pdf.

Rozenas, Artuas. 2011. "Forcing Consent: Information and Power in Non-Democratic Elections." Unpublished manuscript.

Ruotosalainen, Petri J. 2009. Under the Same Shade: Popular Perceptions of Political Change and the Challenges of Consolidating Multiparty Democracy in Tanzania. PhD Thesis University of Gothenburg: Goteborg, Sweden.

Santiso, Carlos, and Augustin Loada. 2003. "Explaining the Unexpected: Electoral Reform and Democratic Governance in Burkina Faso." *Journal of Modern African Studies* 41(3):395–419.

Sartori, Giovanni. 1976. *Parties and Party Systems: A Framework for Analysis*. Cambridge: Cambridge University Press.

Schansberg, D. Eric. 1994. "Moving out of the House: An Analysis of Congressional Quits." *Economic Inquiry* 32(3):445–456.

Schedler, Andreas. 2002. "Elections without Democracy: The Menu of Manipulation." *Journal of Democracy* 13(2):36–50.

Schedler, Andreas. 2006. The Logic of Electoral Authoritarianism. In *Electoral Authoritarianism: The Dynamics of Unfree Competition*, ed. Andreas Schedler. Boulder, CO: Lynne Rienner Publishers, pp. 1–23.

Schedler, Andreas. 2009. Electoral Authoritarianism. In *The SAGE Handbook of Comparative Politics*, ed. Todd Landman and Neil Robinson. Thousand Oaks, CA: Sage Publications, pp. 381–394.

Schedler, Andreas. 2013. *The Politics of Uncertainty: Sustaining and Subverting Electoral Authoritarianism*. Oxford: Oxford University Press.

Scheiner, Ethan. 2006. *Democracy without Competition in Japan: Opposition Failure in a One-Party Dominant State*. Cambridge: Cambridge University Press.

Schlesinger, Joseph A. 1966. *Ambition and Politics: Political Careers in the United States*. New York: Rand McNally.

Schneider, Cathy. 1991. "Mobilization at the Grassroots: Shantytowns and Resistance in Authoritarian Chile." *Latin American Perspectives* 18(1):92–112.

Serra, Gilles. 2011. "Why Primaries? The Party's Tradeoff between Policy and Valence." *Journal of Theoretical Politics* 23:21–51.

Shariff, Ahmad. 1999. Politics and policy in Africa: A Case study of Tanzania's transition to democracy. Phd Indiana University: Bloomington, IN.

Sheffer, Lior, and Peter John Loewen. 2019. "Accountability, Framing Effects, and Risk-Seeking by Elected Representatives: An Experimental Study with American Local Politicians." *Political Research Quarterly* 72(1):49–62.

Shefter, Martin. 1994. *Political Parties and the State: The American Historical Experience*. Princeton, NJ: Princeton University Press.

Shepsle, Kenneth A. 1972. "The Strategy of Ambiguity: Uncertainty and Electoral Competition." *American Political Science Review* 66(2):555–568.

Shivji, Issa G. 2004. "Good Governance, Bad Governance, and the Quest for Democracy in Africa: An Alternative Perspective." *Haki Elimu Working Papers* 4(8):1–8.

Siegel, David A. 2009. "Social Networks and Collective Action." *American Journal of Political Science* 53(1):122–138.

Slater, Dan. 2003. "Iron Cage in an Iron Fist: Authoritarian Institutions and the Personalization of Power in Malaysia." *Comparative Politics* 36(1):81–101.

Slater, Dan and Erica Simmons. 2010. "Informative Regress: Critical Antecedents in Comparative Politics." *Comparative Political Studies* 43(7):886–917.

Smith, Benjamin. 2004. "Oil Wealth and Regime Survival in the Developing World." *American Journal of Political Science* 48(2):232–246.

Smith, Benjamin. 2005. "Life of the Party: The Origins of Regime Breakdown and Persistence under Single-Party Rule." *World Politics* 57:421–451.

Smith, Christian. 1996. *Disruptive Religion: The Force of Faith in Social Movement Activism*. New York: Routledge.

Smith, Heather J., Thomas F. Pettigrew, Gina M. Pippin, and Silvana Bialosiewicz. 2012. "Relative Deprivation: A Theoretical and Meta-Analytic Review." *Personality and Social Psychology Review* 16(3):203–232.

Sousa, David J., and David T. Canon. 1992. "Party System Change and Political Career Structures in the U.S. Congress." *Legislative Studies Quarterly* 17(3):347–363.

Southall, Roger. 2006. Troubled Visionary: Nyerere as a Former President. In *Legacies of Power. Leadership Change and Former Presidents in African Politics*, ed. Roger Southall and Henning Melber. Uppsala, Sweden: The Nordic Africa Institute, pp. 233–255.

Staff. 2016. "Magufuli Relaxes Political Rally Ban, Warns Chadema." The Citizen (Tanzania). Available at www.thecitizen.co.tz/tanzania/news/magufuli-relaxes-political-rally-ban-warns-chadema-2562758.

Stokes, Susan. 2005. "Perverse Accountability: A Formal Model of Machine Politics with Evidence from Argentina." *American Political Science Review* 99(3):315–325.

Stone, Walter J., and Sandy L. Maisel. 2003. "The Not-So-Simple Calculus of Winning: Potential U.S. House Candidates' Nomination and General Election Prospects." *Journal of Politics* 65(4):951–977.

Straus, Scott, and Charles Taylor. 2012. Democratization and Electoral Violence in sub-Saharan Africa, 1990–2008. In *Voting in Fear: Electoral Violence in sub-Saharan Africa*, ed. Dorina Bekoe. Washington, DC: United States Institute of Peace, pp. 15–38.

Streb, Matthew J., Barbara Burrell, Brian Fredrick, and Michael A Genovese. 2008. "Social Desirability Effects and Support for a Female Presidential Candidate." *Public Opinion Quarterly* 72:76–89.

Studlar, Donley T., and Ian McAllister. 1991. "Political Recruitment to the Australian Legislature: Toward an Explanation of Women's Electoral Disadvantages." *Western Political Quarterly* 44(2):467–485.

Sulley, Consolata. 2020. *Intraparty Candidate Nomination in Tanzania: A Gender Analysis*. Berlin, Germany: Friedrich Ebert Stiftung.

Svolik, Milan. 2009. "Power Sharing and Leadership Dynamics in Authoritarian Regimes." *American Journal of Political Science* 53(2):477–494.

Swahili Proverbs. 2014. Available at http://swahiliproverbs.afrst.illinois.edu/proverbs.htm.

Tanaka, Tomomi, Colim F. Camerer, and Quang Nguyen. 2010. "Risk and Time Preferences: Linking Experimental and Household Survey Data from Vietnam." *American Economic Review* 100(1):557–571.

Tarrow, Sidney. 1992. Mentalities, Political Cultures, and Collective Action Frames: Constructing Meanings through Action". In *Frontiers in Social Movement Theory*, ed. A.D. Morris and C.M. Muller. New Haven, CT: Yale University Press pp. 174–202.

Tarrow, Sidney. 1993. "Cycles of Collective Action: Between Moments of Madness and the Repertoire of Contention." *Social Science History* 17(2): 281–307.

Tarrow, Sidney. 1998. *Power in Movement: Social Movements and Contentious Politics*. Cambridge: Cambridge University Press.

TEMCO. 1997. *The 1995 General Elections in Tanzania: Report of the Tanzania Election Monitoring Committee*. Dar es Salaam, Tanzania: TEMCO.

TEMCO. 2000. *The 2000 General Elections in Tanzania: Report of the Tanzania Election Monitoring Committee*. Dar es Salaam, Tanzania: TEMCO.

TEMCO. 2006. *The 2005 General Elections in Tanzania: Report of the Tanzania Election Monitoring Committee*. Dar es Salaam, Tanzania: TEMCO.

TEMCO. 2015. *The 2005 General Elections in Tanzania: Report of the Tanzania Election Monitoring Committee*. Dar es Salaam, Tanzania: REDET.

Templemann, Kharis Ali. 2014a. "Aborigine Constituencies in the Taiwanese Legislature." Unpublished manuscript.

Templemann, Kharis Ali. 2014b. "The Origins of Dominant Parties." Unpublished manuscript.

Teorell, Jan. 2003. "Linking Social Capital to Political Participation: Voluntary Associations and Networks of Recruitment in Sweden." *Scandinavian Political Studies* 26(1):49–66.

Thomas, Tobias, Moritz Hess, and Gert G. Wagner. 2017. "Reluctant to Reform? A Note on Risk-Loving Politicians and Bureaucrats." *Review of Economics* 68(3):167–179.

Thompson, Katrina Daly. 2013. "Representing Language, Culture, and Language Users in Textbooks: A Critical Approach to Swahili Multiculturalism." *The Modern Language Journal* 97(4):948–964.

Thompson, Mark R., and Phillip Kuntz. 2006. After Defeat: When Do Rulers Steal Elections? In *Electoral Authoritarianism: The Dynamics of Unfree Competition*, ed. Andreas Schedler. Lynne Rienner Publishers, pp. 113–128.

Thomson, Alex. 2004. *An Introduction to African Politics*. 2nd ed. London: Taylor & Francis.

Tilly, Charles. 1978. *From Mobilization to Revolution*. Reading, MA: Addison-Wesley.

Tilly, Charles. 1986. *The Contentious French: Four Centuries of Popular Struggle*. Cambridge, MA: Harvard University Press.

Timanywa, Felician. 2017. Kuchunguza ujinsia na matumizi ya lugha katika methali za wakurya. MA Thesis Open University of Tanzania: Dar es Salaam, Tanzania.

Tourangeau, Roger. 1984. Cognitive Sciences and Survey Methods. In *Cognitive Aspects of Survey Methodology: Building a Bridge between Disciplines*, ed. T. Jabine, M. Straf, J. Tanur, and Robert Tourangeau. Washington, DC: National Academy Press pp. 73–199.

Tourangeau, Roger, and Ting Yan. 2007. "Sensitive Questions in Surveys." *Psychological Bulletin* 133(5):859–893.

Treisman, Daniel. 1998. "Dollars and Democratization: The Role of Power and Money in Russia's Transitional Elections." *Comparative Politics* 31(1): 1–21.

Trejo, Guillermo. 2014. "The Ballot and the Street: An Electoral Theory of Social Protest in Autocracies." *Perspectives on Politics* 12(2):332–352.

Treux, Rory. 2014. "The Returns to Office in a 'Rubber Stamp' Parliament." *American Political Science Review* 108(2):235–251.

Tripp, Aili Mari. 2000. "Political Reform in Tanzania: The Struggle for Associational Autonomy." *Comparative Politics* 32(2):191–214.

Tripp, Aili Mari. 2004. "The Changing Face of Authoritarianism in Africa: The Case of Uganda." *Africa Today* 50(3):3–26.

Tripp, Aili Mari. 2010. *Museveni's Uganda: Paradoxes of Power in a Hybrid Regime*. Boulder, CO: Lynne Rienner Publishers.

Tripp, Aili Mari. 2012. In Pursuit of Authority: Civil Society and Rights-Based Discourses in Africa. In *African in World Politics*, ed. John Harbeson. 4th ed. Westview.

Tripp, Aili Mari. 2017. *Women's Activism in Africa: Struggles over Rights and Representation*. Oxford: Zed Books.

Tsubura, Machiko. 2018. 'Umoja ni ushindi (Unity Is victory)': Management of Factionalism in the Presidential Nomination of Tanzania's Dominant Party in 2015." *Journal of Eastern African Studies* 12(1):63–82.

Tucker, Joshua. 2006. "Enough! Electoral Fraud, Collective Action Problems, and the '2nd Wave' of Post-Communist Democratic Revolutions." *Perspectives on Politics* 53(5):537–553.

van de Walle, Nicolas. 2001. *African Economies and the Politics of Permanent Crisis, 1979–1999*. Cambridge: Cambridge University Press.

van de Walle, Nicolas. 2003. "Presidentialism and Clientelism in Africa's Emerging Party Systems." *Journal of Modern African Studies* 41(2):297–321.

van de Walle, Nicolas. 2006. Tipping Games: When Do Opposition Parties Coalesce? In *Electoral Authoritarianism: The Dynamics of Unfree Competition*, ed. Andreas Schedler. Boulder, CO: Lynne Rienner Publishers, pp. 77–92.

van de Walle, Nicolas. 2007. Meet the New Boss, Same as the Old Boss? The Evolution of Political Clientelism in Africa. In *Patrons, Clients, and Policies: Patterns of Democratic Accountability and Political Competition*, ed. Herbert Kitschelt and Steve I. Wilkinson. Cambridge: Cambridge University Press, pp. 50–67.

van Eerd, Jonathan. 2010. "Dominance and Fluidity: Conceptualizing and Explaining Party System Characteristics in sub-Saharan Africa." Presented at the Midwest Political Science Conference.

van Eerd, Jonathan. 2011. "Elite-Mass Congruence in African Dominant Party Systems: The Case of Botswana and Lesotho." Prepared for IPSA ECPR Joint Conference, University of Sao Paolo.

Verba, Sidney, Kay Lehman Schlozman and Henry E. Brady. 1995. *Voice and Equality: Civic Voluntarism in American Politics*. Cambridge, MA: Harvard University Press.

Vicente, Pedro. 2008. "Is Vote Buying Effective? Evidence from a Field Experiment in West Africa." Working paper.

Vicente, Pedro, and Leonard Wantchekon. 2009. "Clientelism and Vote Buying: Lessons from Field Experiments in African Elections." Working paper.

Villalon, Leonardo A. 1994. "Democratizing a (Quasi) Democracy: The Senegalese Elections of 1993." *African Affairs* 93(371):163–193.

Voors, Maarten, Eleonaroa Nillesen, Philip Vermip, Erwin Bulte, Robert Lensink, and Daan van Soest. 2010. "Does Conflict Affect Preferences? Results from Field Experiments in Burundi." *MICROCON Research Work Paper* 21:1–45.

Wahman, Michael. 2013. "Opposition Coalitions and Democratization by Election." *Government and Opposition* 48(1):3–32.

Wahman, Michael. 2017. "Nationalized Incumbents and Regional Challengers: Opposition- and Incumbent-party Nationalization in Africa." *Party Politics* 23(3):309–322.

Wahman, Michael and Jan Teorell. 2013. "Authoritarian Regime Types Revisited: Updated Data in Comparative Perspective." *Contemporary Politics* 19(1): 19–34.

Wantchekon, Leonard. 2003. "Clientelism and Voting Behavior: Evidence from a Field Experiment in Benin." *World Politics* 55(3):399–422.

Wantchekon, Leonard, and Christel Vermeersch. 2005. "Information, Social Networks and the Demand for Public Goods: Experimental Evidence from Benin." Working paper.

Ware, Alan. 1996. *Political Parties and Party Systems*. Oxford: Oxford University Press.

Weber, Max. 1921. "Politik als Beruf." Gesammelte Politische Schriften. Munich: Drei masken verlag.

Weber, Max. 1991. The Nature of Social Action. In *Weber: Selections in Translation*, ed. Walter Garrison Runciman. Cambridge: Cambridge University Press, pp. 7–32.

Webster, Edward. 2007. "Trade Unions and Political Parties: New Alliances, Strategies, and Partnerships." *Friedrich Ebert Stiftung Briefing Papers* (3).

Weghorst, Keith, and Michael Bernhard. 2015. "From Formlessness to Structure: The Institutionalization of Competitive Party Systems in Africa." *Comparative Political Studies* 47(12):1707–1737.

Weghorst, Keith, and Staffan I. Lindberg. 2011. "Effective Opposition Strategies: Collective Goods or Clientelism?" *Democratization* 18(5):1193–1214.

Weghorst, Keith, and Staffan I. Lindberg. 2013. "What Drives the Swing Voter in Africa?" *American Journal of Political Science* 57(3):717–734.

Weinstein, Laura. 2011. "The Politics of Government Expenditures, 1999–2007." *African Studies Review* 54(1):33–57.

Wesonga, Nelson. 2018. "Makerere University's Past Guild Presidents: Where Are They Now?" *Daily Monitor* (Uganda). Available at www.monitor.co.ug/uganda/magazines/people-power/makerere-university-s-past-guild-presidents-where-are-they-now–1790384.

Whitehead, Richard L. 2009. *Single Party Rule in a Multiparty Age: Tanzania in Comparative Perspective*. Philadelphia: Temple University.

Whitt, Sam, and Vera Mironova. N.d. "Risk Tolerance during Conflict: Evidence from Aleppo, Syria." Working paper.

Wilkinson, Steve I., and Christopher Haid. 2009. "Ethnic Violence as Campaign Expenditure: Riots, Competition, and Vote Swings in India." Working paper.

Wilkinson, Steven. 2004. *Votes and Violence*. Cambridge: Cambridge University Press.

Wilson, Matthew Charles. 2014. Governance Built Step-by-Step: Analysing Sequences to Explain Democratization. In *Advances in Sequence Analysis: Theory, Method, Applications*, ed. Phillippe Blanchard, Felix Buhlmann, and Jacques-Antoine Gautheir. New York: Springer-Verlag pp. 213–230.

Wisjen, Frans and Ralph Tanner. 2002. *I Am Just a Sukuma: Globalization and Identity Construction in Northwest Tanzania*. Amsterdam: Rodopi.

Wright, Joseph. 2008. "To Invest or Insure? How Authoritarian Time Horizons Impact Foreign Aid Effectiveness." *Comparative Political Studies* 41(7): 971–1000.

Wuhs, Steven T. 2006. "Democratization and the Dynamics of Candidate Selection Rule Change in Mexico, 1991–2003." *Mexican Studies* 22(1):33–55.

Young, Lauren. 2019. "The Psychology of State Repression: Fear and Dissent Decisions in Zimbabwe." *American Political Science Review* 113(1):140–155.

Zeria, Yael. 2019. *The Revolution Within: State Institutions and Unarmed Resistance in Palestine*. Cambridge: Cambridge University Press.

Index

Printed in the USA
CPSIA information can be obtained
at www.ICGtesting.com
CBHW072220120424
6858CB00004B/139

9 781009 011518